S0-BFB-241

ALSO BY JOSHUA GAMSON

Freaks Talk Back

Claims to Fame

THE
FABULOUS
SYLVESTER

THE FABULOUS SYLVESTER

THE LEGEND, THE MUSIC, THE SEVENTIES IN SAN FRANCISCO

JOSHUA GAMSON

HENRY HOLT AND COMPANY, NEW YORK

Henry Holt and Company, LLC
Publishers since 1866
115 West 18th Street
New York, New York 10011

Henry Holt® is a registered trademark of Henry Holt and Company, LLC.

"The Tomb of Sorrow," from *Ceremonies* by Essex Hemphill, copyright © 1992 by Essex Hemphill. Used by permission of Plume, an imprint of Penguin Group (USA) Inc.

Excerpts from Martin Worman's unpublished "Midnight Masquerade: A History of the Cockettes" used by permission of Robert Croonquist.

Martin Worman's unpublished interview with Sylvester used by permission of Robert Croonquist.

"That's Why Darkies Were Born." Words and music by Lew Brown and Ray Henderson. © 1931 by DeSylva, Brown & Henderson Inc. Copyright renewed. Rights for the extended renewal term in the United States controlled by Ray Henderson Music Company and Chappell & Co. Rights outside the United States controlled by Chappell & Co. All rights reserved.

Excerpts from Maureen Orth, "History of a Hype," *Village Voice*, November 25, 1971, used by permission of author.

"When the World Turns Blue." Words and music by Joe Sample and Will Jennings. © 1977 Chrysalis Music Ltd. and © 1980 Irving Music (BMI). All rights reserved. International copyright secured. Used by permission.

D. A. Powell, "[first fugue]" from *Tea* © 1998 by D. A. Powell and reprinted by permission of Wesleyan University Press.

LIBRARY OF CONGRESS CATALOGING-IN-PUBLICATION DATA
Gamson, Joshua, 1962–
    The fabulous Sylvester : the legend, the music, the seventies in
San Francisco / Joshua Gamson.
       p.   cm.
    Includes index.
    ISBN-13: 978-0-8050-7250-1
    ISBN-10: 0-8050-7250-0
       1. Sylvester, 1947–1988.   2. Singers—United States—Biography.
    3. Disco musicians—United States—Biography.   4. Disco music—
    California—San Francisco—History and criticism.   I. Title.
ML420.S9815G36 2005
782.42164'092—dc22
[B]   2004042380

Henry Holt books are available for special promotions and premiums.
For details contact: Director, Special Markets.

First Edition 2005

DESIGNED BY FRITZ METSCH

Printed in the United States of America
    1   3   5   7   9   10   8   6   4   2

For Richard James Knight

CONTENTS

THE
FABULOUS
SYLVESTER

1.

GET READY FOR ME

When I die,
my angels,
immaculate
Black diva
drag queens,
all of them
sequined
and seductive,
some of them
will come back
to haunt you,
I promise,
honey chil'.

—Essex Hemphill, from "The Tomb of Sorrow"

Back in the 1960s, when Tiki Lofton was a boy, she used to wait until the eleven o'clock flight took off from LAX, right over her grandmother's house, and as the jet vroomed and her grandmother dozed in front of the evening news, Tiki would ease open her bedroom window and climb out to meet Monique Hudson. The plane's tiny wing lights blinked in the California sky, specks of sparkle over unglamorous Inglewood. Tiki always left her necessities—one of her grandma's wigs, preferably red, and an outfit, preferably shiny—outside the window. She would grab her goodie bag, and Monique would show up on the street corner with hers, and they'd head over to one of the Disquotay apartments, like one on Ninety-second and Vermont that Miss Larry had rented, and beat their faces and rat their wigs and listen to music and smoke weed and drink like the teenagers they had recently become.

The apartments were usually big, with two or three people sharing a few bedrooms. But the living rooms barely had furniture, as the Disquotays needed lots of room for other endeavors. On party nights, it was like an assembly line. You'd lie down on the floor and one person would dust your face, and then you'd sit up and Tammi* would do the eyes and blush the cheeks and paint the lips with meringue lipstick. Dooni, who would later become the Fabulous Sylvester, would do your hair and move on down the line: wig, wig, wig, wig, wig. You'd put on two pairs of eyelashes, top and bottom both, just like a cover girl. Your face would be like a picture. You'd slip into a girdle and adjust your water-balloon titties; Monique or Dooni would fix up your outfit; and then you'd head off—a gang of in-charge glamour girls—following the noise to the party in Watts or Compton or wherever.

The first Disquotay bash that Tiki went to was over on 120th and Athens, at Etta James's house, sometime around 1965. Etta, who would later be inducted into both the Rock and Roll Hall of Fame (largely on the strength of her 1961 hit "At Last") and the Betty Ford Center (largely on the strength of her smack addiction), was already a recording star and a friend to many local Los Angeles drag queens, with whom she shared a brazen sensibility and a taste for platinum hair and pumps. When Etta James was out of town, her house-sitter was Miss Foxy, whom the queens called the Jack-o-Lantern, or the Pumpkin, on account of her wide, gap-toothed smile. On one visit to the Etta James residence, Foxy's friend Miss Larry Hines had declared the place "*made* for a party," and sent out the call to gather. Had she known about any of this, says former Disquotay Diane Moorehead, "Etta James woulda killed Foxy and Larry."

Tiki hadn't started dressing yet, and wasn't yet named Tiki. She was still a pretty gay boy, skin pearly smooth and light. To go to that first party, she had worn a cowboy hat, big wide bell-bottoms, and earrings. For Tiki, walking into that particular scene had been like leaving black and white for

*"Tammi" is a pseudonym.

Technicolor. The house, with its swimming pool and fireplace, had stunned her. Women, drag queens, and guys, all sending joyful noises in Tiki's direction; the music had been jumping: Walter Jackson's version of "Lee Cross," Jr. Walker & the All Stars' "Shotgun," "Nowhere to Run" by Martha and the Vandellas, Fontella Bass singing "Rescue Me." Gay kids all perched on gigantic speakers, singing and carrying on. *I said shotgun! Shoot him 'fore he run now.* Folks were dancing, jumping into the pool. *Nowhere to run to, baby,* they'd scream-sung, *nowhere to hide.* "Ooh, I like this," Tiki had said to herself. "This here—honey, where *is* this world?" Within months, she would be a full-fledged Disquotay, made-up, bewigged, bejeweled.

A Disquotay party was an art form. During the week, a few club members would head out to Dolphin's of Hollywood to get the latest 45 or eight-track, often something Dooni had heard on KGFJ, where the Magnificent Montague would cry "Burn, baby, burn!" while spinning something new and hot. The club members would then meet for "music appreciation night," to play records and familiarize themselves with the new material. "Just to get ready, honey, you *had* to," says Diane.

Out on Vermont Street, where there were several black nightclubs, they'd pass out the address of that night's get-together. Or someone would decide to throw a party, and word of mouth would fill up the place. Outside, cars would be double-parked for blocks around, and there was a line to get in. "You would see Cadillacs, Jaguars, Mercedes-Benzes, low-riders, Momma and Daddy's car," Diane says. "You had bulldaggers, femmes, straight men, straight women, wanting just to party," says former Disquotay Jackie Hoyle, "and just to see us."

The Disquotays worked on their outfits the whole week. Some would buy clothes, some would have them made, and some would use whatever was handy. They'd buy makeup and wigs—preferably human-hair ones— or steal them, or pay someone else to steal them. When it came time to join the party they would sit outside on the cars and wait. Every Disquotay wanted to be the last to arrive—the one who steals the show. Everyone wanted to enter with the right song backing them. So they'd wait, sometimes an hour or more, until their tune hit, the song that matched their particular fabulousness on that particular night. Only then would they walk.

Inside, there might be topless dancers on top of tables, straight folks who'd wandered in from nightclubs, and, of course, black drag queens galore. *'Cause I know that beauty's only skin deep, yeah, yeah yeah.* People danced to the Temptations, the Rolling Stones, Barbara Lewis, Wilson Pickett, Martha Reeves, Marvin Gaye. *Ride, Sally, ride.* The Disquotays themselves were more to be looked at than touched. They had taken bubble baths and washed themselves with Jean Naté. They might be willing to get nasty later in the evening, but they had reputations and hairstyles to uphold, and they worked way too hard on their Max Factor to let just anybody mess it up early on.

"We were not allowed to fuck *during* the party, because we were ladies," Jackie Hoyle says. Their parties, though, were unrestrained. "We had the pimps, we had the drug dealers, we had the college boys. We had the butch queens out in the driveways taking care of their business. It was a lot of punks, honey, in the driveway, suckin' all night long," Diane says. "We'd be inside with our perfume and our dresses on, hostessing. We were dancing queens." *It takes two, baby.* Marijuana was still heavily penalized, so some folks would wear big Afros, and upon arrival they'd pull four or five joints right out of their hair. A good song would seem to go on forever. "Four more bars!" a Disquotay would scream, and whoever was spinning would back that record up and start it all over again, seven or eight times, right when it was getting to the good part, teasing you until you were really feeling it, giving it to you just when you really had to have it. *I can't get no. Satisfaction. I try and I try and I try and I try.*

Time at the Disquotay parties went by like nothing, like a dream you thought you might have had. Come four-thirty or so in the morning, Tiki would skip out, Cinderella dashing from the ball, while the other Disquotays were heading off with that evening's admirer, or going out as a pack for breakfast, or soaking their feet in a bucket of water. She would ease back through the window before the five o'clock jet entered its landing pattern over Inglewood. She'd take off her face, hide her clothes, and do her best to flatten her grandma's wig back down to normal. When she woke, it was 1965 and she was a sixteen-year-old boy named Warren again.

The Disquotays—among them Dooni, Tiki, Monique, Diane, Benedetta, Shelley Newman, Jay Freeman, Barbara, Garetha, Tammi, Shirley Floyd,

Jackie Kennedy, Jackie Hoyle, Cleola Balls, Miss LaLa, Miss Louella, Miss Marcia, and Larry Hines, their "founder and lifelong president"—were a cross between a street gang and a sorority. They began gathering in 1963. In their own minds, at least, they were the toast of mid-1960s Los Angeles. This was their fantasy. "*Everybody* wanted to be a Disquotay," says Diane. "It was like Folies Bergère in the ghetto." They were the most fabulous girls around, and the toughest. They could kick people's asses and look good doing so. They would sometimes kick each other's asses just for looking good, in fact. Especially if someone looked *too* good. Tammi, tall and pimply and rarely the center of attention, could go into the bathroom for what seemed like days and emerge a glamour girl. One night she showed up in her pink safari pants, pink fingernails and toenails, and wrap-around sandals. Everyone agreed that this was Tammi's time to shine—everyone except Larry Hines. Wigs flew; nails were broken. History was made.

When the girls competed over clothes and boyfriends—among themselves or with other queens—things could sometimes explode into Jets-and-Sharks rumbles. A run-in with Louella, for instance, or with Duchess, who did her own thing entirely but knew all the Disquotay girls' business, might result in a reading contest of tasty brutality. "They'd be poppin' their fingers," Diane says. "The words would be tripping off their tongues like magic, just like rhythm: 'Look-at-your-hands, look-at-your-feet, look-at-your-neck, look-at-your-eyes, look-at-your-fingers.' They'd bring up news bulletins. They would hit a line just to build to the *next* line. And you'd be laughin' cause they'd be making it rhyme." In such situations, Miss Louella was the most dangerous. When she read you, the half-hidden truths she spat out came so fast and hard your own retorts seemed to flutter away. "She was like a machine gun," Diane says. "She would get you off of her with just her mouth."

Some, like Miss LaLa, might use other means of offense. LaLa, as Duchess remembers her, was "this big old horrible queen, nine feet tall, light-skinned with green eyes, with minidresses on and high heels and feet like garbage trucks, real dumb, and a mean Motorola." LaLa lived with her family in Watts. "The whole family, they were just terrible," says Duchess, hyperbolically. "They were not bad-looking people. They just had little tiny brains, and they were all violent. Even the grandma carried a shotgun." Some of the Disquotays called LaLa the Menace of Society, and balked at letting her into the club. She loved fighting as much as she loved blond wigs and minidresses, and when she was around, someone was going to get their ass whupped. You didn't necessarily want her at your events, since her family had been reported to shoot up people's festivities just for sport, sending people running and jumping out of windows. She often traveled Los Angeles with Cleola Balls, who at six two was a few inches shorter than she.

"They were both jailhouse queens," says Jackie Hoyle, who referred to the two as Red China and Russia, "and they could tear a house *up*." LaLa, in order to expand her own hair options, would sometimes bring a pillow-case and demand the wig right off everyone's head—she was partial to blond human-hair wigs, in particular—leaving behind a roomful of boys in makeup and stocking caps. "Pin your wigs up," the Disquotays would call, "LaLa's comin'."

LaLa eventually bullied her way into the Disquotays, aided by the fact that she could deliver clothing or wigs from a store she'd hit. But though she was tough, she was not invincible. One time, for instance, when Miss Larry Hines and LaLa were fighting over a boyfriend, Cleola held down Miss Hines while LaLa cut off Miss Hines's hair. Queens jumped in cars and buses to console Miss Hines, who was known for growing her own dark, blond-frosted hair and brushing it in people's faces. They found her sitting on some stairs with her hair in her hands, crying. Most were sympathetic, although Miss Louella, upon seeing Miss Hines's big, hairless head atop her tiny body, privately called her "the Screaming Skull." Next weekend, next party: Miss Hines arrived in a wig the same exact color, with the same exact blond frost, and the same exact length, as the tresses that LaLa had chopped off. It was a solid, fuck-you victory for Miss Larry Hines and his adherents, further proof, if any were ever needed, that there is no weapon more powerful than the right hair.

In peaceful times, though, the Disquotays were about the look, the entrance, and the scene. Tammi and Dooni were always flipping through *Vogue* and *Harper's Bazaar* for new ideas. They could recite the names of all the major models: Verushka, Twiggy, Penelope Tree. "We used to name *Vogue* models like they were our relatives," Diane says. "Like it was part of our *duty*." They patterned their makeup and fashions after them, too, and then "would just sit around and glorify each other just for being beautiful."

straw and wearing a natural wig bigger than her own body. But Dooni's creativity was legendary and bottomless. He would sit up at night watching black-and-white movies on television with his baby sisters, sketching the brassy-dame clothes and gestures of Katharine Hepburn (high-collared white blouse, sleek slacks, hands on hips) or Rosalind Russell (purple gown with fur sleeves, purple-gloved hand holding a lengthy cigarette holder).

Dooni was constantly scribbling designs. He would read about princes and queens in exotic places, far, far away from his own neighborhood, and he'd imagine their clothes. He could transform a face beyond recognition and rat a wig like nobody's business. Dooni was tall and big-boned—he fluctuated between pencil thin and slightly chunky—with an oval face that looked good with any hairstyle and skin that was so soft and smooth, people likened it to whipped chocolate. People looked to him for all kinds of support, Marapasa says, but mostly "beauty support." Even among the Disquotays, you would notice Dooni first.

"There's a line of us, and then there's Dooni," Diane says. "We're all lookin' like sisters and cousins, and then there's Dooni. Dooni was always *arranged.* Every detail would be addressed." He would enter a room without fanfare, but all eyes would go to him and return to him. "If everybody had on black and gray, he wouldn't come in red," Jackie says. "He'd have on black and gray also, but his would be constructed totally different than everyone else's. He wasn't going to put on purple, but Dooni's gray was going to be something where you just had to *view* him."

One day in 1968, in their heyday, a gaggle of Disquotays was hanging out at the Clowns, a club on Jefferson where they often met. Dooni was nowhere to be found. He had said he would be there. He had told them that morning, "Get ready for *me.*" You knew what that meant in a general sense—it was both a promise and a warning—but you simply could not predict the specifics. Once, "Get ready" had meant a dress made entirely of paper, the first in a long series of disposable "one-nighter" outfits. For the first-ever Watts Summer Festival in 1966, Dooni had stapled together aluminum pie tins into matching dresses for him and Tiki, and Tammi had made Styrofoam earrings to match. When they walked through the festival people were drawn, confused and squinting in the sun, to the blinding silver light that turned out to be Tiki and Dooni.

Another time Dooni had appeared in a knit dress, bright lipstick and nail polish, and a Batman belt, and once in a babydoll dress, windowpane stockings, and square-toed, big-buckled Pilgrim shoes, his hair in Beatles bangs with so many curls on top that his head looked like a chocolate fountain. He could wear a full-length sequined gown, or two odd-shaped pieces of fabric glued together just so. He was known to have worn a snazzy dress cinched with a big wide camping belt, into which were stuck a knife, fork, spoon, and canteen. He would tear out a page from *Vogue* and put it in his purse one day, and the next he would look a lot like that picture.

He might be a teased-up redhead, or he might have a huge black natural or maybe just a bun sitting there like an upside-down bowl of pudding. When Elizabeth Taylor did *Cleopatra* in 1963, Dooni was the first to have her bangs, and when *Funny Girl* came out, in 1968, Dooni had Streisand's frosted, frothy hairdo. For a while in between, partly to trick LaLa out of stealing the wig right off his head, Dooni wore a platinum-blond wig and rubbed the top with black shoe polish, so it looked exactly as if his own roots were growing out from a dye job.

With his big eyes, Dooni often had an expectant look. Like all the girls, he would certainly have two sets of eyelashes on top of his own, but for Dooni, the word "eyes" didn't quite go far enough. He called them "aye-ees": Once he arrived with checkerboard eyelids he'd seen in *Vogue*, another time with eyelids decorated in Star-Spangled Banner glitter; in both cases, he had made earrings to match. His feet were so big and wide that some of the Disquotays called them "yams," or "dinner rolls," or "aircraft carriers"; his pumps were from the Tall and Smart Shop. Since Dooni's fashions, hair, and face were irreproachable, a queen who wanted to read Dooni usually went after the huge feet. "Can't you chisel those damn things down?" a Disquotay would ask. "Kiss my ass," Dooni would reply. If someone asked him what size shoe he wore, he would tell them, tartly, "*My* size, honey."

"With Dooni," Diane says, "it was always an ongoing saga. *What's she going to do next?* Dooni would come on a pogo stick, it didn't matter. She was her only competition, 'cause *nobody* was on her level. Dooni could always walk away with the spotlight, honey, without even making a big deal out of it." Sometimes, Tiki says, it seemed as if Dooni had come from outer space. Legend has it that he once won a prize at a ball wearing a sheet, a rose, and angel hair from a Christmas tree, and all he did was twirl the rose and spin around.

✿   ✿   ✿

When years later Dooni became a big star named Sylvester, fans and friends alike would know him for his movie-scene entrances and his What's-she-going-to-do-next-ness. On stage in San Francisco, London, or New York, he would rise into a spotlight as if he was ready for his close-up: round, dark face framed by a sparkling headdress; head tilted upward into the light; silver-shadowed eyes closed, as if to accentuate that he was not beholder but beheld. Or he would come down a staircase and pull out a jeweled mirror while everyone waited for him to start singing "You Are So Beautiful" to himself. Or he would let his band tease the audience with a Sylvester song they had danced to many times, the instrumental refrain of one of his huge hits ("Mighty Real" or "Disco Heat" or "Do Ya Wanna Funk"), entering only when he was certain that the crowd had worked its way to near frenzy.

Or he would see the proper backdrop and make a picture of himself for whoever happened to be around: if steam was coming out of a grate in Manhattan at night, he would pause to let it roll up his full-length white fur coat; if someone was selling silver balloons in San Francisco, he would buy some in order to raise a hand into the air and release them into the blue sky. In the Paris airport during a European tour some thirteen years after the Disquotays' heyday, Sylvester's bandmates would look toward the tubed escalator and watch Sylvester descend in his white fur, silver pumps, and a diamond tiara, carrying a handful of French *Vogues*. No one could dream herself up quite like Dooni.

Back in 1968, waiting outside the Clowns on Jefferson, few of the Disquotays saw stardom in Dooni's future. He was one of them, and though they heartily believed in themselves as stars, they also had reliable evidence that most Americans viewed them with less enthusiasm. Still, Dooni was Dooni, and when he was late that day at the Clowns, the Disquotays were wound up, jittery in that way you turn when you're getting ready for something you know you can't get ready for, like a tornado or a spanking or a first kiss. Then they saw Miss Dooni: pigtails, an A-line dress, licking a big sucker, gliding down the streets of South Central on his way to the Clowns. On roller skates. And not in a rush, either.

✿   ✿   ✿

Later, when everyone was sick or dying, on the day 1986 turned into 1987, Sylvester—who had not been Dooni for almost twenty years—made an appearance on *The Late Show,* where Joan Rivers was hosting a festive New Year's Eve. High on his head was a poofy, shoulder-length red wig he'd bought on Seventh Avenue in New York; friends called it his Lucy Ricardo wig, and it indeed resembled the hair of a slutty Lucille Ball emerging from a wind tunnel. One of Sylvester's lapels sparkled with a silver design, and bracelets twinkled and jangled on his wrist. Backed by a mostly white band and two big black women singers, he sang "Someone Like You," a pop song that was getting good radio play, though nothing like what his big disco hits had gotten ten years before. He jumped and danced as he sang, but his voice was off: scratchy and strained, as if his chops weren't quite right.

Sylvester plopped down on the couch next to the preceding guest, the Tony Award–winning actor and seventies game-show fixture Charles Nelson Reilly. It was hard to imagine a queenlier trio: Reilly, whose childhood nickname was Mary; gossipy Rivers, the drag queen without a penis; and Sylvester. After a bit of chitchat about jewelry and furs and Sylvester's boyfriend, Rick, Sylvester reminded Rivers and Reilly that they had all three done one of the earliest AIDS benefits together several years earlier, before AIDS benefits were the thing to do: "The two of you," he said, and "me, that black drag queen you always talk about." Apparently, Ms. Rivers did not hear the warning in his words or the hurt he had felt at being reduced to a label. "What do you wear in real life, when you just want to be Mrs. Rick?" she asked, plainly assuming that Rick played mister to Sylvester's missus. Sylvester laughed, despite the hint of strained patience on his face, and spoke vaguely about having "something for everyone." Joan Rivers persisted. "So what did your family say when they found out you were going to be a drag queen?" she asked. Sylvester gave her a look. "I'm not a drag queen!" he exclaimed sharply but with a big, full-toothed smile, sitting in his wig, makeup, and jewelry. He threw his head back and held his arms to his chest in a small self-hug, laughing. "I'm *Sylvester!*"

Joan Rivers stumbled and stammered a bit ("But—well you sometimes— I know—sometimes . . .") as Sylvester stepped back in to smooth out the conversation. He looked up toward the ceiling for a second. "What did my parents say," he repeated, and then he looked at Joan Rivers and explained the situation as nicely and succinctly as he could manage. "When I was little I used to dress up, right? And my mother said, 'You can't dress up. You can't dress up. You've gotta wear these pants and these shoes, and you have to, like, drink beer and play football.' And I said, 'No, I don't,' and she said, 'You're very strange,' and I said, 'That's okay.'"

That's as pretty a summary of Sylvester's philosophy as you ever could see: *I said, "No, I don't," and she said, "You're very strange," and I said, "That's okay."*

2.

LIKE AN ANGEL CAME DOWN, HONEY

Dooni was not a drag name; Sylvester's little brothers named him that. Where Dooni grew up, in the heart of nearly all-black South Central Los Angeles, if you were given a nickname as a child, people would have to think long and hard to call up your given name later in life. Males, in particular, seemed to get renamed early on, and it was not unusual to find grown men around Watts and Inglewood going by names like Frog or Boy. Dooni's father was named Sylvester James, but everyone knew him as Sweet. In 1947, newborn Dooni was also given the name Sylvester, but it wasn't until he became famous that folks he grew up with in Watts knew him by that name.

Boy was Dooni's uncle Willie James. Dooni's cousin was called Flute. Dooni's brother, John Wesley, was known as Dudda. His stepfather, born Robert, was called Sonny. But when it came right down to it, the men were neither here nor there for Dooni. In later life, although friends met and heard about his mother, grandmother, and sisters, few of his closest friends recall Sylvester mentioning male family members at all. He hardly knew his father, and when other family members mentioned him Sylvester would cut them off, refusing to talk about "that lowlife." His stepfather, Sonny—whom his mother married when Sylvester was in his early teens— was a man of few words with little warmth for Sylvester, and they could easily avoid each other while in the same room. Dooni was raised by fierce women.

Although Dooni's mother did not tell her children much at all about her childhood, bits and pieces of information have survived her. Letha Weaver grew up in a tiny settlement a few miles outside of the tiny Arkansas town of Palestine. Her family was, relatively speaking, well off. "The one thing they had," says Letha's cousin Esau Joyner, "was land."

14

They were farmers. Back in the day, Joyner says, Letha's grandfather owned thousands of acres and even had sharecroppers. "They didn't consider themselves rich," says Joyner, "but they weren't poor people." Letha's mother, Gertha Weaver—she never married, so she kept her family name—was sickly, and the family did not think she could manage a child. When Letha was just a baby, Gertha switched roles with her own sister, Julia: Julia, known to family as JuJu, took in Letha and became her mother, while Gertha became an auntie. JuJu's husband, a man named Egypt Morgan, served as Letha's father. ("If you was kind of uppity-uppity, you had to marry a Morgan," says Esau Joyner, a Morgan cousin.)

Around the late 1930s, Julia and Egypt Morgan, and some of the Weavers, migrated to Los Angeles, part of the massive Great Migration of blacks out of the South. They bought a place in Watts, and after about a year, when they were settled in, JuJu and Egypt sent for their girl, Letha. According to family lore, Letha left Arkansas for Los Angeles in 1940 with nothing but a suitcase and a sign around her neck. She was nine. Gertha had packed Letha up, written Julia Morgan's name and address on a piece of cardboard, strung it over Letha, and put her on a train bound West. JuJu met Letha at Union Station, and took her to their house on 114th street, in front of a big Baptist church.

By the mid-1940s, Letha Weaver had grown into a ferociously pretty young woman: easy smile, deep dimples, and skin that people wanted to touch; she was tall and elegant, too. She'd taken up with Sylvester "Sweet" James, and it wasn't long before she married him. Letha and Sweet moved into a small cottage JuJu and Egypt Morgan owned right behind their own house, and Letha James, still in her teens, started to have her children. Sylvester Junior, born on September 6, 1947, was her first, and within three years she had two more baby boys: John Wesley in November of 1948, joined a year and a half later by Larry.

At first, Letha's house was full of kids and not a whole lot else. She worked cleaning houses in upscale Baldwin Park; when money was tight, she made do with cornbread, beans, and all kinds of gravy, and sewed clothes for her kids. Sweet wasn't much help.

Folks remember Sweet as thin, with a medium-dark complexion and a constant smile; aside from that, he is a vague figure in family storytelling, a cameo player. "I met him, but I didn't know nothing about him except that he was her husband," says Esau Joyner. "He was a guy that was always on the move." Sweet could often be found outside, hot-rodding old cars.

"Sweet was worthless," says Dreda Slaughter, whose sister and Letha were good friends. "I don't even think he worked. When you went over there, you could see Sweet laughing and talking, and nothing in the house—the bare necessities, you had a bed—and then the kids running around. And Letha still had that smile."

Sweet didn't stay around long. "He was a player, and I imagine everyone knew it," Dreda says. "Just as nice as he could be, friendly, and full of crap." When Dreda was going to Compton College, she'd see Sweet riding a girl around in his car, pretending like she was his cousin. He was a shiftless man, a bit of a hound dog, a playboy sweet like cake. Letha James, for all her smiles, was growing up into someone much different. She was becoming a woman who, when it came to her family, did not *play*. Nor would she be played. You were there like you said you'd be, or you were going to get gone. Sweet was gone when Sylvester Junior was still in diapers.

For a little while in the early 1950s, Letha James and her kids moved to Aliso Village, a downtown housing project, and then back into the Morgan house on 114th Street in Watts. Theirs was its own black world, although it had become that relatively recently. When the Morgans moved there in the early 1940s, Watts had been a mixed neighborhood, with blacks, Mexicans, and whites in roughly equal proportions; by the late 1950s, Watts was 95 percent black. Police abuse was common: half the respondents in a 1950 survey of Watts residents reported that they had been "slapped, kicked, etc." by the police. Although a third of Watts's people lived in public housing by the end of the 1950s, many blacks owned their homes. Letha's street had modest houses, with long front yards where kids could play and cars could park.

Sweet was still in the neighborhood; over the years, he would cross paths with Letha and her children at church, or stop back by the house, trying to get back in the picture. Letha was not interested, and neither was Dooni. If he missed having a father, he certainly did not let on. "Sylvester just didn't talk about him," his little sister Bernadette says. "He just didn't care for him at all."

Letha James did not lack the means to carry on without Sweet. JuJu was there, right down the street, to take one, two, or all three of the boys for hours, days, or months. Sylvester described her as the woman who raised him, as much as his own mother had. Letha also had her church and her God, both of which were there before, during, and after the men. Letha was serious church. On Sundays, she would take the three boys on the streetcar, and they'd stay at church all day, breaking only to eat fried chicken with the other congregants. At home, she rarely allowed any music that wasn't religious. "We didn't go to parties, we didn't dance, we didn't smoke and drink and do all those things in our household," Letha told the filmmaker Tim Smyth in her last interview, for a documentary about Sylvester, a few weeks before she died in 1998. "I can do all things through Christ. It strengthens me. And I tell them all if they have the strength and desire, the Lord will give them the strength to accomplish whatever their goal was."

Letha was a strict and doting mother. She did not direct her children toward any particular goals, but watched them and pushed them to see what gifts God had given them. Appreciate yourself first and then you can appreciate others, she taught them. Choose your friends wisely, she said, and just in case she kept a close watch on their choices. Nothing is easy, Letha taught them. She said: You have to work hard for anything you're going to get. She said: Trust in God. And always, always make sure you've got something for yourself. "God bless the child that has his own," Letha would say, repeating it until it sounded like something they had always known. Appropriately, Dooni was raised on the gospel according to Billie Holiday.

When Dooni was a little boy in the early 1950s, the Palm Lane Church of God in Christ was on 119th and Compton. It was actually the back end of the pastor's house, covered up and screened in, with pews and a pulpit, a choir stand and a piano. Referred to as "the Back Porch" by congregants, it held more than a hundred people, and it was always full. Pastor Harold Conedy was an excellent and much-loved preacher, so services were often standing room only. Some folks came only every other Sunday, to free up space. Dooni and the other children were always in the front rows; they would give up their seats to older people politely, if a bit too eagerly, and run out to play. Dooni's uncle Boy played guitar, and Boy's wife played the piano.

Palm Lane was Pentecostal, one of many branches of black fundamentalist Holiness churches where letting the Holy Spirit take over the body was a hallmark of religious experience. Music was the main path to that ecstatic condition. The choir sang two songs in the morning and two at night, and everyone else sang and beat hands and tambourines all along the way. The music was Thomas Dorsey–Mahalia Jackson–style sanctified gospel. George Crawford, a gentleman encountering black gospel music in 1929, described it, not admiringly, as "jazzin' God": the sound coming out of such church windows was "conglomeration itself—a syncopated rhythmic mess of tune accompanied by strumming guitars and jangling tambourines and frequently punctuated by wild shrieks and stamping feet."

As Anthony Heilbut put it in *The Gospel Sound,* "most of the old Holiness tunes are similarly simple and repetitive," emphasizing rhythm and voices that could rise and rise until people seemed to overflow out of themselves. At Palm Lane, the songs usually began with a slow chant and erupted from there, the voices punctuated by claps, hmmm-hmmms, yesses, hallelujahs, moans, and hahs. If the right hand went up in the air, the left foot stomped the ground to match.

The music and the lyrics mostly aimed at redemption—*Take my hand precious Lord, and lead me home; There'll be peace in the valley for me someday*—but they also made clear that you could not get there alone. As the music writer Craig Werner says, "Gospel redemption breaks down the difference between personal salvation and communal liberation. . . . If we're going to bear up under the weight of the cross, to renounce the Devil, if we're going to survive to bear witness and move on up, we're going to have to connect. The music shows us how." There was plenty of room for soloists to tear up the room, but for every call there had to be a response. Deliverance, where Dooni came from, was a group thing.

It was also a lengthy thing. A Palm Lane service was an all-day affair, starting at eight in the morning and often keeping on until late at night. Folks would get up to testify, which could easily last half the morning. "They said that you couldn't shout or testify unless you lived free from sin all week and you hadn't done no wrong," says Dreda Slaughter, one of the few Back Porch congregants still at Palm Lane today. "I figured I lived right all week and I hadn't done no wrong, so it was *my* time to shout. And I was shoutin'."

Reverend Conedy would start preaching at around one o'clock, and the man could preach. "When they put him up to preach, oh, man, there wasn't nobody leaving," Slaughter says. When he was done preaching, around two-thirty or three, and people had done some more shouting and testifying and singing and getting happy, only then did the congregation dismiss. By the time they got to eat something, the children were achy with hunger.

Once fed, the kids had to be back at six for the young people's service, and then turn it back over to the adults. "Those that didn't get a chance to testify that morning, they got their chance that night," Dreda Slaughter says. "So you're gonna shout, and you're gonna testify, and shout. Then you gonna sing, then you gonna shout, take up the offering. Then the choir gonna sing, then you gonna sing, then you gonna shout. Then he's gonna preach. Then after we get through with that he'd make an altar call. We'd have a tarrying service for all those who want to be saved and those that want to be with the Holy Ghost." The music—Dooni's uncle Boy on guitar and his wife on piano—hardly stopped. "If they shouted all night long, Boy would be playing that guitar, and that woman would play the piano till her hands would swell. As long as we shouted, he would be playing that guitar and she was going to be on that piano." Sometimes they wouldn't finish before one or two o'clock in the morning. "I think that's why I'm so tired and sleepy right now," says Slaughter, "because my young life I was up all night at church. Boy, we would have *church*."

The services Dooni and his family attended at the Back Porch were not held only on Sundays. The worshippers also met on Tuesday nights, and if there was a revival, they would be there until the early hours of the morning Monday through Friday that whole week. If you wanted to, you could be at meetings or choir rehearsals or outings almost every day of the week. Once in a while, too, there'd be a "shut-in," where folks shut themselves into church and fasted and prayed for three days and three nights.

However exhausting, Palm Lane—which moved in 1954 from the Back Porch to a building on South Central Avenue—was a place of ecstasy. Time was different. Hunger could turn into lightness. A person could get swept away, and words could come tripping off tongues in magical rhythms. You could feel awe, and something like possession, just banging a tambourine and singing a song. You might feel the plural becoming singular. James Baldwin's classic description of a similar church in *Go Tell It on the Mountain* is probably the closest one can get, on paper, to what it felt like to be at Palm Lane. "The Power struck someone, a man or woman," Baldwin wrote in 1952, when Dooni was five; "they cried out, a long, wordless crying, and arms outstretched like wings, they began to Shout. Someone moved a chair a little to give them room, the rhythm paused, the singing stopped, only the pounding feet and the clapping hands were heard; then another cry, another dancer; then the tambourines began again, and the voices rose again, and the music swept on again, like fire, or flood, or judgment. The church seemed to swell with the Power it held, and, like a planet rocking in space, the temple rocked with the Power of God."

Over the coming decades, as Dooni left the church and grew into Sylvester, he carried church with him, often re-creating in his perform-ances and his music—like any great soul singer—the same sort of swelling and rocking. Baldwin's description of one man, Elisha, dancing, could eas-ily apply to 1970s gay discos: "It seemed that he could not breathe, that his body could not contain this passion. . . . His hands closed into fists, and his head snapped downward, his sweat loosening the grease that slicked down his hair; and the rhythm of the others quickened to match Elisha's rhythm. . . . And so, for a while, in the center of the dancers, head down, fists beating, on, on, unbearably, until it seemed the walls of the church would fall for very sound; and then, in a moment, with a cry, head up, arms high in the air, sweat pouring from his forehead, and all his body dancing as though it would never stop."

This was Letha's world, and the center of Dooni's when he was a kid, a planet rocking in space: a place where music could knock down walls, where bodies sought a power they could not contain, where God and dancing blended and the sound of conglomeration was the sound of redemption. "That's all he knew, was to shout and preach and pray like he saw them doing in church," Letha said, looking back.

Like a lot of church kids, Dooni was banging on the piano and singing by the time he was three. It turned out he could sing quite well, pretty and soprano-high, and he seemed to have made a decision very early on that he would be heard. "If you said no," his mother said, "he was determined to let it be yes. That was just his own personality." You had to be eleven to join the choir, but Dooni, years too young, would wait until the choir came marching in and jump into line from the pew. Someone in the choir would put him out, but usually he would come right back in the side door. They'd put him out again, and he might still slip himself back in. "He just would *make* them listen to him, 'cause he was so determined to sing," his mother said. When little Delmer Ray Cox, one of the other Palm Lane kids, died, Dooni sang "My Buddy" at the funeral. He didn't know the words, so he just sang the same lines over and over: *My buddy, my buddy, your buddy misses you.*

When Dooni was six years old, he was way too short to reach over the podium, so folks at Palm Lane would put him up on a milk crate, and he would sing "Never Grow Old," a hit at the time for the teenaged Aretha Franklin. *I have heard of a land on the far away strand, 'tis a beautiful home of the soul; built by Jesus on high, where we never shall die, 'tis a land where we never grow old.* Sometimes he and Letha would visit other churches, milk crate in tow; Dooni was "a little Stevie Wonder with vision," his sister Bernadette says. On occasion, he joined the choir along the California "gospel highway," the multidenominational circuit of churches and auditoriums that, since the early forties, had been bringing in gospel acts. "Everywhere he went he made a name for himself singing 'Never Grow Old.' When he got through, everybody would be shouting," his mother said. "He would just almost *dismiss* church." Then he would run off and play in the parking lot.

But Dooni wasn't a star at Palm Lane. In fact, in most ways he was a pretty typical church boy. "He wasn't a wonder," Dreda Slaughter says. "He was just a little kid banging around church, trying to sing, beating the tambourine like we all did." He loved an audience, for sure, but back then, he was just a pretty-eyed little boy standing on a milk crate, in his Sunday best, singing out.

In the woman-dominated Palm Lane Church of God in Christ in the mid-1950s, little boy Dooni was a bit of a mascot. Letha, who by this time had become a licensed dietician with a job at Morningside Hospital, dressed her sons like small churchgoing men: suits, ties, short haircuts, shiny shoes. Still, the older girls knew Dooni was a little different from his baby brothers. "He was feminine," Dreda Slaughter says. "He was as pretty as he could be, just like his mother. He wasn't rough like the other boys. He was prim and proper. We were always hugging on him and kissing on him, because he was so cute and always bouncing around and doing cute little things."

One day in church, Dooni was sitting with a girl around his age, Sister Wilson's niece. "Dooni," Bishop Conedy said from the pulpit, "I see you sitting there with that young lady. I want you to keep up with her. You all stick together. Just hang in there." The church broke into laughter. Maybe it was imagining the two little children in grown-up roles, the same kind of funny as dogs playing cards or kittens dressed up like kings. Or maybe it was the recognition that Dooni, who was as pretty as Sister Wilson's niece, might just need a little extra encouragement to hang in there.

His family knew, of course, that Dooni was his own kind of boy—"born funny," as Esau Joyner puts it—even if no one yet gave it a name. When they were still very young, Dooni and Larry and John would play baseball, shoot marbles, race go-carts, ride bikes. They learned how to swim and fish. By the time Dooni was eleven or so, though, he had lost interest in such things. He preferred his grandmother's company to his brothers'. He stayed inside a lot, reading encyclopedias, listening to music, and playing his grandmother's piano. "Why don't you want to come out and play with us?" they'd holler. "He wanted to do things you normally would see a girl doing, you know," Larry says. "He would be in the backyard and he always wanted to bury something. Or he played with dolls."

Neighborhood kids took to teasing Larry and John about their brother. "He act like a girl!" they'd say. "He's going to be a girl." Letha, who did not encourage shame in her children or division among them, explained that Dooni was not going to be a girl. "He is going to be a little different," she said, "but that don't make us apart from him."

Dooni did, however, try Letha's patience. He liked to dress up. When Esau Joyner came over to visit, he would often see Dooni walking around the house in his mother's high heels. Sometimes, starting when he was around six or seven, Letha would find Dooni rummaging through her closet. "What are you doing with that on?" she would ask, perhaps unsure what to make of her baby in her shoes and jewelry. "Oh," he'd say, without apology, "I'm trying this on." Over at his grandmother's house, he liked to wear JuJu's foxtail furs and hats.

One day in 1959, when Dooni was eleven, he complained of pain, so his mother took him to the family doctor. The doctor examined him, and ordered surgery in the rectal region. Letha Hurd did not really understand the sexual implications, so Dooni explained how he had been injured and, in the process, himself. Even then, he had no shame, although it was a shock for his family. "I was let down and disappointed, in a way," Letha Hurd said later. "Letha didn't know how to handle Dooni," says Esau Joyner, so she tried to get some help from a psychologist, who told her that some people are homosexual, and that her son seemed to be one of them.

"She was so disgusted," Joyner says. "She's from the South. They just wasn't used to that."

It turned out that Dooni had discovered not just God but sex at Palm Lane. By the age of eight, Sylvester later told the journalist Barry Walters, he had been introduced to "the life"—homosexual life—by a choir leader. Sylvester never named the man publicly, and he didn't tell his family about it until many years later. He did not exactly blame the man who had seduced him (no one knows how forcefully); even at eight or ten or twelve, Sylvester did not see himself simply as a powerless victim of abuse. That never seemed to change, though he seemed to realize the gravity of what had happened. When they were grown, Bernadette asked him how he got started in gay life. "One of the choir leaders turned me out," he told her, matter-of-factly. As Sylvester himself described it twenty-five years later to his friend and pastor Yvette Flunder, he was doing what he wanted to do.

"He had sex," Dr. Flunder says, "but he never called it sexual abuse. He never called it that. He was a younger man who slept with some older men. Everybody learns from somebody." In 1981 Sylvester told the writer Lee Hildebrand, "Obviously I had to want it to happen or else it wouldn't have happened." Speaking to Barry Walters in 1988, he did describe the experience as "abuse," yet not as something he regretted. "He did a real number on me," Sylvester said, "but it never made me crazy. I was a queen even back then, so it didn't bother me. I rather liked it."

But at Palm Lane, people began to talk about Dooni. A bouncy and prim six-year-old was charming, but when the child was twice that age people began to wonder. His effeminacy was now hard to write off as child's play, and Dooni wasn't working very hard to be like the other boys. His voice was changing, but he still preferred to sing in the high range. Rumors circulated, too, that he was doing unmentionable things upstairs with a man from the church. Some folks in the church knew, or thought they knew, that the man in question was the organist at Palm Lane, who was married— to "a cute little thing," says Dreda Slaughter—and had a child, too.

According to members of Sylvester's family, those folks were right. Still, no one at Palm Lane seemed concerned about Dooni. Instead, a lot of people just started getting chillier toward him. "The biggest hurt you could ever get is from church people," says Dreda Slaughter. "They slice you and dice you and dog you, and they think they are right and think they are helping you." She says many of the Palm Lane devout turned against

Dooni in part because they had their own sexual truths to keep hidden. "They were so busy making us live right," says Slaughter. "If one of the young ladies had a baby and wasn't married, they talked about us like we had a tail—but they were having them, getting rid of them, and all that." Dooni's family already attracted its share of talk. Tongues wagged when Egypt Morgan, who had been president of the Young People's Worship group, took up with a younger woman and left JuJu behind. Letha had given birth to twin girls, Bernadette and Bernadine, in 1956, by one father, and a boy, Alonzo, by another in 1959; she remained unmarried throughout. She did not tell anyone, including her children, anything at all about the men who were their fathers—not even their names—but at Palm Lane there was considerable speculation.

A child like Dooni was much more scandalous than an unwed mother or an unfaithful husband. To put it mildly, churches like Palm Lane were—and in many cases remain—particularly unsettled by homosexuality. On the one hand, most people would tell you, if you got rid of the homosexuals you wouldn't have much of a choir left. The Holiness church world, and especially its gospel choirs, can camouflage quite a bit of flaming with its own flamboyant spectacle. Anthony Heilbut has even claimed that the gospel world attracts "an inordinate number of male and female homosexuals," because of its theatricality, its anything-goes frenzy, and its repeated calls to witness God's presence even as you face "the whole world against you."

On the other hand, the only accepted church discussion of homosexuality was blunt condemnation; the unstated policy was something like "Don't-ask-don't-tell." Michael Eric Dyson has pointed out that "Sunday after Sunday, with little notice or collective outrage," homosexual church members are still regularly invited to be complicit in their own denunciation. "A black minister will preach a sermon railing against sexual ills, especially homosexuality," Dyson says. "At the close of a sermon, a soloist, who everybody knows is gay, will rise to perform a moving number." He sings, that is, his own "theological death sentence," his presence after the sermon symbolizing "a silent endorsement of the preacher's message."

Dooni stopped going to Palm Lane when he was around thirteen. He was, says his friend Yvette Flunder, "too flamboyant to be on the down-low" and "too real" for his church. No one came right out and told Dooni to leave, but "he was invited out of the church in the ways that church folks can invite you out." In particular, the man—or men—Dooni had messed around with "encouraged him out of the church milieu," says Flunder. That was the hardest part, Sylvester told Flunder: "The people that turned me out turned me out."

When later he talked about his reasons for leaving the church, they had more to do with hypocrisy than with sex. "People really believed in his capability of being able to heal and bring joy to people," Sylvester later said of the man with whom he'd had sex. "All these people were carrying on, and he was carrying on with me." Bernadette thinks Dooni was worried, too, that he would damage his mother's reputation at the church, which he knew Letha treasured. "She had a reputation of being a classy, elegant church woman, and a single woman raising six kids," Bernadette says. "He didn't want them pointing fingers, saying, 'See, this is what happens when you have so many kids with so many different men: One of them's going to turn out wrong.'" Dooni, she says, did not want to be the one who went wrong, who brought shame on his mother.

By the time Dooni left Palm Lane, Bernadette says, "he didn't trust the church—the pointing of the finger, the judging." He knew, more explicitly than most, where those pious pointed fingers had just been.

In 1960, with six children aged three to thirteen, Letha James became friendly with her next-door neighbor, a man eight years her junior named Robert Hurd, known as Sonny. (Although they had no biological children together, the Hurds later adopted three foster children: Angelica, Charles, and Tammy.) Sonny made a decent living at North American Rockwell, an aerospace manufacturer, where he did maintenance and construction and later became a supervisor. In 1962, after they got married, the Hurds moved together to a nicer house, on Ninety-seventh Street, north of Watts—a small complex, really, with a golden-colored Spanish-style house fronted by two giant cacti, and a detached duplex. It was not very far from where they had been living, but it was a step up. The Hurds were the first black family on their block. A few years later, after the Watts riots in 1965, when whites couldn't leave the neighborhood fast enough and real estate prices started to drop, Sonny Hurd bought up what he could. "All the whites wanted to get out of there," he says. "They was giving it away, so we took it." He bought a triplex, and then later five stores on 118th and Maine, turning himself into a minor real estate magnate.

Letha's younger kids grew up knowing Sonny as their dad, just as they grew up knowing JuJu as their mother's mother and each other as brothers and sisters. It's not that anyone was keeping great secrets. The family simply was what it was: JuJu was the grandmother, Sonny was the father, and that was that. Dooni, though, spoke of Sonny as his stepfather, and it was clear that the two of them lived on different planets. "Me and Sylvester, we wasn't really close, because a lot of things I didn't approve of," Sonny says. "I just left him alone. If I don't like what you're doing, I don't deal with you. We just didn't connect."

As Letha Hurd raised her younger kids, she opted for more rigorous gender training. Dooni, after all, had turned into an unconventional teenager, to say the least. "It was important to her that her kids be raised properly," Sonny Hurd says. "She just wanted the girls to be real women and the boys to be real men." The twin girls, Bernadine and Bernadette, went to private school, took ballet classes, marched on the drill team, and went to church. When they got older, Bernadine rebelled against some of the requirements, pulling her hair back into a ponytail, throwing on whatever clothes came to hand, and wearing no makeup. But Letha sent Bernadette, who stuck close to her mother, to a mostly white charm school on Sunset Boulevard. "It was a requirement for me to be a lady," says Bernadette. "You had to sit right, be presentable at all times. You had to look a certain way, dress a certain way, act a certain way." Bernadette walked with a book on her head, learned when to say "ma'am," "sir," "mister," and "missus," and how to choose clothes and makeup. She made her debut at the Coconut Grove nightclub, in the Ambassador Hotel on Wilshire Boulevard.

Even the neighborhood girls were under Miss Letha's watch. "I would hate to see Letha coming," says Dreda Slaughter. "She always tried to make me a refined young lady." Letha practiced what she preached, though. Both she and JuJu were known for their immaculate turnout and their stately carriage. Letha liked to look like a respectable lady, and she liked her girls to do the same. JuJu was partial to foxtail stoles and fur-collared coats. "Letha made dresses and things she would wear, and you thought she bought them," Dreda Slaughter says. "She kept Bernadine and Bernadette looking so good, those little girls would come out looking like they were walking out of Nordstrom's." After Sonny's arrival, looking good became even easier. Sonny knew how to rake money in, and he believed in spending it. "Do what you got to do when you want to do it" was his philosophy. Letha Hurd got a credit card and a checking account, and she was not afraid to use them. She drove a Mercedes. She once paid cash for a seven-thousand-dollar sable coat in Long Beach. She might buy several eight-hundred-dollar hats at a time, and she was known to drop a few thousand dollars on a suit. Bernadette once watched her enter a shoe store in San Diego and leave with seventy-eight boxes of shoes in tow; they barely fit in the Mercedes. At church, people waited to see what she would be wearing from week to week. They had to get ready for her. "They knew she was going to be the best-dressed thing there," says Bernadette.

When they went out of the house, especially to church, Letha and JuJu wore coordinated outfits: hats matched gloves matched handbags. "It was not something to do," says Bernadette. "It was a *must*."

Dooni took after them.

Dressing is, of course, an important form of communication. But for some—for women like JuJu and Letha, for instance—dressing is a conscious, elaborate act of self-expression, pride, pleasure, and duty. And for some black women, nothing is quite as important as what they put on their heads on Sunday.

On Sunday mornings at many black churches, ladies work their hats. There are, Craig Marberry wrote in the introduction to *Crowns* (a book of portraits of black women in church hats), "platter hats, lampshade hats, why'd-you-have-to-sit-in-front-of-me-hats, often with ornaments that runneth over." There are hats with all kinds of fur, and hats that look like spaceships. Typically, the best church hat is one of a kind and just showy enough to make people look. Peggy Knox, one of the women Marberry interviewed, talks about "hat-queen rules." She points out that a good church hat is big enough to make it difficult for someone to get too close, which is just as well, since the effect of the hat is better at a slight distance. A hat needs respect. "Listen, never touch my hat!" Ms. Knox says. "Admire it from a distance, honey."

Church of God in Christ women, such as Letha and JuJu, are known for their hats. "Some of us think there's going to be a section in heaven just for us and our hats," says a C.O.G.I.C. woman, Charlene Graves, in *Crowns*. No one ever said glamour and holiness were incompatible, but every woman must find her own dividing line. "I never get so dressed up that I feel like the Lord can't use me," says Ms. Graves, "'cause He will knock that hat right off your head and knock you out."

Sometimes, as Dooni blossomed, he seemed to want nothing less than to take his rightful place, after Letha and JuJu, in a long line of noble hat queens, to keep alive what would turn out to be a slowly dying art form. The principles, in any case, were there for the taking: Coordination is a must. Don't let anyone get too close. (Admire me from a distance, honey.) Seek your own kind of excellence. Never get so dressed up that you are useless to God.

Not surprisingly, Letha Hurd did not actually view Dooni's forays into dressing up as gestures of respect for her and her mother and their grand tradition of righteous black ladies. Nor, in his youth, did she accept homosexuality. Sylvester later claimed they fought a lot, though his sisters do not remember any fights; Robert Hurd says, "They fought a little bit, but it was just a thing that went on."

"If you don't like what's going on in my house, leave," Sylvester recalled his mother telling him one night when Dooni was in his mid-teens.

"Thank you, I've been waiting for this for years," he said, taking the you-can't-fire-me-I-quit position, and left.

No one quite recalls where he went, and for how long, but chances are his first stop was his grandmother's house. JuJu always took him in. "My grandmother was the first person to tell me I was gay," he said later. "She knew some queens in the thirties, and they were her running buddies. So I couldn't put anything over on her."

Letha Hurd was no pushover, but neither would she cut off any of her children completely. From the early 1960s until he left Los Angeles for good in 1970, Dooni drifted in and out of the Hurd household. Bernadette can remember his presence at many important moments. He was at Letha's when Martin Luther King Jr. gave his "I Have a Dream" speech in 1963, recording it on his reel-to-reel tape player; he and Bernadette listened to it over and over again, amazed "just to have a black man *near* the White House." He was at Letha's again, just visiting, when King was murdered five years later, taping again while everyone sat quietly. He was visiting when Robert F. Kennedy was shot; the family was watching television, and when Dooni started crying, so did his twelve-year-old sister. But he came and went as he pleased in those years, more a cautious guest than a resident. "He would be there," says Bernadette, "and then the next thing you know he'd be gone. He would just float in and float out—gone for a week, back, gone."

Many of the nights he was back at his mother's house, Dooni spent in front of the television. The Hurds had a black-and-white TV, but with a screen that went over it with blue, red, and green, to make it a sort-of color television. He had to sneak to the back of the house, and keep the sound down, but if there was a Ginger Rogers or Fred Astaire movie, it was worth the trouble. A Mae West movie was even better. Mae West could *wear* a hat.

Dooni seemed to think in movie scenes. His sisters became his living princesses, full-color, pint-sized actresses in his fantasies. He was responsible for their matching names, to begin with. When Letha had given birth to the twins, on Valentine's Day in 1956, she had asked her then nine-year-old son, who liked to make things up, to name them. Exhibiting a precocious appreciation for symmetry—and perhaps the mildly punitive flair of an eldest child—Dooni had named them like two little dolls: Bernadette and Bernadine, Dette and Dine for short. By the time they were six or seven, he found occasions to put them in full makeup, big hair, and lots of jewelry.

Dooni was closer to Bernadette; Bernadine, who had been very sick as an infant, spent the first five years of her life at JuJu's house down the street. Sometimes Bernadette had felt out of place as the only girl child in the house, and the feeling stuck with her. "I don't think I'm supposed to be here," she once told Sylvester. "You're supposed to be here, but you and I are different," he said. "Always remember that." When she woke up the next day, he was gone. "I was the one he always dressed, and he did my hair, and he would always make me feel special and important," she says. "I knew when he was gone I'd just have to go back to doing what I have to do."

Once, Dooni brought home a gross of flat-back rhinestones—white, pink, and blue—a pair of men's platform shoes, and some glue, and he and Bernadette made rhinestone platforms while they watched TV. He sewed custom clothing for their dolls. If they were fortunate enough to discover a dead bird, Dooni would make a bird-sized coffin sprayed with gold and lined with lace and rhinestones. On such occasions, he insisted that the girls attend the bird funeral dressed appropriately and that they mourn convincingly and in accordance with custom. He dug a hole, and put the open casket inside. They sang a hymn. Dooni briefly preached about the bird's life. He instructed the twins to break down into tears and moans, and they complied. "We buried it and we cried," Bernadette says. "Sang a song and cried, bitterly."

Bernadine got her own occasional Dooni makeovers. When she was nine, she played the main character, a swan, in her ballet recital. Letha made her costume: a lavender tutu over a petticoat. Dine's bird legs poked out from underneath. Dooni was called upon to do her hair and makeup. "Look up," he instructed her, as he worked on her eyes. "Pout your lips," he said. "That's just a little too much," her mother said, and Dooni dabbed a napkin on his tongue and rubbed off a bit of rouge. When Dine got to the recital, nobody recognized her—not her teacher, not the other tutu'd children. Her little cheekbones were bright red, and on her eyes were false eyelashes, black liner, and thick, thick shadow; on her head, a bouffant wig, ratted up. She was, you might say, the only swan in drag.

For her part, Bernadette thought of herself as the ugly duckling in the family, mainly because she wore thick glasses. "You know, you're beautiful with your glasses on and you're beautiful without them," Dooni once told her, outside in the backyard. "You try to count the number of people that have glasses on. There's not very many, so that makes you very special." Right then, one of their other brothers pushed Dette, knocked off her glasses, and bounced a basketball on them. She was panicked—unable to see, certain her mother would be furious at her for the broken glasses. Dooni sang to her, as he often did, to calm her down. *When you wish upon a star,* he sang, in a high, soft voice, *makes no difference who you are. If your heart is in your dreams, no request is too extreme.* Other times, when she was sad, he would make up a song from scratch, and he would call it "Bernadette."

Bernadette couldn't wait to be big enough to fit into Dooni's rhinestone platform shoes. She had grown up an introvert, but when she was finally getting set to go to her high school prom, she made her own dress and got herself a pair of blue platforms. "I rhinestoned my blue platform shoes," she says. "I mean, I *rhinestoned* 'em." Then she put on a pair of natural-tone stockings and rhinestoned those, too, gluing the stones on and then pulling the stockings off right before the glue dried. She washed the glue spots off her legs and hung the stockings up to dry. The next day, she went to the prom, twinkling and elevated and just a little too much.

✳   ✳   ✳

Somehow, Dooni managed to attend Jordan High School—one of three almost all black schools in South Central Los Angeles—though neither his family, nor his friends from the time, can recall talking to him about it or seeing him there. Eventually, in 1969, he would even graduate, at the age of twenty-one. In a graduation photo that became legendary among his friends, Dooni would wear a blue chiffon prom dress, and his hair in a beehive. Although his daytime education remains a mystery, both the advanced age at which he graduated and the dress he wore are a testimony to the more street-based night schooling he pursued in his middle and late teens, as a member of the Disquotays.

Dooni had met some of the future Disquotays at school and at gay parties around town, starting when he was about fifteen. Just as other kinds of gangs had formed in inner Los Angeles at the time—the Gladiators, the Slausons, the Businessmen, often engaging in violent clashes—Dooni and his friends formed themselves into the Disquotay club. Once he stopped living full-time at his mother's house, he lived mostly in and among the Disquotays. He grew his hair and wore lots of bracelets, and he glided through his life in Los Angeles like a butterfly, restless and beautiful and sometimes high. For a while, he lived out on Sunset Boulevard with Benedetta Barzini, born Ray Albertini, the only white gal in the bunch. For a while he lived with Jay Freeman, who always had good jobs. He was on and off various other people's couches. He had "sort of a reputation for being a moocher," says the former Disquotay Marapasa. He lived for a spell with Miss Duchess out on La Brea, though she eventually threw him out because "he didn't have no pennies."

Like many of his colleagues, Dooni found ways to get by without pennies. In May of 1968, for instance, he was arrested for "petty theft with a prior conviction of petty theft." Among the exhibits presented by the People of the State of California were the items Sylvester James, Jr., was accused of stealing: a bra, a girdle, and hose. When such events befell him, Dooni would simply disappear for a few days, returning to tell his friends he had been "on location, filming a movie," Los Angeles drag-queenese for doing jail time.

Dooni wandered from job to job. He once said that his first job was at McDonald's but that he was fired because he refused to wear a hairnet. "I can't think of anything bad about Dooni," Duchess says. "Other than that he could be lazy. He didn't want to work, but he didn't want to turn no tricks, either." For a little while, Dooni worked at the airport, collecting money at the parking garage, and for another little while at a department store, and on and off at a hair salon. He worked hair and makeup at a mortuary, where he could try out new ideas on corpses. Even if he wasn't bringing back a lot of money from the mortuary, he would bring back morbid, hilarious stories, like the one about the dead woman whose large breasts would not sit right in her low-cut funeral dress and had to be sewn together with needle and thread. He told his sister Bernadette that he could do hair and makeup for any corpse except a baby's.

When in doubt, or when he ran out of money, or when he just wanted a home-cooked meal, Dooni always went back to his grandmother's house, often avoiding Letha's. Jackie Hoyle, a Disquotay who was working as a clerk for Los Angeles County, recalls that Dooni would sometimes sit in front of his mother's house, wary of going inside. "If Dooni was hesitant to go into his mom's house, we didn't want to drag our asses in there," says Jackie. "But every time Dooni went to JuJu's door, we were right behind him, because she loved *all* of her children. Whatever Dooni wanted to do, and however he wanted to do it, it was okay with her. He could go in there dressed, or with his face made up. That was her grandson." When, many years later, Julia Morgan sat next to Rod Stewart at a Sylvester show in a Los Angeles club, she turned to Stewart—or so Sylvester told the story—as Sylvester emerged in a platinum blond wig and sequins. "See him?" she said. "That's my grandson. I made him his first dress!"

Over the years, among Disquotays and family alike, Dooni developed a reputation as a peace-loving individual with whom you did not want to mess. The Disquotays routinely argued, Jackie Hoyle says, "over trade, dresses, wigs, records—petty shit, typical sista-girl shit, just verbal cat-fights." Dooni, who did not stir things up, often intervened. "Why y'all arguing?" he'd ask. "Y'all don't have to. You got better things to do. Cut that shit out. Come on, let's do somethin' else. Let's go somewhere." He was too focused on excelling to be bothered with trifling.

If necessary, though, Dooni would fight, and if he did, watch out. "Dooni wouldn't run away from anything with his face in his hands," says Hoyle. "Not when you're from Watts and went to Jordan, no. Nobody could steamroll her; her feet were too big." Bernadette recalls a time when someone had beat up on their brother Larry, and Dooni and John went down to take care of business. "You know what, don't mess with Dooni," her brothers told her proudly. "He will kill you. He doesn't *play*." His own brothers didn't always heed their own warnings about Dooni, though. Dooni would show up to Disquotay gatherings with a story of John or Larry calling him a "punk," which he would not tolerate.

"I had to pop my brother tonight, girls," he would announce upon arrival.

"Oh, well," they'd say, and return to fixing their wigs.

Most of the time, though, Dooni was out being happy. He sang a lot, and often spoke with stylized precision, as if being recorded. "Dooni was in a Doris Day musical, and it was ongoing," Diane Moorehead says.

Dooni hitchhiked around town in drag, went to Disquotay parties, smoked weed; he kept busy, he said, being "the dark queen on Sunset Strip." He would meet up with the Disquotays at black clubs like the Clowns, the Hyde Park, the Belmont, the Bucket of Blood, and the only black gay club, the Horseshoe. Sometimes, he would just ride buses and shop downtown, alone. "She didn't need nobody," Diane Moorehead says. "She was a magnet, honey. She would attract, like flies to shit. Dooni knew everyone, and Dooni would go everywhere. Dooni was everybody's friend. There was no stopping her."

Dooni's boyfriend, on and off in the latter years of the 1960s, was Lonnie Prince. Lonnie, as Diane Moorehead renders him, was chocolate brown, curly-haired, clear-eyed, and well built. Jackie Hoyle describes him as "a Greek god." It had taken Lonnie a little while to hook Dooni, who made the boys work. "Dooni wasn't a quick catch, like some of us," says Hoyle. "If a man was fine, most of us would fuck within the hour. That didn't swoop Dooni. It wasn't just fuck-at-first-sight for Dooni. The guy would really have to impress her, date her and stuff like that." While the other girls would be looking at Lonnie, says Hoyle, "foaming at the mouth, fanning, giggling like geisha girls," Dooni would be turning the pages of a magazine. It took Lonnie Prince a few parties before Dooni was impressed, and then the two of them became the It couple. "They were like the hot couple on campus at high school," says Moorehead, "like the cheerleader and the quarterback."

When he and Lonnie were off again, as they often were, or when he was simply in the mood, Dooni went tootling around town with Duchess. Duchess had originally wanted to be called Melinda, but along the way, some admiring boys pulled the "you are my duchess" line from the pop song "Duke of Earl." The name stuck, perhaps because of Duchess's commanding and imperial demeanor. She grew up in a big Spanish-style house in the Wilshire district of Los Angeles, the child of upper-middle-class professionals. She started dressing at fifteen, and like Tiki used to climb out of the window at her mother's house—she'd tie sheets together and shimmy down the side of the house—to go to gay parties. When her mother noticed she was "just a little too sweet," her parents bought her big barbells for Christmas, and insisted that she work out every Saturday morning. "That is never going to happen," Duchess told them. Soon thereafter, they sent her to juvenile hall. Duchess ran away and got her own apartment, which for a while became a sort of halfway house for local queens. Even when she was in boy clothes, people mistook Duchess for a lesbian; dressed as a girl, she looked very girl indeed. Just in case, though, she carried a straight razor and some mace.

Duchess had met Dooni around 1965 through her first boyfriend, Billy, who lived around the corner from Dooni's family. They became inseparable friends, though Duchess found the Disquotays, with their "blue hair and roller skates and lights on their tits," far too Barnum and Bailey. "I am not doing that kind of show, honey," she said. "I am not wearing that shit. I just want to be a pretty colored girl." Duchess appreciated Dooni's sense of style. "Dooni always had taste," she says. "He was a block from the tracks, baby, but he was miles from the people over there."

Duchess paid her way partly by using the face and body God gave her, enhanced by balloons filled with chicken blood she bought from the chicken man on Exposition and Western. The blood was warm and heavy enough not to slosh like water. The men were never the wiser. "I had no pussy to sell, okay," she says, "and I *still* was selling pussy. I knew how to work it." She'd get in a man's car, get paid up front, and then slip away to "change her lipstick." Or she'd ask him to pull his pants down around his ankles so she could suck it right then and there, and then tie his shoelaces together and slide herself out the window. (Dooni did not hustle, though Duchess was famous for trying to "corrupt everybody into doing it," says Diane Moorehead. "She missed her calling. She should have been a pimp.")

Dooni and Duchess were their own little club, the two most unclockable queens in town; you knew they were boys only when they wanted you to know. Dooni was proud, and Duchess was even prouder, of their ability to pass as women—"fish," in the queens' English. "There were so many different little times that we would be out passing ourselves off as fish, and we would see other queens who didn't look real, and we would walk *away* from them, honey," Duchess says. Most of the girls wore deep layers of orange-ish makeup, which looked very pretty at night but made them look like pumpkin people in the daylight, but not Duchess and Dooni, whose smooth skin looked pretty with just a touch of makeup, day or night. Most of the girls couldn't have passed if they'd wanted to. "Miss Diane," Duchess says by way of example, "used to look like ten men being arrested. Blind men would know she was a man." Others had to disappear into the bathroom for hours to become girls, but not Duchess and Dooni. "I got up, brushed my hair, and put my lipstick on," says Duchess.

Dooni and Duchess would date boys who thought they were girls, and "hot cock" with them in cars, letting them kiss and touch them through their blouses but never letting them feel inside the clothes or below the waist. If they liked the boy, they might meet his mother. "Now you just come back, dear," boys' mothers would tell these nice, sweet girls. When they went out as fabulous black girls, shopping downtown or lunching at the Beverly Wilshire, they wished to be noticed as fabulous black girls. Once, at a restaurant that few black people frequented, they arrived wearing blond wigs cut in Twiggy hairstyles—short, boyish, parted on the side—micro-miniskirts, and utility belts on their hips. They were seated at a table behind a plant near the kitchen. "Oh, no, honey, this isn't working for me," Duchess said, eyeing a table in the center of the room. The maître d' allowed that he thought they would be happier where he had seated them. "Oh, no, honey, I don't think so, no," said Duchess Twiggy.

"You don't want us to make a *scene*," Dooni Twiggy added drily, and loudly, as the rest of the patrons looked on. "We want to be *very* visible," he said.

After a while, Duchess grew impatient with paying Dooni's way on such outings. You have to do *some*thing, Duchess would tell Dooni. Dooni agreed. "I'm going to be a star," he said. Such dramatic, self-aggrandizing declarations were about as typical among the Disquotays as false eyelashes, though. Anyway, future star or not, a girl had to pay the rent.

Most people figured Dooni would turn out to be a hairdresser, or maybe a fashion designer or a makeup artist. Others, however, were not surprised when years later he became a famous singer. He was always breaking into song in his churchy falsetto, or humming along to a tune while the Disquotays were spraying their wigs with Aqua Net. Getting ready to go out, he'd sing "You Are My Sunshine," or Aretha Franklin's version of "Blue Holiday"; on the bus bench at Western and Century he'd burst into "Don't Rain on My Parade" to the traffic. *Blue blue blue blue blue holiday, my heart's in pain!* On a barstool at the Black Continent on Adams and Crenshaw he'd do Barbara Acklin's "Love Makes a Woman" louder than the jukebox. "He would hit a note, but nobody said, 'Go on and sing it, baby!'" says Jackie Hoyle. "We would not tell Dooni, 'Sing that for me Dooni, *please.*' No. It was not like that." Sometimes, some Disquotays would just tell him to shut up his singing so they could hear the tune. "Dooni's screeching again," they used to say. "You sound just like somebody stepped on a cat's tail."

Dooni sang anyway. "He'd stop the party and *make* people listen," says Marapasa. Usually, at parties, he'd wind up in sing-offs with Larry Hines, whose soprano voice was trained, sharp, and clear, to see who could hit the highest note in a given Aretha song—"sissy kung fu," Marapasa used to call it. The party would stop, and people would cheer for a kung fu note from Miss Larry or Miss Dooni. A winner was never declared, and folks went back to dancing.

By 1969, the Disquotays had begun drifting apart, partly because they were getting too old—nineteen, twenty, twenty-one years old—to button their dresses. "They all turned into basketball players overnight," says Duchess. "When you are fifteen and sixteen, honey, even the toughest boys still got some little sweetness in them. But even hormones are not going to make Jim Brown soft. They all started getting hard, the jaws got tough, the razor bumps got harder. It was becoming the truck drivers' convention." Larry Hines and a few others had gone off to college; other people moved away; still others started working regular jobs. The ones who wanted to become women started toward surgery. Some, like Jackie and Benedetta, just didn't want to drag anymore.

Dooni, too, was moving away. He had moved back in with his mother and stepfather for much of 1969. Unlike Duchess, who had always felt herself a woman, and who in 1974 would officially become one through surgery, Dooni also enjoyed being a boy. "He wanted to express that feminine side, and it was very, very strong," Duchess says. "But I don't think she ever wanted to be a woman." Dooni enjoyed using his penis rather than tucking it. For Duchess, penetrating men was something to try, but Dooni "really, really liked it." Dooni still wore lots of jewelry, but his drag became a bit more androgynous: big bell-bottoms with a peasant blouse, maybe, and a colorful head scarf. Some days, he would paint his face into a beautiful woman's, then go out in boy clothes.

He went to rock concerts and rock clubs with Ray Albertini, who had recently stopped being Benedetta. Dooni was becoming a hippie, one of the few black ones, and began introducing himself to new friends as Sylvester. Still, he was often mistaken for a beautiful, dark hippie chick.

Dooni and the Disquotays wandered the streets of South Central in the 1960s done up like women, and threw ferocious gay parties in neighborhoods whose strongest institutions were conservative black churches. It's tempting to see them as fearless and heroic, defiant sissies who were forerunners of Stonewall and sixties counterculture, part of the dawning of gay liberation and African-American civil rights organizing. Los Angeles, after all, had long housed a gay and lesbian subculture and was the birthplace of the Mattachine Society, one of the first "homophile" organizations in the country, founded in 1951. It was also a major civil rights center, with a fifty-year-old chapter of the National Association for the Advancement of Colored People, a branch of the Congress of Racial Equality, black representatives on the city council, and a recent history of effective desegregation efforts. It was a growing Black Power center, especially after the Watts riots in August 1965—when racial inequalities and divisions, detonated by a routine traffic stop, erupted into a six-day uprising involving an estimated 35,000 participants and a military response by some 16,000 police officers, county deputies, and National Guardsmen. Thirty-four people died, more than a thousand were injured, and several thousand were arrested; 261 buildings were burned. Shortly thereafter, the Black Panther Party opened a Los Angeles chapter.

But even if those movements had shown any interest in black drag queens, the Disquotays were hardly interested in anything as dour and poorly dressed as a movement. Their defiance was more matter-of-fact. During the Watts riots, Sylvester said, "while everybody else was burning and looting, me and my friends were grabbing wigs, hairspray, and lipstick. No food or TV sets—just fun stuff." Then, while the neighborhood burned, the Disquotays ignored curfew at a house party. They only stopped dancing when the National Guard came pounding on the door.

If there was an ideology of the Disquotay Party, it was Be fabulous. Be the party. Look good. If there was a purpose, Diane Moorehead says, it was "the boys—what else?—the fellas!" As for the Black Panthers, the Disquotays' main interest was in the ones they dated, "on the QT side," says Jackie Hoyle. Nor did the Disquotays really think in terms of courage. "We weren't scared—scared of what?" says Moorehead. "Honey, we looked like girls. We weren't fearless. We were grand! We were fabulous!"

Fabulousness has a *je ne sais quoi*, like other indefinable things— beauty, love, star quality, good television. You know it mostly by encountering it. Most forms of excess are fabulous, at least when they are admired, and especially when they exceed or defy expectations. Some fat people are just overweight, for instance, but fat people who can really dance are fabulous; sometimes a senior citizen is just elderly, but with lots of rouge, dark sunglasses, and the right hat she can be fabulous; a lavish meal is fabulous if upon its presentation you have to stifle a laugh. The word itself comes from *fabulosus*, Latin for "celebrated in fable." As a personal attribute, fabulousness involves extravagance (which others sometimes interpret as showiness), and extreme, committed self-possession (which others often mistake for haughtiness). As a state of mind, it may best be understood by reference to a physical stance: you are fabulous if at any moment you can stop, rest your weight on one leg, and plant the other foot slightly ahead, raise your hands in a here-I-am vee with palms flat toward the sky, tilt your head back slightly, look upward into the middle distance, and know that applause is forthcoming. You are even more fabulous if you do not ever actually take this pose, but simply walk through life with the attitude it implies. Sequins don't hurt. The sea parts for the fabulous.

Warren Lofton, the boy who was to become Tiki, first met Dooni in Etta James's bathroom. When Tiki tells the story now, it sounds like a visitation from a fairy godmother or a lesser-known saint. Though she wasn't wearing women's clothing yet, Tiki was nonetheless being "fish," sitting down on the toilet to "twinkle." In walked a beautiful black woman in a black dress, her hair in a French roll. She had silky dark-chocolate skin, an oval face, and big feet. Tiki was shook, not having been around women in bathrooms, and started to flex up. "Oh, pay it no mind, sit down, girl," said the woman, introducing herself as Dooni. "Don't worry about it. I'm not a woman." Tiki could not believe it—*Where is this world?*—though Dooni was treating her just right.

"Ooh, chile, you're a cute little somethin'!" Dooni said to the boy on the toilet. "Mmmm. You'd be really pretty in drag. I've seen the others, but you, there's something I see in you."

Tiki was then still just a "plain little gay child," she says, but once he was under Dooni's tutelage it didn't take long for him to become a dynamic girl, the newest Disquotay turnout—"new tuna," in Disquotay parlance. Dooni first brought Tiki out at a party as a "challenge queen" to Duchess; she arrived that evening, not coincidentally, in the same outfit as Duchess. She became, Diane Moorehead says, "the Barbie Doll baby darling" of the set.

She was, however, still unnamed, still Warren. The next week, Dooni took her out for her first public street excursion as a pretty girl, giving Warren the name Jeannette Washington. Jeannette had a cold, and her voice was mannishly hoarse. "Well, shut up then," said Dooni. "I'll talk for you." Boys were honking and yelling, but Dooni instructed Jeannette to pay them no mind. Boys stopped them and asked their names. "She's a girl from Pasadena," Dooni told them, as his companion gave a little cough and jiggled a box of cough drops. "Her name is Jeannette, but she can't talk on account of she's got a sore throat."

In the crowd of Moniques and Benedettas and Doonis, the name Jeannette Washington quickly struck Dooni as dowdy and wrong. "I don't like that name," Dooni announced after Jeannette had attended a couple of parties as Jeannette. "Jeanette Washington? That's not carryin' on. Plus, you look a little bit Oriental or somethin'." Soon afterward, when the two of them were watching the Troy Donahue show *Adventures in Paradise* on Dooni's grandmother's television, Dooni seemed unusually interested in Donahue's adventures, which at that time involved a boat. "That's it!" Dooni called, pointing to the TV screen. "Kon-Tiki! Your name is Tiki!"

And so it was, and ever shall be.

In 1967, when Tiki's hormone breasts first got big enough to show off, she debuted them at a Disquotay party, while Dooni screeched over Martha and the Vandellas' "Honey Chile" and played the tambourine, running his thumb across the skin while tapping syncopation on top of a regular beat, as if it was church. "Dooni turned that party out with just one record and one tambourine," Diane says. "I will *never* get over it. It was just like an angel came down, honey. I thought I had passed on to a whole different level." While Tiki lifted up her shirt and bounced her pretty new titties to the boom-boom-boom, Dooni and Martha Reeves sang about the shiftless, lazy, hound-dog, amount-to-nothin' playboy they just couldn't live without, about the kiss that's sweeter than the cake that Grandma used to make, about honey chile, sure about to drive you wild.

3.

SEQUINS AT NOON

On a trip down to Hollywood in the early spring of 1970, a San Franciscan named Reggie Dunnigan walked into the Whisky a Go Go, a rock-dance club that had opened in an old bank on the Sunset Strip seven years before and had already become known as the place to be for up-and-coming musical acts and general madness. Jim Morrison and the Doors had been the house band there; go-go girls danced in cages. That night, Reggie was wearing a blond wig and a bandleader costume with big brass buttons. He saw, standing along the wall, a tall, dark, and handsome person with pierced ears, wearing a blunt-cut wig, men's pants, and a dress with the front cut open to make a smart little jacket. "We both just like zoomed in on one another," he recalled many years later, "because we were like men with sort of female touches around the edges." They were also two of only a few black boy-groupies at the Whisky. The man with the female touches introduced himself as Sylvester.

Reggie and Sylvester started dancing, and Reggie told Sylvester about the scene up in San Francisco, where he and a gaggle of assorted individuals had started putting on Busby-Berkeley-on-drugs shows at midnight, calling themselves the Cockettes. The Cockettes, a "hippie glitter gender-fuck troupe," as one of them later described the group, were only a few months old. They had done a few shows at the Palace Theatre in North Beach: *Paste on Paste* included a beautiful man named Hibiscus lip-synching to Ethel Merman, a queen named Big Daryl instructing a novice in how to put on coconut breasts, some folks dancing to the Rolling Stones, and the whole cast singing "You'll Never Walk Alone" to the Virgin Mary as a finale. Their sets were made from cardboard, their budgets were in the fifty-dollar range, their makeup was freaky. They wore dresses made out of curtains and used scripts that were not much more than lists of sets.

Glitter was a must. Audiences were enthusiastic—about the shows, about themselves, and about the passing of joints and jugs of wine.

None of this sounded half bad to Sylvester.

Reggie gave his new friend his address and phone number in San Francisco. "You *have* to come to San Francisco," Reggie told him. "You are wasting yourself in Hollywood. No one could appreciate you more than we." Around the same time, Goldie Glitters, another Cockette who knew Sylvester a bit from Los Angeles, threw a toga party in L.A. Goldie thought Sylvester would be a fabulous addition to the Cockettes, and at the toga party he, too, invited Sylvester to San Francisco.

If Reggie were alive, he and Goldie could, and probably would, catfight for credit for Sylvester's arrival in San Francisco. Most likely, the invitations just piled up on top of Sylvester's restlessness and curiosity. He'd been hearing about the San Francisco scene for a while, from hippie boys in rock clubs wearing satin bell-bottoms, ladies' blouses, and platform shoes. The Disquotays were done; he had worn out his welcome at Duchess's apartment; and he was tiring, he later told the researcher Martin Worman, of "doing hair by day and dressing to go out at night," seeing the same old places and the same old people. "I was just getting too crazed in Los Angeles," he said in 1972. "I was carrying on too much. I had to go someplace higher than Los Angeles, where I could do what I wanted to do and dress the way I wanted without getting the news."

The identity options in Los Angeles were clipping him. "You could be a drag queen, a transsexual, a gay guy," Marapasa says of the Los Angeles scene in which she and Dooni were running. "But there was no room for anything else. In retrospect, it was a little provincial. He was more than just a drag queen or a gay guy or a transsexual; he was all of that." He didn't want to be Dooni anymore, anyway. He had already edged away from *Vogue*-model-on-roller-skates drag, and toward the kind of male-female concoction he'd been wearing the night he met Reggie at the Whisky. He was ready to be someone new, whoever that might turn out to be.

Sylvester took a trip up north not long after meeting Reggie. San Francisco, with its dramatic poise, its frilly Victorian gingerbread houses, lacy and colorful and primped for a night out, was so far from the modern flatness and dulling grays of Los Angeles. The two-story pastel Edwardians cozied up to each other, tall enough to catch the sun but not tall enough to block it. Late afternoon brought woolly fog rolling in over hills and bridges as if it were on its way to somewhere, and then lay relaxed on top of the city, as if it had arrived. The city could make one feel optimistic and open, and also vaguely European, as if one ought to be sipping red wine in a sidewalk café and considering new possibilities. "I could be any kind of person at all, and no one cared," Sylvester said later. "Los Angeles is a role city, but San Francisco is free." Like most people with hearts, Sylvester fell right in love with the place. It was the beginning of 1970, he was twenty-two, and things were up for grabs in his life—in the whole country, for that matter.

Sylvester went back down to Los Angeles, packed his stuff, and kissed his mother and grandmother and sisters good-bye. He made sure to tell his baby sister Bernadette that he wasn't leaving because of anything she'd done. "San Francisco is where I can do what I'm here to do," he told her. By Wednesday, he was living in San Francisco.

How Sylvester wound up actually joining the Cockettes is another story on which there seems to be some disagreement. Kreemah Ritz, a Cockette known then as Big Daryl (and then, briefly, as Harold Thunderpussy), remembers that Sylvester was crashing with Tomata du Plenty, an acquaintance who was himself a visitor, on the floor of a huge Victorian flat on Hayes Street. Tomata, Kreemah recalls, brought Sylvester over to the Cockette house on Haight Street for a visit. A Cockette named Tahara recalls that Sylvester had just moved into a flat with two roommates at the top of a long staircase, where he had a few unpacked boxes and a mattress on the floor. Tahara had been seeing Sylvester regularly at the Stud, a bar south of Market Street where "everybody far-out went every night."

One night, Tahara recalls, Sylvester invited everyone at the Stud to his flat for a party, and Tahara showed up with about thirty other people. Word got out that Sylvester did Billie Holiday impersonations. Sylvester pulled out a little square hi-fi and put on a Billie Holiday album. "Wait, no, hold on," he said, "I have to do it with a gardenia in my hair." He found a white flower and put it in his hair, and restarted the record. "Wait, no, hold on," he said, "I have to put on a cut-on-the-bias dress." Finding just the thing, he put it on, restarted the record, and sang with Billie. "You have to be in our show at the Palace Theatre," Tahara said, and the next day brought him over to the Cockette house on Haight Street.

There, both stories converge. People were wandering in and out, so Sylvester made himself at home. He was wearing bell-bottom Levi's, a floral shirt tied up at the bottom into a little halter, platform shoes, and a black do-rag knotted up into a bun in the back. Kreemah heard him tinkering at the house piano, a thirty-five-dollar thrift-store purchase that people only played as a joke, since it was badly out of tune. "Sylvester sat down and started playing, and all of a sudden it didn't sound like the same piano anymore," says Kreemah. A few Cockettes stopped their horsing around and wandered down to see what had happened to the piano. Sylvester began singing bits of this and that, his bracelets clanging away, sounding something like Aretha.

Some of the Cockettes had been talking about doing a mock gospel show, *Radio Rodeo*. Being mostly white boys and girls, they weren't certain they knew how to make it work. "We didn't have any soul in us, but we were going to act like we had soul," Kreemah says, so he asked Sylvester if he wanted to be in the production. Kreemah and a fellow Cockette, Scrumbly Koldwin, sat down at the piano and sang their rendition of "Amazing Grace." "We sang it just like white folks," Kreemah says. Sylvester was not impressed. "I don't want to be in the show if that's what you are going to do," he said. *Show us*, they said. When Sylvester played and sang, they had never heard anything like it. He stretched out some words into moans, trilling up and down others as if his soul were climbing a ladder, going quiet for a few lines and then building to a crescendo. *Oh, my God*, they said.

Later that weekend, Sylvester and Reggie spent the day wandering into thrift stores in Haight-Ashbury, by then a thriving hippie enclave. By the time they got to the Lower Haight, Sylvester had accumulated on his body a woman's suit, silk stockings, women's shoes, a woman's jacket, and a feathered hat. *Damn*, Reggie said to himself. *This bitch can shop.* "She found everything she needed and put it right on and just wore it in the street, brazen," Reggie later recalled to the filmmakers Bill Weber and David Weissman. "And looked incredible."

For every show, the Cockettes moved their piano down two flights of stairs from the Haight Street flat and drove it over to the Palace Theatre. That afternoon, Reggie got a call from Scrumbly telling him he needed help with the piano, so he and Sylvester took a bus up to North Beach. They unloaded the piano from the back of the truck. Scrumbly was there, Hibiscus was there, a bunch of Cockettes were there. Sylvester was in his suit, stockings, and hat—which, of course, immediately impressed the

Cockettes. They got the piano into the theater and set up for a *Radio Rodeo* rehearsal. No one arrived at any established time for such things. The concept of rehearsing, not to mention the notion of punctuality, was too establishment; "every rehearsal a performance, every performance a rehearsal," the Cockettes liked to say.

Passing the time, Sylvester sat down at the piano. "I hadn't a clue that he was talented and musical or anything," Reggie said. "I thought he was just some queen. He started playing piano and it was the old-fashioned, tinkling kind of piano that made you feel you were in 1920, and it was fabulous. Everyone turned around and our jaws were dropped. Then she started singing, and she was singing gospel music and in a falsetto voice that sounded like a woman, and his face when he sang was relaxed and beautiful. Everybody was on the floor. They couldn't believe it." He played the Mickey Mouse Club song as a gospel prayer, slowing down each letter and circling around it like he was spelling the name of Christ Himself. Lightbulbs and whispering went off among the Mouseketeers who were present and the others straggling in. He just *had* to be in their show.

Sylvester wasn't so sure. By the time of his visit, the Cockettes had improvised their way through *Paste on Paste,* and then a version of *Madame Butterfly* with cruddy kimonos and a fifteen-foot fan-dancing geisha. That weekend, a couple of Sylvester's friends took him to the Palace to see the Cockettes' latest, *Gone with the Showboat to Oklahoma,* a promiscuous mix of musical Americana that included a Mammy drag queen in a bandana, who was servant to a Scarlett O'Hara played by a pale young man named Johnni. Johnni, the ex-Cockette Martin Worman recalled, had "natural Scarlett O'Hara ringlets," and was wearing a see-through hoop skirt and "just the lower half of his bloomers, jauntily revealing his fat cock and balls and succulent buns." The show started late, but no one seemed to notice. The audience was noisy, giddy, standing on the seats calling out and screeching and making their own fun and only half paying attention to the stage. During the show, Scrumbly, wearing "breasts made of football halves, and a hoop skirt made of hula hoops," picked up a 7-Up can that an annoyed patron had thrown onto the stage and swigged it "in a parody of butch machismo." Later, the Day-Glo *Show Boat* set collapsed, to the audience's delight, just as a line of chorus girls moved downstage singing, in multiple keys, "Life Upon the Wicked Stage." Upstairs in the balcony, some people seemed to be having sex. Sylvester had never seen anything quite like it, not even in church, where in a different way people could get carried away. He was excited, and put off. "I was really, really scared," he said later. "It was nothing I wanted to be part of."

If you're going to San Francisco, Scott McKenzie sang to pretty much the whole world in 1967, be sure to wear some flowers in your hair. People talked about San Francisco in the late 1960s as if its streets were paved with flowers and weed and acid, as if music there grew on trees. Groups like the Sexual Freedom League were advocating, as a means to peace, love, and happiness, going "naked most of the time," having "five or six orgasms a night" with as many partners as you pleased, and "fucking freely with both sexes." People heard stories, especially after the 1967 Summer of Love, and they just showed up. "San Francisco was a tremendous collection of misfits, of people who were aliens in their own family, the lost souls, really," says Fayette Hauser, who grew up in suburban New Jersey, went to art school in Boston, pitched a tent in the woods near Aspen in 1968, hitched a ride to San Francisco when Colorado got too cold, and became a Cockette. Around the time Richard and Pat Nixon were getting settled in the White House, Fayette was moving into a series of rickety flats. "I just discarded everything that was a remote remnant of my suburban past," Fayette says in *The Cockettes,* a film by David Weissman and Bill Weber.

The people Sylvester met that weekend in 1970, Fayette among them, were unabashedly strange and weirdly familiar. They had names like Hibiscus, Scrumbly, Harlow, Sweet Pam, Big Daryl, Dusty Dawn, Gary Cherry, Link, Pristine Condition, Goldie Glitters. They were men, women— "fruit flies," the women were sometimes called—and in-between. A few smudged children were also present. All of them, basically, seemed to be making themselves up as they went along. They crinkled their noses at any scent of normalcy, and they seemed to live without rules. They happily had sex with whomever they wanted, did hallucinogenic drugs, wore flowers in their hair, and listened to unusual music. Everybody stayed at each other's houses, mostly run-down Haight-Ashbury Victorians serving as communes; the floors were often so crowded at night that people had to step over each other to find a spot. The Haight was gritty and foggy, almost spooky sometimes, but it was theirs and they loved it. Their houses regularly caught on fire, from candles, incense, and pot.

Most of all, they liked to play dress-up. "You completely communicated through drag," says Fayette, who favored black lace and exposed breasts. Sometimes they were just too stoned to communicate with words, anyway. Every day, some constellation of people on drugs would exit the house, and go be what Fayette calls "mythic figures that walked the street." From their imagination they would pull visions that the culture had tried to lock out. Then they would try to wear them. "The point was to turn it inside out, really," Fayette says. "We were deliberately entering the imagination. People speak about their dreams and their fantasies and their desires, but it was all cloaked in. They were speaking about it but they weren't fully out there living it. So that was our job, was to realize that aspect of ourselves, to bring it into materialization. That's a big job, and we were committed." The psychedelics helped.

Sylvester agreed to be in a Cockettes show. A few weeks later, he performed his version of the Mickey Mouse Club song for a screaming crowd at the Palace, wearing a cowgirl skirt. It was like running off with the circus, and like coming home.

In 1964, with the pictures to prove it, *Life* magazine had declared San Francisco the "gay capital" of the United States of America. The city, especially North Beach, was dotted with bars that were gay or gayish: the Silver Dollar, the Fickle Fox, the Golden Cask, the Purple Onion, the Hungry I, the Paper Doll, Finocchio's, Ann's 440, and Mona's, where "girls will be boys." If you had the money, you could spend your time with cabaret people in spots like Chez Jacques and Sutter's Mill and the Venetian Room. You could dress up and go to the Oak Room at the St. Francis Hotel, which was quite gay, and at the piano bar at Dolan's.

For a cheaper and dirtier time, you could sample a bar near the wharf, where there were more military men available than you could shake a stick at. Or you could visit the Capri on Grant, or the Black Cat Cafe, a bar that had been a site of underground mixing since the 1940s and of nascent gay politics since the 1950s. Allen Ginsberg once described the Black Cat as "totally open, bohemian, San Francisco," an enormous bar with a honky-tonk piano, filled with "all the gay screaming queens," the "heterosexual gray flannel suit types, longshoremen," and "all the poets." In 1961, a Black Cat employee, José Sarria, who performed campy satirical operas and led bargoers in rounds of "God Save Us Nelly Queens," had run for city supervisor.

You could live an uncloseted life in San Francisco, but even there, for a lot of people, the late 1950s and early 1960s had been about stealing pleasures and avoiding police. In 1955, the police chief ordered the sex crimes squad to "get rid of this offensive mess" of homosexuals; in 1961, around fifty men and women were arrested in anti-homosexual bar sweeps every week, part of yet another very public campaign against San Francisco's "sex deviates." When he was eighteen, the poet Aaron Shurin used to come into the city from Berkeley and go to an unmarked door on Sutter Street that he knew was the Rendezvous. "You knew that's where people went," he says. "It was kind of collegiate, crewneck sweaters, very pressed. And terrifying, a nouveau hell. It was extremely brutal, extremely repressed, still tragic—it was still Judy Garland and Barbra Streisand, the ethos of tragic inevitability. You scurried into the Rendezvous and you scurried home, as if you had a fedora to hide your face."

By 1965, businesses owned by and catering to homosexuals had sprung up along Polk Street, and the first gay community center had opened in the South of Market neighborhood in 1966. By then, though there was certainly a big homosexual audience for Streisand, you could also find spots where crewnecks, fedoras, and tragedy seemed totally out of place. For Aaron Shurin, that spot was the Capri, which by 1967 was a gay hippie bar. At the Capri people hung out on the street after closing time. People leaned on cars and talked and maybe smoked a joint. "At the Capri, you stood outside in the street together, on your home turf, talking, making liaisons, having friendships outside in the open, in the air," Aaron Shurin says. "For me, it was deep, because it wasn't governed by pain, it wasn't governed by loneliness. It didn't live under the sign of loneliness. It lived under the sign of something new, a new light and a new order that was just being named."

After the Stonewall rebellion in New York in 1969, that new order became known, of course, as Gay Liberation. That was a name for something that had been building in San Francisco—which by 1970 had become, as the political activist Carl Wittman put it, a "gay refugee camp"—for more than a decade. Gay Liberation and hippie countercultures were intimate comrades, especially in San Francisco. Both wanted a world where people did it if it felt good, loved whoever they wanted, whenever they wanted, however they wanted. Homosexuality, as one of the most repressed forms of joy, was a particularly ripe path to revolution; an acid trip, poetry reading, or rock concert might work just as well.

The overlap between Gay Liberation and hippiedom was not just one of philosophy but of everyday life. At the Café Flore, a café on Market Street that had become a sort of informal Gay Lib community center, you could meet people taking a break from an anarchist study group or a sissy study group. The men who went to the Stud bar, which by 1970 had replaced the Capri as the nighttime center of gay bohemia, might be simultaneously planning that night's sex and the next day's guerrilla theater. "We met, we organized, we sang, we danced, we fucked, and it was all part of a project, a comprehensible and totalizing project," says Aaron Shurin, who had begun publishing poems like "Exorcism of the Straight/Man/Demon" in the new gay literary journals. "We were the soldiers of ecstasy."

When Sylvester went to San Francisco in 1970, he moved to one particular intersection of gay life and hippie life. The Cockettes were soldiers of ecstasy, but not the study-group kind. Their project involved very little of the meeting, organizing, and comprehensibility, and a whole lot of the singing, dancing, and fucking. If communes, hippies, drugs, homosexuals, and drag queens were increasingly unremarkable in San Francisco at the time, the Cockettes nevertheless combined them all into an unprecedented stew. "The weirdest thing was that they were Communist drag queens," says the filmmaker John Waters. "Bearded, transvestite, drug-crazed, hippie Communists."

It might be said that the Cockettes' origins can be traced to the making of cum bread. In 1967, Hibiscus, who had been born George Harris III in Westchester, drove to California in a white VW van with the poet and beatnik Peter Orlovsky and a few others. He had been a child model and a bit-part actor in Florida, where his family had moved, and later in the off-off-Broadway avant-garde world in which his father operated. At the time, he said later, "I was still very Brooks Brothers—you know, short hair and lots of madras shirts." He was pretty and blond and eighteen. Along the way, the van stopped for a Washington, D.C., peace march, where George, with *Life* magazine cameras snapping, became the kid who put flowers in the rifles of the National Guardsmen.

In San Francisco, George grew his hair, became a vegetarian, wore long robes and headdresses, and, he said, "lived the life of an angel." By 1969, he had joined the Sutter Street commune, established by the editor and writer Irving Rosenthal, a comrade of Orlovsky, Orlovsky's lover Allen

Ginsberg, and William Burroughs. "He slowly metamorphosed from a young uptown faggot," Rosenthal recalled in a memoir, "to the airy spirit that later dubbed himself Hibiscus." He began sticking fern leaves in his turbans, which eventually became "tropical islands of vegetation." He went barefoot. He wore "full rag drag full-time: torn gowns, flowing coat linings, and tattered scarves," and "his room became a jungle of drag, items of personal adornment, photos, make-up, illustrations cut out of library books, love letters, incense, and Vaseline." His fellow Cockette Reggie once described Hibiscus as "Jesus Christ with lipstick."

The Sutter Street commune was part of a food-buying cooperative that included many of the hundreds of communal households that had sprouted in San Francisco by the late 1960s. It was an ideologically serious place, committed to Free Everything. The commune had emerged partly out of the Diggers, a mid-1960s group of radicals, based mainly in Haight-Ashbury, who were against private property and for doing your own thing. The Diggers themselves had evolved out of the San Francisco Mime Troupe, and in addition to setting up free clinics and distributing free food every day at four P.M., they put on free shows in the streets and in parks. They distributed free Digger Paper manifestos, too, which combined political critique with druggy poetics. One proposed "a FREE PUBLIC structure in the Panhandle where individuals can swim in vinyl pools filled with Vaseline, WAIL LOVE to downcast brows, and carry on as much as they want until they think it beautiful to stop." The author of another flyer claimed, on bright orange paper, to have "suffered from an awful frenzy of collapsed assumptions," and continued: "Needless to say, REVOLUTION NOW—now spinning—now now—invisible—now floating—somewhere—outthere—waiting to grind someone's brain."

The Sutter Street commune espoused the Digger Free philosophy, which they articulated weekly in a free intercommunal newspaper of "practical, philosophical, and household tips." They called their paper *Kaliflower*—borrowing from "Kaliyuga," a Hindu term for Dark Age—to signify a "flower growing out of the ashes of this current age of destruction." The commune took the same name. Thursdays were Kaliflower Day: the commune members would deliver groceries to the other households, along with *Kaliflower.*

Hibiscus was a Kaliflower delivery boy and he enjoyed every moment of it. He liked to pick roses out of the garbage in Union Square, he later told the writer Mark Thompson, and run around singing his old Broadway favorites, such as "You Are Beautiful," from *Flower Drum Song*, and "If I Loved You" from *Carousel*. He also liked to turn his grocery-and-*Kaliflower* delivery into a little show. With a couple of friends, Ralph and Jilala, he formed the Kitchen Sluts. They would deliver the produce and paper to a commune, scrub down the kitchen, and, transforming those present into audiences, perform vaudevillian floor shows. Then Hibiscus would present the household with cum bread, made from dough into which he had masturbated, alone or with his most recent sex partner. "The making of the bread was rather controversial," Hibiscus said later. "It was a whole spiritual thing for me at the time, although a lot of people didn't like it."

Even if they were uncertain about the bread, many of the various communes' members adored the theatrics. In fact, as Worman—who became a Cockette and later a doctoral student studying the Cockettes—described it, many of them already "lived in costumes inspired by their daydreams" and "enacted scenes and musical numbers at home." The Kitchen Sluts had delivered to and performed for Big Daryl and his friends in a flat near Schrader and Page Streets, for a group at Bush and Baker that included Scrumbly and Link, and for the Lyon Street commune in lower Pacific Heights, where Fayette Hauser, Nicky Nichols, and Harlow lived. They recognized in each other an affinity not just for communal living, but for dressing up and slapstick theatrics. "I like to watch people on the streets, to become them, to change their lives," Hibiscus wrote to his brother in 1969. "All the children of paradise."

They ran into each other in the streets, in Golden Gate Park, and at the Palace, a Chinese-deco theater opposite Washington Park in North Beach, which showed kung fu films in Chinese during the day. In 1969 the owner, Mr. Chew, agreed to let a couple of film students, Steven Arnold and Michael Wiese, show underground, ignored-classic, and avant-garde movies at midnight on Fridays and Saturdays. The Midnight Films—later renamed the Nocturnal Dream Shows by Wiese and Arnold and their business manager and booker, Sebastian—were much more than movie shows. They were scenes. The Palace had a carnival-style bronze box office in front of a neon marquee, and its interior was all fading elegance: a two-tiered balcony, Oriental carpeting with a swirling-comet design, and a lobby with red and chartreuse tiling, rattan chairs, and a candy counter.

Arnold and Wiese did everything they could to make it a merry, trippy place. The pair wore costumes and face paint and tuxedo tails. They made up ornate, gorgeous flyers with detailed, hand-drawn, mythic beings from other worlds: satyrs and totem poles and insect-human offspring; a Middle Eastern–looking figure sitting in front of a hookah, smiling and looking up into the eyes of a quarter moon, smoke rising around his headdress; a creature with breasts, two different sets of horns, and long flowing hair beneath a spiky halo, holding up mermaid-finned legs as out of her long penis droplets drip-drip-dripped onto the words "Midnight Films." That the audience would get high was assumed.

The audiences at the Palace showed off strange finery in the aisles and at Mr. Chew's now-lucrative candy counter, which attracted so much hanging out and stoned munching that regulars referred to it as the "candy counterculture." They yoooo-hoooed to one another across the theater. "It was like an insane asylum in there," says John Waters.

The Nocturnal Dream Shows quickly came to include little stage performances between films, and sometimes Wiese and Arnold and Sebastian just threw parties. In his dissertation—he died before he could complete it—Worman described their Halloween costume bash in 1969, in which many future Cockettes joined the spectacle. A man named John Rothermel wore a red ball gown, red satin bell-bottoms with a teal brocade sash, and red alligator pumps, and "his very long, dark brown hair fell over his exposed shoulders, back, and hairy chest."

Hibiscus arrived "wearing a shocking pink Jayne Mansfield gown with beach ball breasts, Kabuki makeup, and glitter in his beard, topped by a floor-length bridal veil trailing fifteen feet behind him, and carrying armfuls of dead roses." Goldie Glitters, "a tall, imperious queen," wore a Grand Ole Opry ball gown with the price tag still on. They, along with other members of the audience, were invited to strut their stuff onstage for prizes. Hibiscus and two young men "sang a nonsense song a capella and took off their clothes," winning no prizes. Goldie received a "large dead flounder and held it like a lady at arm's length, between two black-polished fingernails." John Rothermel "hiked up his dress over the footlights, and took a giant step onto the stage from the orchestra pit." The audience howled, delighted by the move, and John was awarded a cheap San Francisco souvenir. "From the beginning," Rothermel later told Worman, "the audience condoned, appreciated, and glorified itself, so that anything that was tradition-breaking, like crawling up over the footlights, provoked a great reaction." The Palace was becoming a freaky community center.

❂   ❂   ❂

A few months later, the Nocturnal Dream Shows producers announced a New Year's Eve program to welcome the 1970s. It would be a "Futurama Costume Gala," with a science-fiction program booked by Sebastian, including a Flash Gordon flick and H. G. Wells's *Things to Come*. On stage, the poster promised, would be the Golden Toad and the Floating Lotus Magic Opera Company, two "hippie gypsy tribal" bands that had been playing in city parks and schools.

At dinner at Kaliflower on the last night of 1969 with a dozen friends—Sweet Pam, Goldie, Fayette, Ralph, Big Daryl, Scrumbly, Rumi, Dusty, and a few others—Hibiscus announced that everyone there was invited to be part of the New Year's stage show. Hibiscus said he was bringing a 45 of the Rolling Stones' "Honky Tonk Women," and they would dance. Ralph grabbed the key to the drag room, and they dressed up with whatever they could find in the house—the place was brimming with wigs and feathers and thrift-store gowns and jewelry—put glitter on facial hair and genitals and nipples, and set out for the Palace. "Thirteen of us got together and decided we wanted to do a show," as Kreemah Ritz tells it. "We didn't think anything would happen."

As the Golden Toad was finishing, Hibiscus and his crew took the stage and danced around to Mick Jagger in front of an audience of about six hundred people. Nothing was planned. They were slap-happy kids in their living room, prancing in undies and their mothers' shoes and lipstick, mooning and flashing the world. Worman recounted the extravaganza: "Hibiscus wore a fringed lamp shade on his head, coconut halves for breasts on his bare chest, and a grass skirt with nothing underneath. Kreemah sported a platinum marcelled wig done up with red cock feathers, and a red velvet Empire dress, and danced tango-style with one of the satin palm trees. Harlow's natural blond hair fell in pre-Raphaelite cascades. She wore emeralds at her ears and neck, and a backless silver satin gown cut low in front, and a white fur fox draped over her shoulders that allowed her to discreetly flash her breasts. Dusty Dawn wore pigtails and a sailor blouse, and swayed to the music while exposing her breasts. Scrumbly also flashed, lifting his hoop skirt to jump through a hula hoop." The audience, dressed up and tripping and dancing themselves, was whooping for more, and anyway those on stage seemed entirely uninterested in vacating, so the sound guy simply put "Honky Tonk Women" back on and they danced some more, this time joining up in a kick line for a short drunken-Rockettes cancan. They had taken off most of their clothes.

Asked for a name, they called themselves, of course, the Cockettes.

It was just another night of hey-fellas-let's-put-on-a-show. "It was, 'Here we are, androgynous freaks up here dancing! Thank you and good-night!'" says Scrumbly. "We just danced all dressed up in drag," Hibiscus said. "We just did it, got off the stage, took a little more LSD, and went out for food," says Kreemah. Soon, though, the Palace Theatre started getting calls wanting to know when the dancing boys and girls were coming back. The Cockettes were offered 50 percent of the door. That amounted to almost nothing, but no matter. They had danced all dressed up in drag, flashing sequined cocks and boobs and asses, and they were adored for it. They were *it*: living hallucinations, making pretend and breaking rules, kicking high.

By the summer of 1970, having pulled together a few successful Palace shows, the Cockettes were becoming the San Francisco counterculture's vaudeville. But the Cockettes were much weirder than their beatnik and flower children siblings. Their productions were, Allen Ginsberg once said, "part of a large-scale spiritual liberation movement and reclamation of self from the homogenization of the military state." A *Ramparts* writer praised them for their capacity to provide "a glimpse of the beyond." Says Jann Wenner, who attended the Cockettes while editing *Rolling Stone* in San Francisco, "This was *way* beyond counterculture." Barbara Falconer, who profiled them for *Earth* magazine, wrote: "Each of the Cockettes is a way of going crazy. Each is the embodiment of a myth, a dream, a fantasy, a possibility of myself, should the tenuous bolt that holds me together, that keeps me from sliding from Here to There, ever give way. Insanity seems contagious when I'm around the Cockettes."

Performing with the Cockettes, one of them told Falconer, "is like going into a mental ward and trying to organize a talent show." The Cock-ettes pulled their shows from a scrapbook, kept by Hibiscus, in which they pasted their imaginings. *Hair* they weren't. Their shows, with names like *Hell's Harlots, Journey to the Center of Uranus, Elephant Shit—The Cir-cus Life,* and *Tropical Heatwave/Hot Voodoo,* were mobbed. Few of them can remember a performance when they were not on drugs.

Just over a year after Stonewall, before Gay Pride parades existed, as heterosexuals were starting to dabble in "swinging" under the rubric of sexual liberation, the Cockettes were messing with sexuality much more radically than organized gay groups or wife-swappers ever did. "It was total sexual anarchy," John Waters says, approvingly. "The very definition of things like gay was under suspicion at that point," says Joel Selvin, a longtime San Francisco music journalist and scenester. "Pan-sexuality was what was going on. It was an adventure. It was an experiment. The Cockettes were really part of that; their gayness was less significant than their outrageousness."

The Cockettes' home life was as scrappy and genderfucky as their Palace performances. "Reality is fantasy and fantasy is reality to the Cockettes," the journalist Maureen Orth wrote in 1971. "Their life style is carefully contrived to blur if not actually diminish the distinction between the two." LSD was so common, says Sweet Pam, that "we almost brushed our teeth with it." You slept until noon if you felt like it, and when you woke up, sentences like "Look at this nail color!" and "How many pairs of lashes are you wearing?" would float your way. Everyday life with the Cockettes, Sylvester said, was "like living on stage. I mean, you lived in glitter and you ate glitter—the whole thing was glitter."

In fact, they ransacked the city for glitter, which was "about the only thing we paid money for," John Rothermel said. The Cockettes cobbled together the cash they needed for their shows, got their costumes from a thrift shop owned by a straight Cockette named Marshall, and bartered for materials and services. Big Daryl was the only Cockette with a regular job, doing accounts for a plumbing supply company. Most of the Cockettes lived off welfare checks, odd jobs, little scams, food stamps, or boyfriends. One, John Flowers, contributed his student loan. Fayette had saved five hundred dollars to go to Europe, which paid rent for a year. Scrumbly once drove to Santa Cruz, registered as a new resident and father of seven—he was, of course, neither—and collected months' worth of free food from the county welfare department.

But the Cockettes lived optimistically. As Marshall says in *The Cockettes*, "We really did believe there'd be a revolution any minute." Everybody tried to get on Aid to the Totally Disabled, or ATD, which was intended for the completely insane but became, as John Waters puts it, "a grant, actually, from the government, to continue your insane lifestyle in San Francisco." Waters himself, a Cockette sympathizer, was denied ATD.

He refused to get undressed for the physical; had a friend impersonating his mother call in and pronounce, "I hope he dies in Vietnam"; told the shrink, "I never have sex 'cause it smells," and responded to the inkblot test by screaming, "You just want me to talk dirty, don't you?" He was told, "You're insane, but not permanently. Sorry." In his eligibility interview, Divine, the huge drag-queen star of Waters's films, told the ATD officer he wanted "tits bigger than my head."

"Well, the Cockettes," Sylvester liked to say. "When you walk down the street and you see somebody sitting in a mud puddle, and they invite you to jump in and you do—that's the Cockettes." Sylvester, jumping right into the puddle, moved into the "Haight Street Chateau," the name the Cockettes gave their main commune, where most of them moved after the flat on Bush and Baker burned down in a grass-skirt-on-fire incident. It was the middle flat of a three-flat Victorian, filled with overstuffed couches, unusual fabrics hanging on walls and windows, and people. Any space that could be a sleeping area had become one. Each of the five bedrooms slept four or more people, and each had a loft or two, with a sleeping area tucked underneath. Alcoves were demarcated by beaded curtains.

Sylvester shared a room with Tahara and Sandy, whom Tahara describes as a mildly retarded queen who sucked her thumb. Sandy slept in a loft, and Tahara slept to one side. Sylvester moved in under the loft and put up heavy floral curtains as a partition on two sides. He decorated his little space at the Haight Street Chateau with a cobbled-together 1920s-to-1940s mélange: Egyptian deco items; a little round table covered with doilies and linens and dripping with tassels and fringe; a dresser covered with cosmetics and sheet music; and a shelf with framed photographs of a couple dancing, of Pearl Bailey, and of himself in a posed portrait. He painted hieroglyphics on one wall. He had tried acid in Los Angeles, liked it, and now he tried it some more. "I use lots of psychedelics," he said. "Psychedelics keep me together."

Sylvester, like Tahara and sometimes Sandy, would bring men back to the room from the Stud—usually, Tahara says, "white hippie guys with long hair." The roommates would hear each other having sex, and once Tahara walked in to see, through a gap in Sylvester's curtains, Sylvester straddling a white hippie guy with long hair.

Sylvester was known in the house for the way he often started his sentences on a high, chirpy note; for his witty retorts; and for his bossiness. If someone was doing or wearing something he didn't like, he would be the one to say, "Girlfriend, stop that," or "Girl, take that off." He sometimes spoke dismissively to others about the Cockettes. "Oh, don't listen to her," he might say to a new friend he brought over to the house, waving a hand in the direction of a chattering Cockette. "She's absolutely crazy." To most of the Cockettes, a dress was a dress. Sylvester patiently explained that dresses in the 1930s—the period they were emulating in their shows— were actually cut on the bias, with tight tops that flared out into fullness at the bottom.

Sylvester shared the Cockettes' affinity for outrageous flaming, their celebrations of sex and of gayness, their love of acid and good hash, and their bent movie-musical fantasies. Like them, he was making himself up, fantasizing a self into existence. But he usually stood a few feet back, *among* the Cockettes but never quite *of* them. His drag and makeup, for one thing, were almost staid in comparison with the Cockettes'; they pre- ferred facial designs that were almost like war paint, and clothing that didn't make sense. Sylvester wore simple period dresses on stage, and cre- ated the face of a sane, pretty woman. At the Haight Street Chateau, one person might be dancing around the living room in a diaper while another made sounds through a vacuum-cleaner tube. Sylvester would be in his room, in his bell-bottoms/halter-blouse/platform-shoes/do-rag/bracelets outfit, carving hips out of foam.

Sylvester was the only black person in the flat, and he kept to himself a lot. "Sylvester always kept himself a bit aloof, at least from me," Sweet Pam says. "He was like a mini-god." The communal lifestyle left little space for quiet heart-to-hearts—there were almost always three or more people in a room at once—and Sylvester rarely spoke of anything per- sonal. Sometimes he would be quiet for days, responding to queries with a polite, "I'm all right." After less than a year, Sylvester moved to a dark, quiet, triangular house on Market Street with John Rothermel and another Cockette, Daniel Ware. They had a windup phonograph on which they played their old records.

Although he was as flaky as the rest of them—showing up late for rehearsals, or not showing up at all, if he had encountered the right boy or the right hash—Sylvester was also too forward-looking to fully enter the

Cockettes' free-form, messy, anarchic life. "I was in the lifestyle for a penny and for a pound, and for me the Cockettes came out of my lifestyle," Fayette Hauser says. "But for him, it was the other way around. He had other things to do. Sylvester was never a hippie like we were. He didn't want to toss it all away. He wanted to sing in drag, and that's what he did with the Cockettes. He was interested in being an artist."

Sylvester was uninterested in food stamps and welfare—God bless the child that's got his own—or in rebelling against glamour. His bag was to pretend he was a star, and he expected others to play along. "Everybody else was drinking Southern Comfort thinking they were Janis, but I only drank champagne," Sylvester said. "Imported. Somebody brought me a bottle of domestic champagne backstage, I would say thank you and send it back." He wanted real furs, not musty, moth-eaten Salvation Army stoles. He named his German shepherd–Standard poodle mix Greta, and later got himself two borzois, Russian wolfhounds, somewhere between pets and fashion accessories. "I was always the glamorous thing, on and off stage," Sylvester said. "I really believed for a certain time that I was Josephine Baker. In my attitude, in my everything, I *was* Josephine Baker. I'd go out with a headdress and a sort of silly costume, and men would open and close doors for me, light my cigarettes. I wouldn't get out of a car until someone opened the door for me."

Still, he was not above riding through his new city with his new friends on a flatbed truck, being crazy. As Worman tells it, at the Aquarius Day Parade in August 1970—a countercultural hodgepodge of queens, flower children, and rock-and-rollers, where the lead float was the band Black Sabbath—the Cockettes rode a truck "dressed in no particular theme but mixing mini-skirts and evening gowns, combat boots and boas, rags and rhinestones." Realizing that spectators had recognized them, they thought they might be expected to do a bit more than wave and moon. Someone wondered aloud what to do. "Scream, girl!" Sylvester said. They screamed, and the crowd screamed back.

The Cockette utopia was one in which the love party erased any differences: we are all freaks under the skin, sisters in glitter. "We didn't even look at differences," Scrumbly Koldwin says. "Nobody ever talked about race," says Fayette. "Everything went right past that. People were totally individuated, and you met people on that level. People were expressing themselves as their individual persona, and that's who you related to, whether they were black or white, gay, straight, bisexual." But theirs was a mostly white world, except for a couple of "Chocolate Cockettes," as they were called, Lendon and Reggie, who no doubt did sometimes look at differences—their chocolateness defining them in a batter whose vanilla flavor went entirely unremarked. (Lendon and Reggie, like many of the Cockettes, are no longer living.) "You talked about the white experience, not the black experience," Tahara says. "You'd talk to a black guy the way you'd talk to a white guy." Many years later, in an interview, Sylvester claimed that the Cockettes "wouldn't let me in, and I thought it was because I was black." He and Lendon and Reggie he said, "used to get together and talk about it, but none of them would believe it."

That Sylvester's screaming-Josephine persona was specifically and matter-of-factly black further distinguished him from the Cockettes. Although he was not an overtly political sort, Sylvester's utopia was one in which blackness, his blackness, large and silky, *was* looked at and attended to, applauded, and set off beautifully against a white background. Sylvester was a Disquotay in Cockette drag. He would be inimitable *and* unavoidably black.

Sylvester had begun studying, in fact, "the transition of black music from gospel to spiritual music to blues and jazz," thinking he might write a book. He'd discovered "the really obscure people that people know nothing about," and wanted to incorporate them into his act. He never got around to writing the book, and sometimes got the facts wrong, but he threw out the names of the obscure as if they were his relatives, as if it were a duty. "Take the 'St. Louis Blues,'" Sylvester would tell *Soul* reporter Archie Ivey a couple of years after his time with the Cockettes. "W. C. Handy wrote that for a female impersonator, and Ethel Waters was the first black woman to ever sing it. Earl 'Snakehips' Robinson—one of the greatest dancers in New York in that era—was a known homosexual. He was written up as a 'credit to his race.' People like Etta Moten. She sings '[Remember] My Forgotten Man' in the movie *Gold Diggers '33* and she does this big dance number in a Fred Astaire and Ginger Rogers movie, *Flying Down to Rio.* Nobody's ever heard of her, and she just about *made* the movie. Very few people know about the actress Ivie Anderson or that Hazel Scott speaks eleven languages. There are these people who made major contributions to entertainment that are just shunned. MGM released all the big Broadway musicals and cut out Etta Moten's parts. How many people know that Stepin Fetchit had seven Cadillacs, one with his name on the side of it in neon lights? These things impress me, because there is definitely a whole cultural thing that has gone on in the theater-music world. There are definitely Black stars—real stars."

He intended to be one of them. Sylvester dreamed of himself, he said, as a dark brown "superstar—1930s style," attended to by "a lot of maids," sipping French champagne, dripping in rose petals, riding in a white Packard. He imagined himself a blues chanteuse from an era when "black stars were black stars, not imitating white stars." He was well prepared, he would say. "My grandmother gives me her old dresses to wear, tells me stories, teaches me dances like the Big Apple and the Black Bottom," Sylvester said. "I want to do as near a possible recreation of what black audiences saw in Harlem or on the South Side," he told *Rolling Stone* in 1971. "My dream is to have my own tent show like Ma Rainey had, with kids dancing like they did in *Connie's Hot Chocolates of 1927,* or the *Blackbirds of '28"* and "an orchestra all 65 years old or over."

"I'd like to put on a show so total you'd be transported," he said. He wanted to do songs, he said, like "Marahuana"—a 1934 song about how only sweet marijuana can "bring my lover back to me, even though I know it's all a fantasy"—and "That's Why Darkies Were Born." The latter song was recorded by Paul Robeson in 1931, and later by Kate Smith. It went like this: *Someone had to pick da cotton, someone had to pick da corn, someone had to slave and be able to sing: That's why darkies were born. Someone had to laugh at trouble, though he was tired and worn. Had to be contented with any old thing—That's why darkies were born. Sing, sing, sing when you're weary, and sing when you're blue. Sing, sing. That's what you taught all the white folks to do.*

4.

JADED LADY

When Peter Mintun first met Sylvester in the spring of 1970, he thought Sylvester was a cool girl. Peter was twenty years old, living in a commune whose glue was a fondness for old things—old records, old phonographs, old appliances, old cars. "We were like hippies who lived in the twenties," he says. "We lived in a house that didn't have anything modern in it. Nothing in it was made after World War II." Peter played the piano for singers, parties, and silent movies at places like Berkeley's Pacific Film Archive, under the nom de plume Peter Arden. He wore suspenders and bow ties. His friend John Rothermel had suggested that he come play piano for the Cockettes. Peter had seen a Cockettes show and had a laugh, and he considered himself a go-with-the-flow sort, so he agreed.

Peter went to the rehearsal, waiting for a couple of hours for people to show up. As folks wandered in, Peter's eyes widened. "These people are *so* unusual," he thought. While a smattering of Cockettes fiddled with this and that, and Peter played a tune that sounded like 1930s Harlem, a tall black woman in a cap and jeans and a blouse sat down with Peter. "Can you play 'Stormy Weather'?" she asked. Peter could, and he played it, and Sylvester sang. Did he know "The Carioca" from that old Dolores del Rio–Fred Astaire–Ginger Rogers film *Flying Down to Rio*? He did, indeed. They talked about the scene they both loved from the movie: as Fred and Ginger are learning the forehead-to-forehead Carioca dance, the orchestra switches into a Harlem swing, and the camera turns to a black woman, who sings "The Carioca" and disappears. "Wow," Sylvester said, "I didn't think anybody else knew that." *It has a little bit of new rhythm, a blue rhythm that sighs; It has a meter that is tricky, a bit of wacky-wicky*, he sang. *Two heads together, they say, are better than one. Two heads together, that's how the dance is begun.*

61

This was Peter's stuff—vintage, undervalued, ready to be dusted off and brought back to life—and it was a warm treat to find someone else who knew it and loved it so well. He played an Ethel Waters tune, and Sylvester sang in a blues falsetto, and then they did the Fanny Brice song "I'd Rather Be Blue," which Barbra Streisand had revived in *Funny Girl*. *I'd rather be blue over you than be happy with somebody else*, Sylvester sang. *I need a little "ah," little "ooh," little "oh."* After what seemed like hours, Peter suggested that maybe they should get together and work up some routines for the show, and Sylvester excitedly agreed. "It wasn't for another few hours that I realized he was a guy," Peter says. "His hair was in a cap and I thought he was a black chick."

With Peter, Sylvester carved himself a niche at the Palace, neither exactly a Cockette nor exactly not one. Occasionally over the next year and a half, he played a character in a show, often playing up his blackness—a distinguishing feature, for sure—to the point of explosion. He collected Negrobilia (Aunt Jemima kerchiefs, watermelon potholders, Mammy cookie jars), and seemed to enjoy playing clichés campily on the stage. "He would take the ultimate stereotype and put it out in the air and let everybody see it, poking fun at it, tongue in cheek, by doing it," Peter Mintun says. "No other black performer was doing that at the time." In *Tinsel Tarts in a Hot Coma*, Big Daryl played Brenda Breakfast, sitting at a luncheon counter, and Sylvester played Mabel, a randy granny in forties drag. "Mabel, set the table," said Brenda Breakfast. Out came Mabel in a huge fat suit, with gigantic tits, gigantic hair, and a gigantic ass—a shuffling Mammy waving a feather duster at a one-dimensional cardboard table. Mabel said "Fab-u-lous!" a lot and sang "Blue Plate Special," offering up a "hot hamburger with plenty of goo," while pretty-boy hamburgers, hot dogs, mustard, and ketchup danced around her.

In *Tricia's Wedding*, a spoof film made by Sebastian—the booker of the midnight Palace shows that had occasioned the Cockettes' birth—Sylvester played both a tearful Coretta Scott King and an African ambassador, Miss Uma Guma. As Mrs. King, he wore a veil made from a black petticoat, a pillbox hat, and a black ladies' suit. Reefer was freely available, and Sylvester had been "puffin' and puffin'" all day. The film, which coincided with the 1971 wedding of Tricia Nixon, ended with a spiked-punch acid-freakout orgy. "When we got to that final scene, where somebody pours LSD in the punch and all the guests start tripping," Sylvester recalled, "all I kept saying was, 'I'm havin' a dream. I'm dreamin'. Is this a dream? I'm havin' a dream.'"

As Sylvester grew into the role he'd chosen for himself—vintage blues diva—he developed it with the same intensity and rigor he'd brought to his *Vogue*-model-come-to-life in Watts a few years before. He had already taught himself a lot about old blues and jazz singers, and went roaming San Francisco record stores looking for new material. Friends like Mintun and Rothermel, avid record collectors, had taken to making him tapes of obscure or classic old tunes. He read biographies of blues singers. One of Sylvester's favorite lines at the time—amongst the Cockettes, embellishment was an art form that extended beyond clothing—was that he was Billie Holiday's cousin once removed. For a short while, he performed "Songs from the Golden Years (1928–1945)" under the name Ruby Blue (sometimes, for that Parisian feel, "Rubi" or "Bleu"). He had his photo taken wearing a fluffy white coat, a strand of pearls, a faux-diamond choker, and a beaded headdress, with small strings of white beads hanging along his dark neck. In the picture, he smiles placidly, face tilted up, looking from under false eyelashes into the distance. He signed it "Miss Rubi Blue, 1925." Around this time, he dressed himself up and got himself a job at the Rickshaw Lounge, in Chinatown, singing with Peter at the piano bar for Chinese patrons who thought he was a chanteuse. He was playing at it, but he was not messing around.

Sometimes Sylvester could play the prima donna so well you'd almost think he was one. He was hard to pin down for solo rehearsals, leaving Peter waiting for hours and then arriving with an exhausted "Oh, chil', I had the most fabulous night at the baths! Chil', I'm worn out!" But he always arrived with a very clear idea of what he planned to do and what he wanted others to do to make it look right. You did it his way or it didn't happen. "I am going to do 'Sleepy Time Down South,'" he announced at one rehearsal that summer. He had seen an old movie where, behind the singer, many white-gloved hands moved against a black background, like a flock of unusually shaped doves. "Now you all sit back there," he said to the Cockettes, pointing to the back of the stage, "and I want you to wear the white gloves and move your hands like this." He bought them all white gloves—with what money, who knows. When the time came, he sang the song (*I'll find heaven in my mother's arms, when it's sleepy time down South*), a flock of Cockette hands danced slowly under a black light, and the crowd stomped. "He was always the boss," Kreemah Ritz says. "He just did his thing and did it well."

Sylvester did not take kindly to Cockettes flouncing around onstage while he was singing, as they were wont to do, or to the amateur-hour mishaps. "Sylvester," says Sebastian, "took care of Sylvester." During a performance of the Cockettes' October 1970 show, *Les Cockettes Folies des Paris,* while Sylvester was singing "Someone to Watch Over Me," Hibiscus took to the stage in a zebra-skin costume, dancing around and eventually wandering into the spotlight. Sylvester watched out of the corner of his eye, and his face went steely as he finished the song. After his number, Sylvester left the stage to boisterous applause, and waited in the wings for Hibiscus to come offstage.

When he did, Sylvester slapped him right across the face. "Don't you ever do that to me again," he said. "You do not come out in my song and upstage me." He pushed Hibiscus into one of the dressing rooms and kicked him over and over. Another time, a local artist made a beautiful butcher-paper backdrop for Sylvester: a giant bluebird with notes coming out of its mouth. As Sylvester was singing, the rolled-up paper began to unfurl behind him. The audience, keen appreciators of the unintended, applauded so enthusiastically that Sylvester had to stop mid-song. The next night, he insisted that the bluebird be lowered before his song began. He was not about to be upstaged by a piece of paper.

Sylvester made sure he had his own little space apart from the mayhem and sloppiness of the Cockettes, so he could re-create a musical moment from another place and time. He wanted the stage to himself; as he put it later, in simple diva-ese, "My shit was better." (Many of the Cockettes were admittedly tone deaf, or bad dancers, and to a person they were hams.) Most of the time, Sylvester came out as a sort of specialty act in a guest-star interlude toward the end. Whether it fit into the plot or not, a slot would be made for a black nightclub scene, and Sylvester would emerge into a spotlight. His appearances brought to mind the black guest-star spots in 1940s and 1950s movie musicals—the swinging "El Carioca" scene in *Flying Down to Rio,* for instance. Dressed up as an old-time blues singer or just as Sylvester in a good dress with a flower in his hair, he would sing an African-American period piece like "God Bless the Child,"

"Stormy Weather," "Skylark," or "When It's Sleepy Time Down South" while Peter played piano.

"It was always the most magical moment, when he was on stage singing," says Fayette Hauser. Tahara would stop what he was doing and go sit on the side of the stage to listen, just to feel the goose bumps that Sylvester's voice gave him. Very often, Peter Mintun says, Sylvester was "the only thing anyone remembered from those shows" once the drugs wore off. From the very beginning, Sylvester demanded attention, and from the beginning he got it. "He was this little gleaming song in the middle of all this fucking outrageousness," says Joel Selvin. "Sylvester would come out and sing with this incredible voice, and you never felt like he was being campy," says John Waters. "He did it for real. You felt Sylvester could have just as easily done his act in the Apollo as he could in the Palace." Sylvester's performances, Mike Freedberg wrote later in *Soul* magazine, "were like the reverse of comic relief."

In *Pearls Over Shanghai*, Sylvester played Petrushka, the "white Russian." An admirer, played by Sebastian, summoned him. "Shine, lady flame, you can eclipse the moon tonight," Sebastian called. "For me you are the star that sets the world alight." Sylvester entered in a backless white silk gown with a three-foot train, and white peau-de-soie shoes that his friend Nicky Nichols had found. "The dress was high-necked, cut on the bias, and draped over the shoulders," Sylvester recalled years later. "Yards and yards of fabric. Shiny white silk against black skin. Nicky showed me how to glue my tits on, and my hair was in perfect waves. I wore an egret-feather headdress. I was in heaven."

Sebastian threw himself at Petrushka's feet. "Stop kissing my feet," said Petrushka. "Rise and give me your name, and show me what you've got in your basket." The tittering audience watched as Sebastian offered diamonds from his basket. "I have so many men right now, too many," Sylvester-Petrushka objected, but as the music began, she agreed to take the admirer's hand, his heart, and maybe his money, too. "For though you think I'm your angel from above, I'm just a jaded lady, and you a fool in love," Sylvester pronounced grandly, and then leaped up into his high register, singing an old tune called "Jaded Lady." When the song was done, the audience stomped, hooted, stood, screamed, fawned. "He would get five-minute ovations," Kreemah Ritz says. He would stand there and soak it in like sun.

At *Hollywood Babylon*, crowds lined up under klieg lights, and vintage limos dropped various Cockettes (starlets, fading movie queens, gossips, gigolos) in front of a red carpet, then drove around the block, picked up some more, and spilled them out. The show featured a pulpy song set in a Hollywood lesbian bar; a Cockette named Rumi, in a chiffon headdress, singing "Stranger in Paradise" to Johnni, a boy dressed as a harem girl, on a set meant to recall DeMille; Scrumbly and Kreemah, the Nelson and Jeannette of the Cockettes, singing the duet "By a Waterfall," in front of a human waterfall of naked, tinsel-covered bodies; Dusty Dawn singing "I Want to Be Loved by You" as if underwater, while cutting out paper dolls.

Then came Sylvester. He sang "Big City Blues"—a song from *Fox Movietone Follies* that Peter had found—channeling Billie Holiday and Bessie Smith with his drag and his falsetto screech-and-growl. He was outrageous, for sure, but not silly, and the Palace audience was undone. Like many of the numbers Sylvester chose then, "Big City Blues" is a high-spirited song about low spirits. Its lyrics talk about wandering the city amid crowds of people who seem to belong to one another, wondering *why am I alone*, wondering *where are my people*, while the music, the banging piano and the insistent voice, says *I'm doing just fine, I will be just fine.*

If being a vintage blues nightclub singer suited Sylvester, it wasn't because he was especially sad, although one suspects he brought his share of melancholy up to San Francisco. He had, after all, left a lot behind in Los Angeles, and closed the door tight behind him. He disclosed to his new friends nearly as much about his first twenty-two years in the world as his own mother had disclosed to him about her Arkansas beginnings. Reinvented selves are always trailed by ghosts of previous ones.

But there is no reason to think his loneliness and longings were so pronounced that he just had to express them in song. Contrary to the name, singing the blues is not really about wallowing in sadness. Although the blues is about being down, dogged, heartbroken, and struggling, blues music itself is about making people feel good. There is rarely much self-pity or resignation in the mix. "More often than not," Albert Murray notes in *Stomping the Blues*, "even as the words of the lyrics recount a tale of woe, the instrumentation may mock, shout defiance, or voice resolution and determination." Blues music is, Murray also points out, less about an expression of the singer's actual suffering than it is about mastering "a very specific technology of stylization": the "blue notes" created by "a slight flatting of third and seventh intervals of the scale," a twelve-bar chorus, a call-and-response pattern, simple progressions.

Sylvester, who taught himself music by listening to it, knew all that, no doubt. What he wanted was to reproduce the music—to master the technology of stylization, to participate in the tradition. Maybe even more, he wanted to reproduce the movie vision in perfected detail, to make you feel you were looking at a 1927 Hot Chocolate or listening to a '28 Blackbird. What he wanted you to know and admire, really, what he wanted to become for you and for himself, was a black woman, glamorous and brazen, with a strong voice and her own money. His blues were usually stomping, not melancholy.

Sylvester's blues-jazz star persona was less a masquerade than a lived homage. If his Disquotay self was him, his mother, his grandmother, and Twiggy rolled into one, his woman of the blues was an amalgam of black star personae from the twenties, thirties, and forties—Lena, Bessie, Josephine, Billie. There was a lot for him to admire about blues women. *Wild women are the only ones who get by, wild women don't have the blues*—so Ida Cox put it in her 1924 song about hard-drinking, tough-singing blues singers like herself, Ma Rainey, Bessie Smith, and Alberta Hunter. Wild women blues singers did not let a man or the church get in their way. They stared down racists sometimes, or just ignored them. They made good money. They had no qualms about going out and getting sex and telling all about it. *Papa likes his bourbon, mama likes her gin*, Ma Rainey sang, *Papa likes his outside women, mama likes her outside men.*

Bessie Smith cocked her hip when she growled about the man who betrayed her, and she would tell you about how the world owed her "plenty lovin'" and how she "go out collectin' most every day." (She was known to go out collecting from women, too.) Josephine Baker brought Parisians to their feet wearing nothing but a skirt made of sixteen bananas, and the only thing more fabulous than being loved by the French is an edible outfit. Working in a quieter blues idiom, Billie Holiday sang about the "strange fruit" of Southern trees, *black bodies swinging in the Southern breeze.* Lena Horne, who had been a Cotton Club singer, a Blackbird of 1939, and the featured vocalist of the all-black Noble Sissle's Society Orchestra, said the kinds of things Sylvester had grown up hearing. "Always be smarter than the people who hire you," she said. And: "It's not the load that breaks you down, it's the way you carry it."

Even their songs of despair left you off somewhere else entirely. They could make you feel the hard times, but all the while they were chasing the blue notes with words about the good, good loving their man was missing, or with the timbre of their voices or a shake of the ass, or just with the way the flower in their hair picked up the spotlight. Sylvester made an excellent lady of the blues.

None of the music that could be heard at the Palace Theatre bore much relation to what the rest of the world was listening to at the time. In 1971, the Top 40 included many genres: singer-songwriter folk rock like Carole King's "It's Too Late" and James Taylor's "You've Got a Friend"; soul and rhythm-and-blues artists like the Temptations, Al Green, Isaac Hayes, and Bill Withers; rock like Janis Joplin's "Me and Bobby McGee" and the Rolling Stones' "Brown Sugar." If anyone dominated the charts, it was the families Carpenter ("Superstar," "Rainy Days and Mondays") and Osmond ("One Bad Apple," "Go Away Little Girl," "Sweet and Innocent"), who were to the Cockettes as God is to the devil. The soundtrack that attracted the largest audience was *Jesus Christ Superstar*, which was not exactly musical comedy.

In fact, it was that distance from the center of America that carried Sylvester into the spotlight. A black man reviving music from another era in white gowns and high voice, singing of lovin' dat man of his: it would be difficult to create a more fitting star for San Franciscans who wanted nothing to do with the America of smiling, shiny-toothed Mormons in matching outfits and emaciated, lite-rock-singing girls-next-door. Sylvester was their bad apple, and he was delicious. He was developing quite a devoted following.

At the beginning of 1971, Sebastian arranged for Sylvester and Peter to have their own show at the Palace. They had done a gig a few months earlier at a rock club called the Family Dog (with Sylvester as Ruby Blue in a long white gown, and Peter in tails), but the audience there didn't seem to get it. The audience for "Sylvester Sings!" at the Palace, two nights in January and two in February, was much the same as for the Cockettes shows. They paid their two dollars and turned out in force. Sylvester was all falsetto fantasy: Billie Holiday at Carnegie Hall, Josephine Baker at the

Folies Bergère. "The audience was fantasizing as much as the performer," Peter Mintun says. "The performers were fantasizing that they were in front of a very important audience in a major city, at the peak of their career. And the audience, they'd been smoking grass and dropping LSD, and they all wanted to believe they were at this fabulous event, like a 1930s movie of a concert."

Sylvester's solo performances were as simple as the Cockettes' were cluttered. Peter sat at an old upright piano on stage; Sylvester stood, in an almost elegant gown, and sang numbers like Billie Holiday's "Don't Explain," Ethel Waters's "Nobody Knows You When You're Down and Out" and "Am I Blue," Bessie Smith's "Black Mountain Blues," standards like "Stormy Weather" and "Over the Rainbow." He added rare tunes like "Laughing on the Outside," an old Sammy Kaye song. He sang the fast-tempo "Carioca," occasionally throwing in some gospel phrasing at the end of a line. He covered a few newer ones, like Hal David's and Burt Bacharach's "This Girl's in Love with You," and Leonard Cohen's "Hey, That's No Way to Say Goodbye," which he transformed from a depressed poet's self-pitying dirge to a fierce, sad, done-me-wrong love song. Peter played a solo while Sylvester left to change gowns.

"When you've got a lot, you seem to have more friends than you usually do," Sylvester said to the audience at the Palace when he came back. "They come around and talk to you and invite you places that you've already been. Take you out to good times with your money, and invite you out to go somewhere but come to your house to get dressed." Audience members called out their assent. "They do it, I know," Sylvester continued. "But somebody once said God'll bless the child that's got its own. If you got your own you ain't got to ask nobody for nothin'. I'm gonna tell you that I'm one and I've got my own, and God'll bless you if you've got your own." He sang in a sweet falsetto: *Them that's got shall get, them that's not shall lose, so the Bible said, and it's still news. Mama may have, Papa may have, but God bless the child that's got his own.*

While Peter tinkled along on the piano, Sylvester pattered some more: "How many of you know today, you can have everything you want, a person who calls themselves your best friend don't have nothin'? When you don't have nothin' then they ain't your friends no more." Voices called out from the mostly white crowd, churchlike, *mmm-hmms* and *That's rights.* "They'll stand around your door," Sylvester said. "When all your money's gone, after they done drank and shot up and dropped every dime you dropped, you see 'em walking down the street and they act like they don't know who you are. Those friends don't come around you any more." Then he sang in his natural baritone: *Don't get greedy and don't take too much, no, hmmmmm. Your mama may have, and your, your papa may have, Lord, listen, God bless the child . . .* He and Peter paused for a moment, and then Sylvester shot back up into a raw falsetto that sounded almost like crying: *. . . that's got his own.* As the audience whooped and hollered, Peter pounded out the last few bars.

Solo shows were a lot of work to pull together, but the $100 or so they got from their gigs at the Palace, or at little bars like Gold Street, was all Sylvester needed for rent, food, and "items"—the clothing, jewelry, and accessories he liked to have on him or around him. Sylvester still performed sometimes with the Cockettes, though, not least because the audience was big and adoring. In one show, Sylvester took the stage in eight-foot butterfly wings he'd constructed out of pink chiffon, glitter, and sequins. Peter played the 1926 Gershwins tune "Someone to Watch Over Me." It is a song of wistfulness, and Sylvester sang in a register, rhythm, and directness from another era, like a scratchy album on some old boardinghouse Victrola. *Oh how I need someone to watch over me,* he sang, slowly moving his long, fragile wings.

Sylvester loved being driven around hilly, foggy San Francisco: doors were opened, cigarettes were lit. Kreemah Ritz had a blue '47 Cadillac Fleetwood, and naturally he switched the *e*'s and *o*'s on the back. Kreemah, dressed in a chauffeur outfit, would drive up and down Polk Street in the Flootweed, with Sylvester in the backseat, wearing a blond shoulder-length wig and blue velvet dress and elbow-length lace gloves, waving out the window as if people should know who he was. Sometimes, offering drugs and a fun ride, they would manage to pick up a cute guy whom, Kreemah claims, Sylvester would "fuck in the back of the car, up and down the hills, while I drove around."

Other times Peter Mintun, who had moved down to Mountain View, doubled as chauffeur. Peter and his roommates had, between them, a '25 Dodge, a '25 Chrysler, a '29 Lincoln, a '38 Buick Packard, and some '50s cars, and Peter would drive one of the cars up to San Francisco and collect Sylvester. "Peter would wear a tuxedo," Sylvester said, "and I would get dressed in my gowns and we would arrive at the theater in his '38 Packard with my Russian wolfhounds. I mean, we were really living this fantasy life." Or Peter would drive Sylvester down Market Street near the Castro, which was starting to turn gay gay gay. Sylvester might bring a little bottle of Jack Daniel's, and he'd smoke his Benson & Hedges Menthols and pick his teeth with a toothpick. He would insist that Peter slow down for the cute boys, who were maybe a little scared by the sight, and Sylvester would call out, falsetto fabulous or deep tenor, "Yoo-hoo, honey! Want a ride?"

Sometimes, during the day, Peter and Sylvester would tootle around San Francisco looking for photo opportunities and laughing. "We'd go to someone's mansion in Pacific Heights," Peter says, "and I'd park the car so you could see it in the distance, and he would stand on their semicircular colonnaded front porch, and he'd twirl. He had a turban, or a snood—he loved snoods—and a monkey-fur stole, and a long dress and platform shoes with espadrille ties. He'd pose and we'd take pictures. We thought it was magical, gorgeous, glamorous. And we loved blowing people's minds." Other times, instead, Sylvester would just take the train down to Mountain View, in full drag with a little traveling kit and a hat box. Peter would take photos in the garden, of Sylvester in a sun dress and a big straw hat and a wig, one leg lifting slightly behind him, reaching up for an orange in the sun.

5.

BIG CITY BLUES

The Cockettes performed for their first anniversary, on New Year's Eve of 1970, at Bimbo's 365, a North Beach night spot where Rita Hayworth had gotten her start as a chorine and where Dolfina, the Girl in the Fishbowl, appeared through optical illusion to be swimming in the nude. Sylvester joined them as a solo act. The Cockettes raided the club's refrigerator, which contained only champagne and caviar, on which they lived for weeks after.

Sitting on the floor in the front of Bimbo's that night, his red-blond, butt-length hair tucked around and beneath him, was a beautiful, dewy, pink-skinned, heroin-addicted boy named Michael Lyons. Sylvester, singing his trademark "God Bless the Child" in a gray dress and high pompadour— a nice match for the elegant black-and-red Bimbo's decor—stared at Michael throughout the song. When he was finished, he jumped off the stage and loudly declared to him, "You are so beautiful. I am going to marry you." Michael had resisted, turned off by both the drag and the forwardness.

"If he had said, 'I am going to screw your brains out,' I would have gone with him immediately," Michael says, "but marriage to me is a very, very deep thing." Eventually, he gave in. In Michael's telling, Sylvester sent flowers and notes, declared regularly and with great certainty that Michael was the one for him, and sang love songs like "Something in the Way She Moves" directly to Michael from the stage. "I was in awe that he could love me the way he did," Michael says. He loved the way Sylvester smelled, and the way he anointed himself with lotions and oils. Watching Sylvester paint his face, Michael was transfixed.

Within weeks, Sylvester spoke to Peter of Michael as "the love of my life." Their birthdays were six days apart. When they were seen together, they were nearly always touching. "I was fulfilled in every possible way," Michael says.

It is hard to know how much time and heroin have eroded the line between fantasy and reality in Michael Lyons's memories. Michael remembers that when they met, Sylvester was sixteen, when in fact he was twenty-two; that they had sex three times a day, every day; that Sylvester was worth an impossible twelve million dollars by the time they broke up three years later. But in Cockette-ish San Francisco, as Maureen Orth noted, distinguishing fantasy from reality was hardly a priority. "It was like we were in the movies all the time," Michael Lyons says. But they brought a couple of different scripts.

In one hand, each held the roses-and-love-songs, you-and-only-you, no-sex-before-marriage fantasies of coupling; Michael brought it with him from his traditional New Orleans family, and Sylvester from the black-and-white movies that had inspired his earliest daydreams. In the other hand, each carried the screw-your-brains-out, love-whomever-you-want-whenever-you-want ethos of the flower children. "Both of us felt completely free, and yet we were committed to each other in this special way," Michael says. Along with those all around them, they were redrafting the play from the opening scene: the lead would be a sexual revolutionary who was also a swooning lover, the set an orgy room with a picket fence.

That spring, in a ritual joining of the two fantasies, Sylvester and Michael were married in a ceremony in the Shakespeare Garden in Golden Gate Park. They wore identical white tunics and flower garlands in their hair. Wally, a Cockette, had stolen flowers from a cemetery, and many of the attendees—Cockettes, drag queens, hippies, and miscellaneous hangers-on—wore thrift-store white wedding gowns. Drugs enhanced the event. This being a Cockettes-style marriage, no particular obligations were implied, sexual or otherwise. "Well, I can't live without other people," Sylvester said in a conversation about monogamy, and Michael felt the same way. "Don't ever tell them that you love them," Michael said. "You say that only to me." Sylvester agreed, for the time being.

Michael claims not to have slept with Sylvester before the Shakespeare Garden event. That night, he recalls, Sylvester pulled up his white wedding dress, to Michael's horror. "He had this huge black penis and he wanted to stick it in my little pink twat," Michael says. Michael injected some heroin, and the night was lovely.

When Michael moved in with Sylvester shortly thereafter, in the Market

Street apartment he shared with two Cockettes, it was a bit of a step down. Michael had been living in a spacious flat in the Mission district with gas lights, lace curtains, and Oriental rugs. Sylvester's place was horrifically messy, the floor of his room covered with glitter, hair shed by Greta the dog, sequins shed by outfits, outfits shed by Sylvester. They were living off very little, and when it came to money, Sylvester was entirely undisciplined. "He would spend everything for that flash," Michael says. "He wanted to flash every single person out, and he didn't care how much money he spent on it." If he saw an "item," he would simply have to have it, even if it meant borrowing from Michael. Anyway, Sylvester knew how to get by and get over. At the Stud, he could always manage to get someone to buy him and Michael drinks and then talk his way into a free bus ride afterward.

Together and alone, Sylvester and Michael implemented the sexual revolution as thoroughly as possible, which wasn't so much tawdry as sweet. They went to the Ritch Street baths together, and gave each other to friends as birthday presents. "Oooh, brother got around," his friend Giana says of Sylvester. "He wasn't ashamed at all, honey, not at all. Honey, anything you could imagine under the sun, Sylvester dipped and dabbed and tried all of it." Sylvester liked to tell people that he wanted to be reincarnated as a bicycle seat, and he once joked to Michael that when he died he wanted all his gold jewelry melted down into a giant phallus, and then he wanted that golden phallus planted up his butt for eternity. When they wandered the city, Michael liked to wear the "cock coat" Sylvester and Nicky Nichols had made: the sleeves were dotted with pink cellophane cocks, and on the back was a large, padded pink one spurting rhinestones.

Sylvester wearied of the Cockettes. At a Cockette meeting after the performance of *Les Cockettes Folies des Paris* in which Sylvester slapped Hibiscus—the de facto leader of the Cockettes—Sylvester had raised to the group the sensitive subject of the zebra skin, which Hibiscus would don at any given moment during a show. "The show is lagging," he said. "It's lagging. And then the fucking zebra comes out." He paused and pursed his lips. *"Again."*

He was never especially fond of Hibiscus. Hibiscus, as Fayette describes him, was "dirty, funky dirty, stinky dirty." He stank not because of an ideological commitment to stench, but because "he really knew no boundaries whatsoever, and that's what he was *interested* in." In early 1970, he had left the strict confines of Irving Rosenthal's doctrinaire Kaliflower commune—too many rules, too little drag—for the Haight Street Cockettes house, but he was still the guru of anarchy, the expert in the right way to let it all hang out. Hibiscus was, to Sylvester, "that scary queen." Hibiscus was all over the place, whereas Sylvester knew just where he wanted to be, and when, and in what outfit.

Sylvester was not alone in his frustrations. As they had become more popular, many of the Cockettes wanted the shows to be more professional, and they had begun writing full scripts and insisting on rehearsals and on getting paid. For *Hollywood Babylon*, they had even used a director. Hibiscus was against taking money, and committed to freewheeling, unscripted performance. "Hibiscus was against any structure," Kreemah complained to *Rolling Stone* later that year. "He thought we should do *everything* on stage. But he wanted to be the superstar." Hibiscus retorted that the Cockettes "completely suck up people's brains." Soon came a high-drama blowout involving nasty words and some fisticuffs, in which Hibiscus took some like-minded Cockettes with him and founded the Angels of Light, a more underground, spiritually oriented, explicitly political troupe committed to free performance. "The Cockettes are too straight for me," said Tahara, who joined Hibiscus as an Angel, in a 1971 interview. "The Angels of Light do not look back on Burning Sodom. They do not render unto Caesar. They don't see the height of beauty of the present as a dying Marilyn Monroe." Kreemah Ritz—then still known as Big Daryl—announced that he intended to have the "Cockettes" name trademarked.

For his part, Sylvester was tiring of being the blues diva with the one-shot guest spot and tired of living in another era. He was beginning to reimagine himself as the love child of Jimi Hendrix and Janis Joplin, with electric guitars and rhinestones on his platform shoes, feather boas and an Afro. Sebastian had been sort-of managing Sylvester, getting him gigs around town, and another friend, Dennis Lopez, offered to comanage him. Lopez was somewhat better connected. One of his friends, Gregg Gobel—the wealthy son of the comedian George Gobel—was interested in backing Sylvester financially. Sylvester said he wanted a band of longhaired straight boys who could rock and roll and sing high. "They have to be hot," he said. He and Michael would give them clothes to wear, so that they could rock and glitter at the same time.

Sylvester went looking for new singers and found some sisters named Pointer. The Pointer sisters wore halter tops and Afro wigs and love beads. They weren't hippies—that was a white scene, Anita Pointer says—but from a distance they supported the rebellion of the white kids their age, and they lived just around the corner culturally and geographically, in a "funky, funky, shaky flat" on Gough Street that they absolutely loved. Drunken men hanging out on the corner had helped them move a piano up the stairs. In 1971, they were making about fifty dollars a week singing, not enough to buy a car but enough to leave their day jobs.

In the fall of 1971, Anita Pointer got a call asking if they'd like to sing with someone named Sylvester. None of the sisters had heard of him, but a gig is a gig, so Anita took down the address and she and Bonnie and June went to a dank basement rehearsal space. There they found Sylvester, with his slicked-back hair and mass of bracelets. His flamboyance was nothing new—they had gay friends and family members, and they were living in Haight-Ashbury, for God's sake—but his voice was different.

"I was just amazed at how hard and how high and how strong he sang," Anita Pointer says. "His voice was so powerful. He would just wail. Most falsettos are very small and thin. His was really gutsy." He wanted the Pointers to sing above him, and Anita thought the top of her head might just blow off. The Pointers were already dressing mostly in forties thrift-store fashions, so Sylvester just spruced them up with sequined tops and feathered hats pulled from his closet. "He liked what we were doing," Anita Pointer says, "but he wanted it to glitter and shine and all that."

Once, after a rehearsal over at the Pointers' house, Sylvester initiated a "crazy day of dressing up and taking pictures." Anita put on a long gingham dress, and Sylvester threw on one of the sisters' dresses, and the four of them ran around outside, posing for pictures. "We just started playing," says Anita Pointer. "It was just one of those *days.*"

The departure of Hibiscus cleared a path, many of the remaining Cockettes seemed to think, for the big time. Other people were thinking so, too—and talking. The Cockettes' combination of raggedy, flower-child innocence, gay-love ethos, free-form, hallucinogenic style, and junk-shop drag had turned them into symbols for the media and counterculture movement alike. Local press had started to write about them, and in September 1971, Rex Reed, Truman Capote, Gloria Vanderbilt, and Joanna Carson went to see *Tinsel Tarts in a Hot Coma.* "For me, it was just another story, a colorful piece to do," says Reed. "I was there for a wedding with a group of very famous people, and we were told this was what we *had* to do on our free night, that this could only happen in San Francisco. People just sort of wanted to be in on this *happening.* It gave everybody a chance to be a hippie for about two hours before going back to their regular lives." The very famous people were stunned. Reed was struck, in particular, by the presence on stage of a pregnant woman and a dancing baby.

In his nationally syndicated column that week, Reed called the Cockettes "the most unbelievable American phenomenon since Margaret Mitchell. They are the current sensations of counterculture show business, the darlings of the underground press, a landmark in the history of new liberated theater, and if you've never heard of them, some circles would say you're just not alive." The Cockettes, Maureen Orth wrote in the *Village Voice,* were "transforming themselves full circle from society's aberrations to style setters and clowns." Janis Joplin, Alice Cooper, and Tina Turner came to their shows.

The next month they were featured in *Rolling Stone,* which described them as "the satiric cutting edge of Gay Liberation" and "the defiant unisexual wave of the future" located at "ground zero during an explosion of sexuality and hedonism and dope and sensation-seeking unparalleled in American history." The author noted that the Cockettes and Sylvester— already Sylvester was seeing to it that he was named as a separate act—had been "star performers" at the wedding of Raggedy Robin and Raggedy Jane, San Francisco's "famous clown couple," and the "local papers freaked on it." The article singled out Sylvester, "a beautiful black androgyne who has a gospel sound with the heat and shimmer of Aretha's."

The Cockettes caught the fever of their own publicity, and Sebastian contacted the rock promoter Bill Graham, for whom he had worked a few years before. There was talk of a New York Cockettes-and-Sylvester engagement, maybe at Graham's Fillmore East. Graham balked, but not before hooking Sebastian up with Harry Zerler, a wealthy talent scout for

Columbia Records. Zerler got the backing for a three-week Cockettes gig at the Anderson Theatre off-Broadway. Sylvester and His Hot Band would be their opening act.

Sylvester and Michael couldn't afford two tickets to New York, so Michael stayed home to work. "The Cockettes are not going to make it in New York," Sylvester told him, getting ready to go to the airport. "They're just not." He, on the other hand, would make a big splash, launch his career as a rock star, and they would live happily ever after.

Getting ready to go to New York on the last Friday in October 1971, the Cockettes imagined themselves, as always, as characters in an old movie. In fact, they had been asked the month before to star in a movie about themselves called *The Rollicking Ritz Family,* which took its name from vaudeville's Ritz Brothers. Sitting around in their Oak Street flat in San Francisco, they wallowed in the ironic image of themselves, a bunch of druggie hippie freaks, in the tony, highfalutin Manhattan scene, puttin' on the Ritz. Each of them chose a Ritz name. (Only one lasted long-term: Daryl, who put sour cream on everything, built his name from the Spanish word for the substance, *crema,* and remains Kreemah Ritz to this day.) Sylvester arrived at the airport for their trip east in a red sweater vest covered with Ritz crackers.

The departure of the Cockettes for New York made the TV news that afternoon. The Channel 7 story opened with a shot of Pristine Condition putting on makeup, and continued with snippets of people-at-the-airport interviews: some found the scene "strange," others "beautiful," or "far out," or "just unreal, man." The reporter assured viewers that "no one disliked" the Cockettes, proudly claiming them as "San Francisco's most outrageous entertainment troupe."

If you were a regular passenger on that late flight across the country with the Ritzes and the rest of the Cockettes, you would probably have needed a drink. With all the hype, the ranks of the Cockettes had expanded considerably, so there were forty-seven people in their party. Forty-seven Cockettes could dominate a 747 with little effort. Their fellow passengers, says Maureen Orth, who traveled with the Cockettes for ten days, "were just in shock." Link was wearing a mink coat over a beauty-queen sash covered with Girl Scout badges over a one-piece bathing suit. Another Cockette wore a bra made of plastic pumpkins and gold tinsel, and went trick-or-treating through the plane while beating a tambourine. They took over the economy lounge, sang show tunes, posed for pictures with other passengers, and complimented the thunderstruck stewardesses on their "drag." Most of the Cockettes were tripping, of course.

New York City in 1971 was lousy with drag queens. The city has a long history of drag, dating back at least to the 1910s and 1920s, when female impersonators like Julian Eltinge and Bert Savoy were vaudeville headliners and elaborate drag balls were held in the city. In the 1920s, the historian George Chauncey has documented, poets read and drag queens performed in Greenwich Village, and Harlem had "speakeasies where men danced together and drag queens were regular customers." The Village's Liberal Club Ball was "attended by scores of drag queens and hundreds of spectators," and Harlem's Hamilton Lodge Ball "drew *hundreds* of drag queens and *thousands* of spectators."

By the time the Cockettes arrived in Manhattan some forty-five years later, the city's avant-garde arts scenemeisters had once again made drag very cool. The celebration of drag queens was made possible in part by the women's and gay liberation movements with their ongoing attacks on gender conventions. But the art world was less interested in heated gender politics than in the cool celebration of trampled boundaries: between pop and high art, between man and woman. Drag queens were some people's favorite tramplers.

Andy Warhol, one of the most important publicists of drag, was fascinated, he wrote, by "boys who spend their lives trying to be complete girls, because they have to work so hard—double-time—getting rid of all the tell-tale male signs and drawing in all the female signs." It's grueling work, he pointed out, "to look like the complete opposite of what nature made you and then to be an imitation of what was only a fantasy woman in the first place." He put them in his movies. Warhol's "tart trio of drag queens," as the social historian Wayne Koestenbaum calls Holly Woodlawn, Jackie Curtis, and Candy Darling, were immortalized by Lou Reed in "Walk on the Wild Side": Holly hitchhiked her way across the U.S.A., shaved her legs, and then he was a she; Candy came from out on the Island, and never lost her head even when she was giving head; Jackie thought she was James Dean for a day.

That summer of the Cockettes, not far from the Factory, the studio where Warhol did most of his work, the Ridiculous Theatrical Company was also in full bloom. In many ways, the Ridiculous folks, who were also part of the hippie counterculture, were spiritual cousins of the Cockettes. Under the leadership of the playwright, actor, and director Charles Ludlam, they had put on shows—*When Queens Collide, Whores of Babylon,* and *Turds in Hell*—in which "sexual dementia and every conceivable variety of perverse possibility are matters for anarchic slapstick comedy." They sometimes performed at midnight, and used psychedelic lights. "It was improvised chaos," as one troupe member, Black-Eyed Susan, told the researcher Brennan Gerard. "During the all-night extravaganzas," Gerard writes, "boundaries between theater and reality, performer and spectator, actor and character, dissolved as audience members took drugs and took the stage, as performers forgot lines, missed cues, improvised scenes, wandered out into the house, or otherwise discarded the text." Men played women, women played men; Ludlam was famous for his Norma Desmond, and later for his Marguerite, a version of Greta Garbo's Camille.

But unlike the Cockettes, for whom acting was pretty much irrelevant, both the Ridiculous performers and the Warhol Superstars were committed to a camp tradition of good bad acting. For all its use of camp and drag, the Ridiculous was serious. Ludlam's writing and productions became more and more careful over time. His 1970 play *Bluebeard,* which borrowed from *Doctor Faustus,* involved a mad scientist's attempt to invent a "third genital." By the summer of 1971, just before the Cockettes arrived in New York, Ludlam had landed a Guggenheim Fellowship.

The Warhol Factory superstars—Darling, Curtis, Woodlawn—considered themselves actresses, too. While the Cockettes were getting famous in San Francisco, Jackie Curtis and Candy Darling, who'd appeared in Warhol's *Flesh* in 1968, were starring in *Vain Victory* at the La MaMa Experimental Theater Club. Candy played a mermaid in a wheelchair. Holly Woodlawn's role in Paul Morrissey's and Warhol's *Trash* the year before had prompted George Cukor to start a campaign to nominate her for an Oscar; she was following it up with roles in Warhol's *Women in Revolt,* with Candy and Jackie, and another film entitled *Scarecrow in a Garden of Cucumbers.* Ms. Darling, whose screen appearances, Wayne Koestenbaum suggests, could "melt a Popsicle," was "restrained in delivery, abstracted by ruminations on her own minor luster." Her greatest disappointment came when "Twentieth Century–Fox, despite her unsolicited letter-writing campaign, refused to cast her as Myra Breckenridge, and chose Raquel Welch instead." These queens were messy, but they weren't messing around. They were not about living a fantasy, or about being silly, or about turning gender into a sandbox they'd play in on acid and weed. They ruled movie screens and Max's Kansas City, and in their world adults did heroin. They were considered art.

Into this New York the Cockettes flew, dropping from the sky in a poofy cloud of hype.

In New York, the Cockettes stayed at the Hotel Albert on Eleventh Street in the East Village. Some remember it as a nice place, but they were probably high. At the time, Orth described it as a place where "on a good day the hallways smell somewhere between old socks and vomit." Pristine Condition claimed that "the roaches are putting together a road show of *Hello, Dolly!*" But you could score cheap heroin at the Albert, and some took advantage.

Advance warnings, a New York *Daily News* reporter wrote, "have likened the impact of their appearance here with that of Lenin arriving at the Finland station." Truman Capote had announced that their show was "the most outrageous thing I've ever seen," and Rex Reed had wondered aloud if the Cockettes would replace rock concerts in the 1970s. For the week before their show opened, the Cockettes simply took over fancy-hip-avant-garde Manhattan. The first night they arrived, they were guests of honor at a party thrown by the hamburger-chain heir and entrepreneur Errol Wetson at his East Side town house, where attendees included Diana Vreeland and Oscar de la Renta. "I heard about the Cockettes from my friend Truman, and New York's been so quiet, so dead, something's gotta happen," Wetson told Maureen Orth. "I haven't seen the Cockettes perform," he confessed. "I don't have to. I can feel their vibrations." Vibrate they did. "In wild costumes they uninhibitedly danced, sang, romped, and stomped," Orth reported. Reggie wore a white gown with his ass hanging out, and his was among the tamer fashions. "What's so marvelous is that they look happy, truly happy, and that's so rare these days, don't you think?" Vreeland said.

The Cockettes wound up making Max's Kansas City their home away from home. Max's, a restaurant and bar near Union Square that had opened in 1965, had been for several years New York's "salon of the psychedelic era." Artists like Robert Rauschenberg and Willem de Kooning hung out there, and in the back room Andy Warhol often shmoozed with various "superstars" from his Factory. At Max's, Warhol met Valerie Solanas, the woman who would later shoot him. Celebrities littered the place: John Lennon and Germaine Greer, Jane Fonda and William Burroughs, Warren Beatty and Mel Brooks, Michelangelo Antonioni and Bob Dylan. Many of the waitresses were drag queens. By the time the Cockettes hit New York, though, Max's was a bit played out. "In two days they completely revitalized the sagging dragging atmosphere," Orth said. They were allowed to charge their burgers and cocktails. When she spotted the Warhol star Joe Dallesandro at Max's, Pristine Condition "swiped his bread roll, brought it back to the Albert, shellacked it, and sewed it on a hat."

They were all nearly broke and hungry, so the Cockettes ate for free at cocktail parties and graciously accepted a thousand-dollar grant from Robert Rauschenberg. They were invited to a party for the Kinks and the Who at the Waldorf-Astoria, attended also by John Lennon, where they devoured pounds of shrimp. They went to an Andy Warhol party, and one given by *Screw* magazine. "I must have gone to twenty-seven parties with the Cockettes, on the East Side, the West Side, in the Village, in penthouses, lofts, museums and basements," Maureen Orth wrote in the *Village Voice,* "gotten a total of fifteen hours' sleep, met two thirds of the freaks of New York, and began to suspect that all of Manhattan was gay." The Cockettes got a ride in Marlene Dietrich's limousine, and taxi drivers turned off their meters. They received standing ovations in Manhattan restaurants just for being. Although he was a bit more serious about the upcoming show, Sylvester joined in the partying. "He rehearsed more than the other Cockettes," Maureen Orth recalls, "but I do not remember him being *that* different. Even compared to them, however, he was more sulky, definitely the diva."

By opening night, anybody who was anybody knew who the Cockettes were. Even being somebody did not guarantee you a ticket; John Lennon himself had to do some finagling. The *Washington Post* writer Sally Quinn declared their opening night at the Anderson Theatre "*the* biggest off-Broadway opening in the history of New York." In addition to drag queens and counterculture types with spray-painted bodies or whips, or dressed up as Captain America or Queen Elizabeth, there were pop stars, society matrons, fashion icons, movie stars, and literati, pulling up in Bentleys and Rolls-Royces. Filing into the Anderson—a former Yiddish art theater in Greenwich Village—were Anthony Perkins, Peggy Cass, Angela Lansbury, Gore Vidal, Gloria Swanson, Baby Jane Holzer, Allen Ginsberg,

Nora Ephron, Sylvia Miles, Alexis Smith, Rex Reed, Bill Blass, Diana Vreeland, Bobby Short, Taylor Mead, Clive Barnes, Andy Warhol, and Warhol's drag queen stars Holly Woodlawn, Candy Darling, and Jackie Curtis. "Each time you heard a sustained hair-raising shriek," wrote Ed McCormack in the counterculture magazine *Changes,* "you knew without looking that some incredible queen and its entourage had made an entrance." Orth spotted the cast of *Jesus Christ Superstar,* some *Vogue* editors, two princesses, and "the night clerk at the Hotel Albert." There were Cockette groupies who turned out to be, oddly, women. The red carpet was actually clean.

Sylvester and His Hot Band were to open with a forty-five-minute set of gospel-tinged blues-rock. Sylvester would be wearing hot pants, knee-high boots, and loads of mascara. Then would come the Cockettes, with their imported *Tinsel Tarts in a Hot Coma,* whose loose plot involved a bunch of girls heading off to New York City to make it in show business, where they get eaten alive and then head for California.

It is not so much that on opening night the Cockettes were confident in their performance skills or their production standards. It was more that such considerations seemed largely irrelevant: they were already the beloved stars of lower Manhattan, and it had always worked before to just bring their lifestyle and good vibes to a stage. Besides, there had been all those parties to go to.

They'd known there were problems. The Anderson's stage was more than twice the size of the Palace's, so the sets the Cockettes had brought with them had to be remade from scratch. There was no sound or lighting system in place, and no curtain. The costumes all needed upgrading, with cuffs and collars big enough to be seen from the back of the house. To accomplish all this, the Cockettes had six days. At two or three in the morning, between parties, a handful would show up to help build a set piece or hang part of the curtain. Most of them, though, were having too much fun running around town to worry much. They rehearsed, but they never did get around to a sound check or a full run-through. By opening night, the dozen who had been scrambling to bang together new sets and costumes were, as Kreemah Ritz puts it, "just too pooped to pucker." Those who had not were exhausted, too, from carousing. They figured they'd just go up there and do what they were used to doing—dance around, sing, knock over a set or two—and they would be loved. "We just flopped it on the stage," Fayette said.

This was not a great idea. "In minutes, they completely lived down their reputation," Mel Gussow wrote in a *New York Times* review the next day. The Cockettes, he said, proved to be "unburdened by imagination," and offered a "drag show to end all drag shows, the kind of exhibition that murders camp and gives transvestism a bad name."

New Yorkers do not suffer amateurs, or non–New Yorkers, gladly. What had seemed goofily, hippily charming in San Francisco—the Cockettes' looseness, their inability to project their voices or use mikes properly, their tendency to run into sets and into each other—appeared to New Yorkers simply incompetent. "Whereas in San Francisco it had more of an event status, in New York it just seemed tacky," says Rex Reed. "In San Francisco it all seemed wonderful and spontaneous and nutty. Here in New York it just seemed ridiculous, much ado about nothing." Nor did the Cockettes' happy-kids-on-drugs-expressing-whatever-comes-to-them vibe help them much. In New York, "happy, fun, and free" was often seen as the domain of the unhip, the dim, and the dull. Midway through, in what Ed McCormack called "an open and audible declaration that San Francisco drag queens just don't make the grade by New York standards of decadence," Taylor Mead of Andy Warhol's Factory called out, as if invoking the name of God, "Where is Jackie Curtis?"

By the time the opening night show was over, those who had stayed to watch the whole thing filed out of the theater, as one observer put it, as if leaving a wake. "It's three years old, and it's boring," a woman leaving the theater commented, and then corrected herself. "It's *five* years old, and it's boring. It's no good just being a drag queen anymore. Anybody can do that." Many had actually fled shortly after the show began. Rumors circulated that Angela Lansbury had stood up, said, "Let's get the fuck out of here," and had taken a whole row with her. "My God," said Rex Reed, whose column had made this bomb possible, "this is worse than Hiroshima." Gore Vidal had the last, dry word. "Having no talent is not enough," he commented, paraphrasing a line from *Gypsy*.

The Cockettes got better over the next few nights, switched to the glitzier *Pearls Over Shanghai* the next week, and performed through the run of their two-week contract. But the damage of opening night was irreparable. The Cockettes were eaten alive, and headed back for California. The *Berkeley Barb*, which had run Cockette-friendly articles the year before, welcomed them home a couple of weeks later with the head-line "Cockettes Crumble: Lay $50,000 Gotham Egg."

The only person who hadn't laid an egg in New York City in November 1971 was Sylvester. He had gone to all the major parties and done quite a bit of shopping, but he had also rehearsed every day with his band, on stage, for two hours, while miscellaneous Cockettes and workers ham-mered sets and strung up curtains around them. The day of the opening, Sylvester's background singers had disappeared and then reappeared, but Sylvester rehearsed them until the minute the doors were opening.

"Here is a close friend of mine who performs his beautiful love on stage," a Cockette had announced on opening night, and out came a white guitarist in a "velvet frock-coat English fop style," a white bassist in "the straggly Woodstockian pioneer style," a "fat black drummer," and a trio of black women dressed in "simple blouses and long church-going skirts" who provided a "raunchy kind of syncopated oop-shooping." The band cooked, Ed McCormack recounted, and then out came Sylvester, "half-naked in hot-pants and boots," looking like "an athlete who got side-tracked into ballet." Sylvester did "unprecedented things with his voice, shrieking with great (if shrill) soul, hitting new highs with all kinds of impressive oop-shooping and verbal tapdancing." He played the piano on a ballad, "whisper-singing like Nina Simone and tinkling the ivories like a cocktail jazz pianist on a baroque streak."

Sylvester introduced "God Bless the Child" with a version of the monologue he'd delivered at his Palace Theatre shows, about friends who invite you to dinner and then ask you to pay. He received, in return, squeals and hoots. Jumping up from the piano, "enormous rusty-colored Afro bouffant bounding buoyantly with every step," Sylvester danced right into an up-tempo tune that "had almost everyone in the house going bananas, jumping up and down like a jack-in-the-box in their seats." People who weren't jack-in-the-boxing were dancing in the aisles, while Sylvester was "jumping up and down, banging shit out of his tambourine and singing in his shrill shriek, some wild-ass chorus scream, over and over and over." He left the crowd in a froth, and they stood and stomped on the floor and screamed for more. For an encore, he chose the Rolling Stones' "Midnight Rambler"—*he don't give a hoot of warning, wrapped up in a black cat cloak*—into which he periodically threw some gospel phrasing.

"Remember," Sylvester said, dripping sweat, "if no one else cares about you, we do." He exited blowing kisses.

And so had Sylvester made a beginning of what was certain to be the Cockettes' end. "They loved Sylvester, even after forty-five minutes," the *Village Voice* reported after opening night. The New York *Daily News*, while savaging the Cockettes, commented that "the hit of the show actually was its curtain raiser, a former Cockette." His act, the reviewer said, "is professional and tightly organized." The *Times*'s Gussow wrote that Sylvester "wailed and shouted rock and soul like an Aretha touched with Sumac." In *Changes*, Ed McCormack declared Sylvester "infuckingcredible."

At the next show, his head perhaps swelled by the reviews and the screaming audience, Sylvester began with a tart acknowledgment of the disastrous opening night. "I apologize for this travesty that I'm associated with," he said from the stage. Some of the Cockettes were angry and others were simply dismayed. Sylvester had given not a hoot of warning.

Sylvester and His Hot Band did four more shows, but on the seventh night Sylvester walked out onstage and folded his arms. "I gotta be here," he said, "but I don't gotta sing." He told the audience that the show for which they'd paid $6.50 could be seen for a pittance in San Francisco. And while the Cockettes scrambled to get themselves ready to go on early, Sylvester "put the producer and Sebastian down," the Cockettes' lighting technician Tom Nieze (known as "Technical Tommy") wrote from New York to Peter Mintun. Some people threw things at Sylvester from the audience. "Suckers!" Sylvester said, and walked off the stage. "It floored everyone," the Cockette Dusty Dawn wrote to a friend. Sylvester would never again appear onstage with the Cockettes.

"Sylvester did us, and himself, in," Dusty Dawn said at the time. From the few hazy reports that remain, it seems that Sylvester was being advised by Dennis Lopez to cut and run from the Cockettes' New York disaster. Sebastian, who held Sylvester's contract, had refused to release him; in walking off stage, Sylvester was plainly choosing to side with Lopez and Lopez's patron Gregg Gobel. He must have seen his escape from the Cockettes as a narrow one, worth leaving friendships and ovations behind. He flew back to San Francisco with his band and kudos from the major New York papers, and a glimpse of just how big the big time must be—and what it took to get there.

Upon the Cockettes' return from New York the next week, Kreemah Ritz was asked by a *San Francisco Chronicle* reporter what he thought about Sylvester's behavior. Kreemah replied, mock-dramatically, "He'll never work in this town again."

Few of the Cockettes ever performed in that town, or any other, again. By 1972, the crazy colors and new shapes of psychedelics and hallucinogens were fast being knocked out of the San Francisco scene by edgy, buzzing, estranging drugs like PCP and speed. The wind that had carried the Cockettes to San Francisco prominence seemed to suddenly die down. They put on a few more shows in San Francisco—good ones, say loyalists who stuck with them—but fizzled out in the fall of 1972. The *Rollicking Ritz Family* film project was dropped. Soon, two Cockettes would overdose on drugs together while watching an episode of *Star Trek,* and Hibiscus himself would pack his bags and go back to New York.

They had thought they might just be liberating spirits, reclaiming selves from the homogenization of the military state, kicking loose preconceived notions, giving a glimpse of the beyond. They had thought they might just be the defiant unisexual wave of the future. But the sea on which they had risen seemed to be drying up beneath them—though some of them kept right on riding.

"We were all a little drunk on possibilities," the novelist Robert Stone has said of the 1960s acid-and-liberation culture on the West Coast. "Those who cared most deeply about the changes, those who gave their lives to them, were, I think, the most deceived." Soon, the playful visions of revolutionary flower children would come to seem to many like an innocent cover; the revolution had not materialized, and the grown-ups had simply gone about the business of war and Watergate. "Sex, drugs, and death were demystified," Stone says. "The LSD we took as a tonic of psychic liberation turned out to have been developed by C.I.A. researchers as a weapon of the Cold War." Many merry pranksters would come to suspect that "the prank was on us."

A glimpse of the beyond, it turned out, was all they were going to get.

6.

SCRATCH MY FLOWER

Sylvester came back from New York floating on a cloud. On stage in Manhattan with screaming crowds on their feet: his life was a real fantasy, full of kissy promises. Where the Cockettes had been rudely awakened from their dreams, Sylvester had had one of his come true.

There was certainly no reason, at first, for Sylvester to come down. Not long after his return from New York, *Rolling Stone*'s editor, Jann Wenner, who had seen him perform, got it into his head that Sylvester should make a record. Wenner got some money from A&M Records and to produce the album hired Ben Sidran, a white jazz musician who had recently published his doctoral dissertation as the book *Black Talk: How the Music of Black America Created a Radical Alternative to the Values of Western Literary Tradition.* "Jann said he had a feeling Sylvester could become a star, and I had the feeling that if Jann put *Rolling Stone* behind it, my dog Harold could be a star," Sidran recalls in his memoir, giving some indication of his respect for Sylvester.

Sylvester showed up at the studio in full drag: a "long flowing dress, hair piled high and neckline plunging." Sidran liked Sylvester's baritone, but Sylvester "refused to use it, insisting instead on this piercing falsetto which, at times, was interesting but often veered off into the horrific," and sounded "downright bizarre" coming out of the body of a "six foot cross-dresser." They recorded "several heart-wrenching versions" of Leon Russell's "Superstar," a recent hit for Karen Carpenter. "Sylvester was so excited about making a record, being in a studio, and he sang with no restraint," Jann Wenner says thirty years later from his offices at Wenner Media. "I mean, he blew his voice out. Every single take we were doing was the final take." *Don't you remember you told me you loved me, baby?*

Sylvester sang. Between takes, he and Sidran's wife, Judy, chatted about makeup and fashion.

Jann Wenner did not, in the end, manage to interest A&M Records in the Sylvester demo, and Ben Sidran was evidently more drawn to Jann Wenner than to Sylvester. But Sylvester was encouraged nonetheless. For the first few months after the New York City trip, with the Pointer Sisters and his Hot Band, Sylvester was getting gigs in the many small rock clubs around town, places like the Boarding House, the Orphanage, the Shed, and the Keystone.

Sylvester's act was more insane than lucrative. He had one big foot still in Cockette culture and the other in the rock scene. "No matter what people say," Sylvester said when the curtain rose at the On Broadway one night in February 1972, "things are always the same." Pristine Condition ran up and down the aisles twirling batons and calling out nonsense incantations, and a dog sat onstage for much of the gig. *They are the eggmen, I am the walrus, goo goo goo joob,* Sylvester sang. Sylvester, the Pointers, and the band members made about $10 apiece. At one show Sylvester and His Hot Band did at a San Francisco warehouse, live chickens ran around the stage, a man jumped through a flaming hoop, and people streaked. "But when he started singing, they would listen," Anita Pointer says. "Sylvester could catch anybody's attention with that voice." *We got to make this land a better land than the land in which we live,* Sylvester and the Pointers sang. They syncopated their voices together like hand claps: *Yes we can, I know we can can, Yes we can can, Why can't we?*

Sylvester and His Hot Band were invited to record two cuts for a KSAN compilation album on Blue Thumb Records, *Lights Out: San Francisco.* The album appealed largely to local stoners. "Light your incense, clothes off, get yourself and your Koolaid together and boogie in the dark," wrote the producer, Voco, on the album notes. With the bass player Kerry Hatch and a couple of other musicians—including the future Journey guitarist Neal Schon—Sylvester recorded "Hey, That's No Way to Say Goodbye" and, backed by the Pointer Sisters' tight, three-part harmonies, a song he wrote called "Why Was I Born?"

Sylvester intended to set aside his vintage blues lady, but the lady herself seemed reluctant to leave. "Tonight we're going to rock out, so I want you to get yourselves prepared now," he told a Palace Theatre audience in early 1972. "Dance. Don't sit there, 'cause I don't want this to be like a sit-down concert. This is not like the old Palace shows I used to do. This is something new and different, so I want your reactions to be new and different. So if you feel like dancing or screaming or shouting or jumping, do." He went immediately into his slow, bluesy version of "No Way to Say Goodbye," and from there into a slow, gospelly tune about standing by a friend no matter who they may be, and from there into a slow, gravelly blues tune about how nobody wants me. On most songs he accompanied himself on piano. He ended with "God Bless the Child." There wasn't a whole lot to rock out to, really.

That summer, Josephine Baker was playing at the Circle Star Theatre in San Carlos. Sylvester went to the show, and afterward he talked his way backstage. In Miss Baker's presence, he could barely speak. He still wanted to be her. He did take away advice, or so he would later say. "The illusion you create onstage is *all*," Miss Baker told him. That same summer, he went to see Bette Midler, too, at the Boarding House on Bush Street. "You've *got* to see how she performs," he told Peter Mintun, dragging him along, as if he wanted help figuring out what Midler had that so affected an audience. Accompanied by an unknown pianist named Barry Manilow, Midler sang some of the tunes Sylvester had already been singing—"Am I Blue," "Superstar"—brazen and raunchy and more than getting away with it. Maybe he wanted to be her, too. He was shedding the blues chanteuse for a rockier incarnation, trading sequined gowns for sequined hot pants, but for now he was floating, not sure just who to be next.

By the winter of 1972, the Pointer Sisters had ventured out on their own, though they would sometimes sing background for Sylvester at hometown shows. Sylvester and Dennis Lopez had reconstituted the band, first hiring Kerry Hatch and then adding four rock and rhythm-and-blues musicians in their twenties from Los Angeles, where the talent pool was bigger. Recruiting musicians, Dennis Lopez talked a lot about "glam" this and "glitter" that—British "glam rock" or "glitter rock" being all the rage—but they were clearly looking, Hatch says, "for a band that could play well enough to get a record deal." At the auditions, Sylvester, overflowing with scarves and bracelets, smiled shyly at the musicians, and fervently played the piano. Neither he nor Dennis said much about what kind of music they were after, so the musicians just jammed. They were all hired.

The plan seemed to be that Sylvester would be "as outrageous and in-your-face and radically flamboyant as possible," Hatch says, the band would "make the music legitimate enough to sell records," and they would all be famous and make tons of money. They were something of an odd match, Sylvester and the five longhaired straight white boys, but the new Hot Band could play. Dennis and Sylvester figured the musicians could at least *look* as if they belonged in the same world as Sylvester, so the band members awkwardly added sequins, beads, and occasionally lamé to their onstage wardrobe. "Sylvester had a big box of clothes, and everybody had to wear something from that box," recalls the sax player Chris Mostert, who had come from a band called Pollution, along with the trumpet player Bobby Blood and the guitarist James Q. "Smitty" Smith. They competed for the tamer, manlier items in the box, like the denim jacket covered with rhinestones.

Sylvester and the band—now "the" rather than "his" Hot Band—shuttled back and forth between clubs in Los Angeles and San Francisco. They played Bimbo's 365 a lot. They played with Merry Clayton at the Keystone in Berkeley, and shared a bill with Stevie Wonder at the Whisky a Go Go in Los Angeles, where Sylvester had been a groupie just a couple of years before. They played some of the standards Sylvester had done over the past few years, and the Beatles' "Blackbird"; "Somebody Loan Me a Dime," a song by the Chicago bluesman Fenton Robinson; Wilson Pickett songs that Sylvester had danced to with the Disquotays, like "Hello Sunshine" and "Stagger Lee." Sylvester's soul-shouts turned James Taylor's "Fire and Rain" from a smooth downer into something more fiery and wet, and his high voice brought something like pain to Neil Young's "Southern Man" lyrics about burning crosses and cracking bullwhips. The band was tight, with horns and, the Hot Band drummer Travis Fullerton says, the sound "of a kickass roadhouse rhythm-and-blues band." Together they built crowds into such a fever that their gigs sometimes resembled riots.

Genderfucky outrageousness was quite the ticket in 1972. Detroit-born Vincent Furnier, renamed Alice Cooper, had a hit that year with "School's Out." Onstage, he wore drippy, spidery black eye makeup, black panties and maid outfits and Girl Scout uniforms and silver jumpsuits. His "shock rock" props included an electric chair and live snakes and chickens. British glitter-glam rockers like Bowie, T. Rex, and Roxy Music were making waves for wearing glitzy costumes and makeup. Their shows were spectacles: elaborate sets, glammed-up young audiences. They were attracting crowds with androgynous images. Glam rockers sometimes presented themselves as strange, made-up characters, too. Just a few months earlier, Bowie had introduced Ziggy Stardust, his hard-rocking, shiny-clothed, sexually voracious, drug-loving Martian. "It became very dangerous," he said later of Ziggy. "I got hopelessly lost in the fantasy."

For that Halloween weekend, Bill Graham booked Sylvester and the Hot Band as the opening act for David Bowie at Winterland, a former ice rink that had been converted into a 5,400-person arena, where Jefferson Airplane and the Grateful Dead had played. It was their biggest gig yet.

When Bowie failed to sell out his two nights at Winterland, he shrugged it off. "They don't need me," David Bowie said of San Franciscans. "They've got Sylvester." Bowie had a point. Bowie and Ziggy must indeed have seemed a bit redundant in a city whose soil was already so thoroughly mixed with glitter that its indigenous culture included a built-like-a-linebacker black man in a spangled headband over a floppy wig and tasteful makeup, wearing blue sequins and a toga split up to his waist, lost in a Josephine-Baker-as-rock-star fantasy, wailing in gospel-falsetto backed by a bunch of straight white guys with rock-star haircuts and rhinestones playing kickass roadhouse blues-rock. "I want to *destroy* reality when I'm performing," Sylvester said.

For his encore on the second night of the Bowie run, Sylvester became the first person to fly inside Winterland. He hired a technician who had flown Mary Martin in *Peter Pan* to rig the cables. He made twelve-foot, sequin-covered butterfly wings. At the sound check, Sylvester and some of the Hot Band practiced the flight: Sylvester would run eight steps and then leap off the stage, as several men hoisted him into the air from backstage, sending him out over the audience and back again. That night, as the band played the final rollicking song, Sylvester ran and jumped and flew across the theater, like a big-boned, glittering brown Tinkerbell.

In early 1973, Sylvester and the Hot Band were signed by Bob Krasnow to Blue Thumb Records. Krasnow hired Ben Sidran, who had not seen Sylvester since the failed Jann Wenner demo session, to produce. Blue

Thumb, though based in Beverly Hills, had a renegade San Francisco spirit: an appreciation for eccentricity and any music that could make you shake your ass. It was, says Sidran, "the epitome of inmates running the asylum." Bob Krasnow's office was dark gray, with a "floor-to-ceiling painting of Jimi Hendrix" and a barber's chair. The label's eclectic roster included Ike and Tina Turner, actor and female impersonator Charles Pierce, Captain Beefheart and the Magic Band, the Crusaders, the zydeco musician Clifton Chenier, Dan Hicks and His Hot Licks, Lenny Bruce, and Tyrannosaurus (soon to be T.) Rex. "We were all just having a good time," the Blue Thumb producer Tommy LiPuma said later. "There were a lot of good chemicals going around at that time, and it was one big hang." Sylvester would fit right in.

Sylvester invited Peter Mintun for a trip down to Los Angeles to record "Gimme a Pigfoot (And a Bottle of Beer)," an old Bessie Smith song, for the Blue Thumb album, and to do another Whisky a Go Go gig. "You're going to make lots of money," he told Peter. Peter was skeptical: the last time they had planned a gig together, Peter had written up a contract stipulating a payment of $134.40 and "exact times and dates for rehearsals"— and Sylvester had done the shows without Peter. Still, for what was starting to seem like old times' sake, Peter joined Sylvester for the trip.

Blue Thumb put up Peter and Sylvester in the Hotel Continental, and just the name made them feel as if they were in a 1930s film. Sylvester already had his drag together, of course, but they needed something for Peter, so they wandered over to the Western Costume Company on Melrose Avenue. After they found some white tails for him, they wandered the aisles pulling at the tags, which listed the history of the costumes; Sylvester screamed for Peter to come see a Debbie Reynolds outfit, and Peter called him over to stand in the presence of Jackie Gleason's suit. It was all very old-Hollywood. They wore dark sunglasses. The next day, they recorded at Capitol Tower, the thirteen-story round building at Hollywood and Vine where Ella Mae Morse had once recorded "The Cow Cow Boogie" and Billie Holiday had once sung with Paul Whiteman's band. Peter played piano while Sylvester sang "Gimme a Pigfoot."

In the afternoon, Sylvester stopped by his mother's house for a visit. His twin sisters were only sixteen, but Bernadette was dead set on going to the Whisky that night, so Sylvester spent much of the afternoon making her up to look older. "When he made me up, there was no place I couldn't get into," Bernadette says. She and Letha went with Sylvester to the club, and sat backstage with him before the show.

That night at the Whisky, Sylvester first brought Peter Mintun up to the stage for a medley of songs including "Pigfoot." *We all gather at the Harlem Strut*, Sylvester sang, *and what we do is tut tut tut.* The audience was polite, but uninterested in strut and tut. "It wasn't what that crowd wanted to hear," Peter says. "They wanted rock." Peter knew that Sylvester was closing the door on his vintage blues persona; that night, Peter felt the door close quietly behind him, as well. It was the last time he played piano on stage with Sylvester, and he went home the next day.

The rest of the night Sylvester and the Hot Band gave the crowd at the Whisky the rock they wanted. The next day, the critic Richard Cromelin praised the excitement level the band generated. "It's time for everyone to get ready for Sylvester and the Hot Band," he wrote, raving especially about Sylvester's voice, "an unusual instrument, high and nasal, unconventional in its phrasing and almost eerily Eastern in some of the strange notes he slides through and around." If the album Sylvester and the Hot Band were recording "comes anywhere close to the energy level they create in the flesh," Cromelin predicted, "they're going to be one of '73's first and biggest smashes."

Sylvester would name that first album *Scratch My Flower.* In the right upper corner of the album cover is a scratch-and-sniff flower sticker scented with gardenia. The back cover shows Sylvester in front of five longhaired white men. They all have their arms crossed. In front of them Sylvester sits in silver flapper drag, a gardenia in his wig, the toenails of his huge bare feet painted red. On the front cover, he sits in shiny silver pants, a black sequined blouse, rhinestoned platform sandals, and large red sequined gloves. His lips are slightly parted as he looks at you, and he holds a cigarette in a long black holder. Even now, if you scratch the album's flower and move your face up close, you can smell it, pretty and hopeful and sweet.

Distinguishing fantasy from reality is a reasonable endeavor, but as a goal it is also sadly modest. It is a necessary step in the more ambitious project of bringing fantasy and reality into contact. There are moments when what is imaginary is also true. These are probably what wise people mean by magic. Creating or even just recognizing those moments requires an enormous talent, uncommon intuition, tremendous dedication, extraordinary faith, and hard work. It can take a whole lifetime, maybe more.

Sylvester's strategy—as a Disquotay, as a Cockette—had always been to send fantasy ahead and let the reality catch up. The one thing Sylvester knew he wanted to be, and deserved to be, was a star. "Being a star is first of all knowing that you're a Star; the rest will take care of itself," Richard Cromelin said at the time. "Sylvester is always the Star. A Star sitting at dinner in the hotel coffee shop, a gorgeous ring on each finger and an art deco lady-walking-her-greyhound pin on his jacket; a Star soaring over the audience in the Palace Theatre on 12-foot butterfly wings, totally destroying the acid-tripping queens below; a Star shining through the crowds back in the dressing room; a Star jogging through Golden Gate Park every morning."

The day the Blue Thumb advance came through, Sylvester cashed the entire check and grabbed his new friend Cassie.° Sylvester and Cassie, the wife of one of the band members, had become fast girlfriends. Cassie, who had been a model, happily took fashion instruction from Sylvester, seeing him as a woman who knew her stuff. "Honey, the bag's not working," Sylvester would say when Cassie walked into a gig. Or, "What's with the fake eyelashes? You've got beautiful eyelashes. Just be yourself." Sylvester had taken to knocking on Cassie's hotel room door at seven in the morning and calling, "Get up, my darling! We're going looking for the items of life!" Cassie would get dressed, and Sylvester would typically make her undress and redress. "No jewels, my darling," he would remind her. "Dress down. You look too good for making deals." Off they would go, to flea markets and hole-in-the-wall shops, to bargain for deco jewels and shawls and candlesticks.

For some time, Sylvester had been eyeing a Volkswagen Bug with a Rolls-Royce grille, so the day the record money came through he and Cassie headed straight to the car dealership. Cassie was six foot one; Sylvester was wearing a bit of makeup, a short natural, a T-shirt and jeans, and big hoop earrings. When they walked into the dealership the salesmen scattered like mice. "I want this one," Sylvester announced, pointing at the car. Cassie suggested that they take a test drive and find out about financing. "No, honey," Sylvester said, "I want this one." Cassie rustled up one of the frightened salespeople. Sylvester put the cash on the table, got in the

°"Cassie" is a pseudonym.

Volkswagen with the Rolls-Royce grille, and he and Cassie drove right off the lot.

There was some money left over, and Cassie insisted that they go to the bank and open an account. "She would have spent that money in a day, on herself and her friends," Cassie says of Sylvester. At the bank, Sylvester wanted the checks to say only "Sylvester"—a diva needs no second name—though the bank insisted on his full, legal name. "I've got a checkbook! I've got a checkbook! Let's go write my first check!" he called. He wrote his first check for an eleven-dollar diner lunch. Cassie asked whether he knew how to balance a checkbook. "Honey, I don't have to worry about things like that," Sylvester said, with a wave of the hand.

Later that day, Sylvester and his lover Michael took a limousine down to Polk Street and meandered. They popped into every store that caught their eye, and Sylvester bought expensive gifts for his mother, Michael, himself, and miscellaneous others, and threw them into the limo. "Sylvester thought the payroll would never end," says Cassie. "The world had become her apple. In her mind, when the recording contract happened, it was like the fantasy came true. In her mind, she was the diva. She was Diana Ross."

Sylvester's diva-tude extended to the Hot Band, which was not always a bad thing. Gregg Gobel was still a backer, and Gregg had his father George's credit card. Other musicians they knew went to gigs in converted school buses with uncomfortable seats, and ate badly; for the first year or so with Sylvester, the Hot Band flew to out-of-town gigs, and both they and Sylvester arrived at engagements in limousines. They ate well and drank cocktails. "That was an important part of how the whole project was presented, and it included us," Chris Mostert says. "It had to have that glamour."

Sylvester and Michael Lyons soon created a home life befitting a diva, moving into a building on Pacific Heights that had once been a women's prison. They had a houseboy. They burned through the Blue Thumb money quickly, but were helped along by a series of friends who were using some of their family money to hang out in San Francisco; one was a Ritz Hotel heiress, and another, a girl named Greg, was a Bank of California heiress. They threw elaborate dinner parties. Metal scarves were draped over lamps; candles were lit. The apartments in their building were filled with other glammy, kooky people, and some had balconies facing a courtyard. "Sylvester was their star," says Kerry Hatch. One imagines him stepping out on his balcony to be adored: a small theater, but a good crowd.

When everyday life seemed less than fantastic, Sylvester would toss Michael a fringed jacket or a fur and say, "Here, put this on." That seemed to cheer Sylvester up. "If it looks like you've got too much on," he loved to say, "put more on." Sylvester would get dressed up in sequins and a headdress and a parasol and walk through a crowd, Michael trailing a few feet behind. The rest would take care of itself.

Sylvester was still something of a child when he made his first album, with movielike daydreams of applause. Dennis Lopez and Gregg Gobel—band members remember them mainly as pleasant, passive, overwhelmed, unprofessional, and absent—had only a tad more music-industry experience. All three envisioned Sylvester as an ultra-glamorous megastar, but beyond that they offered up no particular musical vision. "He was not at the helm musically at all," says Kerry Hatch. "There was no guiding force." Ben Sidran, who produced *Scratch My Flower*, was arguably not the best man for the job. He considered Sylvester's vocal talent "kind of marginal" and his falsetto often "excruciating." Sidran, Hatch says, was "trying to produce something that was completely out of his element."

Sylvester was, in a sense, out of his element as well. "I love them so much, my boys," he would say to Cassie about the band, but he was reluctant to tell them what to do. At rehearsals and recording sessions, Sylvester would sit around the studio, "just being a diva, smiling coyly," recalls Travis Fullerton. "Why do I have to be here?" he would ask. "I'm not singing today." Sylvester left everything but vocal decisions to the producers and the band. "He partially trusted us to do the right thing," Kerry Hatch says, "and he partially just didn't give a rat's ass if we did the right thing or not. He had his own social world and everything else came second. The first thing on his mind was what fun thing he was doing at that moment. He just wanted to be glamorous and have a party." He knew Diana Ross did not sit around the studio all day.

At the Blue Thumb sessions, Sylvester was like a casual visitor to someone else's reality. He brought his own world with him: sometimes his little sisters; sometimes Michael Lyons, with whom he would loudly talk about their sexual exploits from the previous night; sometimes people Sidran described as "his band of androgynous whackos," hangers-on who filled the studio with "a lot of drama, a lot of scarves and ankle bells and lipstick all around." When it was time to sing, he would float in looking tired—a visiting band had rented Marilyn Monroe's mansion, and it had been fabulous, he might report—and do his thing. He preferred singing in cars or at home to singing at rehearsals. "Oh, honey, rehearsal is so not fun," he explained to Cassie. When Sylvester was frustrated he stamped his feet or yelled or just left, and the band members would look at each other, shrug, and go back to playing their music. Ben Sidran found Sylvester "bitchy, star-struck, arbitrary, self-impressed, and, from time to time, simply evil"; Hatch saw Sylvester as "a temperamental woman"; Mostert saw him as a "genius without common sense"; Fullerton saw him as a "shy boy, wanting to be adored." Everyone agreed he was a prima donna; only some understood that that was the whole point.

The Hot Band, which had become a tight-knit crew, had already started to fill the vacuum left by Sylvester and his managers. They hoped, Kerry Hatch says, that "the vehicle of Sylvester's outrageousness"—"Aretha Franklin as a drag queen," as Hatch saw it—would "launch all of us into some bigger stardom." They adjusted to the fact that their vehicle came with "instability, craziness and all of this emotional flamboyance."

Scratch My Flower came out an unlikely, uneven, jagged-edged potpourri of covers from different genres and time periods, mostly culled from Sylvester and the Hot Band's show set: James Taylor, Ray Charles, and Lieber and Stoller; Neil Young's "Southern Man," along with a Sylvester arrangement of "My Country 'Tis of Thee" with funk bass and Hendrixish guitar; "Gimme a Pigfoot," with its barrelhouse piano; the Procul Harum hit "A Whiter Shade of Pale," and "God Bless the Child." The album had little of the fire and focus of the live shows. "It was all over the place," says Kerry Hatch. Sidran refused to have his name attached. It was nobody's dream come true.

"The producers didn't understand Sylvester at all," says the Hot Band drummer, Travis Fullerton. "And I think the band may have hijacked her dreams."

"I think a lot of people enjoy my show because they don't understand it," Sylvester said of his act with the Hot Band. "And rather than criticize it, they just get into it." That seemed about right. If the vinyl version of

Sylvester and the Hot Band was, as *Rolling Stone* once put it, a "shrieky outré" event, the live act still created fevers. The shows attracted some gay men and, much to the band's delight, many beautiful straight women. Touring, though, was hardly glamorous—especially after George Gobel cut off Gregg's credit card. They played big cities, like Atlanta, Detroit, and New York, but on several weeks-long tours, they played mostly in places like Kenosha, Wisconsin; Des Moines, Iowa; Joplin, Missouri; and Dothan, Alabama. They stayed in Ramadas and Holiday Inns, and traveled by Winnebago. They usually had one roadie.

Most of the time, especially in the South, they felt like a traveling freak show. People with shotguns in their pickup trucks would see the long-haired band members and yell out of their windows: "Hippie, go home!" "Longhairs, you look like girls!" At their hotel in Dothan, the manager stopped them on the way out. "I just got to ask y'all," he said, "when y'all get up in the morning and look at yourselves in the mirror, how do you stand it?" In such towns, Dennis Lopez would often get so shuddering and stressed that without telling anyone he would just jump in a car, head for the airport, and take himself back to the safety of San Francisco, leaving the band trying to figure out where the next job was and how to get there.

After a show, when people commented to band members about how good "that black girl singer" was, they would simply say, "Yeah, she's good," and leave it at that. Longhaired men were an unusual sight in most of America in 1973, but husky black queens in colorful outfits and head scarves made no sense whatsoever. When Sylvester walked through a town or into a restaurant or a Holiday Inn, heads snapped in double takes, narrowed eyes followed, mouths dropped open, bodies stopped dead in their tracks. "Oh, they just don't know," Sylvester would comment to Cassie. "Pay it no mind."

Sylvester mostly just went about the business of being Sylvester. If salespeople in a department store would not wait on him, he would snap his fingers and call "Excuse me! Excuse me! Excuse me!" until they came around. Once in Joplin, Missouri, Sylvester walked into the hotel coffee shop where Kerry Hatch and his visiting uncle—"a total redneck, Archie Bunker deluxe," as Hatch describes him—were eating breakfast. Sylvester, in bangles and mirrored jeans, his eyes bloodshot and droopy, sat right down and put his head on Kerry Hatch's shoulder. "Oh, my dear," he sighed. "What a *night.*" Hatch's uncle could not speak for minutes.

ester had enough years as a black queen to know how to get by. within minutes of arrival, even the trashiest hotel looked like a place from Sylvester's world: scarves over lampshades, Indian fabrics on the walls, candles burning. If a town had a bathhouse, Sylvester would be there; if there was an available gay man, Sylvester would do him. When a town seemed particularly unwelcoming, he simply holed up in his hotel room until just before showtime. In one city in the South, Sylvester later told friends, he was escorted out of town by two sheriffs. "There's two things we don't like down here, boy," they said. "And you're both of them." Sylvester left quietly—he might be crazy, but he wasn't stupid.

Back in California, where they were on safe cultural ground, Sylvester and the Hot Band were quickly integrated into the "Bill Graham Presents" circuit in the Bay Area, playing venues like Winterland and Berkeley Community Theater and Stockton Civic. They toured with Bay Area soul fixtures Tower of Power, who had established themselves with the hit "You're Still a Young Man"; with Lynyrd Skynyrd, whose "Freebird" was already becoming a rock anthem; with a psychedelic folk-rock band called It's a Beautiful Day; they were invited to tour with Billy Preston, who had several hit records, including "Nothing from Nothing" and "Will It Go Round in Circles," and who had played keyboards on the Beatles' *Let It Be.*

Sylvester and the Hot Band opened a lot of other people's shows, but almost never headlined. They were something like gregarious, gorgeous bridesmaids at the wrong wedding: you loved them to death, but you weren't quite sure what they were doing there. None of this sat too well with the diva: not the finger-snapping for service, not the cheap hotels, not the holing up, not the long car rides, not the boring talk about money, not the rehearsing, not the second billing. "Sylvester didn't understand why he couldn't instantly be Marilyn Monroe," says Kerry Hatch.

It is debatable whether a place yet existed where Sylvester could make sense. More likely, it would have to be made up.

Certainly his managers were at a loss as to how to package and sell him and make him a star. He was trying on various musical hats, often piling one on top of the other in unusual combinations. "Nobody knew what they were looking at, or what they were listening to," says Kerry Hatch. He was black and gospel-singing, but with an all-white rock band, playing to what the music writer Joel Selvin describes as "blue jeans–wearing, rock-and-blues-singing, white, middle-class hippies with long hair who dressed badly." He was overtly and unapologetically gay, with an audible lisp, but projected an image that, Richard Cromelin wrote, "encompasses an extensive portion of the sexual spectrum transcending rigid categories and obliterating distinctions." His own label's publicity materials pitched Sylvester as everything but the kitchen sink: the "coming together of outrageous ideas, colors, philosophies, glitter, lights, and a wildly unique hot rock, with a touch of 20s and 30s blues." The publicity sheet invited comparisons to Bowie, but then lazily asserted that while "Bowie is white, English, and cerebral," Sylvester is "black, American, and definitely earthy."

Reviewers seemed to be struggling to make sense of Sylvester. The only precedent reviewers had for interpreting a flaming black rock-and-roller was the pompadoured, desexed, tutti-frutti Little Richard, who by then seemed almost like a novelty act. Reviewers took pains to point out that although he might seem like Little Richard's younger, taller sister-brother, Sylvester was a real musician. The *San Francisco Chronicle* assured readers, for example, that Sylvester's was "a cooking band, not a freak show," great at "taking a small crowd and transporting it with energy." *Variety* praised "the black transvestite" whose "performance is serious, not campy, a turn that can cook."

Sylvester was not much help, partly because he was determined to ignore boundaries that did not suit him. "I can be a man if I want to, or I can be a very beautiful woman," he said. He was also still figuring out how to be odd and respected at the same time. "I don't mind at all being called bizarre," he told an interviewer in 1973. By the next year, he seemed to have changed his mind. "I'm not strange," he said. "People try to explain me off as weird, and into the whole glitter rock scene. I might wear costumes and dress up, but that's me. I have no great message to deliver to people. And I'm not concerned about being at the forefront of any revolution through music or any other means." That same year, he was strange again, but mainly, he said, to entertain: "If it takes sequins, if it takes feathers, if it takes makeup, I'll put it on because that's what I'm there for."

By the time Sylvester and the Hot Band recorded their second album, *Bazaar,* in late 1973, Sylvester's managers had lost control of the band. The album was, as Kerry Hatch says, "more satisfying for us as a band," and "more honest in terms of what we were doing: R&B with an outrageous singer." *Bazaar* included some songs Sylvester had been performing in shows, like James Taylor's "Don't Let Me Be Lonely Tonight" and a song called "She," which felt like his mother: *My, my she sure could sing. She had faith and she had believing. She led all the people together in singing. And she prayed every night to the Lord up above, singin' hallelujah, oh, hallelujah.* The album also included two songs by Kerry Hatch and one by his bandmate guitarist James Q. Smith. It could have been called *The Hot Band featuring Sylvester.*

By now, some of the Hot Band members had concluded, as Hatch puts it, that Sylvester was "a nut case" who was living in a "fantasy world." He arrived at the studio one day while they were playing a chord progression, and started singing along, as if improvising, about how the same folks you misuse on your way up you'll see on your way down. They whittled their jamming into a song: the band wrote the music and Sylvester wrote the lyrics. When they tried it out at Whisky a Go Go, one of the members of Little Feat was there. The song Sylvester had been improvising, it turned out, had been written by Allen Toussaint and recorded earlier that year by Little Feat.

Sylvester does not appear on the back of the *Bazaar* album cover. Instead, there are pictures of the band members, and beneath them their own cryptic inside joke: "Why is the Hot Band smiling? Because they have S.O.M.F." ("S.O.M.F." was Hot Band code for Sit on My Face.) On the front is a photo of Sylvester, with long flowing hair, turquoise Indian jewelry, and light makeup. He is not smiling.

When Sylvester opened for Billy Preston at the Santa Monica Civic Auditorium in early 1974, he fluttered onto the stage in a silver-sequined, high-slitted dress. The *Los Angeles Times* reported the next day that he and the band had "outrocked" Preston, stealing the show with an "electrifying soul-gospel sound" and "uninhibited cavorting and prancing." For the second show, Sylvester donned his twelve-foot sequined butterfly wings and his harness and got ready to fly. Rather than a run and a leap, he walked to the side of the stage and took a single timid step. With no momentum, he swung out a bit, crashed into the side of the stage, and then hung there, just above the third row, twisting and dangling in the cable, wings drooping. "Boys, boys!" he yelled, as people in the audience grabbed at his broken wings. "Put me down, boys!" Sylvester was lowered into the crowd, and the fans mauled him. When he got back to the dressing room, the Hot Band guys howled and cried with laughter. "He looked like a hooker on a bad night," says Kerry Hatch. His wings were in tatters, clothes torn, makeup smeared. "Oh, my dear," Sylvester said, flopping down on a chair with great ado. "Oh, this is just crazy. I'm just out of my mind." The next week, Preston's management called Dennis Lopez and withdrew the tour invitation.

By the end of 1974, Sylvester had fallen out of his dreams with a thud. Neither of the Blue Thumb albums had sold well—nothing compared to the Pointer Sisters, who had signed with Blue Thumb the same year as Sylvester, gotten tons of radio play with "Yes, We Can Can," made several network television appearances, and become the first pop act to perform at San Francisco's War Memorial Opera House.

Earlier that year, Bob Krasnow had given Sylvester a chunk of money—rumor put it at twenty-five hundred dollars—to buy a piano so he could write songs at home. Sylvester spent the money on "items." That July, when Krasnow called Sylvester and invited himself over to Sylvester and Michael's house, Sylvester panicked. Without telling anyone in the band, he went to Paris. Wandering the Champs Elysées in what he called his "daytime costume," *Rolling Stone* reported, he attracted a crowd that followed him from store to store, calling him "an Ugly American in so many words." The commotion was enough to attract the authorities, who discovered that Sylvester didn't have a return ticket. They kicked him right out of France.

Back home, he found that the entire Hot Band had quit. "We all just said fuck it," says Chris Mostert. Bob Krasnow canceled Sylvester's recording contract.

Sylvester's dreamy relationship with Michael Lyons had deteroriated by this point, along with everything else. Opposites no longer attracted. Michael believed that less was more, and Sylvester lived by the idea that more was better. Sylvester dropped acid, fearlessly moving outward into the world seeking psychedelic colors; he wanted his life heightened. Michael shot heroin, seeking just the opposite: a blank white screen that erased everything for a while, including him. As Michael saw it, everything

Sylvester touched turned to glitter except for Michael himself. "He would go out and be this fabulous, radiant person," he says, "and there wasn't much room for me, except to walk the dogs behind him." Michael cut his hair off to spite Sylvester, who, Michael had concluded, "just wanted a longhaired, beautiful guy to be his trophy wife." Sylvester complained that heroin was Michael's "other lover."

Michael discovered that Sylvester also had another lover, a man to whom Sylvester had given house keys and who would sneak into bed with him while Michael was at work. It was both a violation of their no-sex-with-others-in-our-bed pact and an outright deception. By the time Sylvester took off for Paris in 1974, Michael says, he thought Sylvester looked at him as "just a hole," and about the only thing keeping Michael there was Sylvester's "beautiful big, black, huge, beautifully shaped dick."

When Sylvester took off for Paris, Michael Lyons threw a "huge, week-long, blow-out, boy-girl, suckfest orgy." By the time Sylvester returned, Michael had started working up the strength to leave.

Still, they moved together, into a small, converted-garage apartment on Lombard Street. Sylvester pulled together a new band. Informally, they called themselves the Four A's: brothers Adrian and Amadeo Barrios on bass and drum, a guitarist named Angel Reyes, a keyboard player named Archie White. Sylvester made the band members sequined pants. As background singers he hired two black drag queens, Jerry Kirby and Lady Bianca. A friend named Tim McKenna, who had agreed to be Sylvester's new manager, got them a gig playing Monday and Tuesday nights in a club on Montgomery Street called the Cabaret, which had a small downstairs "Show Room" with table seating, a small stage and runway, and bad acoustics. It featured offbeat acts such as Charles Pierce, and Waylon and Madam—the fey man bullied by his mean-old-snob hand puppet—and now Sylvester.

In December 1974, Sylvester and the band played at the Whisky in L.A., hoping to land a recording contract. Nobody bit. An L.A. *Times* reviewer called the band "tepid and inferior," and Sylvester's performance "lackluster." The band members stopped playing with Sylvester after that.

That same month, Michael paid his bills and moved to Hawaii.

Sylvester scrounged and borrowed money to get out of town again, and this time tried England for a few months. He took little back from England other than the small-comfort observation that "no matter how bad you think it is over here, it's worse over there." Back in San Francisco, he was close to broke. "Oh, dear, Mary, I was down, down about as low as I could go," he told the *Bay Area Reporter* a decade later. He sold most of his stuff—his faux Egyptian deco, his antique statuettes, an autographed picture of Gloria Swanson. Finally he called his mother and begged her for money. "I didn't ask to be born," he reminded her, "so you've got to pay." She knew he was joking, but Letha sent him a check.

7.

SUNDAYS AT THE ELEPHANT WALK

Back from England in 1975, unable to afford a band, Sylvester conjured up a piano player, got himself booked back into the Cabaret's little basement Show Room, and sang sad old songs for a hundred dollars a night. He soon had a drummer named Sandyjack Reiner, and a keyboardist named Philip, who was a church-trained boy like Sylvester but who was also sometimes so drunk he couldn't make it through the set. Other musicians came and went. Sylvester did his old, familiar Billie Holiday and Bessie Smith channelings and jazz standards. Even the gardenia had started to look a bit fusty, but plenty of folks still came to see him.

While Sylvester was downstairs, Arnold Marvin Elzie was upstairs singing on the dance floor. Arnold sang in church and on the dance floor. *Never can say goodbye, no no no, no no no.* He had big platforms, long bell-bottoms, permed hair, light brown skin, an alto singing voice, and a fake I.D. He traveled into the city from Berkeley, where he lived with his mother and some of his five siblings. At home he might try on his sister's clothes, but at the clubs he was just a "wild glitter hag." He would spray the front of his black hair silver, and then the next time switch to gold. He was too young and too cute to need much makeup. He landed in the clubs that would let him in. Places like Bojangles required an official California I.D., and Arnold's fake one wasn't that fancy; sometimes he went to the Alley Cat, a dark bar with go-go dancers located in an alleyway, mainly because they didn't give him the third degree. He spent most of his nights out, though, at the Cabaret. There they let him right in; if they didn't, some older wild glitter hag would let him in the back door. Anyway, the dance floor at the Cabaret was *the* place. It drew every kind of person you could imagine, especially gays and tourists. You only really heard two words in San Francisco right then, "free" and "fabulous," and on the floor at the Cabaret, Arnold felt both. *Shame shame shame on you*, he sang, *if you can't dance too.*

After his sets, Sylvester would come upstairs to see his friends, cruise cute blond and redheaded boys, and sing on top of the music while he danced. *Gitchee gitchee ya ya da da. Mocha chocolada mama.* Arnold, who always peeked into the Show Room when he went downstairs to the bathroom, had once gotten up the nerve to tell Sylvester how much he admired his singing, but that was about it. They would smile and say hello, quietly recognizing themselves in each other. One night, they wound up dancing to the Supremes. Sylvester started singing. *He calls says get dressed and I put on my best, whoo!* So Arnold did, too. They sang, Arnold taking alto and Sylvester soprano. *He's my man-an-an-an-an-an, yeah!* Sylvester gave Arnold the once-over as they were moving back off the dance floor. "Chile, you can sing, honey!" he said. He invited Arnold to the Show Room the next day at one. Without knowing it, Arnold had auditioned on the dance floor.

The next afternoon, Arnold's friend Leroy Davis offered to take him to his first rehearsal. Leroy was another dance-floor singer, about ten years older than Arnold. That afternoon, when Sylvester needed someone to sing the high part—Lady Bianca was gone, and Arnold and Jerry Kirby sang in the middle range—there was Leroy, making damn sure to fill in the part in a high falsetto from down below the stage. "Who is this child?" Sylvester asked Arnold, looking out from the stage. The next thing they knew, Leroy, Arnold, and Jerry were onstage with Sylvester. They spangled up their costumes, and sang tunes off Sylvester's Blue Thumb albums, Sylvester's favorite Aretha and Billie tunes, and the Pointer Sisters' "Going Down Slow." They weren't making a lot of money, but Arnold still felt glamorous. The night Arnold's mother, Georgia, brought Arnold's sister and brother-in-law to the show, Sylvester came out in a long, tight, sequined green dress and a black wig. They were all shocked at first—they knew Arnold was girlish, but *this* child was just too unusual—and then the music took them over.

In Sylvester's mirrored clothes, Arnold caught glimpses of who he might turn out to be: many years later, Arnold Elzie became the female rock and soul singer LZ Love. Arnold watched how Sylvester put together set lists, how he came in with just a bag of stuff and whipped together some drag in time for a show, how he brought packs of tiny square mirrors and a glue gun and made himself jackets that twinkled in the stage lights. He listened to Sylvester, Leroy, and Jerry read each other—over who was owed money, over who had tried to steal the limelight, over who was just a dirty evil queen—and took notes. From Sylvester, Arnold also learned how to make a headdress from just a bag and a roll of masking tape: he would take a produce bag from Safeway, smash it down over his head, and wrap it real tight with layers and layers of masking tape, so that the bag became a form-fitting cap; then he'd trim it and cut it, and if he felt like it he would tape on Styrofoam pieces to give it height, add fabric or glitter or both. Then he would put it on his head and go be a magnificent, beautiful creature.

Sylvester gradually started making enough money at the Cabaret to hire a couple of musicians, and the crew took trips down to Los Angeles to play the Whisky and the Cabaret, and out to rock clubs like the Long Branch in Berkeley and the Woods in Fairfax. They did some of Sylvester's Blue Thumb album tunes, like "Southern Man," "Friendship," and "She," some Aretha, the Carpenters' "Close to You," all gospeled up. Sometimes they sang at a small bar called the Elephant Walk, at the corner of Eighteenth and Castro, that had opened that year. Sylvester would stand in the back of the cramped, dark room, next to a piano, and Arnold, Jerry, and Leroy would have to sing into their mikes while seated at a nearby table.

By 1975, San Francisco was to gay men and lesbians what Israel was to Jews, only with fewer wars and more parties. It was known as the gathering place of the exiles, the land of milk and honeys. This was the era when the various wings of the gay movement—the ones who wanted to be accepted, the ones who wanted to make noise, the ones who shouted "Gay Power," and the ones who quietly argued "We are just like you"—all had at least one thing in common: they all advocated coming out of the closet. Not surprisingly, a lot of people did just that; at the very least, liberation seemed to promise less shame, more love, and better sex. It also, of course, often meant being suddenly reviled by nearly everyone who had thought you were straight.

San Francisco was, now more than ever, where you went to come out and be gay. If people came out in the diaspora and were cast out of their families, they went to San Francisco; or they picked up and moved to San Francisco in order to come out among their people. The annual Gay Freedom Day Parade, begun in 1972, was an Independence Day festival with elaborate costumes and floats—in 1975, the Empress Doris rode an elephant—and every kind of homosexual imaginable, including almost-naked ones. The other big holiday was Halloween. San Francisco, Edmund White once wrote, is the place "where gay fantasies come true."

The city, he also wrote, served as "a sort of gay finishing school, a place where neophytes can confirm their gay identity." It was filled with potential mentors, insistent that learning could be fun. There were gay softball teams, gay newspapers, gay churches, gay choruses, gay moving companies, and a gay tap-dance club. Being gay in San Francisco was a full-time occupation.

If you lived in the Castro neighborhood in 1975, it might have seemed as if you had fallen asleep in a run-down, working-class, mostly Irish neighborhood and awakened in a gay male shtetl. Gay florists, gay restaurants, gay bookstores, and gay Laundromats had suddenly sprouted. Grocery stores had morphed into bathhouses. The maternity store was on its way to becoming a clothing shop called All American Boy. The Castro Theatre, where Mae West had opened her first live revue, had become an artsy movie house, routinely filled with men who would collectively recite the bitchy lines coming from the mouths of Joan Crawford ("There's a name for you ladies, but it isn't used in high society—outside of a kennel"), Bette Davis ("Fasten your seatbelts, it's going to be a bumpy night!"), Elizabeth Taylor ("Hey, Swampy!"), and Elizabeth Taylor quoting Bette Davis ("What a dump!"). Gay bars lined the streets, and most nights they were full; they closed at two in the morning and many opened again at six. Quite often, two guys with short hair and flannel shirts would pass each other on the street, turn their heads, and wind up making out within minutes. In the Castro, "cocksucker" was a term of endearment.

The Castro was, as Frances FitzGerald put it in *Cities on a Hill,* a "liberated zone," part of "the avant-garde of the sexual revolution and the revolutionary change in sex and gender roles," a "kind of laboratory for experimentation with alternate ways to live," and "a carnival where social conventions were turned upside down just for the pleasure of seeing what they looked like turned the wrong way up." At the Castro Street Fair, which began in 1974, men dressed as "Betty Grable look-alikes, as Hell's Angels toughs, as nuns on roller skates, and as men in Brooks Brothers shirts and tasseled loafers." All this dress-up was play, but also "a meditation on the arbitrary nature of gender roles and costumes; it was also real life for men who found themselves in the excluded middle of the terms male/female."

At any time of day or night, folks could stop by Andy's Donuts for "a hot cup of coffee and/or a hot man," as one regular put it, and for a sheet of "cosmic information" from Janet Planet, also known as Cosmic Lady, who was nearly always there. On weekends, Castro Street was so filled with people that cars had trouble getting through the neighborhood. The Hibernia Bank at the corner of Castro and Eighteenth Streets was reno-vated, and the plaza in front newly paved; on warm days it became "Hiber-nia Beach," where boys in short-shorts and a few girls sunned themselves, chatted, and cruised. The Castro villagers knew one another by name or by face: the couple who owned a health food store, the kids who worked at the jewelry store, the folks who ran the pizzeria, the ones who owned a beauty salon, the guys who ran the camera store. They had their own neighborhood political chieftain, Harvey Milk, one of the camera store guys. That year, Milk had received the endorsement of the Teamsters and 52,649 votes in a second bid for the Board of Supervisors. He'd lost, but in the Castro they called him the Mayor.

At night, and on Sunday afternoons, the gay San Franciscans' pastime was their own brand of folk dancing. It must not be an accident that what brought them together as a group was dancing. A dance floor may very well be the closet's antithesis: all that flailing, sweat, bright lights, noise, and unapologetic throbbing. As a collective experience, sharing a beat can almost be like sharing a heart. In dance clubs around town—the Cabaret, soon renamed the City Disco; the Shed; the Mineshaft; Toad Hall, the Cas-tro's first dance bar—differences, for a moment, didn't seem to matter. "I remember dancing at the Mineshaft," the historian Allen Bérubé says in the documentary film *The Castro*. "Those moments when you'd smoke a joint, and there'd be all these lights and fans and this wonderful disco music, where you felt this beat that really united you, I had this kind of spir-itual moment or vision where I said, 'This is what it could be like.' You could see what it could be like, and be inside it, and feel it, if we were totally free."

The sound that most brought people together, that really gave them a glimpse of what it could be like to be totally free, that pumped out of bars in the Castro, was that of a black soul diva singing over a thumping beat: Donna Summer, Diana Ross, Melba Moore, Candi Staton, Gloria Gaynor. The gay men who came to San Francisco after Stonewall were mostly not living under the long-suffering stars of Judy Garland and Marlene Diet-rich. As Barry Walters has written, they were on the lookout for their own heroes, and "for the generation of young men who grew up with the Supremes and discovered gay lib, R&B singers became the new divas of choice. Early 70s soul sisters had one major thing in common with gay men—their suppression exploded in a torrent of sensuality. These aggressive black women provided the nighttime dancing sound track while they captured both the alienation and the fervor that gay men understood."

Sylvester had started hanging out in the Castro sometimes, and most of the Castro villagers knew who he was. At the second annual Castro Street Fair in 1975, from the corner of Market and Castro Streets, you could look up at the still hills of Diamond Heights, or down the other way into the heart of the Castro, where the crowd, mostly men in jeans standing shoulder to shoulder, pulsated slowly. In the windows of apartments lining the street, men held beers and called out to people below. Some of them wore only jockstraps. A stage was set up at the corner of Market and Castro, and on it Sylvester and three black queens performed. *I can live without love if I wanted to,* Sylvester sang, and stepped back to let Arnold take a verse. They moved into Mary McCreary's "Singing the Blues." *You got me singing the blues, and I'm paying all my dues,* they sang with fervor, in headdresses made of Safeway bags and masking tape.

Working hard for no money can wear thin quickly, and with great regularity Sylvester and his backup singers Leroy and Jerry were getting on each other's last gay nerve. They would light into each other almost daily, and not for laughs, and then give each other the I'm-not-talking-to-you-ever-again-but-I-*know*-you-hear-me treatment. Arnold steered clear. One night at the Long Branch, things were so chilly that none of them said a word or looked at any of the others onstage, and the next day Sylvester fired the lot of them. He called Arnold and offered to keep him on, but Arnold chose to go his own way. "He just knew it was hitting rock bottom," says LZ Love, who Arnold became.

A few months into 1976, Sylvester moved into an apartment in the Castro with his houseboy-turned-roommate David Brewer and his old friend Marapasa. They couldn't quite afford it, but no matter. When heiress money was unavailable, Sylvester would use his local celebrity to find a grand apartment, and then he would simply skip the rent part. "By the time the landlords got the court involved and served papers, six months had elapsed," says Marapasa, "and he was on to the next fabulous house, living there another six months without paying the rent." Anyway, his public, such as it was, would never know. "Even when there wasn't a pot to piss in, he was fabulous," says his friend Brent Thomson. When they went downtown to shop at Lane Bryant, which sold clothes for big girls, Sylvester would wear a full-length fur coat, and he would bring along his borzois—long-nosed, long-legged, clean-toothed dogs whose silky coats draped toward the ground like Sylvester's. "There was nobody that didn't see you," Brent says.

Soon, Sylvester's new boyfriend, a tiny Puerto Rican man named Willie Sanchez, moved into the apartment. Sylvester had met Willie a few months before at the Long Branch in Berkeley. He had sat through many shows by himself, stars in his saucer eyes, just watching Sylvester, not hiding his desire. He had bad acne, little feet, a pile of dark curls, big brown eyes, and an amazing ass—"he was all eyes and ass," Marapasa recalls. He lived with his parents. One night, he had found Sylvester in the Long Branch dressing room and introduced himself with a little giggle. They had made out for a while, and Sylvester had taken him home. Within a few weeks, Willie's thick black hair was slicked back like a forties mati-nee idol's; he sported a neatly trimmed beard and mustache; his eyebrows were plucked and his skin was clearer. "Sylvester fixed him right up, honey," says LZ Love. Sylvester and Willie were a sight, especially in the white, jeans-and-flannels Castro: a petite, swing-hipped Puerto Rican with a tall, hefty black man wearing scarves and bangles and eyeliner, flanked by two long, thin, imperial dogs, whom Sylvester had trained to prance like queens, stand with their noses in the air, and pose.

Willie was not known as an intellectual or a conversationalist, and like Michael before him—and like Sylvester's boyfriends to come—he mostly played puppy to Sylvester's alpha dog. Willie worked as a waiter, and at home he took on a domestic role, cooking and cleaning. He and Sylvester would bring home boys, and sometimes girls, and do them together. They also had a giant black dildo known as Johnny. When record executives came to the flat to meet with Sylvester, Marapasa would usually find a way to bring out Johnny the dildo and set him down on a table when no one was watching.

"They thought Sylvester was just a big ol' freak, which he was," says Marapasa. "But he was trying to at least maintain a professional facade." As the record company guys did their best not to look at Johnny, Marapasa and David and Willie would leave the room and peek out the door, stifling giggles until they wound up screaming and rolling on the floor. "Johnny was never washed or anything," says Marapasa, "and Johnny was greasy and had carpet fibers on him." Each time, Sylvester would beg Marapasa and Willie and David not to do it again, but they couldn't resist. Each time, when the men in suits were gone, Sylvester would play the furious diva, shocked and disgusted at the behavior of her underlings, waving Johnny menacingly like a floppy, dark rolling pin.

At home, Sylvester continued to live with a diva's generous narcissism and his own brand of exhibitionist introversion. One day he might bring a gift, or take his friends out shopping; another day he might barely speak. Once, Marapasa recalls, Sylvester had managed to pick up a couple of bucks, and he brought home some Kentucky Fried. Willie, David, Marapasa, and their friend Alonzo, hungry as could be and smelling the greasy breading, watched in amazement as he began unpacking it and eating it, one pinky in the air, pretending they weren't even there. "He just *ate* the chicken, honey," Marapasa says. "We still talk about that today, how he just *ate that chicken.*"

Sylvester, now almost thirty, still seemed to be waiting for something. Once, a friend from the neighborhood, Giana, went with Sylvester and Willie to a party thrown by a minor socialite, a fancy gathering with a few celebrities in the mix. They were all dressed up. Giana watched from a window as Sylvester and Willie sat at the top of the stairs, just sitting there staring into the magnificence. *I should have all of this*, she thought Sylvester's look was saying. *I should be living like this.*

Early in 1976, Tim McKenna, Sylvester's friend and manager, asked Brent Thomson to help him jump-start Sylvester's career. Brent and Sylvester later grew close, but for now she was just a friend of a friend of a friend who had worked a bit in the music industry. She had left a marriage and show horses and become a lesbian. She and her first girlfriend, Peggy, had moved that year from Los Angeles to San Francisco, where they lived in the back of a Victorian house on California Street with a fireplace in the kitchen. They started their days with LaBelle's "Nightbird" on the record player, and they ended it the same way. Brent spent most of her time hanging out with gay men, shuttling between Castro Street and the Café Flore a few blocks away. "It was like getting invited to a big party and getting to stay and stay and stay," she says. She had time, and she had money from her family and from her divorce.

Brent adored Timmy McKenna, who could have been a poster boy for the Castro. He and his boyfriend, John, owned an art deco furniture store on Castro Street. Warm and soft-spoken, he had an all-American white-boy look—mustache and dirty blond hair, khakis and Izod shirts. Brent was impressed by Sylvester, too. The first time she had seen him, a few years back, Sylvester's bass player and lead guitarist were both so drugged up that while one had crawled across the stage unplugging all the amplifiers, the other had passed out entirely; Sylvester, glancing back, had kept on singing to nothing but drums. Brent converted the basement of the California Street house into a recording studio and started getting Sylvester work where she could. "Girl, if this doesn't work out in the next five months," Sylvester told Brent, "I am going back to crankin' hair."

Brent's was not an easy task. Although Sylvester could always pull together a band and some singing queens, musicians were not knocking each other down to get to him. The money was bad and the promise of a gay, feminine falsetto singer uncertain. The first to join and stick around was Sandyjack Reiner, the drummer. Reiner tried to recruit a guitarist he knew and liked, Tip Wirrick, but Tip went to one show at the Cabaret, took one look at Sylvester's semi-drag and the background singers' full drag, and politely declined. "He was kind of doing his androgynous 'I'm not really a drag queen but I'm obviously not a straight man' kind of thing, and he had these black drag queens doing backup," Wirrick says. "I was a nineteen-year-old straight boy who had not really seen a lot of this. I was just so flabbergasted." (Wirrick, who is a music producer and composer, has long since replaced the nickname Tip with his given name, James.)

Brent convinced Sylvester over the next few months to get rid of his drag, and his drag-queen background singers, entirely. "Nobody is giving out recording contracts to drag queens," she reasoned. "Besides, touring will be a lot easier without all those wig boxes." Sandy Reiner called Tip Wirrick for another look-see. "It's different now," Reiner said. "He's going for a record deal." Sure enough, when Tip went back to the Cabaret, Sylvester had short hair and a three-piece suit.

Less freaked out, sufficiently wowed, and needing a job, Tip reconsidered. He wasn't blown away by Sylvester's voice, but he was impressed with the way the audience was wrapped around Sylvester's finger within a few minutes. Sylvester was quiet and seemed somehow smaller offstage, Tip thought, and though they didn't have a whole lot to say to each other, he and Tip worked well together musically. Now he needed some vocal backup. "I want two *big* girls that can *sang*," Sylvester told Tip. Then, as if seeing the picture in his head, a scene from his own movie, he said, "And I want them on either side of me."

If that didn't work, Sylvester had another plan. He got himself an application to the San Francisco College of Mortuary Science. He would be either a mortician, he thought, or an international superstar.

Martha Wash was born and raised in San Francisco, in the Western Addition. She started singing when she was a few years old, first in church and then in school choirs. She got a lot of support. "Church people are good about that," she said once. "If they think you just *hum* good, they'll put you up on chairs and tables and encourage you." Wash was a soprano, and her voice could kill you dead right where you're standing. When she was seventeen, her gospel choir at Poly High School raised $25,000 from bake sales and car washes and donations from their parents and Mayor Alioto, and she and thirty-five other black kids toured Europe for two weeks, singing. In February 1976, she was just out of high school, singing with a gospel group called NOW—for News of the World—living at home, and looking for a job, when she got a call from a friend telling her to audition for Sylvester.

Martha Wash had seen Sylvester perform at the Berkeley Community Theater in 1974, when he'd opened for Billy Preston. She had not been ready. He had worn his sequined hot pants, his black net top with winglike silver shoulders, and his curly black Shirley Temple wig. For his encore, Aretha Franklin's "(Sweet Sweet Baby) Since You've Been Gone," he'd changed into a floor-length lavender sequined gown. While everybody else was moving, Martha had just stood there with her mouth open, staring. *Who is he?* she'd thought. *Who. Is. He. What is he? Who is he?* "He just kind of got away with me," she says. "I had never seen anything like it or anybody like him before. He was this big, beautiful woman. He blew Billy Preston off the stage and he wore me *out*." She'd talked about it to friends for the next couple of days, and gone on about the business of being a teenager.

Heading over to the audition out near the hospital two years later, taking her big self downstairs into a cramped, half-dark basement, she did not put two and two together. Sylvester was there, in jeans and some bangles, and two white girls who had just finished their audition were chatting with

Brent Thomson and Tip Wirrick. "I was growing weary from seeing these little tiny birdlike girls come in and doo-bop around," Sylvester said later. "Then Martha came in, I took one look at her and *knew* she could sing." This was all new and strange to Martha, coming out of the church, but she sang a song and then bantered with Sylvester a bit. Martha had no idea that Sylvester was the big, beautiful woman who had gotten away with her that night in Berkeley; it would be days before she figured that out. But Sylvester knew who she was, even though he had never seen her before.

When he later told it, Sylvester buffed and polished the story down to its sparkly essence: "I just asked her to sing one or two notes, and she sang them. I said, 'Sing this note,' and she sang at the note, and said, 'I have to go to the bathroom. I'll be right back.' When she came back, she sang the note, and sang above the note." Whether it was a couple of notes or a song, what Martha sang was more than enough. Sylvester looked at Tip, and Tip looked at Sylvester. *There's one,* their eyes agreed. Sylvester told the white girls they could leave, and turned to Martha before they were even halfway up the stairs.

"Stop, girl," he said. "Oh, honey, you're the *one.* You're hired, girl. Now, do you know another woman as big, black, and beautiful as you, who can sing like you?"

"Oh, yeah," Martha Wash said, "I've got the girl for you." She phoned Izora Rhodes.

Martha and Izora had been singing together in News of the World for just a little while, but they'd known each other for years from community choirs. Having known Martha since she was a "snotty-nosed brat running around church singing her behind off," Izora called Martha "the baby." On account of her girth and her seven children, Martha called Izora "Mother Earth." Martha went to the Church of God in Christ, which was just across an alley from Izora's Baptist church. Sometimes they could hear each other's choirs drifting across the open space.

Izora was an alto, and when she felt the spirit—sometimes even when she didn't—she could bring up a growl that started down low and roared up out of her like a rough wave. Like Martha, she'd been singing since she was a little girl, before her family moved to San Francisco from Texas. She'd led the San Francisco Inspirational Choir, studied classical music at the San Francisco Conservatory, taught piano and voice, worked the key-board at all kinds of churches. She'd done time as a bartender and a nurse's aide. In 1976, she was raising her girl and her six boys on her own, with help from her parents and godparents. (By the time she was all done, she'd have eleven children and a new husband's last name, Armstead.) Martha was a big girl, but Izora was even bigger.

Izora had seen Sylvester perform once before, too, at the Cabaret. "It wasn't no big thing," she says. "I'd been around the gay life all my life, from church. A lot of gay people going to church and in choirs and singing, so that was nothing new. That was no big thing—especially not in San Francisco." When Martha called her, she went down to Sixth and Judah, a neighborhood that was always foggy, where Sylvester often used a dank basement rehearsal space. She started down the stairs, "my big butt getting ready to go through the door," Izora says, and Sylvester looked up, took a glance, and said, "Come on." He hustled her back out to his car before she even had a chance to catch her breath. Izora got into Sylvester's Volkswagen, taking up most of the backseat, and Sylvester and Martha got in the front. They drove across the Golden Gate Bridge, since Sylvester was due at a keyboardist's house in San Rafael to practice songs for a demo tape. Izora and Sylvester and Martha had their first rehearsal right then, in the car going over the bridge, singing to the radio and then finding their parts in a couple of gospel tunes. Martha and Izora would just fall in on either side of Sylvester's falsetto lead, Martha's soprano riding on top of his, Izora's alto rolling in just under. "We went in the studio the next night," Izora says, "and we was with him ever since."

Professionally, Izora and Martha became the Two Tons o' Fun, but Sylvester called them "the girls." They called themselves "the tons," or sometimes "tonnage." They called each other "heifer." They did not care what you thought, and anyway they could shut you up and knock you down with a couple of notes. "They used to come to rehearsal and each of them would have two bags from Burger King," Brent Thomson says. "They would sit there, and as soon as they had eaten their Whoppers, it would be time for them to sing. And they'd just throw those mouths open, full of hamburger, and hit every note just like that. Just hit every note." They joked a lot, but they were no joke. They knew they were sexy—men had been known to drop to their knees, declare their love, and offer them bags of weed. They could move their bodies. If you were waiting for the skinny girl in the tight gown to come out, you could die waiting.

Sylvester christened Izora the Queen Mother, and it fit. "I had so damn many children," says Izora, who was known to swear like a sailor. She took care of everyone, and something was always on the stove at her house. She treated Sylvester like her own. "That was my baby," she says. Usually they'd rehearse at Sixth and Judah, or sometimes in Brent's basement, or sometimes in Izora's mother's basement on Lyon Street, which had a grand piano and Izora's kids in every available spot. At rehearsals on Lyon Street, the kids would be running around, jumping on Sylvester, tickling him until he waved his orange-polished fingernails at them. "Miss Izora," he would scream, "come get your monsters! Come get your little war orphans off of me, Queen Mother!" Izora would run them upstairs, but they'd be back down soon enough.

Soon after they joined up, Brent got Sylvester and the Two Tons a couple of out-of-town gigs, in Portland and Seattle, where they played places like Shelley's Leg, a gay bar owned by a woman named Shelley whose leg had been blown off by cannon fire at an annual parade and who had used the settlement money to buy the place. With all those mouths to feed, Izora still worked two jobs and Martha, who was a secretary at UC Hospital, wasn't about to give up her day job either. "We weren't making squat," says Martha.

Sylvester's three-piece suit disappeared, piece by piece, in a weeks-long striptease: the vest disappeared in one show, a few sequins in its place; the jacket dropped out of another show, replaced by some feathers. It was as if, flanked now by his two large bodyguards, Sylvester could let himself be. Brent never knew how far he might take it. Usually Sylvester wore loose, low-cut, flowing shirts that underemphasized his girth; short hair; a bit of makeup; and lots of jewelry. But if the mood struck, Sylvester would dress up "in full regalia," Izora says, and he and the Tons would "come down the aisle carrying on," right past Brent, who was "clutching her heart and having a hissy."

Sometimes on the road Sylvester would bring someone into the bed next to Brent's in their hotel room, and other times he'd go into the bathroom by himself, and for minutes Brent would hear the agreeable sound of a dozen bracelets clinking up against one another.

Something clicked and sighed into place when Sylvester and the Tons got together—something that wasn't there with the Hot Band white boys, for all that they could cook; something that wasn't there with Peter Mintun, for all the beautiful oldness he and Sylvester shared; something that wasn't even there with his black drag-queen singers, for all the fierceness they projected. Izora and Martha were whom he came from and who he was. "Martha and Izora, and that kind of black, that's what I call basic black," Sylvester's friend Yvette Flunder says. "Cornbread and black-eyed peas. That's the kind of black folks that he liked being around. He was very basic black and for real, like his mama, and he had no shame about being a black man. He's a fried-fish, fried-chicken person. You'd do with quiche and paté, and he'd have you eating fried chicken." Martha and Izora didn't look down on themselves, partly because they had been singing to God for their whole lives, and they would read you up and down if need be. They were women who got their own. They sounded right with Sylvester, and looked just right, one on either side of him. Plus, next to them, Sylvester, who had grown quite round, looked positively svelte.

On stage, Martha and Izora were not off to the side or swaying and coo-ing way back where you might forget about them. The Tons had about as much in common with Dawn as Sylvester had with Tony Orlando. Nor were they edging themselves into his spotlight. "Now, he's always going to be the diva, and you ain't going to top Sylvester, anyway," Izora says. "But we all came from church. If you're in a choir, you're all up there in the front, and the lead might just step out and do something a little bit, but you all are up there. You didn't trip about being the lead. And when it was your time to lead, you sing your ass off and then you fall right back into what you're doing. When you do background, you push whoever's leading. You made them sound good." Without having to talk about it, the three of them could summon spirits. They went to "a place where Black People live," as Amiri Baraka said of rhythm and blues, "a place, in the spiritual precincts of its emotional telling, where Black People move in absolute openness and strength."

When they went to that place, they would need to look good, too, so Sylvester dressed them and made them up. When he could, he made them outfits that were shimmering and bright—reds with gold, blues with silver, oranges—or buy something off the rack at Lane Bryant. He wanted them to help him create a scene you'd remember. "And we did look fabu-lous," Izora says.

Within weeks of the Two Tons' arrival, the band was joined by John Dunstan, a bassist who had been playing with a group called Anna Rizzo and the A Train, and a keyboard player named Dan Reich, who had worked with a theater-improv group called the Wing, sold encyclopedias, and played in a Top 40 lounge band. Reich auditioned at Izora's mother's house, with Martha Wash in the room. "Okay, sit down and play," Sylvester said. Reich asked what he should play. "Just play," Sylvester said. Reich went with a gospelly arrangement he'd come up with of Randy Newman's "Sail Away," a sardonic song in which the narrator bamboozles slaves to cross the ocean with promises of freedom and watermelon. "That's fabulous!" Sylvester said, and, after another song or two, "You're the guy."

Reich was "not the greatest player in the world," he says, but that didn't seem to be what mattered to Sylvester. What Sylvester appreciated, Reich came to think, was his ability to "pull things out of a hat, turn on a dime, just be in the moment," to "not be concerned with what came before or what's coming up, but just ride the wave and be aware of what's going on right then." The band was what some musicians call a "feel" band, and Sylvester was a "feel" singer. No one used sheet music, and not all of them could read music, anyway. They would just start playing, find the feel, and adjust it from there. Sylvester would never talk about measures-per-bar or chord progressions, but he knew what he wanted to hear. "You should come in with a bum-bum-*bum*," he would say, or, "I'd rather hear bada-*ba*da-bada-bada." They mostly communicated nonverbally, with sound.

The band's riding-the-wave groove; Sylvester's girlish, raw falsetto rubbing up against the Tons' gospel harmonies; the look of Sylvester and the Two Tons in bright flowing robes: with all this happening, the act quickly spawned a new local following. They played gay bars like the Stud and the Endup, and that summer of 1976 they landed a regular job playing weekend nights at a small, trendy nightclub on Polk Street called the Palms. The Palms was a long bar with a teeny stage and lamps on the table. Mostly, they did covers—Leon Russell's "Song for You," Aretha Franklin's "Day Dreaming"—but they also started trying out songs that Tip Wirrick and Sylvester had been cooking up. They'd play two or three sets a night, an hour or so each, sweating like crazy. Each set began with the band playing for a few minutes, building up some heat for Sylvester's grand entrance. The nights they played were packed to the streets, with a mix of straight, gay, old, young, white, and black.

If, in the middle of a set, Sylvester had a feeling for a song that wasn't on the set list, they would do that one: if you feel it, sing it. If, in the middle of a song, he felt something coming on, the band would sense and then see it. Sylvester had trained the band to keep a close eye on him, so that he could use them for dramatic effect, James Brown style. "We never knew what he was going to do," Dan Reich says, "so we had to be ready for him." If the impulse seized him, he would raise a hand and then drop it, and the band would thump to an immediate halt so Sylvester could testify a bit. "I want you to know that I love you," he would say, and signal the band for another thump. "Loooooovvvvee," he would wail, floating a few phrases of song in the unmetered time. "Loooooooovvvve!" Thump. Then he would raise his hand, bring it back down, and the band would start back up again. Sometimes, Izora would do a tambourine solo.

The crowd pleaser was a bouncing song called "Over and Over," written by Ashford and Simpson, which Sylvester had seen the duo perform on *Soul Train*. The band would start, laying down a groove, and then Sylvester would start singing (*over and over, time and time again, you can't be nobody's lover till you're somebody's friend*), and then in would come Martha and Izora on top of and behind his voice (*be nobody's lover! be nobody's lover!*). Sylvester and the Tons would escalate, and escalate, and escalate, building to "this incredible sort of surge," John Dunstan recalls, "until you're in rapture." When Sylvester really got going, he would jump, jump, jump, and jump, the jumps getting higher as he did. The crowd almost always went with him to another place.

Sylvester, the band, and the Two Tons o' Fun began playing again at the City Disco, where Sylvester had played the basement back when the place was still the Cabaret. Now he moved upstairs.

Martha Wash took a trip over to Honey Records in Oakland in late 1976, to audition for some gospel studio work. Honey was a small company run in a converted Safeway market by Harvey Fuqua, a former fifties doo-wop star with the mellow, slick Moonglows ("Sincerely," "Shoo Doo-Be Doo," "Most of All," "Ten Commandments of Love," "See Saw"). Etta James, who dated Fuqua in the 1950s, described him as "a cool character," then sporting gold teeth, a "honey-molasses voice and a debonair manner," and hair that fell into his face when he sang. "He could come on like a Kentucky gentleman," James wrote. "Other times he had the crafty conman moves of a pimp." He'd written "Someday We'll Be Together" and "If I Could Build My Whole World Around You." He'd made his name in Motown, producing Marvin Gaye and songs like "Ain't No Mountain High Enough," and marrying Berry Gordy's sister.

Fuqua had left Motown to go out on his own, then spent several years at RCA, then went back out on his own again. He and Nancy Pitts, a former RCA artist developer who became his business partner and lover, were on the lookout for musicians in the Bay Area, which they saw as "virgin territory." They were starting, Fuqua said, back at "square one." Honey would produce and develop the artists, and their neighbor Fantasy Records would help promote and distribute the albums.

At her audition, Martha mentioned to the Honey Records duo that she was singing with a guy named Sylvester, and that maybe they'd want to come to a show. Nancy Pitts thought she was talking about Sylvester Stallone, so out of curiosity, and since Harvey was out of town, she took herself out that night to the Palms to see the show. Driving through the rain across the bay into San Francisco, Nancy kept thinking about *Rocky*. At the Palms, she barely had time to register that Sylvester James was the exact opposite of Sylvester Stallone. The minute he opened his mouth, she knew she had to have it. "It was like a force," she said. "You know how you get a gut feeling that this is what you've been waiting for?"

Nancy Pitts found a pay phone, called Harvey Fuqua, and told him he had to come back into town right away. She invited Sylvester into the office the next day. Sylvester, strapped for money, had to take BART and a bus to get to Honey, but he wasn't about to tell Nancy that. "I was grand and I was lovely, and I was good enough at living off the illusion," he said. "I knew I had to be fabulous." After the meeting, he took off his heels and walked from the studio all the way back to BART. "Fuck it," he thought to himself after the meeting, trying not to worry. "I'm not going to be bothered. If it's going to come, it'll come. If not, I'm not going to die."

It took Nancy a few weeks to coax Harvey to the Elephant Walk in the Castro, where Sylvester was again performing, now with the Two Tons. "What I saw on stage were two big women, looked like they must have weighed a ton each—great, gospel-singing, gorgeous hunks of women," Harvey Fuqua said a couple of years later. "And I saw an all-white backing group and they were dynamite. I said, hey, they got rhythm, too. And I saw Sylvester, an extravaganza of immense talent. And the people were going crazy. I'm standing there in a suit and everything and I'm getting destroyed. I said, wow, that's it. Whatever we're doing, close it down as soon as possible. I wanna work specifically on this man here. There's only two people in this business that I've worked with who have really, really got it: Marvin Gaye and Sylvester." Sylvester signed with Honey and Fantasy. Fuqua would produce, and Pitts would be his manager. All their eggs would be in Sylvester's basket. Brent Thomson and Tim McKenna moved aside, relieved that someone—especially real music industry insiders, both black—could make Sylvester a full-time job.

In February 1977, Sylvester and Izora and Martha and the band went over to Fantasy to record. They walked through the high-ceilinged lobby, where gold records—mostly belonging to Creedence Clearwater Revival—hung on the wall, and into the 24-track studio. Harvey Fuqua was a "feel" producer: he cut the musicians loose and, as Dan Reich puts it, let them "find that groove where the magic happened." Cocaine and pot were available at the sessions, and their use was encouraged. As one musician said, "It would help us get into a head space where we could just focus on the music. We'd get in these head zones where we had blinders on." Among the songs were two versions of "Over and Over," one a three-minute radio cut and the other a longer album and twelve-inch dance-club cut. For eight minutes, the band chnnk-a-chnnk, chnnk-a-chnnked and Sylvester and the Tons sang and howled, looping their voices around each other, calling and responding. They did it all in one in-the-pocket take.

Sylvester's first album on Fantasy came out in the middle of 1977. The original cover showed Sylvester in a dark suit, seated against a black-and-white-striped background, with subtle but visible eyeliner, rouge, and lipstick. Finding that stores in the South would not stock such an album—even *Billboard*'s review began by asserting that "the androgynous cover art is startling"—Fantasy executives had the art department reshoot the photo. In the new one, Sylvester stood in a white suit and red-framed tinted sunglasses in front of white octagonal tile, holding a rose. If he was wearing lipstick, it was not visible.

Sylvester included two slow love songs that the singer and Tip had written together—slow songs tended to bring out his sibilant esses—and three more written by Sylvester. On Sylvester's favorite, "Tipsong," he sang wistfully of *lying underneath the stars, just you and I, everything so nice, so nice, so nice.* On another tune, Martha and Izora chatted with each other. "Honey girl, I can't *begin* to tell you what I been into," said one Ton. "Well, I got a little time, so tell me about it," said the other Ton, and they sang a song, by themselves, to each other, about being *down so low getting up ain't crossed their minds.* Most of the songs were dancy; with the horns and strings Fuqua added, the sound was closer to Marvin Gaye than to KC and the Sunshine Band. Songs like "Never Too Late," one of Sylvester's compositions, and their "Over and Over" cover, came close to re-creating the zeal of their live shows. On "Never Too Late," the horns and the Tons and Sylvester all echoed each other: *Never too late! Never too late!* "Over and Over" included a Tip Wirrick guitar solo, and horns and violins for punctuation. It built to a raving culmination, with hand-clapping, whistling, doo-doo-doo-dooing, dipping voices, and what sounded like the pleased, excited sounds of a congregation of partygoers.

At a record-release performance at the Old Waldorf, three fans presented Sylvester with roses. He was still in silver lamé and "prancing like a madman" that night, one *San Francisco Chronicle* reviewer noted, but Sylvester had "all but abandoned sex confusion and wildly extravagant costumes for a more traditional approach to rhythm and blues." Most reviewers of the album made a similar point. "For his Fantasy debut, a conscious effort was made to normalize him," a *Rolling Stone* reviewer wrote, while praising the "contemporary gospel-disco flow" and "pervasive gentleness" of the record. A brief *Rolling Stone* profile, accompanied by a picture of Sylvester holding up a Little Jimmy Scott album, presented his taste in music (jazz, gospel) and equipment (Kenwood KR-2600 receiver, Panasonic SL-20 turntable, Pioneer CT-F2121 tape deck). "Sylvester," the review asserted, "has let his music replace his glitter." This, to the delight of the Fantasy publicity department, was the phrasing of choice: Philip Elwood, in the *San Francisco Examiner*, approvingly noted that "gradually music has replaced glitter." Sylvester's "driving intensity as a lead vocalist," Elwood continued, "now overshadows his gaiety." Even a local gay paper, the *San Francisco Sentinel*, soon noted that since Sylvester's "former image as a classy but draggy 'freak' limited his audience appeal, he now appears on stage in casual male sportswear."

His managers' strategy, for sure, was to market him as a plausibly masculine rhythm-and-blues singer. "It seemed to me like Harvey and Nancy were trying to manage this thing they didn't really understand," says Dan Reich. Nancy Pitts tried to keep Sylvester "invisible" at first, she says, to make it more likely that radio stations would play the music. "When we started out," she says, "you never saw a picture of Sylvester. There were no photos."

Sylvester, who thought in pictures, could hardly be counted on to be invisible for long. "When I conform too much it makes me nervous," he told *The Advocate* that year. "I want to play the San Francisco Opera

House. *I am going to play the Opera House.* It's going to be a fabulous show with a full orchestra, lots of costumes, lots of lighting, and lots of everything. Lots!" Then, in an aside, he proclaimed for all to hear his simple philosophy of muchness and moreness, applied by Disquotays and Cockettes and Sylvesters the world over: "Whenever you think you have on too much, you should put on more, just to be safe."

"Lo and behold," Sylvester said in October 1977, "everything I'd been looking and working for did come." "Over and Over" was a major hit in Europe and Mexico, and a minor one in the United States. "I don't know when I'll get excited," Sylvester said. The crowds got bigger, and the jobs got better. He and the gals opened for the Average White Band in Berkeley. They went down to San Diego to play at a gay club called the Ball Express, where the air was so foggy with sweat, smoke, and amyl nitrate that when they looked out at the crowd they saw a bucket of wet, writhing flesh. The band got headaches from the poppers and smoke, but Sylvester didn't much mind. "I always encourage people to smoke at my shows," he said, "so that the lights will do little fuzzy things, because it creates a softness for me on the stage."

With help from Fantasy, Fuqua and Pitts arranged a tour to, oddly, Louisiana and Mexico City. The disillusionment set in quickly. At the club they played in New Orleans, the Nitecap II, Sylvester and his crew went on early in the morning, after a Top 40 band and a drunken, foul-mouthed local musician. It hardly felt like the big time, but they enjoyed themselves just the same. Harvey Fuqua brought Marvin Gaye to one of their shows, and they all got to shake a legend's hand. Izora found the best red-beans-and-rice joint in town and went there every day. The band members trashed their hotel room and paid off a security guard with cocaine. Cheered by the band, Martha and Izora took a dip in the pool at two in the morning. Sylvester, ready to be indulged, drank champagne in his own hotel suite and schmoozed with gay fans after the shows.

Sylvester had insisted that the band members wear one-piece skintight black polyester suits with silver diagonal strips on the legs. The suits were not ideal for playing music: the strap hurt, and the suits held on to the sweat of the energetic shows and turned rancid on the way from one gig to the next. After New Orleans, the troupe stopped in a small Louisiana town gymnasium, where they performed to a small crowd of unimpressed high school girls. The smell of the band's unitards mixed with that of high school vomit.

In Mexico City, things seemed to be looking back up. All over town, they saw postings for "Sylvester y Su Banda Show," and they were wined and dined in the Zona Rosa like big stars. For Sylvester it was a glimpse of the glimmer, and he and Martha and Izora laughed their way through most of it. In Mexico City, they performed "Over and Over" live on television, singing over their own LP. *Over and over, time and time again,* Sylvester was singing, with Martha and Izora getting ready to jump in with the backgrounds. *You can't be nobody's lover, nobody's friend.* Just as he was getting ready to repeat the first line, the record got stuck on the "O," but he didn't miss a beat. *Oh, oh, oh, oh, oh, oh, oh,* he sang, his eyes opening wider and wider with each *oh,* watching the laughter spread from Izora to the rest of the room, until even the camera was shaking. Sylvester just went on singing to the scratch.

On the first night in Mexico City, the two-thousand-seat theater was half full with a giddy, adoring crowd. The next night, though, only about a hundred people showed. Members of the band soon discovered that although some nine hundred free tickets had been distributed for the opening night, the shows had attracted almost no actual ticket buyers. The local promoter had then skipped town with what little money he had made. After going unpaid, the venue owners threatened to seize the band's instruments. Each of the next two nights, Sylvester and the Two Tons and the band played to dinkier and dinkier crowds, with fewer and fewer instruments. They did the last show with a grand piano and a tambourine. "Don't blame us," Harvey Fuqua and Nancy Pitts told the band.

A rift had already quickly grown between the management and the band; Dan Reich says the musicians felt that "as time went on, Harvey and Nancy indulged Sylvester more and more and gave us less and less." The band members were not about to accept a verbal agreement from Harvey Fuqua and Nancy Pitts. Reich and the others drafted an agreement for Fuqua, Pitts, and Sylvester to sign, guaranteeing them payment for the tour upon return to San Francisco. "Harvey was one of those guys that if you let him take advantage of you, he would," says David Frazier, who had joined the band as a percussionist on the first album. Fuqua had once hired Dan Reich and some other band members for a gospel record, and, Reich says, paid them with a six-pack of beer. Nancy Pitts, whom some band members called "the Pitts," was fine, they said, as long as there was no money in the picture. But when she started calling you "honey" or "darling," Frazier says, you would do well to "watch your wallet."

At first, Sylvester, Harvey, and Nancy refused to sign the Mexico City agreement, Dan Reich says, but the band sat outside Sylvester's suite for hours, and eventually got the signatures. After everyone else had left for the airport, the band members found that the hotel owners had not been paid and would not allow them to leave; Fantasy Records had to send bailout money.

A few nights later, back in San Francisco, Sylvester had a meeting at his apartment and summoned band members one by one into a room and shut the door. "We are not amused," Sylvester said to Reich, Reiner, and Dunstan, siding with his management. "Your services are no longer required." He kept on Tip Wirrick and David Frazier. "The people you walked over on your way up," David Frazier reminded Sylvester, "you are going to see on your way down."

Soon, Sylvester let Willie Sanchez go, too. Few people were surprised. He was thanked as "spiritual advisor" on the album, but most band members saw Willie as an "airhead," a "boytoy," or a "sweet, giggly queen." He wore pants with a zipper that went from the top button all the way underneath and back up over his ass to his back. When he introduced himself, he laughed after he said his name. He was fun and sweet, and Sylvester spoke to him with tenderness, but no one was under the impression that he was Sylvester's peer. Sylvester found Willie an apartment, gave him furniture, and quit him.

Sylvester did not sell nationally very well, in part because black radio stations did not pick it up. "He was informally blacklisted because he was gay," says Leslie Stoval, who met Sylvester in 1978, when she was just out of Stanford and in her first year as a deejay at KRE, a radio station in Berkeley. (In 1979, KRE would become KBLX.) "Black radio is just very macho, and they weren't ready to give this gay man his place. They didn't want to deal with it." Still, Sylvester had more money than ever before. "Money won't change me," Sylvester sometimes told friends. "It'll just amplify my trip." Whenever he got a royalty check, Sylvester would come home beaming. "Ooh, honey," he told Marapasa, "we are going to *eat*." He had always said he wanted to move up onto a San Francisco hill—and to have enough rent money to stay. A few months later, he had enough cash to trade his VW for an Audi and move into an apartment in lower Twin

Peaks, just above Castro Street, which he decorated with a deco mirror and pictures of Lena Horne, Billie Holiday, Josephine Baker, and Bessie Smith. "I'm going to move higher up there," he told an interviewer for a local paper, pointing toward the top of Twin Peaks. "I'm not going to move from San Francisco, but I want it at my feet."

"By the time I was fifteen I had been through five marriages and divorces, none of them my own," says Jason Williams. "I have three mothers I've met, two I haven't, a father, one stepfather I know of, and one real sister." He was born in Oklahoma and moved to Roswell, Arizona, when he was four; when he was thirteen, he moved to Dallas with his mother and her new husband. He and his stepfather did not get along in the least, and his biological father agreed to take him in, so at fifteen Jason moved again, this time to Phoenix. His stepfather berated him all the way to the bus station. From the steps of the Greyhound bus, Jason declared to his mother and stepfather that they would never see him again as long as they lived. "I was a grand little sissy," he says, "and not well, mentally." In Phoenix, Jason lived in a household without music, which his father thought was the devil's handiwork. When he was eighteen, he got his hairdresser's license. A few years later, he moved to San Francisco, and he has not moved since.

In San Francisco, Jason got a job at the salon at I. Magnin and threw away his jeans and all but one pair of cowboy boots. In 1973, he had seen the *Scratch My Flower* poster in the window at Gramophone Records, with Sylvester all covered in red sequins and jewelry and holding a cigarette holder in a gloved hand; he had fallen in love. *I've never seen anything like it,* he'd thought, although he himself at that moment had been dripping with Indian jewelry. Jason paid his two dollars at the Elephant Walk to watch Sylvester and his two bearded, pink-eyelashed "wild mad black queens" perform. He went to see Sylvester at the City, where "you never knew what it was going to be." He admired the voice and the style both. Over the years, he would see Sylvester on the streets on his Vespa, or just walking down what some people called the boulevard, the stretch of Castro and Market Streets where you went to promenade. He thought they were destined to be friends, and he was right.

Jason didn't fit with the gay in-crowd dominating the Castro. "Living in the Castro was very disturbing," he says. "It was a real meat market. I felt like I had to douche to go buy a quart of milk." He didn't own a flannel shirt, didn't see himself as "hot and hunky," didn't fix his pants to feature his penis; he wore jewelry, admired high fashion, and wanted a relationship. He liked to lay out pretty things around the house, trinkets and necklaces and crystal jars, just because they were pretty things. You might go into his house and see a thin, three-foot vase filled with purple orchids. He was a grand sissy.

A grand sissy—cousin of the diva; a particular brand of queen—takes all the things the world says make him valueless and insists they do the opposite. Told that boys don't play with dolls, he becomes a doll himself. Told that boys don't wear jewelry, he finds the biggest tiara of all. Told that he is a faggot, he says, "That's Miss Faggot, to you." Sylvester became a comfort to Jason, his own secret Patron Saint of Sissies.

For all its beauties—the supportive, we-made-this-ourselves communal life; the throwing off of stigma and shame; the unabashed embrace of desire—by 1977 the Castro was quickly becoming insular and homogeneous. The counterculture types—the arts queens, the radical faeries, and the politics queens, "the broken sequined remnant of the Sixties," as Edmund White called them—found themselves edged out. Their sexual revolution, as they saw it, was being co-opted by men who wanted the sex without the revolution. To Aaron Shurin, who was "hanging out with drag queens and doing drag and worshiping the goddess," the Castro had become home to an enemy vision. "The tradition I was in was an underground socialist and psychedelic tradition," he says. "You couldn't say that about the Castro. The Castro was where gay men came to realize their bourgeois dreams. It didn't take very long to realize we were outnumbered." The faeries, drag queens, and radicals called the other men Clones, and the name stuck.

Edmund White describes a night out in San Francisco around then that began with a trip to a birthday party in a store that had been turned into a dance studio. In the window were doll replicas of the king and queen of mid-1970s camp, King Tut and Bette Midler. Many of the guests were in drag: one man, who chewed gum and did the Twist, wore "a mohair turtleneck sweater, long teased bubble-dome blond hair with a fringe of bangs in front, a black straight skirt over black slacks and black boots trimmed in white fur." The star of the party, Ambisextrous, had outlined his beard with Magic Marker and wore "a red bathing suit and black bra over red tights, gold lamé spike heels, a diamond question-mark over the crotch, and butterfly glasses studded with rhinestones." Bums wandered in off the street, and there were belly dancers, and "everyone ended up on the floor in a puddle, sick with laughter."

From there, White went to a disco, where he found men with "the celebrated look of the so-called Castro Clone": a "strongly marked mouth and swimming, soulful eyes (the effect of the mustache); a V-shaped torso by metonymy from the open V of the half-unbuttoned shirt above the sweaty chest; rounded buttocks squeezed into jeans, swelling from the cinched-in waist, further emphasized by the charged erotic insignia of colored handkerchiefs and keys; a crotch instantly accessible through the buttons (bottom one already undone) and enlarged by being pressed, along with the scrotum, to one side; legs molded in perfect, powerful detail; the feet simplified, brutalized, and magnified by the boots." The emerging Castro Clone culture was about gender, and it was about fucking, but it was pretty much the opposite of gender-fucking. It was, White noted, "an image of homosexual desire potent enough to have crowded out all others." It was a vision of sameness, of short-haired white men and no beads at all, of a gay culture that was not strange.

Many people found the Castro-centered gay culture unwelcoming, to say the least. Women mostly found themselves uninvited. Queens didn't fit unless they covered up their nelliness with a mustache and packed it away in jeans. "The scorn directed against drags is especially virulent; they have become the outcasts of gay life, the 'queers' of homosexuality," White wrote. "Our old fears about our sissiness, still with us though masked by the new macho fascism, are now located, isolated, quarantined through our persecution of the transvestite."

Guys who weren't white often found themselves invisible men, or were turned away from bars because they didn't have three pieces of ID. "The Pendulum was where the black folks hung out, and that was it," says LZ Love. "If you were in the Castro, if you wasn't in the Pendulum you ain't right. If you black and if you don't want to be seen as some white-loving queen, you better be at the Pendulum." Many black gay men didn't feel welcome at other Castro bars, or comfortable at places that threw "Gone with the Wind" parties with plantation camps and Confederate flags. "I get off the bus, and I look around," says Brian Freeman in *The Castro*, "and there's all these very kind of buffed, mustached, white men in their late

television and town hall debates; he had also recently dressed up in a clown suit and called out "I'm a supervisor" to tourists on cable cars, and then conducted political meetings without taking off the outfit. He liked to begin his speeches by saying, "My name is Harvey Milk and I'm here to recruit you." Harvey Milk often got death threats, and he had been worried about getting shot even before taking on Briggs. "If a bullet should ever enter my brain, let that bullet destroy every closet door," Milk had said in a tape recording he'd made the year before and labeled "In Case."

That May, Sylvester sang at Harvey Milk's birthday party. In June, just before Sylvester's new album came out, Milk waved from a convertible in the largest-ever Gay Freedom Day Parade: around 300,000 people spilled over the sidewalks and into the streets. Milk had encouraged a man named Gilbert Baker to create a flag for the gay and lesbian movement, and Baker had sewn together an eight-color Rainbow Flag; two thirty-by-sixty-foot flags flapped over United Nations Plaza in San Francisco.

Sylvester wasn't one to turn down an invitation from Hollywood. In the spring of 1978, he was invited to audition for the rise-and-fall-of-troubled-rock-star biopic *The Rose* at Studio One, a disco in West Hollywood, on the recommendation of the star, Bette Midler. Unbeknownst to him, Sylvester said, Midler "had my records and she heard me sing before." The producers were looking to hire miscellaneous drag queens for a scene in which Rose, the boozy, Joplinesque singer played by Midler—who herself, of course, was only a few DNA strands away from a drag queen—goes back to a drag bar she used to frequent in the old days. They already had a Barbra–Streisand–in–her–"Hello gorgeous"–period drag queen, a Bette-Davis-as-demented-Baby-Jane drag queen, a generic Mae West drag queen, and a frizzy-redhead Midler-as-Rose drag queen. They wanted a Diana Ross, too. The other two candidates at Studio One that day were exact replicas of Ross, skinny and pretty, but the producers thought it would be hilarious to have a Diana who tipped the scales at around two-twenty, so Sylvester was hired.

In the movie, Rose enters the bar and encounters an old drag queen, played by an old drag queen named the Queen Mary, who has a very tall hairdo. "Oh my God," says Rose, "your hair's got a hard-on." At the bar, the emcee is the Bette Davis drag queen, who welcomes Rose back by introducing the queen in Rose drag. The two Roses scream at the sight of each other, then scream a duet of Bob Seger's "Fire Down Below," about street-walkers and johns who have nothing in common but the fire down below. In the middle of it, Sylvester bursts through the two of them in a red sequined sleeveless Supremes gown, grabs the mike from the faux Rose, and sings along with the real one. Shortly, Mae and Barbra show up, and the faux Rose joins back in, and the five of them dance and sing, falling all over each other like a bunch of well-coiffed Cockettes. Sylvester's drag Diana towers over Rose, and for a while Sylvester dances behind Bette Midler, dipping her and holding her up in his big arms.

It took several days that May to film the sequence, which was shot in an old nightclub in the basement of a seedy hotel in downtown L.A. Sylvester said he enjoyed "the fantasy of being in Hollywood making a film," but he would not make another movie, he said, "unless I'm starring." The shoot was decidedly unglam. "My dear, we hung around for days waiting to do one shot, from early morning to late at night," Sylvester later complained. "The studio was small, the ceiling too low, and all those hot lights—my makeup just ran off me." Most of the time was spent doing a lot of nothing, and the time in front of the camera went by so fast it almost seemed to Sylvester that it hadn't happened at all. His company was not Miss Midler, but a squad of seasoned bar drag queens, who sat around swapping stories about filthy drag bars they'd played in places like Omaha and Toledo. Sylvester laughed along, but he did not contribute any stories of his own. He was shy, for one thing, and he also just wasn't a female impersonator. His mind seemed to be elsewhere. He was eager to get home and finish his new album, and he wanted "a total new concept and a total new feeling about the music," he said.

Bored with his own sound, Sylvester took himself to the *Billboard* Disco Forum in New York in mid-June—Mayor Ed Koch had declared it "Disco Week" in the city—and sat in the back of the room just trying to figure out what was making disco such a big deal and how it all worked. "There were all these big stars, making millions, and they were all sitting on this dais and winning all these awards and they told me that I wasn't good enough, big enough, or anything enough to even *be* there, let alone sit close," he said a year later. "But I said, 'Someday I'll be there. I'm not even worried about it.'"

Sylvester had only recently come to take disco seriously at all. "When disco came I was skeptical as to the importance of it," he said. "When I began there was Gloria Gaynor, the first, and I liked her. But then it was everything from 'I Love Lucy' remakes to standards, and it was all instrumental disco and a pounding sound. A lot of performers were left out. Then there was back-up singers' disco, which was back-up singers with an orchestra; and then all of a sudden, singing *stars* came in again, with disco *stars* and disco groups. And that's when I started to like disco again." Disco, he conceded, was not exactly Billie Holiday, but he thought maybe he should, as he put it, "do a disco record and throw our record in the pot, too." The decision was partly calculated—disco was like an open cash register right then—and partly a matter of what the hell.

By 1978 what was known as disco included much formulaic, Manilow-ish music to which white suburban people were dancing at Arthur Murray studios and strip-mall discothèques. But disco music, like jazz and rock, was actually black music. It had begun as "party music" in black and Latino underground clubs in the late 1960s, and by the 1970s had migrated to mixed underground clubs in New York like the Loft, mostly black gay clubs like the Paradise Garage, and mostly white gay clubs like the Tenth Floor. It took elements of rhythm and blues, soul, gospel, and funk, and added orchestrations and sometimes big-band horns. Early party music came out of Motown and Philadelphia International groups like the O'Jays and MFSB, whose "Love Is the Message" became the *Soul Train* theme song in 1974. New multitrack recording technology had made it easier to add in distinct instrumentation, the music writer Barry Walters points out, and "brought out new elements of style—the hissing high hat, the guitar that was scratched and plucked, the bass drum on every beat, the Barry White strings that would go up, up, up."

Popular songs tended to let you know when they were ending, but DJs had started to create long, continuous, seamless mixes with instrumental breaks and ups and downs, and the structure of party songs was transmuted into a repetitive cycle that reminded you only of the present. The messages weren't cognitively complex or even especially deep; they were as idealistic as hippiedom, and they moved from your body to your soul to your mind. Words were important but basic, subordinated to movement; in fact, as the cultural critic Richard Dyer put it, disco was "often little more than an endlessly repeated phrase that [drove] beyond itself." Often, the rhythm and words were about getting your *push, push, in the bush.* Sometimes they told you that as long as you knew how to love you would survive, and the fact that you were dancing proved it. Often they simply advised a trip to *boogie wonderland.*

"Disco music is dance music and a lot of the time it doesn't require much of singing," Sylvester once pointed out, "but the right singing in the right place." The vocals in a lot of disco were subservient to its sounds and rhythms. As Albert Goldman wrote, when the voice was used it was used "in its abstract dimension as song, chant, or shout rather than in its literary-intellectual aspect as statement, prophecy, or jest." The vocalist, Walters says, "had to communicate through the voice what the lyricist didn't have the words to say." To be remembered within the loose, sexual structure of most disco music—build, build, build, build, climax, drop, drop, quiet, build, build, build, climax—the singer had to "get under your skin, as well as in your pants."

In 1973, the same year that *Billboard* introduced the term "disco hit," party music had started to cross over from clubs into the Top 40 by way of "Soul Makossa," a song by a Cameroonian saxophonist named Manu Dibango. When the Love Unlimited Orchestra's "Love's Theme" and the Hues Corporation's "Rock the Boat" made it big the following year, the music industry started to smell the money. Most record companies opened "disco departments" responsible for crossing club disco over to the radio, and from there to white and heterosexual record buyers. Those departments were staffed largely by men who came directly from the gay club scene; they would go from weekends dancing on Fire Island right into work on Monday. In 1975, the first disco labels were formed, producing special, long 12-inch mixes for DJs, like Donna Summer's "Love to Love You Baby," a big hit for Casablanca Records. And a lot of people learned how to do the Bump and the Hustle.

Many kinds of music were labeled disco over the next few years—almost any music with a hundred and twenty-five beats per minute, or with a four-four kick drum and heavy strings and shakers, or with at least two beeps and two toots. There was funk-and-soul disco, by groups like Sister Sledge, Taste of Honey, and (sometimes) the Jackson Five, and individual artists like Gloria Gaynor, Barry White, and Evelyn "Champagne" King, in which you could hear strong echoes of Motown and gospel; there was spacey, lengthy, machinelike European stuff, heavy on the strings and synthetic effects and light on the melodies, by producers like Giorgio Moroder (the force behind "Love to Love You Baby") and Jean-Marc Cerrone (who made hits like "Love in 'C' Minor—Part 1"); there was Top 40 disco, from groups like KC and the Sunshine Band, the Bee Gees, and individuals like Rod Stewart, with shorter, safer, radio-ready songs that prom bands could easily play.

By 1978, disco had crested into a giant wave of pennies, and almost everyone was trying to ride it. Disco and its related enterprises brought in an estimated gross of eight billion dollars, which even now is a preposterous amount of money. About two-fifths of *Billboard*'s Top 100 singles and albums were disco. New York's WKTU went all-disco and suddenly became the most popular radio station in the country; within six months, the number of disco stations quadrupled. *Saturday Night Fever* had been a hit film of shocking proportions the year before, generating the best-selling soundtrack ever, and giving a boost to polyester suits, the Bee Gees, and that dance move in which you point a finger to the sky and then back down at the earth. Dick Clark hosted a show called *Le Disco*. Rod Stewart and the Rolling Stones had disco hits. Dolly Parton, *Charlie's Angel* Cheryl Ladd, the porn star Marilyn Chambers, and *Sesame Street*'s Cookie Monster had all cut disco records, and soon Ethel Merman would release an album with disco versions of songs like "There's No Business Like Show Business" and "Everything's Coming Up Roses." It wouldn't have been surprising to hear that a disco version of the Mourner's Kaddish was on the way, or that Mrs. Betty Ford was working on a disco album.

Disco moved gayness, camp, and androgyny even closer to the American mainstream than the glitter rockers had done. For instance, Grace Jones, dark and tall and angular, got her start as a model in European magazines, and by the mid-seventies was a flamboyant gay-club fixture with a series of disco hits. Her songs had what used to be called a gay sensibility. She sang "I Need a Man" in a way that implied that she didn't need him for much besides sex. With the disco producer Tom Moulton, she took self-pitying Broadway show tunes like "Send in the Clowns," "What I Did for Love," and *Annie*'s "Tomorrow"—and then, brilliantly, the classic Edith Piaf wrist-slitter "La Vie en Rose"—and turned them into something you danced to. Sexy genderfuck was one of her signatures: she claimed that she resulted from a "genetic mixup between her and her twin brother"; wore her hair short and sharp; often dressed in animal skins, gorilla suits, or men's tailored suits with breasts revealed. She presented herself as an unsmiling dominatrix-diva. Academics would later suggest that she "boldly interrogated both racial and sexual stereotypes associated with the black female body" and "played with iconic signs of 'the primitive,' and transformed these signifiers and her body into a site of power." The gays adored her, in any event. By 1978 Grace Jones had crossed over, and the straights, although perhaps a bit frightened, loved her too.

The gayest musical act ever, of course, was the Village People. They'd been created by a Frenchman named Jacques Morali who, upon seeing a dancer in costume at a New York gay bar, had concluded that "the gay people have no group, nobody to personalize the gay people, you know?" He put six men in macho drag and made them into a disco team: construction worker, cowboy, GI, biker, Indian, and cop. "Every time I was speaking to somebody good-looking," Morali told a *New York* magazine writer, "I say, 'Do you sing?'" He recruited some of the People through an ad seeking "gay singers and dancers, very good-looking and with mustaches." One review called them "a faggot high school band," but they were an unexpected hit singing of mainstream American institutions, such as the YMCA, where "they have everything for young men to enjoy," and the navy, where "they want you" and "need a hand." The Village People were awarded *Billboard* Disco Forum's Group of the Year award in 1978, beating out the Bee Gees. "Y.M.C.A." spent six months on the charts, hitting Number 2. That year, the Village People also performed on a float in the Macy's Thanksgiving Day Parade.

Disco's royal palace, Studio 54, had opened in New York the year before, and in its first year had made an estimated $7 million. Studio 54 had a long, red-lit, gold-ceilinged, mirrored entryway; a chrome bar; lots of lilies and couches; a main dance room with multiple levels and a man in the moon over it, who would light up when a giant spoon lowered under his nose; pouty, pretty-boy bartenders; and famous people. Sometimes, working the door, the co-owner Steve Rubell would tell people to go home because they were ugly or because he thought they wanted to get in too badly or not badly enough, but he was also committed, like disco more generally, to a sort of fruit-salad aesthetic. "You want a little bit of everything," Rubell said back then, "the pretty girl, the celebrity, the guy who's a model, the kid who turns hamburgers at McDonald's." Those selected for entry on a special night, like a celebrity's birthday, might see zillions of white roses (Liz Taylor) or white ducks (Dolly Parton), or elephants— white (Bianca Jagger) or gray (Liza Minnelli). Grace Jones might enter on a motorcycle, or on the shoulders of a gaggle of very attractive men in loincloths, carrying her like an African queen and then writhing while she coolly sang *La vie en rose, la vie en rose, la vie en rose.*

In 1978, in other words, the disco world was brimful of strangeness, gayness, mixing, dress-up, drugs, androgyny, and excess. It included items like Disco Lashes, false eyelashes painted with multicolored glitter. It was a pretty good bet that in these environs nobody was going to run screaming from a black guy wearing womanly clothing and singing gospel disco like a sexed-up church girl.

Sylvester and Harvey Fuqua, having fired or lost most of the band that had played on the first album, had quickly gathered up a new one: a drummer named Randy Merritt, a keyboard player named Michael Finden, and an eighteen-year-old bass player named Bob Kingson had joined Tip Wirrick and David Frazier. They rehearsed for weeks in Finden's basement in the Fillmore neighborhood.

The band members worked and played enthusiastically, but they didn't all necessarily share Sylvester's sensibilities. Sylvester still planned to make a "concept album about Harlem in the twenties and thirties," he said, with songs like "Harlem on My Mind" and "Sleepy Time Down South." Sylvester would bring to rehearsals obscure, decades-old recordings by black women and insist that the band play them. "They were always duds," says Wirrick. Some of the band members had decided that they all sounded the same, too, and invented a fictional character to blame them on: "Oh, God," someone would report before a rehearsal, eyes rolling, "Sylvester's bringing in a Magnetta Washington song." Sylvester never let on whether he heard the band joking about Magnetta Washington, but it didn't really matter. If you didn't like it, you could just walk away. You would not be missed.

Tip Wirrick, the veteran of the band, was loosely serving as its leader. He'd show up at rehearsals with some songlike thing in his head and insist that the band play around with it, hoping to turn it into an actual song. The band members called these his "exercises," and they teased him pitilessly about them. One day, Tip arrived with a nondescript, mid-tempo rhythm-and-blues ballad he'd written the night before in his tiny studio apartment on Thirtieth Street. It was simple, just a few chords without a melody. The song excited no one, not even Tip.

About ten minutes before rehearsal was supposed to end, Sylvester blew in with a small entourage. "What have we got?" he asked. He listened to the latest exercise, and impatiently waved for the band to stop. "No, no, no," he said, shaking his head. "What are you doing? Like this." He stomped his foot fast and hard, and signaled to the band to pick up the beat. Sylvester instructed the drummer: pound the kick drum on the quarter notes, psss-psss-psss the high-hat cymbals on the off-beat eights, hit the snare on two and four. Tip had already been thinking along the same lines: that if they used a bouncing bass an octave below the piano, which was what seemed to be working on radio at the time, they might have a hit. "You're going to hate me for this," Tip told the bass player, Bob Kingson, "but please, please just play the octaves." Kingson made up a bouncing bass line. *Voilà*: disco.

While the band played, Kingson says, "Sylvester proceeded to create the melody and lyrics on the spot. He just blasted this thing out of himself." He sang words on the chorus, but on the verses he just la-la-la'd. Tip Wirrick thought, "If we can get this on the record it'll be a hit." Kingson thought, "My God, we're going to be world famous." Kingson called Harvey Fuqua the next day and told him they had the single for their new album. Fuqua listened to the song, and cautiously hedged his bets for a couple of weeks. Then, one day, he pulled Kingson aside. "'Mighty Real' is badder than a motherfucker," he said.

Sylvester, though, was casual about the whole thing. "We put this disco beat on it, and I really didn't think much about it," he said later. "I didn't think the song was that hot." For weeks, he didn't even bother writing down the lyrics he'd come up with. When he later put them on paper, the words to the song, "You Make Me Feel (Mighty Real)," were not exactly Dylanesque. "There weren't a lot of words," Sylvester said, "but they said exactly what was going on: to dance and sweat and cruise and go home and carry on and how a person feels." "Mighty Real" was a thrown-together, homegrown ditty, in which Sylvester meets someone on the dance floor, brings him home where it's "nice and dark." The music is in him and he's still "real hot," and he gets kissed and it feels real good, and he knows "you'll love me like you should."

They had the single, but only morsels of *Step II*, the album they were working on in the summer of 1978, were decided before Sylvester and the band went into the Fantasy studio. Tip, Sylvester, and the band pretty much made up the rest of the album in the studio. They'd start playing, feel it, and see what happened. They didn't know how to make a record.

Harvey Fuqua, whom his ex-partner Nancy Pitts calls a "musical genius," certainly did know how. He had been mentored by Alan Freed, the rock and roll DJ and TV-show host who became one of the most important promoters of rhythm and blues—and who in 1962 pled guilty to two counts of commercial bribery. Fuqua had a hand in the hit-making of Stevie Wonder, Diana Ross, Marvin Gaye, David Ruffin, and Tammi Terrell. He'd worked at Motown and RCA Records, and had founded his own record labels. He had hits with the Moonglows, with whom he would later be inducted into the Rock and Roll Hall of Fame. He was no slouch.

But in the studio with *Step II,* Fuqua did not always seem entirely engaged. He was famous among band members for falling asleep while they were recording. They'd play a song, and then through their headphones they'd hear Harvey ask for another take. "And you'd finish the song and think you totally nailed it," says James Wirrick, "and you'd look in the control room, and there's Harvey with his hand on his balls, asleep." Someone would ask him what he thought of the take, and he'd wake up, a bit startled, and say, "One more please." When they wanted to crack each other up, the band members would pretend to snore, hand on balls, and then jump awake mumbling, "One more, please."

The band's teasing of Harvey was affectionate, but they did not rely on him for direction. "It was a lot of loose, sloppy ends," says the percussionist David Frazier. "He would allow things to stay on the tracks, time warps and bad notes, just flagrant mistakes. Whole beats would be missing, and it would slow down. People were looking at him like, 'Dude, you can't leave it like that,' and he would say, 'Well, we'll take it out in the mix.'" That became another band inside joke: when one of them screwed up, someone was likely to shrug and say, "We'll take it out in the mix."

Sylvester, the Two Tons o' Fun, and the band recorded most of the slower B-side cuts down in Los Angeles. They did a Burt Bacharach–Hal David song called "I Took My Strength from You" that Sylvester's friend the singer Frank Loverde had turned him on to: *Think about the good things, think about the good things, think about the good things,* Sylvester sang. They put on a tune about gratitude that Sylvester had written with his keyboard player, Michael Finden. They added a song Sylvester had written with Harvey Fuqua that began with a gossip session about Sylvester himself. "Child, have you heard the latest?" one Ton asked.

"Ooh, ooh, what's going on now?" replied the second Ton. "About Sylvester breaking up, he done broke up with a— Girl, it's a mess. Honey, he can tell you better than I can. Sylvester, you gotta tell me please about this, honey." Sylvester stepped in and sang the story of how he got a letter, dialed the number but it was disconnected. "I was so *through,* child," he said. He just didn't know what was going on or if it was something he said, but he did know that "I need you, need you, baby, yes I do."

On the A-side of the album, there were just two songs. In addition to "Mighty Real," Sylvester and the crew tossed on the album a song Eric Robinson—a pianist and singer who joined the group for the album—had written called "Dance (Disco Heat)." It opened with another spoken exchange, this time between Sylvester and Martha in an imaginary disco. "Got a match?" Sylvester said in his deep voice, over steady drum and bass, and Martha mmm-hmmed that she did. "It's a fabulous club," he said, and she agreed. "Look at all the fabulous people. You wanna dance?" Martha said she'd love to, and off they went to get down and party a little bit. *Cookin' on my feet to the disco beat,* the Tons sang. The song was mostly Martha and Izora singing fast lyrics about *movin', groovin', slidin', glidin', rockin', reelin',* and Sylvester coming in on the chorus to insist that you dance with him in the *disco heat,* commanding you *Dance! dance! dance! dance! dance! dance!*

Sylvester heeded that advice regularly, just as he'd been doing since he was a teenager. One of his regular gigs was at a disco, the City, where he had been dancing for years. The City had been the place gay men and the people who loved them went to dance. It had a glass tile bar lit up from the inside, and a lighting system with sixteen hundred bulbs. By 1978 it had become pretty straight, and gay people were going to places like the Trocadero Transfer and Dreamland, but the City crowds still cheered for Sylvester.

The lighting guy at the City Disco was a wee, bouncy, literate, unassuming blond named Patrick Cowley—a "little cosmic cookie," his friend Linda Imperial called him. Cowley was not especially musical, but he was a whiz with a synthesizer and was starting to do some hip stuff with synthesized sounds. One night, Patrick invited Sylvester over to his house to hear some of his synthesizer music. "I totally flipped out," Sylvester said. It was the sound he'd been looking for. He played "Mighty Real" for Patrick, and Patrick totally flipped out. Patrick came into Fantasy and added boingy synthesizer on top of the "Mighty Real" that Sylvester and the Two Tons and the band had recorded, and did the same for "Disco Heat." He was right on time.

Sylvester saw "Disco Heat" as just another "funny little disco song." Some of the others involved were even less impressed with it, and indeed with the whole album. If you listened closely to "You Make Me Feel (Mighty Real)," you could hear it speeding up and slowing down, coming out of time and back in again. "I listen to the record now and I think it's godawful," James Wirrick says. "I really thought that thing was a piece of shit when we did it," says David Frazier of the album.

The cover of *Step II* shows two feet on a pink tile floor. One foot is Sylvester's, in a tan Ralph Lauren shoe from Wilkes Bashford, and next to it is a woman's dark, red-nailed bare foot kicking over a crystal glass, spilling its champagne. Dennis Gassner, the Fantasy art director, had loaned the crystal for the shoot, and he and his team had rigged a thin wire to tip the glass just slowly enough to photograph the sloshing champagne. They broke four of Dennis's crystal glasses. They had planned to hire a foot model to do the kicking-over pose, but Nancy Pitts had nixed that— Fantasy had given her a tiny budget, and fifty bucks is fifty bucks. The bare foot is hers, no extra charge.

Days after the album was released that summer, it was as if they had simply taken a snapshot from Sylvester's new life as a worldwide disco star: enough champagne and crystal to waste, and pink tiles for everyone's feet.

Sylvester popped into stardom with suddenness and force, like an ember that has smoked for a while and then without warning ignited. For a few minutes, his life became one of those star-is-born, oh-my-God-that's-my-song movie montages. As a child, he had no doubt imagined it all something like this, corny and glamorous, maybe sketched out the scenes on a notepad. The song begins, and here is Sylvester, staring at the portable radio in his Laundromat, screaming and throwing his socks in the air. *When we're out there dancin' on the floor, darling.* Cut to the tinny speakers of an Audi, and then to Sylvester driving in a beret, grinning to himself. *And I feel like I need some more, and I.* Cut to Sylvester signing autographs on the streets of San Francisco, a large ring flickering and bracelets shivering. *Feel your body close to mine, and I.* Cut to sweaty men dancing, eyes closed, fists up, and shirtless. *Know my love it's about that time. Make me feel.* Cut to Sylvester, arriving at a gig in New York City in dark Jackie-O sunglasses while bodyguards hold back reaching hands. *Mighty real. Make me feel.* Cut to Sylvester and a radio interviewer, both wearing head-phones, their heads thrown back in laughter. *Mighty real.* Cut to the *Bill-board* charts, dates flapping by as the song shoots up the charts. *You make me feel.* Cut to *ABC Sunday Night Football,* going to commercial as fans dance. *Mi-i-ighty real. You make me feel.* Cut to Sylvester, in a white sum-mer fur, getting on the Concorde, landing in London! Paris! Rome! *Mi-i-ighty real. I feel real. I feel real. I feel real. Wooooh.*

"Feeling real" is an interesting notion, and a lot more was packed into that little song than Sylvester's simple lyrics let on. On the one hand, to be real is to be authentic, down-to-earth, not fronting. To feel real is to let out something you recognize as your genuine self: free of social airs and pretensions, unafraid, unhidden, honest. This was the realness people—especially gay people, so accustomed to closets—felt from Sylvester him-self, as he sang joyfully about sex in the dark with another man. Yet to some people—those in the drag-queen culture in which Sylvester was reared, for instance—to be "real" is to pass in a social role that has been denied you. In the 1980s Harlem drag balls made famous in Jennie Livingston's *Paris Is Burning,* for instance, "realness" trophies were awarded to those who most effectively approximated something they could only dream of being: an executive; a town-and-country aristocrat; supermodel; superstar. To feel real, in this sense, is to make the costume into your skin, to bring the fantasy self into actual being. This was the realness people might have felt watching Sylvester become a diva before their eyes. Perhaps, in the end, realness simply means refusing to be denied, being exactly who you feel yourself to be, occupying your space with all your might.

Realness is relational, too: it does not happen without love. Margery Williams's famous children's story *The Velveteen Rabbit* taught this lesson in a slightly more sober, sentimental, and sexless manner than Sylvester did, but it is nonetheless one of the better meditations on realness. When the toy Rabbit asks what "real" means, the older, wiser Skin Horse answers, "It's a thing that happens to you. When a child loves you for a long, long time, not just to play with, but REALLY loves you, then you become Real." The Rabbit wants to know if it happens all at once, the way some toys get wound up. "It doesn't happen all at once," the Horse replies. "You become. It takes a long time. That's why it doesn't often happen to people who break easily, or have sharp edges, or who have to be carefully kept. Generally, by the time you are Real, most of your hair has been loved off, and your eyes drop out and you get loose in your joints and very shabby. But these things don't matter at all, because once you are Real you can't be ugly, except to people who don't understand." The children of San Francisco loved Sylvester, and they understood, and they made him Real.

In mid-August, Fantasy rushed Sylvester to London with only four hours' notice, to pounce on the quick ascent of "Mighty Real" in Europe. Sylvester went straight from the plane to Radio London. The Brits, it turned out, couldn't really get enough of Sylvester. British publications described Sylvester as suggesting a "younger, plumper Eartha Kitt" and "a plump Tina Turner," both remarks no doubt meant as compliments. That night, he sang at three London discos—the Royalty, the Sundown, the Global Village—where he was met by mobs. People followed him from club to club, so the crowds got bigger as the night went on. "Sylvester caused riots," said a reporter, Sharon Davis, who hung out with him that week. The club appearances were quick and repetitive—hand the DJ a tape, sing "Mighty Real," hand out signed photos and posters, smile at the fans—but Sylvester didn't seem to mind. He carried a folding fan with him wherever he went.

Over the next week, Sylvester performed in Camberley, spoke with a lineup of reporters at the Montcalm Hotel, went clothes shopping, and performed at the discos Hammersmith Palais, Bangs, and Gullivers. He was photographed for *Sounds* and interviewed by Sharon Davis for *Blues & Soul,* performed and signed autographs at two more discos, and shared a buffet lunch with twenty DJs. He appeared on Capitol Radio, *Top of the Pops,* and *Newsbeat,* did some more press interviews, window-shopped at Harrods, judged the semifinals of the EMI Disco Dancing Competition, and then performed "Mighty Real" to a capacity audience of twenty-five hundred at the Empire in Leicester Square. When Sylvester taped a video for the song, Davis, the magazine reporter, noted that he designed the three costumes he used "in a matter of minutes," and then "cut [them] out, and sewed them together in between eating dinner, answering the phone, and getting showered." That night, exhausted, he made one more disco appearance, at the Lyceum, in front of three thousand people. It was a busy week.

Sharon Davis, to her surprise, found Sylvester to be "a warm, considerate, introvert man who cringed at authority, bullies, and heat." When he wanted her to shut up, he smacked her on the knee with his fan. When she told him that his single was a hit on the British charts, he asked, "Does this mean I can buy the couch and two armchairs in Harrods window?" Not long after his visit, Sylvester appeared as *Blues & Soul's* full-color pull-out centerfold, in a curly reddish wig, light makeup, and a beaded, sparkling shawl of reds, blues, and greens, holding a fan. Britons who could name Sylvester's producer, backup vocalists, and first single were eligible to win a Sylvester package, consisting of his first two albums, a Sylvester badge, and a Sylvester fan "perfect for cooling yourself down after a rigorous dance floor session—or whatever!!"

Before he left, Sylvester sent Letha Hurd a postcard of the sunset over the Tower Bridge. "Hi Mom," he wrote in curvy script. "I'm here again. But this time with lots of money and fame. Love to everyone. Your son, Sylvester." Then he flew home. He needed to go do nothing for a minute, just walk the dogs.

That Sylvester realized his diva fantasy through disco is actually quite fitting. Good disco, like a good church service or a good hippie gathering, could melt away differences for a while, send you flying outside yourself, let you glimpse something beyond this world. Sylvester himself pointed out that disco was really the same sort of thing he was up to ten years before with the Cockettes—and really, although he didn't say this, his whole life—since disco was about how "everyone can be strange and live out their fantasies on the dance floor."

Still, he wasn't quite ready for stardom when it came. "I've always lived out my fantasies of being whatever I wanted to be—I did all the things that I thought stars do," Sylvester reflected later. "When I actually became one it sort of freaked me out."

But he got used to it. "Dance (Disco Heat)," the funny little disco song about cookin' on your feet in the disco heat, went to Number 1 on the U.S. and British dance charts and quickly crossed over to the pop Top 20. Most people who heard it noticed parts of their bodies moving. "You Make Me Feel (Mighty Real)," which at first Fantasy did not much promote in the United States, by the end of the summer became the Number 1 disco song in most of the country's major cities. It hit the Top 10 in England, Italy, France, Belgium, Germany, Spain, Holland, Switzerland, Mexico, Brazil, Venezuela, and Hong Kong. *Step II* went gold, and Fantasy released

Baby Sylvester, with an unidentified neighborhood woman and girl, Los Angeles, circa 1948. Sylvester was raised on the gospel according to Billie Holiday: God bless the child that's got his own. (*Courtesy of Bernadette Brown*)

Sylvester, nicknamed Dooni (top), at home with his brothers John (left) and Larry (right), Los Angeles, circa 1957. Neighborhood kids took to teasing Larry and John about their brother, saying he acted like a girl. (*Courtesy of Bernadette Brown*)

Dooni at home in Los Angeles, circa 1957. When Dooni sang "Never Grow Old," at church and on the gospel circuit, everybody would be shouting by the time he was through. (*Courtesy of Bernadette Brown*)

Julia Morgan blowing out her birthday candles, surrounded by family, Los Angeles, circa 1954. Dooni is on the right, holding a cup; his mother, Letha, is in the back center, next to his very tall grandfather, Egypt Morgan. "My grandmother was the first person to tell me I was gay," Sylvester said later. *(Courtesy of Bernadine Stevens)*

Sylvester as a teenager, Los Angeles, circa 1962. Soon, he would leave home and become a member of the Disquotays, a gang of in-charge glamour girls. (*Courtesy of Bernadine Stevens*)

Sylvester, not long after moving to San Francisco, circa 1970. "Los Angeles is a role city, but San Francisco is free," Sylvester said. (*Courtesy of Peter Mintun*)

Sylvester on a trip to the suburbs of San Francisco in 1971. "He'd pose and we'd take pictures," his friend Peter Mintun said. "We thought it was magical, gorgeous, glamorous." (*Courtesy of Peter Mintun*)

Sylvester in his hippie days with the Cockettes, San Francisco, circa 1971. "Psychedelics keep me together," Sylvester said. (*Photograph by Clay Geerdes. © Carol Kossack. Used by permission.*)

Sylvester with three Cockettes, San Francisco, circa 1971. "When you walk down the street and you see somebody sitting in a mud puddle, and they invite you to jump in and you do," Sylvester said, "that's the Cockettes." (*Photograph by Clay Geerdes. © Carol Kossack. Used by permission.*)

Sylvester, wheeled by Tim McKenna, Nitsa Elite (right) and Tony Elite (far right), in San Francisco's Gay Freedom Day Parade, June 26, 1988. "All my business is done," said Sylvester, who died six months later. (*Photograph © Rick Gerharter. Used by permission.*)

Sylvester at San Francisco's War Memorial Opera House, March 1979. "You are a
star, everybody is one," Sylvester sang on the album released that day. "You are a
star. You only happen once." *(Photograph by Phil Bray. Courtesy of Fantasy, Inc.)*

a special promotional pressing of "Mighty Real" on bright pink vinyl. Fantasy gave elaborate parties with *Step II* this and *Step II* that, and gave away bottles of wine with *Step II* labels.

Rolling Stone called the *Step II* album "as good as disco records get," and the *Los Angeles Herald Examiner* called it "the very best disco being made just now." Sylvester, the reviewer Ken Tucker wrote, had become "that very odd and rare thing, an original artist working in disco." Over the next months, Sylvester and the Two Tons and the band—which now included Patrick Cowley—appeared on *Dinah Shore, American Bandstand*, Don Kirshner's *Rock Concert*, and *The Merv Griffin Show* (twice). Sylvester invited Dinah Shore's other guest, Charo, into his dressing room and lifted her up in front of the cameras; their photo appeared in papers in St. Louis, Grand Rapids, and Dallas. On his first visit to *Merv Griffin* he wore a dress, and on his second he presented Griffin with a gold *Step II* album; their photo appeared in Cleveland, Shreveport, and Houston. On *American Bandstand* he wore a pelt skirt.

Sylvester, the Two Tons, and the band were not home a lot. Harvey Fuqua got a new drummer; he hired a saxophone player named Marc Baum and a trombone player named Dan Reagan, and off they went to support the album. In Europe that fall, audience members sometimes got so excited that they'd rush the stage and carry Sylvester, Martha, and Izora above them through the crowd; the first time it happened, Izora thought they were under attack, so she rolled up her sleeves and put up her dukes. In Germany, the crowds tended to be sedate, but it turned out they loved Sylvester so much that some German gave him a fur coat.

At concerts in England, where Sylvester wore a black tunic with silver sequins and a glittering silver snood, "all hell broke loose—a great deal of floppy-legged dancing in the aisles, girls and boys leaping on the stage to kiss Sylvester and one or the other of the Tons." In Venice, Sylvester and his crew played at a high-tech club with a chrome floor and state-of-the-art disco lights, attended by the chic-est of the chic. Elsewhere in Italy, fans clamored after Sylvester on the streets as if he were dribbling money or chocolate bars or true love behind him. "It was like the Beatles or Jimi Hendrix," says Marapasa, who was with him in Rome. "They treated Sylvester like a god," Marc Baum says. Fans almost tipped over his limousines in their frenzy, clawing at the windows, screaming "Sylvestri! Sylvestri!" Some people cried. In France, it was pretty much the same thing, only a little more elegant. "Sylvestre! Sylvestre!" called the French.

Back in the States, they joined the California Jam tour, sponsored by an R&B radio station, with soul artists like Evelyn "Champagne" King, Peabo Bryson, and Atlantic Starr. The tour was just a few days long, but Sylvester rose right to the top. "Our first night, in Concord, we were the opening act," Robert Kingson says. "By the final show in Long Beach, we were going on last." Their whole show consisted of just two songs, "Mighty Real" and "Disco Heat," which Sylvester stretched to nearly a half hour each, bringing the energy down, then taking it back up, down, back up again. When, in the middle of "Disco Heat," Izora emitted the guttural wail, "Get on your feet and dance to the beat and dance!" kids screamed and jumped out of their seats and danced in the aisles. Two songs, and the audiences were worn out.

In November, Sylvester and the Two Tons o' Fun and the band opened for the Commodores ("Three Times a Lady") in Oklahoma; played with the O'Jays ("Use Ta Be My Girl"), War ("Why Can't We Be Friends?"), and L.T.D. ("Back in Love Again") in Texas; headlined a disco convention in Miami. In December they played two nights in Philadelphia, opening for Ashford and Simpson; the Roxy in Los Angeles, where Sylvester, the *Los Angeles Times* reported, was cheered by gay-and-proud guys in short hair and T-shirts who "appeared to be greeting a messiah." They also did gigs in nearly every disco in New York City, including one where you checked your clothes at the door.

That November 7, while Sylvester was on the road, the Briggs Initiative—California's Proposition 6—was defeated by a two-to-one margin, but the celebration in San Francisco was short-lived. Twenty days later, a former city policeman, fireman, and supervisor named Dan White walked into City Hall. White, whose liberal colleagues outnumbered him on the Board of Supervisors, had resigned from the board, changed his mind, and then heard that Mayor George Moscone, a Harvey Milk ally, did not intend to reappoint him. He went to Moscone's office and shot him in the shoulder and pectoral, and then twice in the head. At first, Moscone's secretary thought she was hearing a car backfiring. Then, White went down the hall and shot Harvey Milk in the hand and wrist—Milk had thrown his hand up in front of him—and then in the chest. As Randy Shilts wrote, White then fired a fourth bullet at Milk, which "sliced into the back of his head and out the other side, spraying blood against the wall." Even so, White fired one more bullet into Milk's skull.

When Dianne Feinstein, then the president of the Board of Supervisors, announced that Moscone and Milk, who had become a major figure in the national gay rights movement, had been shot and killed, seasoned reporters loudly gasped. As word spread across San Francisco, many people met it with desperate belief, and then with desperate grief. Many made their way down to the Castro. That evening, a crowd readied to march from Market Street to City Hall; most held candles stuck into upside-down paper cups, and walked slowly and numbly, as one man beat a drum. The crowd grew to around forty thousand and filled the street all the way from the Castro to the Civic Center.

At City Hall, Joan Baez sang "Swing Low, Sweet Chariot," and a few folks made speeches. What most people remember, though, is just standing there, in such quiet that the only thing audible was an occasional sob, and in such darkness all you could see were thousands of little flames. Most people left their candles to burn on a statue near the City Hall steps. "In the morning," recalled Harvey Milk's former speechwriter, Frank Robinson, "you couldn't see the statue at all, only a small mountain of candle wax."

In the New York area that December, Sylvester opened for Chaka Khan at the Capitol Theatre, wearing a silver sequined robe, a feather boa, and black high-heeled boots. "The drooping tendrils of the nouveau afro framing his wide, subtly made-up, baby-soft face gave him the look," wrote Vince Aletti, "of a somewhat slimmed-down, somewhat freaked-out Roberta Flack." At first, the mostly black, mostly straight crowd seemed to be at a loss. Unlike male falsetto soul singers they'd heard—love men like Eddie Kendricks or Donnie Elbert, say, or Smokey Robinson—Sylvester was clearly not trying to win over the ladies with feminine softness. Sylvester sang, as Guy Trebay put it, "like a street girl—sassy, hot, skirt hiked up, paying it no mind." That night, he took a look at the audience. "Sometimes folks make us feel strange, but we're not strange," he said. "And those folks—they'll just have to *catch up*." Then he sang them the Quincy Jones soul classic "Everything Must Change." *Everything must change, nothing stays the same*, he crooned with confidence. *Everyone will change, no one stays the same.* He moved into "You Make Me Feel (Mighty Real)"; the audience still seemed to be responding with "a mixture of caution, confusion, and amazement." But then they caught up: by the middle of the set, "they greeted his remarks with an immediate roar of approval and support," Aletti reported. "Sylvester was no longer mystifying, he was mighty, mighty real." By the end of the set, they were on their feet dancing to "Disco Heat." "Miss Thing stole the show so completely," says Bob Kingson. You wouldn't have wanted just then to be Chaka Khan, who found out, as a New York *Daily News* reviewer wrote, "why nobody in his right mind follows Sylvester."

Sylvester, John Rockwell soon wrote in *The New York Times*, "gives a show that makes most performers look positively dowdy," and the *Daily News* said he was "on a transcendental par with such talents as Celia Cruz, Bruce Springsteen and Patti LaBelle," and made "David Bowie look like Lawrence Welk." In *Melody Maker*, Simon Frith reported that Sylvester, "a sexual utopian who seems, miraculously, to have made it," had "put on the best show I've seen for ages." On fast songs, he stamped his right foot and waved his left hand; on slow ones, he seemed on the verge of tears. "I used to marvel at the moments Sylvester had in his show," says Marc Baum. "It was an old gospel showbiz kind of thing. There was the fun moment, there was the big energized moment, there was the touching moment—he was a master of the touching moment. He used the same lines every night, but I would have sworn it was spontaneous. He meant it each night. It felt like it was just Sylvester and the audience, and that this was that special moment, and it was; a tear would come to your eye. The feeling was authentic, and it was also pure unadulterated show business." They would usually close with a version of "Dance (Disco Heat)" that went right into "Never Can Say Goodbye." Sylvester would leave the stage waving, and the band would keep pounding the song's tag until, after letting the tension build and build, Sylvester would come bouncing back. Then, to bring the crowd back down, he would sing the ballad "You Are My Friend," dedicating it to the audience. That was his touching moment. "It killed every night," says Baum.

Touring wasn't all movie-glamorous, of course. In Amarillo, Texas, Sylvester's dressing room was a cattle stall with curtains. They hated him a lot in places like Hollywood, Florida, where he played a disco called the Limelight. "The performance was lifeless as a boulder," an irritated local reviewer wrote, citing as evidence yawning audience members counting the ice cubes in their drinks. The reviewer likened Sylvester's anger to that of an elephant, and his ego to that of a whale. Sylvester, who was always on some kind of diet, could not have liked the elephant/whale business, but he didn't pay yawning audiences much mind. "If an audience is having an awful time," he said on another occasion, "I say, 'Fuck them.' I turn to my girls and my band and we have an absolutely fabulous time with each other."

Disco, Sylvester once said, was "simply a means to an end for me." His long-term goal, he liked to say, was to do absolutely nothing. A friend, the Fantasy publicist Terri Hinte, once did an astrological chart for him (he was a Virgo). "He has a very plain, quiet chart, nothing ostentatious," she says. "I just want to go places and be strange," he said.

When he imagined himself doing nothing, of course, it was usually in an exotic setting. He planned to "go to Egypt, lie in the sands, and swim in the Nile, hang out, and do nothing." In the meantime, he spent most of his San Francisco do-nothing time with his new boyfriend, John Maley, a model he had met at a show in San Francisco late in 1978. John was tall, white, Catholic, shy, and handsome. Their relationship had begun as "a combination of courtship and getting into bed," John Maley says, and then quickly deepened into love. A few months after *Step II* hit, John had moved into Sylvester's Castro apartment. As the money flowed in, the two of them moved into a larger, fancier apartment on Corbett Street, up the hill on Twin Peaks. From their living room, they could look out over the Castro, past the city to the Bay, and over the water to places beyond.

Sylvester was invited back to New York for the 1979 *Billboard* Disco Forum in February. He had already collected a couple of trophies at the National Disco Awards in Boston, where he was Best Male Artist to Donna Summer's Best Female. At the *Billboard* Forum, he won the awards for Top Light Radio Single, Top Heavy Twelve-Inch Single, and Top Male Vocalist. The year before, he hadn't been able to get a table. Now he blew everyone away in a live performance and sat on the dais at the Roseland Ballroom with the Village People, Grace Jones—who was like Sylvester with the parts reversed—and Cher, who presented him with the award for Top Male Vocalist. At a *Billboard* Forum party, Sylvester roller-skated with Cher.

Rolling Stone listed him as one of the top thirty "prime movers" in the "pop revolution" of disco. In the *Village Voice*, Robert Christgau, the rock critic's rock critic, called "Mighty Real" a "genuine classic" and declared that "Sylvester is a star," which pretty much made it official.

Sylvester made plans to get his teeth fixed and to have his cheeks injected with silicone, to make himself "even *more* lovely." He had his little boobs—which had been enhanced by his use of hormones back in the Disquotay days—readjusted to suit a man's chest. Then he went to get rid of the bump on his nose that he'd always asked photographers to airbrush away. Rumor had it that he went to the same plastic surgeon as Cher, and that he arrived holding a photo of the nose of Miss Diana Ross.

9.

FLAME (ON THE DANCE FLOOR)

Although the folks at Fantasy were certainly thrilled to have a hit record on their hands, they couldn't even begin to wrap their arms around Sylvester. Sylvester wasn't interested in competing with the "middle-of-the-road disco people," he said, but with the stars in the disco big league—Giorgio Moroder, Donna Summer, Linda Clifford, Cerrone, Grace Jones. "If you are going to compete in that league," he told a *San Francisco Bay Guardian* reporter, "you cannot be safe." Fantasy had the largest jazz catalog in the world, and made its biggest money from Creedence Clearwater Revival and *One Flew Over the Cuckoo's Nest*. It was a conservative, cautious, jazzy kind of place. An employee who was around at the time remembers Phil Jones, the president of the company, as your basic "racist, sexist homophobe." He was known to read *Reader's Digest*.

Sylvester didn't usually complain to anybody about Fantasy—he was grateful and loving his life—but when the company released a 12-inch disco mix of "Disco Heat" without his consent, Sylvester was livid. Listening to it at Harvey and Nancy's East Bay pad, he threw himself on their bed and cried. "It took four months for us to mix that record," he said. "And then to have somebody just roll the tape, and these effects just *come* in, and *go* out, and lots of fabulous things are left out: the panning, the effects, the way you play with the electronics." What really pissed him off, just destroyed him, was the way someone else was credited with the "concept" of the mix. "I died, I cried, I flipped out," he said. He threatened to walk on desks and scream and break things. In fact, band members heard that he walked into a Fantasy executive's office, threw a pile of the records at the wall, and broke one on the man's desk. "I'll never have that done to me again," he said. "*No one* conceptualizes me. *I* am the concept."

Sylvester was constantly conceptualizing. In case you weren't planning on seeing his show, Sylvester—promoting himself in the British publication *Sounds*—could sell it to you it in such a way that you more or less had to change your plans. "Izora Rhodes is just enormous, and so real," he said in 1978. "She sings and dances and sweats and shakes. Martha Wash has these huge tits that just come out like this, and shake from side to side when she sings, and she's got the nerve to have a shape from the waist down. I'm putting them in skin-tight dresses, like the Supremes. That'll be unbelievable, with them singing, all these butts and bellies and tits sticking out and shaking, and me being absolutely crazed." Indeed, Sylvester conceptualized Martha and Izora on a day-to-day basis. "No one was telling him what to wear," says Izora Rhodes Armstead. "He will make *you* go home and tell *you* what to wear." He made the Tons matching gowns from red-and-gold Chinese fabric; he even had them in spandex for a while. Or he would just cut up a sheet and glue some things onto it. The Tons had Peaches-and-Herb braids before Peaches and Herb, and Patti LaBelle white fingernails before Patti LaBelle.

In case you weren't sure you wanted to buy his next album, he'd be happy to give you a preview of that, too. It was going to be, he said, sex disco—like Donna Summer's sixteen-minute, oohing, multiple-orgasm-simulating hit "Love to Love You Baby," only not so timid. "I want to have someone fuck on the record and record it, the sounds," he told *Sounds*, although he never did produce such an album. "Not moaning and groaning, but the sounds of sex, the sounds of touching, the actual sounds of penetration. Nice music and close miking. It's not gonna be a record for sex. It's a record for dancing, with sex."

Sylvester had a clear Sylvester concept, too. He used his outside like a canvas, and although he was often just plain Sylvester, and at home he was usually a jeans-and-T-shirt-and-jewelry kind of guy, his preferred mode of public representation remained royal: movie queen, queen bee, grand diva. You could come to his house dressed as the Queen of Sheba, he said, because he would probably be Cleopatra. When he was "on"—talking to a reporter, appearing on a talk show—he often played the Great Lady off-stage in her dressing room. He spoke definitely, as if he were writing the words down with a fountain pen dipped in ink. "And that is the way it should be." "And I have concluded that this is what I shall do." His gestures were grand, "almost like a parody of formal gestures, and the speech was regal, almost imperial, almost like a parody of formal speech. It sounded like what you would see in the movies," recalls the comedian and writer Bruce Vilanch, who knew Sylvester from *The Rose* and later from appearances on the television music show *Midnight Special,* which Vilanch sometimes hosted. When Sylvester was invited to perform at the Royal Palace in Rio, someone asked him what he was going to do once he got there. "I don't know." He shrugged. "Be royal, I guess."

On stage, Sylvester would often design a movie moment for himself. At the Hammersmith Odeon in London in 1979, Sylvester performed mostly in a tinsel tutu and striped blouse over black tights, "an asexual outfit of multi-sexual promise," as Simon Frith reported. He emerged at the end, in a "black leotard and tattered robe," to sing an "end-of-show ballad, sweeping-up music, image from a thousand films—the deserted stage and dead dressing room, the public star, the private grief." It was very Judy Garland at Carnegie Hall. When he was finished, he walked the catwalk into the audience with a crown on his head. "Some people ask me why I wear a crown," he said. "I say, every queen must have a crown."

But a scene did not necessarily require an audience. Beautiful is beautiful, regardless of who is watching. On a visit to New York that same year, Sylvester was sporting a long white fox coat he'd just picked up in Germany. He'd performed at the Garage, and was on the way to a bar in a white limousine with New York friends Tom and Ed when he spotted steam coming out of the sewers. "Stop the car, please," Sylvester called to the driver. "Get this," he said to Tom, who had a camera. He stepped out of the limo into the dark, and Tom followed with his camera. Sylvester stood over the steamy sewer in the street in his white fox coat, waiting for the flash to light up the scene.

Many years later, in a letter to a San Francisco newspaper, a man named Paul Wynne recounted a similar moment he'd witnessed in the Castro on a cold, rainy Valentine's Day afternoon around 1979. "I was watching the world from a window table at a neighborhood bar," Wynne recalled. "Outside, a man at the corner was selling silver Mylar balloons at $3 a pop. Sylvester appeared. A week earlier, at the same time and nearly the same place, I'd watched him sporting in black leather pants and full-length white sable coat. This day, he was indistinguishable from others bundled against the cold. He bought a balloon, then stepped to the street and let it go, like releasing a captured bird. It wasn't a big 'look at me' gesture. He loosened his fingers and a shining heart zig-zagged up through a leaden sky toward the heavens. Sylvester watched his offering a few moments, turned, and walked on."

What picture Sylvester would create of himself on any given day was something of a mystery, which was sort of his whole point. "Some days he was butch, other days it was full queen," says David Frazier. "I had no idea who I was going to see from day to day, and I don't think he did either." He had an entire room devoted to his "drags," and he would regularly rummage through it and run wild. But around the house, where he was constantly building something or taking something apart, he was often quietly masculine, "not the raging queen that people thought he was," says John Maley. He still often downplayed his costumes to the press—"You do what you have to do to do what you want to do," he'd say, or "People pay for fantasy"—but he never stopped playing dress-up of one kind or another. He'd talk to a reporter about his "new butch image" while wearing eye shadow. Wearing men's clothing, Sylvester usually looked like a sweet little boy, big-eyed and round-faced. "His butch thing," says his friend Jeanie Tracy, who joined his band as a singer in 1979, "would be fifteen bracelets and hoop earrings and a man's haircut." He wasn't "doing drag," though, says Robert Kingson, "he was being Sylvester."

Even androgyny had become a bit troublesome in much of gay male culture at the time, where being "butch" had high status and "queen" or "woman" was a status insult. "Butch" was moving from subversive role to coercive ideology, setting the tone for decades of gay culture to come. Many men seemed to have forgotten that the hit song "Macho Man" was satire. Being butch became a lot of work, too. The "butch" man, gay or straight, lived—lives—with the constant threat of revealing the queen he had suppressed. He reined her in, leashed her, but if he did not watch out she would strike at any moment, crossing her leg at the knee, laughing at too high a pitch, letting it be known that she liked to be penetrated.

To Sylvester, butch was and always would be no less ephemeral and put-on than feminine drag—though for him, at least, a bit less fun. Butchness might occasionally be useful as a strategy. If people needed to see a man, he might be willing to be one for a while; if they needed to see a woman, he might bring her out. "Are you a girl?" an uninformed fan yelled out at Sylvester's Roseland appearance on Memorial Day of 1979, where Sylvester was dressed androgynously in blue sequined pants and a patterned T-shirt. "Honey," Sylvester replied, "tonight I'll be anything you want me to be." Butchness might just suit his mood on a given day. When he felt like a woman, he was flattered to be mistaken for one; when he felt like a man, he was flattered to be mistaken for one of those, too. But Sylvester had no use for butch as a dogma or a way of life. It was not fabulous, or free, or *enough*. Gender was an everyday choice.

People mistook Sylvester's feminine side for his whole being at their own risk. Sylvester once told Yvette Flunder about the time a couple of men broke into his house while he was asleep; they tied him up, put him in a closet, and started stealing his things. In the closet, it dawned on him that they were stealing his drag—"and my jewelries, child," he told Yvette; he seemed to find a sudden strength. *Now, I may be a queen*, he thought, *but I'm also a two-hundred-and-ten-pound man*. He managed to untie himself, then grabbed a dowel from the closet, burst out, beat the living daylights out of the robbers, and called the police. By the time they arrived, he had the thieves tied up. Don't mistake him for a feather. Don't think just because he's a queen he can't handle his business. And if you want to see what butch looks like, just *try* to steal his jewelries.

"What is butch?" Sylvester would ask his friend and tour manager Robert Pintozzi when the right trigger walked by: a guy in work boots and flannel, an older woman with a cane she wasn't afraid to shake, a little girl in a plaid skirt with a soccer ball, or a drag queen rumored, like most drag queens, to be a voracious top. His tone was mock reflective; his index finger rested mock thoughtfully on his cheek. Or Sylvester would be in the dressing room trying on a new outfit—leather pants or a fedora—and ask Robert if he thought it was butch enough. "What *is* butch?" Robert would respond, after a little pause. Patrick Cowley played the what-is-butch game, too. Sometimes he would put a drumbeat on the synthesizer, and they'd sing a little "What is butch?" song. It was a joke, but also the question of the decade, and none of them once considered proposing an answer.

In the "Mighty Real" video Sylvester made in January 1979, a bikini-clad dancer jiggles through the intro, then points her finger behind her as if to say, "And now, the fabulous Sylvester!" Sylvester sings to you as he walks slowly down a flashing staircase, in a slimming black tunic, black leather pants, and a smart little black leather jacket. His lips are glossy, his hair is in tight black curls, and you can see the gap between his front teeth. He leaves the room, emerging next in a cocktail bar, where several men in teensy-weensy white shorts and tank tops walk in a circle while Sylvester walks toward you in a white suit open at the neck, with sunglasses hanging from one pocket, carrying a white fan. In the next scene, he is in a loose jacket decorated with squiggly lines of silver-black sequins and white tassels at the elbows, and a toque of the same material; on his left hand are six white bangles, and there are two on his right. He is fanning himself rapidly, as if all his flaming has made the room hotter. Then he's gone again, presumably to change his outfit, and in his place are five women in white hot pants doing a short, calisthenic-y disco-dance routine. Sylvester finishes up the song in his black leather pants, this time with a shiny gold open tunic-vest and an invented item of clothing around his waist—a sort of waist-kerchief—also of shiny gold, and then takes his leave, heading back up the stairs in yet another tunic-vest, this one loose-armed and multicolored and sparkly. He *was* the concept.

Really good sex can indicate the existence of God. Some people have also suggested that really good religion reminds them of sex. Michael Eric Dyson, E. Patrick Johnson, and others, for instance, have pointed out that many black church services resemble a sexual encounter: the early part of the service like flirting and foreplay and the eventual ecstasy of a congregation like one gigantic orgasm. Disco was much the same. Barry Walters once called it "the gospel music of sinners," and that's just about right. "The disco scene," Albert Goldman wrote, a bit hyperbolically, in 1978, "may be seen as the often baffling, sometimes sordid, but ever-renewed quest for ecstasy and transcendence." *Saturday Night Fever,* "A Fifth of Beethoven," and roller boogie were all about as spiritual as a plastic bag, but for a lot of people in the hard-core scene, disco was as spiritual an enterprise as it was a sexual one. When it was good, it possessed you, as though you'd been hooked in to something larger than you. You felt like a lit flame. Dancing, music, sex, and God all seemed to come in one package.

In fact, add some drugs and some more white people, and subtract some clothes, and James Baldwin's description of Elisha in church could just as easily be a snapshot from a disco, especially a gay one, in the late 1970s: people crying out, voices rising, the place swelling with some unknown power like "a planet rocking in space"; the body unable to contain its passion, turning with fisted hands and pouring sweat, "on, on, unbearably," until it seemed the walls "would fall for very sound," the body "dancing as though it would never stop." Regulars at the Paradise Garage, the gay black and Latino club where DJ Larry Levan worked three turn-tables and a custom-made sound system, called their clubgoing Saturday Mass. They worshipped to Lorraine Johnson ("Feed the Flame"), Chaka Khan ("I'm Every Woman"), Chic ("Le Freak").

You weren't meant to listen to disco alone at home, unless there was a mirror and you were dancing with yourself. At exclusively gay places like the Tenth Floor and Twelve West, some people clanged little finger cym-bals, others spun T-shirts or lengths of fabric like baton twirlers, others banged bongos or wooden percussion sticks. "They lived only to bathe in the music, and each other's desire, in a strange democracy whose only ticket of admission was physical beauty—and not even that sometimes," Andrew Holleran wrote in his novel *Dancer from the Dance*. "All else was strictly classless. . . . It was a democracy such as the world—with its rewards and penalties, its competition, its snobbery—never permits, but which flourished . . . because its central principle was the most anarchic of all: erotic love."

Holleran described the moment at around six-thirty in the morning "when the air was half-nauseating with the stale stench of poppers, broken and dropped on the floor after their fumes had been sucked into the heart, and the odor of sweat, and ethyl chloride from the rags" clamped between men's teeth, the moment the DJ would let fly the first bass beats of a beloved song—"Don't Turn Around," by the Raes, or Anita Ward's "Ring My Bell," or Cheryl Lynn's "Got to Be Real"—and the dancers would scream. At that moment, their faces "blossomed into the sweetest happi-ness" and "everyone came together in a single lovely communion that was the reason they did all they did." Each E-flat, one of Holleran's characters says, was like the thrust of a penis. Dancing could not be separated from communion. Sex could not be separated from dancing. Memories could not be separated from disco songs.

The Loft had the same basic soundtrack, but going there was like going to a party at a friend's house. In fact, it *was* David Mancuso's apartment in SoHo, and you had to be invited. There were balloons, a table with snacks and punch, and a cadre of regulars who knew each other by sight if not by name. It cost three dollars. The crowd was an organic gay salad sprinkled with straight people, brown, light, poor, woman, dark, uptown, rich, man, all of it. People smoked pot but didn't drink much, and they danced to music about dancing to music. *Music is my way of life,* Patti LaBelle testified. *Ain't no stopping us now,* Risco Connection sang. The dance floor became a model for what might modestly be called an entirely new way of living. When the song said *We are family,* it meant whoever was there, ignoring troubles and shaking their asses.

When Sylvester was in New York, the place he went to most regularly was the Paradise Garage, on King Street. The Garage was open to members and their guests only, but it was, as one former denizen put it, "where hunks and hunkesses of color were most at home," and you were graded not for being known but for "your looks, your moves, your style, your spirit" at a particular moment on a particular night. It had a movie room and a unisex changing room and a Buddha room. Its sound system was among the best in the world, and its members thought Studio 54 was a joke. Sometimes, a guy would set up a complete drum set on the floor beneath the DJ booth and play all night. Some people fanned themselves with dollar bills. "One night a record ended and we were left in hot, sweaty, and silent darkness for ten seconds or so," wrote Carlos Perez not long ago on a Web site devoted to Garage memories. "Then the sound of rain started. A thunderclap or two burst out of one speaker, responded [to] by another thunderclap from the speaker on the opposite side of the room; then torrential rains. Before you knew it there was a tropical thunderstorm going on above and around us while a freezing winter wind blew outside the building. . . . And we were in this safe haven expressing ourselves. All was reaching up; celebrating the joy of the sound of rain." When Larry Levan, the DJ, then started playing Chaka Khan's "Clouds," "the place went up in ecstasy, and when he turned the volume down during the chorus, the entire dance floor was humming along, exactly on the beat, in unison, in harmony."

Others describe feeling that God and angels had led them to the Garage, where they entered bliss and found solace, lost their minds, learned to be sexy, uninhibited, beautiful, and open. Khris Lewis's memory is lovely: "i remember when my coworker told me about the garage he was like it's no need for fancy clothes just come as u r—naw i need to put on my best stuff—he was like naw it's not that type of party. . . . he was like listen brother i am telling you come as u are. . . . once i went in i was hooked—after that night and for every day after i learned—to love people for themselves—gay black white—deep down inside we—have something

high priest's robe," says Bruce Vilanch. "To me, he was kind of a Vegas showgirl version of a voodoo priest."

On a good night, when they were really feeling it, Sylvester would say to Izora and Martha, "We had *service.*" The three of them would be "testifying, straight up, bringing the Holy Spirit on," says David Frazier. "They didn't have to talk about it. They would just get onstage and turn the mother out." They might bring in a gospel tune any time, performing or backstage getting ready, like "Mary, Don't You Weep," or "Lord, Keep Me Day by Day." Whether he meant to be or not, Sylvester was part preacher. You had to be moving your body to hear his sermon. I enjoy who I am, where I come from, and what I'm doing. Watch me be me, he said, then go be you. I won't hold anything back, and don't you either. Live your fantasies and be a star; everyone is one. Truth is joy, and joy is truth. I'll sing while you dance.

When Sylvester performed, he usually carried a fan in his right hand. It was hot up there, and he worked that fan like his mother, and her mother, and maybe her mother, too, fanning themselves and amen-ing at church, wearing hats like crowns.

10.

EVERYBODY IS ONE

The title tune of Sylvester's next album, *Stars,* was a flattering paean to the love you feel for yourself on the dance floor. It was written by Patrick Cowley for Sylvester to perform at a big gay dance party, also called Stars, on a pier in San Francisco. *You are a star,* Sylvester sang for about ten minutes. *Everybody is one. You are a star. You only happen once.* Coming out of Sylvester's mouth, the words were entirely believable. He himself was living proof.

"They can drop the needle anywhere on the record and it's perfectly there," Sylvester said of the album, recorded in early 1979. "It's my first completely disco record, and it will probably be my last." The album was a tribute to the genre itself—a "love letter to disco," as the writer Jake Austen has put it. It consisted of just four very long songs, each its own little world. "Body Strong," written by Sylvester and his keyboardist Michael Finden, has no verses, just Sylvester and the Tons repeating "You make my body strong, ohhh," over horns, blipping synthesizer, and kickdrum, with long orchestral breaks. It was, Sylvester said, "a sort of muscledisco song." The slower "I Need Someone to Love Tonight" set up a relaxed, cocktaily ambience meant to be, he said, "hypnotic." The eleven-minute cover of Lieber and Stoller's "I (Who Have Nothing)," originally recorded by Ben E. King in the early 1960s, began with bass drum and church piano, joined by Patrick Cowley's synthesizers, flashing little bolts of sound, then guitar and cowbell. After a long introduction, Sylvester begins singing about how "she" can buy you diamonds and take you to fancy clubs, whereas *I, I who have nothing, I, I who have no one, must watch you go dancing by, wrapped in the arms of somebody else.* It is pleading, lonely, and very danceable. You can imagine the new diamonds shimmering on Sylvester's hand, as he sang the song in fancy clubs.

The "premiere" of *Stars* was celebrated on March 11, 1979, at the San Francisco War Memorial Opera House where, less than a year before, Harvey Milk's memorial service had been held. Sylvester was one of the first pop acts to perform there—the Pointer Sisters and a few others had beat him to it—and the first disco act. But he was the first gay act, unless you counted *Madame Butterfly*. It was, without a doubt, the biggest night of his life.

If Harvey Milk had been the Mayor of Castro Street, Sylvester was its undisputed First Lady, and his success was both victory and vengeance. Sylvester at the Opera House: that sure was a big, fat, juicy kiss-my-ass to the Anita Bryants, John Briggses, and Dan Whites. This is *our* town, it said. Nobody, Armistead Maupin once noted, "embraces eccentricity as unconditionally and as joyously as do San Franciscans." Sylvester was eccentricity made divine. If you'd known about him from the Palace or the Cabaret or just from seeing him around the Castro with his broad, shy smile and his dogs, you also felt as if your cousin had just become a movie star.

People arrived at the War Memorial Opera House in San Francisco like everybody was a star. Tickets had sold out long before, three thousand, two hundred fifty-two of them, and outside the Opera House people were offering five hundred dollars to anyone with an extra. (It would turn out to be the top-selling event in the country that week in venues holding under six thousand people.) It was a Sunday night, so they'd had plenty of time to arrange themselves. Many people showed up in the fancy dresses and sharp tuxedoes they might wear to an actual opera, but a lot of them took to heart the "optional" part of "black tie optional." Jason Williams, for example, who had not yet met Sylvester but would later become one of his closest friends, tucked his pants into high boots, with a full-length peacoat over an eight-hundred-dollar long-sleeved collarless Yves St. Laurent blouse woven with real gold threads; as a "corsage," he wore "The Hulk," a hunk he'd met recently in Los Angeles. They made a splash, but it had taken work: a lot of people heard in Sylvester's voice the call to fabulousness. There were painted dolls of both sexes. There were men in leather and in boas, women in jeans and in pearls; there were not a few shoulder pads. There was ass out, too. People arrived in limousines and taxis and on motorcycles. "They were coming in helicopters and dropping their asses down on Market Street," says Izora. "*Everything* came to that show. You had sissies, you had gay, you had purple, green, white, black, whatever." A Rolls-Royce dropped off one crew, and another piled out of a garbage truck. "I suppose everyone's dream fantasy for living your life the way you want it is to go to the opera," Sylvester said a few months later.

Inside the Opera House, you could smell the arrangements of gardenias on the stage. From above, the audience would have looked like a bunch of penguins wandering through a field of wildflowers. A man in a well-cut leather tuxedo and a dog collar was being dragged to his seat by a man in a matching leather tux. People were lined up against the golden Opera House walls and standing in the aisles and sitting in the aisles. You might have mistaken the ushers in red hoop skirts for drag queens, until you noted their librarian hairstyles and masks of blank shock. The future San Francisco mayor Willie Brown—then a state assemblyman—was in a booth in the Grand Tier near the Fantasy Records bigwigs. Nearby sat City Supervisor Harry Britt, the openly gay successor to Harvey Milk. Almost every self-respecting homosexual man in San Francisco was somewhere in the crowd, along with quite a few for whom self-respect was plainly beside the point. Some were sipping champagne, and the majority of the audience was probably already high on something else—it just seemed wrong not to be. Below the stage, a twenty-six-piece orchestra was tuning up, while on stage the band's equipment sat ready. At the back of the stage was a pink dome that looked like an upside-down, folded-up vegetable steamer. On each side of the stage was a big easel with flip cards like those in vaudeville shows. Each bore a phrase so pure, right, and San Francisco that it probably made some people quit their jobs: "Flowers While You Live."

Letha Hurd was in the front row, surrounded by fancy, rich San Franciscans. She had driven up from L.A. with her son Alonzo, Alonzo's wife, and her daughter Bernadette, who was hanging out with Sylvester backstage. They sat with Sylvester's old friend and hairdresser Barron, and scattered throughout the audience they could see the other family members who'd made it up for the show. Letha wore an excellent hat. Marapasa was in the center section, Row K, not too far from Peter Mintun. Giana from the Elephant Walk days was backstage, doing Martha's and Izora's makeup and giving the white band members some color in their cheeks. Jeanie Tracy, a singer who had opened for Sylvester a few times and whom he'd invited to be one of the pit singers at the Opera House, was checking her costume backstage. Sylvester wanted her and the other pit singer, Sharon Hymes, to wear black, so Jeanie was wearing her strappy shoes and a cute little outfit she'd made herself: boat neck, long sleeves, fitted waist, and a slit-up-the-middle dress that looked like a beautiful black diaper. She was whispering to herself, "Oh, my God, oh, my *God*, oh, my God."

The pressure was a bit much, and Martha Wash had cotton mouth. It was the San Francisco Opera House, for one thing. There were more than three thousand people out there, not a few of them family members and people Martha knew from playing around town and from singing in church. Then, too, it was a hometown crowd: you wanted to give them your best, and they wanted it from you. Martha was used to a six-piece band with her and Izora, not to a full orchestra and pit singers. A new drummer, Kelvin Dixon, had been hired just that week. On top of that, Fantasy was making a live recording of the show, and you never could be completely sure what Sylvester might do.

Sylvester himself seemed collected, but earlier in the day he had been having fits, on account of glitchy sound checks and rushed rehearsals. Nancy Pitts, who was in charge of the show, had assigned to Robert Pintozzi the task of calming him down. Robert had been his friend before becoming his tour manager and then the stage director for the Opera House show, and his presence tended to affect Sylvester like a bath. Everything was pretty much in place, and Robert had figured the show would run itself. Late in the afternoon, he'd joined Sylvester in a dressing room once occupied, they'd told each other with hands covering their mouths, by Miss Maria Callas herself. The place reeked of diva. Sylvester had locked the door and pulled out a little pillbox. "I have been waiting a long time for this day," he'd said to Robert, "and here it is." He'd given Robert a hit of acid, and taken one himself. He'd painted Robert's eyes with thick, exaggerated black lines, like Joel Grey's eyes in *Cabaret,* and then had made himself up. Robert was about Sylvester's size; Sylvester asked him to stand on the small tailor's platform. Robert, tripping heavily on acid and Callas, had tried on the outfits Sylvester would soon be wearing onstage, while Sylvester pinned this and hemmed that. Robert had decided that the one he loved most was the blue sequined number Sylvester would sport in the second act, as he rose on a ramp from beneath the stage into the spotlight, singing "Lover Man."

Sylvester was peaking right around the time the show was supposed to start, and since it's not advisable to jump into a major performance at an ornate opera house in front of a sold-out crowd in your hometown while peaking on acid, Robert saw to it that the show was delayed until the main event could come down a bit. Bernadette watched him put a little white thing on his tongue. "What is that?" she asked. "Quaalude," he said, and checked his makeup one last time.

When the lights finally came down and the band, accompanied by members of the San Francisco Symphony, started playing a medley of Sylvester songs, the crowd jumped to its feet, screaming. Drums rolled, strings gushed, horns blared. You could feel something like gratitude in the room. "You go to most big concerts for what it's going to give you," Marapasa says, "but people wanted to give *him* something." Jeanie Tracy took Sharon Hymes's hand and prayed to God that she wouldn't suddenly forget everything she'd learned in rehearsals. Martha and Izora were supposed to start singing "You make my body, body strong!" before Sylvester came out, but Martha's mouth was so dry she couldn't sing and they missed their first cue. The contraption onstage opened up and became a giant pink fan. "Ladies and gentlemen, Miss Martha Wash and Miss Izora Rhodes," Robert called into the microphone as Sylvester bounded out onto the stage from the wings, his deep red costume flowing and glimmering, his jewelry flashing and jiggling. Martha and Izora followed, singing now, as Robert called, "And the fabulous Sylvester!" "Fucked that up," Sylvester remarked about their entrance, but nobody seemed to notice.

Glitter and sequins require bright light to do their thing. When they catch bright light they come to life and seem to be in constant motion, flickering like sun on the tips of tiny waves. The Opera House managers had told Sylvester not to throw glitter, since it would be hellish to get it out of the cracks in the floorboards. But tell Sylvester not to do something and watch him go do it. Sylvester entered the Opera House stage in sequins, throwing glitter to each side of him, like a princess scattering silver seeds or a fairy dispensing stardust. When it landed on the orchestra some people swore they got to playing even better.

You make you make you make my body strong, Sylvester and the Tons sang. "Come on, Queen Mother," Sylvester said to Izora, mock-impatiently, when the first song was done. "Come on over here close to me," he said to Martha. "There's plenty of room, honey." Then he turned to the audience. "Don't we look lovely?" he asked.

Bernadette, who had returned to sit with her mother in the front row, watched the audience go mad—screams that lasted too long, sounds that humans don't often make, bodies that leaned toward her brother as if for a hug. A *San Francisco Examiner* reporter, Philip Elwood, described the response to Sylvester that night as "a sheet of vocal sound" that reminded him of the West Point rooting section at the Army-Navy game—more of a response, Elwood said, than Nureyev or Pavarotti got. Bernadette found herself crying, so full that she simply overflowed.

Sylvester's Opera House show, like many other Opera House shows, had three acts and lasted nearly three hours. Its design was operatic, too: an elaborate overture and opening act; a quieter, bluesier center; and a high-energy, allegro closing. The evening began with a gospelized version of Lennon and McCartney's "Blackbird." Sylvester bantered about how the song has to do "with animals, y'all, birds, blackbirds." He asked Patrick Cowley to give him some blackbirds, and Cowley made a cooing on his synthesizer. "Chil', that sound like seagulls," Sylvester said. "I want some blackbirds." Some folks laughed. But when Sylvester and Martha and Izora started in—"Ya'll ready, girls?"—singing about the blackbird who is learning to fly, flying and singing into the light of the dark black night, the blackbird who was just waiting for this moment to arise, it wasn't funny at all. People got goose bumps. "Did y'all get the message?" Sylvester asked just in case, and people cheered. "Are you sure you got the message? We're going to do it for y'all again again, just to be sure you got the message," he said, and their voices shot around each other and around the room. *Blackbird singing in the dead of night! Take these broken wings and learn to fly!* You didn't have to know that Dooni had buried birds with broken wings in rhinestone shoebox-caskets; or that Sylvester had declared two years before that he would sing one day at the Opera House; or that he was high as a bird himself right then. *Blackbird fly! Blackbird fly!* All you needed to know was that it was the dead of night, and you were broken and free, and Sylvester and Martha and Izora were flying around you like beautiful birds. *You were only waiting for this moment to be free!*

The next tune was a duet with the pianist Eric Robinson, a delicate medley of Barry Manilow's "Could It Be Magic" and Leon Russell's "A Song for You." Two men making love with their voices, singing come, come, come into my arms: could this be magic? *I've been so many places in my life and time,* Sylvester sang, and the audience hooted, as if to say they knew where he had been and knew he was home. Robinson, in a high, clear, smooth voice, took a verse. Then Sylvester sang his favorite line of the song: *I've acted out my love in stages, with ten thousand people watching.* The house went silent. "Even though there were thousands of people there, it was still quiet," Sylvester recalled later that year. "It was like one person." *We're alone now and I'm singing this song for you,* Sylvester continued, in harmony with Robinson. *And when my life is over, remember when we were together. We were alone and I was singing this song for you.*

Midway through the concert, while Sylvester sat in a chair onstage fanning himself, Harry Britt, on the order of Mayor Dianne Feinstein—whom Harvey Milk used to call the Wicked Witch of the West—presented Sylvester with the keys to the city. He declared the day to be Sylvester Day, which really just made official what everyone in the room already knew.

Throughout the Opera House show, Sylvester took a series of diva poses, which the audience ate like candy. When someone called out "Syl!" he stopped in his tracks, the demanding diva: "Syl? Do you know me? Turn these lights on. I want to see my friends. Shine the lights over here." The lighting guys seemed to be having a hard time. "Uh, the lights dear," he said, looking up to the booth, and when the technicians finally obeyed him, he thanked them "so very much," with a weary, grand outpouring of breath. Later, he was the diva in love, dedicating a song to his lover, "who is here tonight and who I love very much"—possibly the first time a man had ever dedicated a song to his boyfriend from such a prominent stage. (The moment may have been more memorable for others in the audience than for John Maley, who says: "I remember him dedicating a song to me. I don't remember what it was, but it was very touching.") Later still, moving a stool around, Sylvester was the humble diva: "I still move furniture and things. Nothing's changed. I still wear the same old rags, I still do the laundry. Same old me." At the opening of the second "act," he emerged from underneath the stage as his favorite Ruby Blue diva self: wearing the dark blue sequined number Robert Pintozzi had tried on that afternoon and a silver beaded headpiece that dripped jewels, the microphone cupped in both hands, his face turned upward into the light, his eyes blue-shadowed and lashes heavy and skin glowing, singing *lover man, oh where can you be?*

Mostly Sylvester was just singing and being fabulous, giving and getting love. He dedicated "You Are My Friend," a lesser-known Patti LaBelle song, to everyone in the audience, but it quickly became clear that it was a love song between Sylvester, Izora, and Martha. The lyrics are about looking around and then realizing that what you were looking for was there all the time. Sylvester started telling the story of how they'd met (little studio on Sixth Avenue and Judah; first rehearsal in VW going over Golden Gate Bridge) and how the Tons had stuck with him through everything. "You see, I don't know if y'all have noticed it or not, but these women can sing, y'all," he said. "Honey, your ear has to be in your *foot* to not hear these women can sing. They don't need these dresses. They don't need them jewelries"—pronounced as an exaggerated *jewrees.* "They don't need that hair. These women can sing, y'all." The crowd approved. "Martha, you've been around, girl," he sang, "I know that you've been around." Martha responded by singing strongly and sweetly that she'd been around and you were here all the time, but then she let fly a high *yow-oh-oh-oh-oh-oh-oh* that seemed to shoot people straight up from their seats. "Izora, you've been around," sang Sylvester, "I know you've been around." On her turn, Izora leaned way over, and came up with a long, deep *waaa-aa-aa-aa-aa-aa* growl that sent the audience into such hysterics you would not have been surprised to hear people speaking in tongues. "Sing, Auntie!" Izora's niece called out. In between, the three gathered together, sniffling and hugging while the band played the same couple of lines quietly over and over, and afterward they had to blot the tears from their faces. For the audience, it must have been a bit like suddenly being at someone's wedding, tearful declarations of love and all, so intensely intimate and intensely public. "You Are My Friend" became the only hit from the Opera House live album, *Living Proof,* maybe because it sounds like an open heart.

Letha Hurd had just expected to sit there in the audience and be proud, maybe stand up and take a bow, but near the end of the show Sylvester invited her up onstage. The spotlight touched her and the crowd let out its sheet of sound and jumped up and down. When she had made her way to the stage, people threw flowers at her feet. Sylvester kissed her, and the two of them paraded around the stage from one side to the other. "I felt like *I* was the lady on stage," Mrs. Hurd told the filmmaker Tim Smyth many years later, "like *I* had did the performing."

In the last act, as "Dance (Disco Heat)" was just getting going, Sylvester asked his audience just what the hell they were doing in their seats. "I could just hear the big roar," the drummer Kelvin Dixon recalls, "and I knew everything was just gone. He just set everybody free. The room started to shake." A few minutes in, Eric Robinson starting changing up the song—it was he who had written it—pounding a gospel chord sequence in the middle of his piano solo. Dixon picked up on it, switching the rhythm over from 4/4 to 6/8 and putting a little more emphasis on the high hat. "The pulse changed," he says. Martha and Izora and Sylvester exchanged glances that said, "Okay, we know where this is going." They had been rehearsing all day, and hadn't been to church. They grabbed tambourines. *Disco sound takes me higher.* They started soul-clapping double-time. "I don't know what happened," Sylvester said later, "but the whole thing changed and we had service."

"You know what, you may not understand this, but tonight *is* Sunday night," Sylvester said as the spirit started to rise up. "That's why we carryin' on like we do, because tonight is Sunday night, y'all." *Dance with me in the disco heat. Dance with me in the disco heat.* "It's church, y'all," Sylvester called out. "We goin' to church, y'all." Izora sang a "My my my my my," and Martha sang "Come on, come on." Jeanie and Sharon kept on with "Why don't you dance?" and Sylvester jumped in with a few repetitions of "Come on and dance" in a deep voice. *Get up and dance.* The spirit got higher and higher, and people were going absolutely nuts, shouting and clapping in double-time and dancing like it was gospel hour. "That shit is hypnotic, that steady rock," says Kelvin Dixon. "It transcended." White folks who were used to clapping on the one and three were clapping on the two and four. "If you didn't feel nothing that night, you would never feel nothing in your life," Izora says.

As they moved into "You Make Me Feel (Mighty Real)," Martha heard a rumbling in the building, and then she felt it under her feet. She thought maybe it was an earthquake: it seemed quite possible that the ground was opening right up in the middle of the show. It turned out to be the vibrations from people dancing up in the balcony—which was visibly rocking and swaying—but it felt like another kind of vibration, too. "While we were singing," Martha says, "listening to the roar of those people and their approval, it's like a spirit when you connect. Everybody's thinking along the same lines and it's explosive. They're feeding us, we're feeding them. We have this eruption of kindred souls." *I feel real, I feel real, I feel real, I feel real, I feel real.* The fire marshals almost shut down the place, and you couldn't be sure if they were worried about blocked exits, the bouncing balcony, or all that flaming.

As the sweaty people in tuxedos and gowns and chaps and boas felt their souls rising up, Sylvester brought them back down into their bodies and into his arms for the big finish. In their last few minutes on stage, Sylvester and the band and the Two Tons turned "Mighty Real" into a hymn, slowing it way down. "Y'all know what I mean when I say you make me feel real?" Sylvester asked. "I mean *real*. I know you must have had someone in your life that made you feel real." Jeanie and Sharon slowly sang the chorus, and Izora and Martha improvised on top of it. *Mighty mighty mighty mighty mighty mighty mighty real*, Sylvester suddenly belted out, bluesily. "Have I got a witness out there?" he asked. "Let me hear you." On Sylvester's cue, each section of the Opera House sang *You make me feel mighty real*. After they had all listened to one another sing, Sylvester signaled the band to bring the sound back up and the Opera House audience to all join in. "Come on, let me hear everybody!" Sylvester called, and then the whole place was singing, and it sounded like they were all holding hands.

When Jeanie Tracy first met Sylvester at Honey Records, where she was writing and producing for Harvey Fuqua's gospel group Voices of Harmony, they'd hit it off right away. She'd heard about Sylvester from her brother and from Harvey and Nancy. One day, she'd been working the phones at the Honey office when a creature in a long coat, careful makeup, and a curly, puffy blow-back hairdo had walked in to meet with Nancy and Harvey. "I thought it was just a big woman," Jeanie says. The lady, who of course turned out to be Sylvester, was in the middle of a story, and everyone was laughing. Jeanie had let on that she was getting ready to have a tummy tuck—she'd lost a hundred and fifty pounds—and the big woman was very supportive. "Oh, girl, that's fabulous," Sylvester had said. He'd told her that when she was through with the surgery, he would give her a sequined gown that would suit her just right. She'd asked him his name, and when he told her she was surprised and embarrassed. "I thought you were a woman," she'd said. "Oh, girl!" he'd said, flattered. He'd noticed Jeanie's diamond engagement ring, and whipped out a loupe from a key chain. "Oh, girl, you did good," he'd said, examining the ring up close.

After the Opera House, Sylvester invited Jeanie to sing with him and the Tons at the Circle Star Theatre in San Carlos, where they were opening for Dionne Warwick. She had learned the material already, so her first concern was what she would wear. She did her best to match the Tons' outfits, and her brother did her hair. Sylvester wanted Martha, Izora, and Jeanie in the dressing room with him before the show. They were all singing gospel songs when they heard a knock on the door. It was Dionne Warwick's backup singers, asking if they could join in. After that, Sylvester asked Jeanie to stay.

Jeanie was the baby, but on tour she learned quickly. Izora made sure she knew the rules. "Doesn't nobody come to see and hear about your problems, number one, and number two, you want to give people a show as if you came out and paid the money," Izora says. "I've come straight from the hospital and did shows, and I've went into the hospital straight from shows. You could even be fighting on the side of the stage—I mean *rumbling*—but when you step out on that stage, honey, you all smiles and you ready to do your job. Then you resume the fight after you get through with your show. That's old-school training."

Jeanie learned how to beat her face in the car—with makeup, that is— and how to sleep almost anywhere. For a model, she could watch Izora, who would sometimes be fast asleep in a chair by the side of the stage getting her makeup done while Sylvester was starting the first song, until Robert Pintozzi told her, "Okay, Izora, it's time," at which point she'd whip off her massive glasses and walk onstage blasting like a foghorn. After a while, Jeanie knew to jump on the note she wanted to sing before Martha or Izora stole her part. If she wanted to, she could do like Sylvester did, and dance by Izora, who was blind as a bat and never performed with glasses, and whisper, "Ooh, look at that *fine* man out there." She learned how to change the lyrics onstage to make Sylvester, Martha, and Izora laugh—"You make me feel mighty ill," they liked to sing, and "Cookin' on my feet with the disco meat"—but to do it without the audience knowing.

The schooling Jeanie received could be boiled down to just a few basic principles. First, watch out for your stuff. Back when she had long fingernails, Izora would sometimes glue a diamond to one. She often sang with her eyes closed, too, which was fine until the night she hit a microphone with her hand and the nail broke and the diamond flew off. She stopped the show and made the band members look for the stone on their hands and knees. "I paid *dollars* for that diamond," she says. She got it back and had it made into an earring so it would remain more reliably attached to her person. Sylvester might throw a boa into the audience, but he knew the location of the boa at all times and would track it down at the end of the show. "They'd be trying to steal his rings off his fingers, and baby, we'll stop in the middle of the *show* and get that shit back," says Izora. "We worked too *hard* to get that shit."

Second, watch out for Sylvester's "tricks" and "trade," who were not always as nice as they were cute. In Italy, Sylvester once met a hot little number, who went looking for him in the middle of the night and got Izora's and Jeanie's room number by mistake. "We wasn't getting up to answer no goddamn door," says Izora. "You didn't even want to go to the toilet, it was so fuckin' cold at night in that town." The hot Italian number proceeded to smash down the door.

Third, watch out for Sylvester's hair. In Brazil, his extensions started dropping off onstage and everyone had to run around during light changes picking them up like little caterpillars.

Fourth, watch out for phony smoke. In Mexico, when smoke started flooding the stage while they were singing "Disco Heat," Jeanie screamed and shot off the stage like a rocket and clear out the back of the building. When she realized it was just a smoke machine, Martha and Izora were already leaning against the wall for support, laughing so hard they were crying. When it came time for the harmony to come back in, though, they were right on time.

Fifth, watch out for your money. When they were doing a show in Indianapolis with Grace Jones, the promoter claimed not to have enough money to pay them. "We won't go on until we get all the money," Sylvester said, standing backstage. Jeanie watched as the promoter brought in money, and Sylvester quietly counted it and said, "*All* the money." Sylvester got his money, and Indianapolis got a show. Martha and Izora could also be a danger to the pocketbook. They would charge interest on a borrowed dollar; they'd charge for half a sandwich if someone was hungry, or a cigarette if someone was out.

Sixth, be on time and on cue, or be prepared to be read. "I got my reading for the day," band members would say to each other. If someone was messing up in rehearsal, they would call out, "Somebody read me! I need to be read!" Often, when Sylvester played the aloof, spoiled, childish diva, Robert Kingson says, "you could see a twinkle in his eye and know it was a joke." When it came to professionalism, though, Sylvester was not joking.

"He was never easy to work with," says James Wirrick. "If he was in a mood—just a cranky mood, a bitchy mood—he was impossible." He'd insist on going over and over a section of a song. "I'm thinking, 'Jesus Christ, Sylvester, it's not going to get better than that,'" Wirrick says. "But it wasn't good enough." He knew what he wanted you to do, and he wanted total commitment, and if you were not with his program you were going to hear about it. He might come up with the parts for the horn section in his head, and sing it to the horn players until they got it; if they blew it in a performance the next day, he would look at them coolly on the bus and say, "I heard you children blowing that horn line. That was *not* what I sang to you." Bystanders would see the look—the mouth would start to sour up, the eyes would get a little bit smaller—and quietly scurry out of the way. But "if he read you," says David Frazier, "you needed to be read."

Jeanie never had to worry about being read. "Sister Jeanie," Sylvester would say when they had some time in a tour stop, "do you want to go out with me?" Jeanie was always up for going out. Usually they went shopping. "We're shopping for Jesus, girl!" Sylvester would say, grabbing her hand. In the year or two just after *Step II,* people screamed his name out from cars and followed him into stores asking for autographs. They followed him up the aisles of the supermarket, looking into his cart. "How does it feel to have people know you like that?" Jeanie asked. "Oh, girl," he said, "you know I always wanted it."

If Sylvester was a big brother to Jeanie, he was alternately mother and boss to the band. He kept after Bob Kingson, who was barely twenty, about his dirty clothes and dirty body. "Am I your mother, Bob?" he asked one day, demanding, to everyone else's great amusement, that Bob lift up his arms so Sylvester could take a sniff. Once, after a fight with Nancy Pitts, Bob cried on Sylvester's shoulder. "He didn't look at us just as hired side men," says Kingson. "If you were in the band, you were in *Sylvester.* Maybe it was ego, but it was also his musical old-school concept: You were just part of him." Here the diva's ego and the mother's generosity met: he took care of the band, even loved some of them, because they were part of Sylvester.

In May 1979, when Dan White went on trial for murdering George Moscone and Harvey Milk, police witnesses described him as "a man among men," a good policeman and fireman and an excellent softball player. Psychiatrists testified that he was depressed and that his consumption of junk food, including Twinkies, was both a symptom of his "diminished capacity" and a contributor to it. There were signs around town saying "Free Dan White." When the prosecution played White's tape-recorded confession, four jurors cried. On May 21, a jury of his peers (all heterosexual, all white) convicted him of two counts of voluntary manslaughter, which carried a seven-year, eight-month sentence. Thousands of people marched to City Hall, chanting "Out of the bars and into the streets," "Avenge Harvey Milk," "He got away with murder," and "Dan White, Dan White, hit man for the New Right." Some smashed windows, and some set police cars on fire. The San Francisco police moved into the Castro with riot gear and clubs. They shut down Castro Street and smashed up the Elephant Walk. Some officers stood on top of the Elephant Walk's bar, swinging their batons and shouting "Sick cocksuckers!"

The Elephant Walk reopened the next day. Harvey Milk's friend Cleve Jones organized a birthday party for Milk in the Castro, and around twenty thousand people showed up. "We'll disco right in the police's faces," Jones said. "We have come here from all the old hometowns of America," he said to the crowd, "to reclaim our past and our future and replace lives of loneliness and despair with a place of joy and dignity and love." The partygoers sang "Happy birthday, dear Harvey," smoked joints, drank beer, danced, and, as the journalist Randy Shilts put it, generally congratulated themselves "on the unique homosexual ability to stage a stormy riot one night and then disco peacefully on the streets the next." When Cleve Jones introduced Sylvester, who sang "You Make Me Feel (Mighty Real)," they roared and danced and danced some more.

Some 150,000 people turned out for the 1979 Gay Freedom Day parade. "An army of lovers cannot fail," read one sign. Sylvester, of course, commanded the main stage that day like their general. Even before he took the stage—a flatbed truck—as David Frazier began kicking the bass drum, and Patrick Cowley and Bob Kingson came in with their synthesizer and bass lines, the crowd recognized "Mighty Real" and let out a thunderous cry. Sylvester revved up the song, then dropped it to a whisper and let it rise again. He jumped up and down and banged his tambourine. Some of the band members say they could feel their own skeletons shaking from the crowd's pounding and bellowing.

❀   ❀   ❀

Sylvester had a tendency to turn women he liked into sisters, and so he did with his friend Leslie Stoval, a DJ he had met the year before. Sylvester had introduced himself to her at a black awards ceremony where, sporting her pearls, she was standing in the corner. Sylvester, wearing a big-shouldered, sequined suit, had walked right up to her, given her a look, and said, "Well, *you* are a lady of quality." He wanted to know what such a lady was doing in the music business. "It's pearls before swine," he suggested.

Soon, he and Leslie were each other's regular date for music industry parties, which they called "industry nights." Neither of them liked to go out alone, and Leslie, "a little glamour girl," became his "little upper-class black girlfriend," she says. She put on her pearls and he his sequins, and they drank cocktails and spoke of Europe. Often, Sylvester would just drop by the radio station and keep company with her. She would sit on his lap and they would sing and chat and play records, including his. They would speak in nice tones, admiring the timbre of each other's voices. Leslie was skinny, so Sylvester always looked to feed her. When her shift was over, Sylvester would bring her to his house to eat marijuana brownies, then take her out for tuna sandwiches, macaroni and cheese, and milkshakes.

Sylvester rarely spoke to Leslie or any of his other San Francisco friends about his childhood, but he never lost touch with his family, either. Letha and the twins came to visit every once in a while, and his brother Larry, too, who was drifting around, landed for a brief spell in San Francisco. Sometimes his grandma JuJu sent up something she had cooked. He attended Bernadine's wedding in Los Angeles, wearing a loose African-print robe and a shoulder-length, swept-back wig. (On other visits he dressed as a man, wearing polo shirts and just a few rings.) He called his mother regularly from the road, just to check in. "Ma, this is me," he'd say. "Hello, me," she'd respond. When he was doing a gig in Los Angeles, he'd stop in and see the family. If he was visiting over the weekend, Letha Hurd made sure he went to church with her on Sunday.

He was closest to Bernadette, who came to see him in San Francisco as often as she could. On one visit, Sylvester dressed her up in his black jacket and diamond ring and they went to the Fantasy studio and took pictures there; then he took her out to dinner and to see *The Rose*. The next day they went shopping, and he bought two pieces of antique furniture, plus hats for both of them at the Emporium; she asked him about sex, and in answer he showed her porn videos. By the next visit, Bernadette had met a man who'd swept her off her feet, her future ex-husband. "Oh, my God, no," said Sylvester when he heard, and refused to meet him. "She's gonna be barefooted and pregnant, and gonna have a house full of kids," he told Letha. "Sylvester never wanted me to get married," Bernadette says. "He thought it would take away all those dreams and ideas and unusualness about me. And it did."

Not long after, Letha's family came together for a reunion in Arkansas. Sylvester was scheduled to perform in Memphis, not too terribly far away, so he came over for the reunion. For the big banquet, he did Bernadette's hair and makeup, Letha's hair and makeup, and JuJu's hair and makeup. Bernadette was struck by how much weight Sylvester had gained and by his teal underwear. They sat up and talked late that night, and Sylvester suggested that they drive to Memphis to see what was going on. It was so dark out there in the country that you couldn't see your hand in front of you, and Memphis after midnight wasn't much brighter. Driving through the city, they thought they were the last people on earth. They made a U-turn and headed back over the Colorado River, and as they did a massive rainstorm went with them.

Bernadette is uncomfortable with the usual scary creatures: rats, snakes, spiders. But her worst fear is of frogs. That night, when they stepped out of the car at the motor home they were staying in, they saw that the rain had brought out frogs. In Bernadette's memory, they were oversized frogs, so many that they were perching on top of one another. The ground seemed to be moving. Sylvester bent his knees and told Bernadette to get on. She rode, screaming uncontrollably, on her brother's back into the motor home.

11.

SELL MY SOUL

Right around the time Sylvester became an international disco star, it was decreed throughout the land that disco sucked. The people who decided this were certain of themselves, and they espoused their cause with an enthusiasm that would have been amusing had it not also been ugly. One night in July 1979, for example, the Chicago rock DJ Stephen Dahl and the Chicago White Sox promoter Mike Veeck organized a "Disco Demolition Night" in Comiskey Park during a doubleheader with the Detroit Tigers. For those who brought a disco record, admission was only ninety-eight cents; the plan was to take all the records, throw them in a Dumpster in the middle of the field between games, and blow them up. Handmade "Disco Sucks" banners dotted the park, and in addition to the fifty thousand or so fans in the stands, ten thousand–odd more milled around outside. Inside the stadium, the crowd chanted "Disco sucks" and threw disco-record Frisbees onto the field during the first game. The day was festive and dangerous; one 45 lodged itself between the shoulder blades of a young woman in a tank top. Outside, John Travolta was burned in effigy. There was much drinking.

After the first game, Dahl—wearing military garb and a helmet and accompanied by a waving blond model named Lorelei—rode onto the field in a Jeep and led his "antidisco army" in another long round of "Disco sucks" chanting. Rock and roll blared. The Dumpster of disco records was blown up, and some describe the little vinyl bombs bursting in air as quite lovely, like a homemade fireworks display. Thousands of disco haters ran onto the field, lit bonfires, and tore down the batting practice cage. Apparently, disco had upset them a lot. The White Sox had to forfeit the second game.

Just why disco caused certain people so much distress is not entirely clear, but the combination of professional sports, military symbolism, a blond pinup, rock and roll, fires, and violence may offer a clue. Sure, some people objected to disco's crass commercialism, some to its formulaic musical simplicity, some to the perceived "Me Decade" narcissism and selfishness that disco came to symbolize; it had quickly become boring, and also tacky, in a sad-not-funny way. But these objections don't seem enough to make people light bonfires. The backlash was largely against disco's original and primary advocates. Despite the Bee Gees and John Travolta, disco was still a genre dominated by black artists, especially women; its core fans were still gay, black, and Latino.

There's something familiar about the scene of white people denouncing some form of black music as stupid, lazy, animalistic, and inferior. Jazz, rock, and hip hop, at least until white artists got in on them, went through similar tribulations. (The General Federation of Women's Clubs crusaded against jazz in 1921, arguing that it "was originally the accompaniment of the voodoo dance, simulating half-crazed barbarians to the vilest of deeds.") Often allied with white critics were middle- and upper-class black folks and black clergy, perhaps because denouncing such music was also a means of marking oneself as refined and righteous. At some point in its history, every kind of music coming from black culture seems to have riled some powerful people.

Disco haters weren't happy about the unabashedly female and gay sexuality of disco music and disco culture, either. As Peter Braunstein wrote in the *Village Voice* two decades later, "The real animosity between rock and disco lay in the straight white male. In the rock world, he was the undisputed top, while in disco he was subject to a radical decentering." Being radically decentered can make you want to blow something up. Disco at heart saw things from the point of view of women—black women, especially—and had high expectations of straight men. If you were a straight man, you were expected to be able to give Donna Summer multiple orgasms *and* to be able to dance. Disco favored sparkle, fever, and *le freak*. It checked out your ass and your basket. "Only by killing disco could rock affirm its threatened masculinity," Braunstein wrote. That "sucks" was the word chosen to denigrate disco is no accident.

In any event, by late 1979 the music industry had dropped disco like an extremely hot potato. Albert Goldman, who had written a book-length tribute to the music and its culture the year before, now declared that disco was "like a cartoon—it's just a consumer product." Disco clubs closed. An *Esquire* writer declared that the in crowd was avoiding Studio

54 "as if it were Cambodia." All-disco radio stations abandoned the format as quickly as they'd picked it up. "Radio was still quite powerful and still ruled by a very conservative old-boy network, and there definitely was a strong 'disco sucks' feeling at the level of radio," says Vince Aletti, who wrote about disco and worked at a record label in the late 1970s. Disco never sat too well with the old boys, even the younger ones.

It didn't help that the industry's earlier attempts to capitalize on disco had involved hiring and promoting openly gay men and African Americans. "It was one thing for us to elbow onto the charts and create a little niche for the gay and black markets," wrote Mel Cheren, who in those days was a record executive immersed in the disco scene, and who is gay. "It was something else for us to grab a third of the whole industry, and threaten to take it over completely." Besides, disco was seen as primarily a producer's medium. Music industry executives and radio programmers preferred hit-making, brand-name artists with long-term marketability; unseen producers with a series of one-hit wonders seemed a less reliable business program. "The 'disco sucks' campaign wouldn't have had any effect if it didn't happen within the industry," says Aletti. "They wanted to go back to business as usual, something that they were more comfortable with—rock and roll."

In the first month of 1980, the top-selling U.S. pop albums belonged to Donna Summer and the Bee Gees, but after that the list was dominated by rockers like Pink Floyd, Bob Seger, the Rolling Stones, Queen, and Bruce Springsteen, and then the next year by R.E.O. Speedwagon, Styx, Foreigner, Journey, and AC/DC. The song that took over America in 1980 was Pink Floyd's rock anthem "Another Brick in the Wall," which was usually chanted while pounding a fist into the air.

It's not that the taste for dance music suddenly died; Europeans and South Americans were still buying disco records, for one thing, and even in the United States disco continued under different names. In 1980, for instance, Blondie's "Call Me," Lipps, Inc.'s "Funkytown," and Michael Jackson's "Rock with You" were Top 10 singles. "A lot of the New Wave music of the early eighties was disco that just didn't call itself disco," says Barry Walters. "It's got the same tempo and the same instruments. It doesn't have the symphony orchestra, but it's got everything else, and you can dance to it. And people like Madonna or Michael Jackson, they were just about as disco as anyone else." But as far as marketing was concerned, the disco tag suddenly became toxic. Major labels scrambled to reclassify, or simply drop, anything that smelled of disco—anything like, say, Sylvester.

The San Francisco DJ and record producer John "Johnny Disco" Hedges was at the 1980 *Billboard* Disco Forum with a bunch of dance records out, a couple of them climbing up the charts. The year before, when Sylvester was taking home all the awards, there had been a brash confidence at the convention, but this year there was an edge of nervous energy. At the New York City Gay Pride parade a few weeks earlier, Hedges took a Polaroid of a gay man standing against a lamppost wearing a "Disco Sucks" T-shirt. "Uh-oh," he thought, and he was right.

Fame is known to be powerful enough to make hatred go limp, but it works more like a narcotic than like surgery: the hatred perks back up after the initial buzz. At first, fame works mostly as a buffer: a star is an individual, above and beyond any social category; a star, by definition, is loved, not despised. But as time wears on, and a famous person becomes more familiar, the shield morphs into a bull's-eye; the star becomes a target for ordinary contempt, magnified and purified by the star's visibility. Often, in fact, the star status gets turned against the star, whose above-it-all elevation becomes another reason to hate her. The dynamic has been especially pronounced with respect to American black stars who have the audacity to behave as if their place is above rather than below.

Sylvester had encountered plenty of racism just by being black and alive; he ignored it, or pushed his way through it if need be. "Sylvester didn't take no shit," Izora Armstead says. Most of the time, though, he seemed content to let other people worry about black and white, while he just went about the business of being himself. He wasn't black in the political-movement sense, any more than he was gay in the political-movement sense; "gay" and "black" were facts of him, but they rarely became his causes. He didn't talk much about race and racism, even with black friends like Tom Martin and Ed Shepard, whom he'd met through a friend after a show in New York City. "Sylvester just *was* a black guy," says Tom. "He loved black culture, but it wasn't an 'I love my culture' kind of thing—he just was. It was just in him."

On occasion, though, being black and famous was enough to invite trouble—as it did in March 1980. Sylvester had flown to New York to perform at Madison Square Garden and the Felt Forum, and to do a bit of recording. Tom and Ed took him sightseeing around town in yellow cabs, and they rode the subway up to Harlem and walked around. They ate deli sandwiches and coleslaw and watched cartoons from a suite at the St. Moritz Hotel, looking out over Central Park. There was still some snow on the ground, so Sylvester wanted to go to the park in his full-length white fox coat "to get some pictures of me playing in the snow," he said. Before he'd gotten around to that, though, he had done an interview and photo session for *Black Agenda Reports,* gone to a party for Patti LaBelle, and stayed up until four in the morning at a studio called Blank Tape mixing some of his tunes. The next day, Sylvester gave interviews at the hotel to reporters from *Soul Teen,* UPI, *SoHo News,* and *New York* magazine. He wore beaded Bo Derek braids and told UPI that although he was "not into material things at all," he liked diamonds "as much as people." After the interviews, Ed hung out with him in the suite, just for company, and Tom came in after work. They listened to some of the recordings Sylvester was working on, Tom and Ed trying to contain their awe.

That evening, Sylvester wanted to get his nails done nearby; Tom and Ed were going to tag along and then they'd all get something to eat and have some fun. They were laughing their way out of the revolving door when two white men claiming to be police officers asked them to step back into the lobby. "That's him," said a third white man as they went in. At first Tom, Ed, and Sylvester thought it was a joke: the only police they encountered regularly were the fashion police, and these men were not fashionable. When the men insisted that Sylvester come with them, though, Sylvester started to panic. "I didn't do anything," he repeated, as he was escorted into a first-floor security office in the hotel. Tom ran up to get Harvey and Nancy.

Sylvester was being held, the men told him, for armed robbery and grand larceny, in charges stemming from the holdup of a coin dealer and a bogus check. The man who'd identified Sylvester ran a coin dealership off the St. Moritz lobby. He claimed to have been robbed that day of $15,000 cash and $10,000 in rare dollar coins by two men, and said he recognized Sylvester as one of them. He quoted to police Sylvester's instructions to "give me the cash or we'll blow your head off," which sounded to people who knew him about as likely as Dorothy giving instructions to slit Toto's yappy little throat. A dealer at another coin gallery, who turned out to be a friend of the first accuser, had then come forward and claimed that Sylvester had bought $30,000 in coins the day before and paid for them with a bogus check from the East New York Savings Bank. The police took Sylvester out of the hotel in handcuffs, and down to the precinct on Fifty-fourth Street, and then to police headquarters. As the police shuffled him toward the car, photographers surrounded him, flashing. Ed threw himself on the car to block some of the photos, but Harvey Fuqua was of a somewhat different mind. "You know," Ed recalls Fuqua saying, "all press is good press."

Sylvester spent the night and much of the next day in jail with six drag queens and the (not yet convicted) murderer of Congressman Allard Lowenstein. The drag queens admired Sylvester's teeth, which he'd had impeccably done several months earlier. They wanted to know just who he was, since a queen with teeth that good has got to be *some*body. Sylvester later told Tom and Ed that the drag queens made him feel protected, but to the press he daintily maintained that he had never before seen the inside of a jail cell, that he felt "distinctly uncomfortable in the presence of rapists, prostitutes, and murderers," that the whole thing "was a nightmare."

The nightmare was probably not so much the jail experience itself. Sylvester had, after all, been "on location" in L.A. County jail as a lingerie-stealing teenager, and street queens were neither unfamiliar nor frightening to him. The shock of being treated by the press as a criminal, though, was a different story. The arrest was all over the TV news: six o'clock, eleven o'clock, the next morning. The newspaper coverage was widespread, accusatory, and riddled with painful puns: "Cops say disco star danced off with stolen coins," said the *New York Post*; "Sylvester's Sour Note," read the *San Francisco Examiner*; "The Check That Bounced to a Disco Beat," said UPI.

The district attorney's office quickly discovered that the robbery charge had been fabricated by one man to support the bad-check charge of the other. A *Black Agenda Report* writer confirmed that he'd been interviewing Sylvester while he was supposedly threatening to blow people's heads off and passing bad checks. The police dropped the charges before the complaint had even been formalized. Sylvester took a lie detector test conducted by a certified polygraphist named Nat Laurendi. (See Sylvester strapped into a device, the needle rattling and the ink dancing on the page.) Reading Sylvester's chart, Mr. Laurendi concluded that Sylvester "did not commit the crime as alleged in the complaint, in the St. Moritz Hotel or anywhere else." Sylvester told a crowded press conference the next day that he was eager to get back to San Francisco and finish his album and relax. (See Sylvester through the medusa of microphones, putting up a brave front.) "I trust God will see me through this," he said. He'd been calm through the whole ordeal, he told a reporter, and his doctor was concerned that he might later explode unexpectedly. Therefore, Sylvester said, when he returned to San Francisco "they'll shoot me up with drugs and get me to cry and freak out." He planned to undergo hypnosis, too, although he never did.

Sylvester and his lawyers claimed that the bad-check scheme was the dastardly deed of a Sylvester impersonator. Although that might have sounded unlikely, a doppelgänger, Michael T. Henson, was in fact caught weeks later. He had on several occasions passed himself off as Sylvester, cashing bad checks and the like, and was arrested after being shot in the foot by an angry jeweler. Sylvester's lawyer, Ted Rosenblatt, made sure to tell the press that Michael Henson, in addition to committing fraud, weighed considerably more than Sylvester.

After he was released from jail Sylvester went to stay with Tom and Ed, where nobody could find him. That he was starring in another scene from another movie, or maybe several—the innocent accused, shielding her eyes from the flashbulbs; the glamorous star befriending the prison gals while New York City cops track a mysterious, fat imposter—would not have escaped him. But Sylvester responded to the arrest with despair so deep and visceral that it frightened his friends. He refused to talk to anyone but Tom, Ed, and Tim McKenna, his good friend and road manager. He vomited and then, Tom says, lay trembling in a heap "for days." He wouldn't even eat.

It is certainly traumatic when admiration is suddenly withdrawn. It is even more sickening to be defamed by ignorant, petty, powerful people just when you thought you were finally being celebrated. Sylvester had blasted through, his voice not just heard but beloved, his shameless refusal of social boundaries transformed from ridiculous to heroic. He had been male and female as he felt them. He had sung at the San Francisco Opera House. But one pointed finger reduced him to the Black Man, who looks like all other Black Men, who are perpetual suspects. If Sylvester had dreamed that stardom would be his protector, he had been shaken awake. He shivered and threw up as if he'd been poisoned.

When the forces you're trying to float above reach up and try to grab you, the best you can do is wriggle yourself clear, go where it's safe, and plot your revenge. Sylvester picked himself up and got ready to go home and record his next album. He joked about it to the press, saying he was going to record "Jailhouse Rock" and call the album *Accused . . . and Exonerated*. Then he sued his accusers for $80 million, dropping the case only after he'd watched them sweat for a while.

A couple of nights before Sylvester's return to San Francisco, he and Ed were hailing a cab on the corner of West End Avenue and 103rd Street, near Tom and Ed's apartment. They heard someone call out Sylvester's name. It was one of the drag queens he had met in jail. Sylvester waved. "Hi, girl!" he called, flashing his beautiful teeth. "You're out!"

Back home, Sylvester was something of a family member at Fantasy Records in Berkeley. He dropped by periodically like a visiting cousin, bearing gifts, dogs, and demands for attention. He'd open up his little pouch of diamonds and show off the new ones. He taught Phil Bray, an in-house photographer and the last person on earth you could picture with a blush brush, how to apply an even base of makeup to a subject and then build the face from there. He always noticed if someone was wearing something new, and Sylvester complimenting your outfit was something like Beverly Sills telling you she liked the way you hum. Even now, the art director, Phil Carroll, proudly remembers Sylvester's commentary on his new hiking boots ("You look great in your Castro clone shoes, chil'!") and on a bright new sweatshirt ("That's a fabulous shade of fuck-me red").

A Sylvester visit also often involved some minor drama, usually around whatever photographs of him were in the pipeline. "He was obsessed with his physical appearance," says Jamie Putnam, who was an assistant art director back in the days when photo retouching was done by hand. "I did a lot of retouching. Even *after* he had his nose done, I always had to do his nose." Once, looking over photos for an early album cover, he'd spotted borzoi hair on the black gauze top he'd worn for the shoot. "The best-trained eyes in the world would not have noticed," says Phil Carroll. "But he saw it. He would not allow a picture of him with dog hair." The photo was retouched. Other sticking points were an angle on his new nose that didn't look quite right, or a fatty bulge he wished would go away. Any photo that made him look fat would have to be airbrushed. He asked nicely, but his perfectionism, inherited from generations of divas he admired, drove some people batty. Once, when Sylvester asked for one touchup too many, Jamie Putnam simply threw his photos across the room. Sylvester could be a pain in the ass, and anyway she had "never understood why he wanted to look like an ugly woman." Sylvester often showed up with his own photos, taken by some well-known photographer in Los Angeles or New York and almost always too expensive or too queeny for Fantasy to use.

In a conservative industry and with disco crashing, the Fantasy Records honchos—referred to by everyone else at the label simply as "upstairs"—were extra concerned about both costs and Sylvester's image. Black record stations in particular were never enthusiastic about playing music by an openly gay—and, as *Jet* invariably and winkingly described him, "flamboyant"—artist. Every time a station turned down his records, "it called into question how he was handling his career," says Terri Hinte, who worked downstairs but was in close contact with upstairs. "They weren't playing the guy's records, because he's too outrageous, too outrageously gay. At the time it really felt like if we did what he wanted to do, he'd just be dismissed. He'd be defined by that and the music would be completely overlooked."

Fantasy wanted to Teddy Pendergrass him. Pendergrass had become a soul star with lady-killer songs like "Close the Door" and "Turn Off the Lights," and he wore open shirts with gold chains. Molding Sylvester into something similar could be a challenge, the Fantasy folks knew; he had, after all, worn skirts on television shows and sung to his boyfriend at the Opera House. As the writer James Earl Hardy has put it, while Pendergrass "had women throwing their panties at him on stage, Sylvester was *wearing* them."

Yet, asked if he would please tone it down a bit, Sylvester said maybe. He liked to live well, he was not above trying things that might get his music heard, and anyway he had by then taken up a stage style more Temptation (white sequined suits, large shoulder pads) than Supreme. Sylvester went along with the Fantasy makeover program in bits and pieces, just as he had tried to do a few years earlier. One great advantage of androgyny is how mutable it makes you: a slight change in clothing, hair, or gait can bring the man or the woman into view. Sylvester agreed to photo shoots with his long weave pulled back into a ponytail, so that it looked like a man's close-cropped hair, and to photos that were glam in a GQ–ish way. Even Sylvester's debonair look, though, was not what you might call conventionally mascu-line. In any photo of Sylvester in boy drag, there was always a tell: the placement of a kerchief; the presence of tassels or horizontal zippers; a couple of bangles; shoes that were just a little too sweet; the way he sucked in his cheeks or held a cigarette.

Sylvester began talking to reporters about his "new image," which involved, one shocked journalist recounted, his own hair, slacks, and "a simple shirt that is almost a T-shirt." Sylvester promoted the idea that "the media have built this disco thing up out of all proportion in my case" and that "there is so much more to Sylvester." He did not like, he said, having to "live up to somebody else's image and concept of me." He claimed— falsely, as any friend or even record company colleague would have known—that the whole fantasy-outrage approach had been "somebody else's idea in the first place, anyway," and that he was relieved to no longer "have to put on an act of being something other than what I truthfully am." He called his next album, released in 1980, *Sell My Soul*.

The last thing I'll do is change up on you, Sylvester sang on the album. *If by chance I reach fortune or fame, I'll still be me, I'll be the same. You won't catch me in those funny games.* But the album felt like a bit of a funny game. Before Sylvester started recording it, he said he planned to experiment with rock and New Wave. He went on to say that he'd be using "top-notch New York musicians" and the New York Community Choir, and "plenty of original material, some that I have written." But *Sell My Soul* turned out to be a tame soul-dance album, with a couple of soupy bal-lads, just one song Sylvester helped to write, no choir, and a puzzling rock-and-roll version of "Cry Me a River." Some of it—songs like "I'll Dance to That," "Sell My Soul," and his cover of "Fever," funked up with cowbells, congas, and bongos—was like a less inspired *Step II*: lots of strings and horns, 4/4 disco beats and funk bass lines, churchy background vocals. It was notable for the absence of familiar musician-friends and the presence of strangers. Martha Wash joined backgrounds on just one song, and Izora on none; Jeanie Tracy sang on a few, James Wirrick played on two, Patrick Cowley on none. Otherwise, the musicians were new. The album was recorded in two weeks.

Mike Freedberg, who the year before had praised Sylvester's vocals for seeming to "visit the outer limits of the universe," wrote that on *Sell My Soul* he "makes his points without charm." It was, the music critic Ian Cranna later wrote, "a very average album." It had the sound of compromise.

❊ ❊ ❊

Sylvester was ambitious and sometimes impressionable, but when push came to shove he seemed constitutionally incapable of selling his soul. "I may be queer," he liked to say, "but I'm no whore." When she heard that Fantasy was trying to make Sylvester over, Martha Wash thought, *Oh, child, please. Good* luck. "You tell him not to do it, he gonna do it, okay? You tell him no, he was *gonna* find him a way to get his point made, some kind of way." He certainly was impatient with attempts to restrict him, perhaps because he recognized that conformity was often not just dull but also, and relatedly, a total rip-off, in that it relied on the questionable judgments of fearful people. He might play himself down to reporters, and give something different a try on an album, but he would no sooner let people dress him up in shame than in a fat-revealing outfit or a black blouse littered with borzoi hair.

For the cover of *Sell My Soul*, Sylvester arranged for a photo session with a gay photographer. He brought in to the record company photographs of spurting champagne bottles: foam shooting all over his face, running out of his mouth and down his shirt. These were to be the cover photos, he insisted. "Up to this day," says Phil Carroll, "I'd say the world is not ready for most of those pictures, including the ones he picked as his first choices." Jamie Putnam found them "grotesque." Terri Hinte, who had just taken over as Fantasy's publicity director, told him there was no way to put these pictures on an album cover and take it to a black music station. Phil Jones, then vice president of promotion and marketing, agreed. Jones had spent years at Motown, and was on the front lines with radio programmers. "We're not going to put that out," he said. "It's suicide."

In the stories Sylvester told of ignoring the rules, his character was not so much a revolutionary as a grand queen (though the difference between the two is smaller than often imagined). He would be imperious, self-righteous, bratty, and well-dressed. One day, toward the end of his time with Fantasy, Sylvester arrived at the offices in a blond wig and gown. He waved to Jeanie Tracy, whose hand on her own mouth was the only thing keeping her together. He walked up and down the halls and sashayed up to the president's office in what might best be described as a minor act of gender terrorism. "Is this butch enough for you?" he asked. "You can change my image, but I ain't changing shit," he said, or liked to say he said.

"This *is* the image." One imagines him turning on his heel, Disquotay hair slapping the air, and marching right out.

Sometimes when Sylvester told this story, his memory costumed him in a "drag queen purple negligee or robe or something." For one of his birthdays, Terri Hinte had sewn him just such a thing, a kimono-style, floor-length bathrobe of sheer, purple, honeycomb-patterned cotton. Terri and Sylvester had a quiet understanding: now and then he allowed her to rein him in for publicity purposes, and now and then she allowed him to let out her reins. Sylvester being Sylvester, their intimacy found its outward expression in clothing, hair, and makeup. One night, he agreed to be Terri's date at a benefit—Bobby Hutcherson, Herbie Hancock, and Wayne Shorter at the Opera House—for a Mark Spitz lookalike named Conrad Silvert who was battling testicular cancer. Sylvester invited Terri to his house to prepare. He smoothed out her frizzy hair with a hot iron and made up her face, which was usually as calm and direct as her demeanor, in supermodel style. She wore baggy dark green raw silk pants and a gold silk blouse, and Sylvester loaned her his café-au-lait-colored cashmere cape and separate cashmere wrap. Both cape and wrap were hemmed with sable pelts. She was so fabulous that a lot of people didn't recognize her. "I've never looked that way," she says. "He just dressed like Joe Blow. So I was the star."

Terri was not the kind to call attention to herself—the job of getting attention for others suited her well—but when Sylvester invited her to Tim McKenna's birthday party, she pulled out a red blouse that she'd bought in Brazil and then had deemed too tiny and too *too* to wear in polite company. Her hair was gigantic, and when Sylvester saw her he fawned and gushed. "He was really the only person I could dress that way for, in drag," she says. She wore the tiny red Brazilian blouse with black linen pants that went zooming outward from a tight waistband and then back down to a tight cuff. "It was just this screaming outfit," she says, "almost like a heart."

Sylvester gave in on the *Sell My Soul* cover, mainly because of his affection for Terri. There would be no spurting champagne bottles. On the actual album cover, Sylvester looks out from under sunglasses. You can barely make out his long braids or the fact that his shirt is cut to reveal the shoulders and has buttons along the top, because half-inch wavy black stripes run across his image.

Like *Sell My Soul,* Sylvester's final album for Fantasy, *Too Hot to Sleep,*
was recorded without the Tons. With Sylvester's cautious consent, Harvey
Fuqua had produced their 1980 album, *Two Tons o'Fun.* It did well, with
club hits like "Earth Can Be Just Like Heaven" and "I Got the Feeling."
Patrick Cowley, whom Sylvester had fired on the grounds that synthesizers were outdated, played synthesizers on the record. Harvey started to
get calls for the Two Tons as a solo act. That same year, they recorded a
second album, *Backatcha.*

As soon as their management contract was up, they were going to go
their own way, Izora and Martha told Sylvester and Jeanie Tracy. Jeanie
cried, and Sylvester pleaded with them to stay, upset that they were aban-
doning him while he was still with Fantasy, where he no longer wished to
be. He'd always featured "the girls" up front with him, even given them a
solo spot at a big show in Madison Square Garden, but now they were
really stepping out. "He cried and tried to get us to stay," says Izora, "but
management had fucked that up completely. The only problem we had
was management." (Neither she nor Martha cares to elaborate.)

They still sometimes performed with him, but in 1981—the year of *Too
Hot to Sleep*—Martha and Izora officially left Sylvester's act. "The management," Sylvester sniffed vengefully to a *Black Stars* interviewer in
1981, "took them away and forced them into this solo career I don't feel
they're ready for." They seemed ready, though. NBC's *Real People* showed
Izora and Martha singing, eating, and chatting. *Ebony* profiled them, with
two pages of the Tons performing, getting made up, sitting around
Martha's parents' house, playing pinball, and bowling. They were a *Village
Voice* centerfold. When they were informed that an Oklahoma gospel act
had been registered with ASCAP since 1958 as Two Tons of Fun, they
changed their name to Two Tons, and eventually to the Weather Girls.

On their next album, 1983's *Success,* on Sony, the Weather Girls would
pronounce "It's Raining Men." A lot of people, especially gay men, were
excited to hear that men who were tall, blond, dark, mean, rough, tough,
strong, and lean were falling from the sky. The song took off, and the
Weather Girls with it. "Oh, Sylvester," someone later made the mistake of
saying to Sylvester in a club where "It's Raining Men" was playing, "they
got you out*done.*"

✿   ✿   ✿

On *Too Hot to Sleep,* Sylvester changed things up again. On the liner notes, he announced that since he, Jeanie Tracy, and his new background singer, Maurice "Mo" Long, all grew up in the Church of God in Christ, they'd now be calling themselves the "C.O.G.I.C. singers."

Some of the songs, like "I Can't Believe I'm in Love," "Can't Forget the Love" and "Can't You See"—the latter two written by James Wirrick, who was back in force on the album—were old-style Sylvester: one a slow-groove soul song, one a ballad, the other a bouncy dance tune, all with Sylvester in falsetto over C.O.G.I.C. gospel call-and-response backgrounds. One, "Give It Up," featured Jeanie Tracy on lead vocals. None of the songs had the orchestral markings of disco.

Others sounded as if Sylvester had stepped back and let another man sing lead. "There is an element of shock value," he said. At a gig at the Boarding House that summer, he began the concert in falsetto and then warned the audience that something new was about to happen. "Don't worry, it's all me," he said, and sang several songs in a straight baritone croon.

Tip Wirrick had been trying for years to get Sylvester to sing in his deeper register, but he had repeatedly refused. The timing was now right to experiment with public maleness: the pressure from Fantasy, combined with the encouragement from Harvey, who loved Sylvester's baritone, met up with the force named Jeanie Tracy. Sylvester and Jeanie had been working on a duet called "Here Is My Love" that Sylvester had written for the album. Sylvester wanted to sing high, but Jeanie wasn't having it.

"Look, there's not gonna be two women up in here," she'd told him. "It's only one, so you've got to be the man now. You need to sing in your deep voice."

"Oh, girl," Sylvester had said, but he gave it a try. There wasn't a whole lot left to lose.

Not only "Here Is My Love" but also several other cuts featured Sylvester singing without falsetto, including the title song, in which he talked between verses about being *too hot to sleep,* about *laying there holding myself* when he'd *much rather be holding you.* His baritone was pretty and surprising, if somehow also blandly George Bensonish. Some of Sylvester's closest friends loved hearing him singing deep: it sounded like the person they knew, and they knew it took courage for him to try out that voice in public. Some strangers were also impressed. A *San Francisco Chronicle* reviewer described Sylvester as "right in the virile baritone mainstream; say, somewhere between Billy Eckstine and Robert Goulet." The caption on the accompanying photo was: "SYLVESTER, Virile baritone."

Many listeners, though, thought Sylvester was doing an unconvincing job of being someone else. Musically inclined people often told him that his falsetto, unlike most, sounded natural. His deeper voice seemed, somehow, less real and less mighty. One critic complained that his baritone was "wobbly and unbelievable," his torch singing "strained and foolish," the songs too "full of esses" to fit the love-man genre he was entering. "It was as though Diana Ross had suddenly begun to take hormones," said the reviewer of the Boarding House performance, though the audience had cheered Sylvester on. "Sylvester," Guy Trebay concluded in a *Village Voice* review of *Too Hot to Sleep,* "is suffering from gender discomfort." Whether Sylvester himself was uncomfortable or others were uncomfortable with his fey incursion into macho-crooner territory, some intangible alchemy slipped away with the falsetto. The baritone was him, too, but without magic.

Sylvester dedicated a song he wrote called "New Beginnings," which opened and closed the album, to himself. He, Jeanie, and Maurice Long made chords with their voices; the song had no words.

The cover of *Too Hot to Sleep* shows a house in the desert. Sylvester is not pictured. In front of the house is a large cactus.

In December 1979, *Black Stars* magazine had featured Sylvester, along with model the Beverly Johnson and singers Freda Payne, Teddy Pendergrass, and Valerie Ashford and Nick Simpson, in a goopy feature on what the stars wanted for Christmas. "All I want for Christmas is to be left alone with someone I love," Sylvester said. He sometimes told people that fame "destroyed my personal life and my romance." It made him and John Maley, he told a reporter, "become something different from what we planned. . . . We could have been very, very happy together—enjoying the success. But the pressures of success, the identity crisis, the ego problem—they've all taken their toll." Some of that hand-to-brow description was probably high-price-of-fame copy for the press. But there was more than a hint of disillusionment, as though the life Sylvester had sought might not be the life he wanted. "It's very sad," Sylvester said, "because I know when it's all over and done, what do you have left but the person you love and who loves you?"

Sylvester's album notes always thank his family and a pile of friends and colleagues, of course; nearly every one also thanks a different man, and each one sounds like *the one*. Sylvester's friends tend to have a hard time recalling his boyfriends in great detail, which may be because the men had much in common with one another—they were generally white, self-doubting, and effeminate—and because they generally disappeared after a couple of years, to be replaced by someone new and similar. Sylvester had a habit of finding wounded men, loving and dressing them up into some semblance of self-esteem, showing them that they could be whoever they wanted to be, and then watching as the relationship grew out of itself.

Sylvester dedicated the *Too Hot to Sleep* ballad "Can't Forget the Love" to John Maley, the same lover to whom he'd dedicated a song from the Opera House stage. It was a good-bye song: *I need your love so desperately, make this moment last. I can't forget the love that you gave to me, oh baby, and I won't forget the joy that you gave to me.* That year, John decided to move to Los Angeles to pursue his career as a model and make-up artist. "The very thing that I fought to keep together was my personal private life," Sylvester said in an interview with Frankie Crocker, "which was the first thing to fall apart."

"She was a lovely man, and I owe him a lot," says John Maley. "He gave me a sense of responsibility within myself, to believe in myself. By his lifestyle I believed in myself, that I could do anything, and I did. He was very helpful and gracious, but a queen doesn't sit there and take a queen's money. I needed to get my own." Sylvester could not argue with that, and he never for a second considered moving back to Los Angeles, so he had to watch John go. Many years later, he told a friend that he had been "truly, deeply, utterly in love" with John. "That bitch took me *through* it," he said.

That same year, 1981, Sylvester met Michael Rayner, an attractive, skinny, insecure, depressed brunette. Michael grew up in Deep River, Connecticut (population: 3,000); he quit college at age twenty, and then got in his car one morning and drove to San Francisco, where he got a job at a heterosexual fern bar in the financial district. Sylvester visited the bar from time to time, and he and Michael would quietly make eyes at each other. In 1981, when they met at a party, Michael was attracted to Sylvester's smile, deep laugh, and manliness. ("There was definitely a strong female side to him," Michael says, "but even if he had the big wig and all the makeup, I still saw a man there.") Sylvester asked Michael to the opera. Michael wore traditional black tie, while Sylvester's formal wear was more interpretive: a white shirt with a brooch where the tie would go. They both wore very long black coats. At dinner, they confessed that they'd been admiring each other from afar; they became boyfriends immediately. After that first night, Sylvester began planning a trip for them to Hawaii.

In San Francisco, though Michael and Sylvester didn't officially live together, they spent most of their time at Sylvester's three-story place on Corbett Avenue, which John Maley had shared until a few months before. The place was all chrome, glass, and lacquer. A French art deco armoire dominated the bedroom, and in the living room a chrome-and-brass deco vase sat atop a glass-top deco table. Over the sofa in the living room was a big red kimono in a Plexiglas frame. Sylvester offhandedly told Michael that he would be laid to rest in that kimono, and that he had already found the lipstick to match. They ate, watched television, and listened to music, and Michael felt peaceful. "Syl was a homebody," says Michael. He thought he recognized a familiar melancholy—not self-hatred but sadness, what Timmy McKenna called a "bad patch." When one of them hit a bad patch, they would just get take-out chicken and not leave the house for days, and it was all okay.

There was much trying on of clothes. Together, they looked a little like Jack Sprat and his wife. Sylvester was in a zaftig period, and Michael was five eleven and a hundred and forty pounds—"a toothpick." Sylvester didn't pay that any mind. "Michael," he said, "one size fits all." Michael loved Sylvester's fox coat, which had an accompanying scarf with red fox-tails hanging off it. That was a lot of coat. Sylvester loaned it to Michael a few times to wear at his job as a cocktail waiter at Alta Plaza, a gay piano bar in Pacific Heights where people wore sweaters tied around their necks. Sitting in Sylvester's Fiat on the way to the bar, Michael was more fox than man, but he swirled into work like a star. Michael did not respond to most people's compliments, which felt to him like pretty lies that confirmed his lowness, but when Sylvester said, "You're fabulous," it seemed simply to be a natural fact. He was Michael, and that was enough. "What you *are* is beautiful," Sylvester said, and Michael believed him.

The sex was great, but out of bed Michael and Sylvester became more like brothers. "It was a lot for me just that someone loved me, and I felt so lucky that I returned it," Michael says. "It's so clichéd, but you can't really like someone until you like yourself." Michael had grown into himself enough to recognize that he was not in love and that he could not be what Sylvester wanted, and he told Sylvester so.

"So it's not like you're madly in love with me," Sylvester said, over a restaurant lunch, when Michael broached the topic. When Michael allowed that he was not, he thought that would be the beginning of the end. "But it *was* the end. For [Sylvester], there was no easing off."

Perhaps Sylvester suffered the curse of the control queen and the narcissist: he chose controllable and adoring partners, only to find that they were not self-possessed enough to meet him where he wanted to be met. But his was also the curse of the generous and gentle-hearted. He used the nurturing talents that Letha and JuJu gave him, teaching people, with just a coat or a diva's self-confidence, that they, too, were loved and fabulous. When he succeeded, they were ready to go out on their own. You ask one person and he'll say that Sylvester just wanted a worshipful housewife; ask another and he'll tell you that Sylvester wanted to give his soul away to someone extraordinary enough to handle it. They are both right, no doubt.

12.

LIVING ON THE LEGEND

People can strive and strive and strive, dream and dream and dream, and when they arrive at the place they had been dreaming of it can turn out to be brilliant for a second, and then all wrong. Something like that happened to Sylvester. He had had his good year, and then it had quickly begun to unravel: he had been treated like a criminal; he had fought with his record company; Izora and Martha had moved on; one boyfriend and then another had moved on, too.

Some people, when their dreams-come-true let them down like this, strive and strive and strive some more, jonesing for another hit of that brilliant moment. Without seeming to think too much about it, Sylvester did something different: he dug deeper into the life of gay San Francisco. It was as if, when stardom disappointed, he learned that the kind of fabulous life he really wanted did not require—indeed, might be inhibited by— being a big star. "You don't have to push me off my throne, honey," Sylvester once said. "Just give me advance notice and I will *move.*" But he didn't so much move off his throne as throw it on his back and plop it back down in the smaller kingdom whence he came.

"They all said disco died," Sylvester said in 1980. "But I don't know. I go out dancing all the time." He had a point. People didn't just stop dancing in the 1980s, especially not black people and gay people, and especially not gay men in San Francisco. What had begun to be in 1978 only became more so. The San Francisco dance music scene, in fact, hit its stride in the early eighties, developing into a full-fledged independent subculture: San Francisco gay men had their own places to dance, their own musical sound, their own way of dressing, even their own record companies. Sylvester kept himself right in the thick of it. Clubs like Dreamland, Music Hall, the I-Beam, and the Trocadero Transfer, which had come into their heyday a couple of years before, were booming. It was not unreasonable to ask a man if he was a Trocadero guy or a Dreamland guy, though chances were you could guess within the first few minutes.

Dreamland was modeled after New York's Flamingo. It was light, bright, and grand; the inside was all white, with balconies and a seashell-like stage a few feet above the floor, where Sylvester sometimes performed. It was known for its state-of-the-art sound system, its pretty faces, and its drugs—cocaine was to much of the eighties San Francisco scene what acid and pot had been to the seventies. People more or less assumed everyone was on one drug or another; some just said they were on MDA, for "Mary, Don't Ask." If you were looking for drugs, you would discreetly make an appointment to see the "night nurse," Mia Lucas, who was also Dreamland's "head girl," working the door and taking phone reservations and eventually managing the place. You were in trouble if you needed a toilet, because the stalls were usually occupied by drug doers.

Trocadero men thought Dreamland men were A-gay posers who didn't really like to sweat. Trocadero got a more acid/speed kind of crowd, and was darker and trippier. It stayed open until ten in the morning. "It was a place to get together with people and get high and spend ten hours tripping," Gini Spiersch, one of the few female Trocadero regulars, said in David Diebold's oral history *Tribal Rites*. The DJ and lighting technician would "get together at the beginning of the night and plan where they would take the crowd and with what songs. They believed that if they could totally control the audio and visual environments, then they could actually control the group consciousness and influence people's trips, which they unquestionably did." If people seemed out of synch or if it seemed a bad batch of drugs was going around, the Troc DJ Bobby Viteritti said, they'd decide what steps to take to turn them back around: a sudden "wild frenzied set" of rough songs with strobes and wild music, then a smoothing out with "pretty clean music," so that "everyone had reunited and cooled out and realigned their heads, like demagnetizing or something." New people went through an informal initiation process, and after that they were called Trocadites. Former Trocadites talk about family, spirit, magic, and euphoria.

Sylvester, of course, went everywhere.

Gay entrepreneurs also threw massive parties—events like "Salute to the Men of San Francisco"—at the Galleria, a three-story, glass-paneled Design Center building, and at the Moscone Center, the Gift Center, and once, even underground at the Castro Muni Metro Station. A lot of the gay parties, perhaps intentionally, seemed to be quoting Rome before the fall. Randy Wallace, who had lived in San Francisco since the 1940s, noticed at one such party that people were passed out all along the perimeter of the dance floor, while in the center, on a raised platform, was a huge golden lion statue. "I was dancing and looked up," he recalls, "and saw a guy getting fucked over that lion."

Although his gospel-soul sound was not much like the prevailing San Francisco speed-disco, Sylvester was still a regular headliner at all the San Francisco parties and clubs. It was he who saluted the Men of San Francisco, and he who inaugurated the Castro Muni station, wearing a suit made of silver dollars. In 1980, he had been the first disco act to play at Davies Symphony Hall. (Among the advertisers in that night's program were several gay bars, two gay gyms, and several men's clothing stores.) The event, "An Evening of Glamour and Glitter," was produced by David Bandy and Gary Roverena, promoters whose evenings, the program announced, have "formed the social centerpiece of most holiday weekends."

Sylvester played at all the clubs, too, in his sequined suits with shoulder pads covering simple shirts open to his chest, or loose, bulk-covering sequined tunics over black pants, and always a bit of jewelry. When he played Dreamland, he and Jeanie and whoever they'd got to sing with them would come in early and sit in the lounge upstairs. Often Sylvester would have no costume planned. He would bring his trunks, pulling from here and pulling from there until he had a look that made sense for the moment. The trunks were kept near enough that he could reach in to add or subtract. His outfit "would evolve through the evening," says Mia Lucas.

Sylvester's performances were only a hop, a skip, and a jump from those of the Elephant Walk in 1976 or even, for that matter, of the Palace Theater in 1972. He began and ended the sets with his dance hits, of course. But along the way he quieted things down with "Lover Man" and "Blackbird," howled hard-core honky-tonk blues, channeled the Marvelettes as if playing a sock hop, and for an encore did the rock-gospel version of "Cry Me a River" he'd recorded on Sell My Soul. Sometimes his hair would fall in front of his face, and he would tilt his head to the side and then back, like a lady in a shampoo commercial. His dancing was bouncy, punctuated by spontaneous hops for joy. When the harmonies were especially tight, you could see his eyes close for a second, Sylvester leaning back a little into the sound and smiling, more to himself than to you. The boys at Dreamland or Trocadero—and the few women— shouted out to him. He knew a lot of them. If someone gave him a bouquet of roses, he and Jeanie Tracy danced and sang and threw rose after rose out into the crowd.

Tom Martin and Ed Shepard, Sylvester's friends from New York, once went out to San Francisco to visit him for a big party where he was to perform. The night before the party, they all played in his drag room on Corbett Avenue, trying on this and that; Sylvester picked out, for the party, a sequined dress with his red kimono over it. The bash was at the Galleria, and the wall-to-wall men made it hard to move. Sylvester stepped out onto the stage. When the light hit the sequins, he spread the kimono sleeves like red wings. Jeanie used to say that Sylvester was about the only person she knew of, other than Michael Jackson, who could walk onto a stage and not do a thing, not open his mouth, nothing, just walk out, and people would start "going in." That night, Sylvester stood, arms open, and the crowd went in.

After Sylvester's performance, he called Tom and Ed and a couple of other friends into the dressing room. "I want you to know I love you all," he said. "I had to say that to you: I love you." He turned to each man in turn and told him why. Then they all went out to the dance floor. The crowd, the kimono, the dancing, the love: it was more than fabulous enough.

After most of the major record companies had dropped their disco departments, it became a lot harder for DJs to find the kind of records people wanted to dance to. In San Francisco, some of those DJs had just up and formed their own record companies. This was, after all, still Oz. They didn't have thousands of dollars to plunk down for a symphony orchestra, so out of necessity they relied heavily on synthesizers, which turned out to suit clubgoers just as well. Marty Blecman, who had been a DJ and mixed records for Fantasy, founded Megatone Records with Patrick Cowley, the slight blond synthesizer whiz who'd helped turn Sylvester's songs into hits a few years before; the first Megatone LP was Cowley's 1981 *Megatron Man*. An investor started them off with twenty thousand dollars, and they ran the label out of Blecman's house, where it was all gay all the time.

Their main competitor was Moby Dick Records, which became known for its sloppy accounting and for being run by Trocadero partiers, many of whom were not really down from their drugs until Wednesdays. In publicity photos, the women wore big hair and sassy smiles, and the men wore mustaches, hair parted on the side, and leather vests over bare chests. Both labels churned out dance club hits and made dance music demi-stars out of acts like Paul Parker, Jo-Lo, Loverde, and the Boystown Gang, a group modeled on the Village People, only gayer. The Boystown Gang's dance hits included disco covers of "Can't Take My Eyes Off You" and "Signed, Sealed, Delivered," and a 1981 song called "Cruisin' the Streets," which began with producer Bill Motley whispering "I didn't think anyone was into that!" and continued for a thirteen-minute gay-porn fantasy orgy and references to "asshole," "cunt," and "dick of death."

The music that came out of the San Francisco gay labels was the soundtrack of the San Francisco gay club scene in the early 1980s. Robotic and synthetic, slightly faster and more mechanical than its more soul-driven New York counterpart, it was more or less invented by Patrick Cowley. The "San Francisco sound" was, like Patrick, up-tempo, highly sexual, drug-friendly, white, and infectious. "The high-tempo, high-energy sound was about sex," says John Hedges, who worked closely with Patrick and produced records for both Megatone and Moby Dick. "Tempo, on the beat, pounding, faster, gay sex. And everybody was tripping their brains out." The music was best on amphetamines.

Patrick Cowley was a sweet, wiseass Catholic boy. He could usually answer all of the questions on *Jeopardy!* and if anyone else got one wrong he would torture them with his rightness. At parties, he mostly liked to watch people. He was also something of a workaholic. He shared a studio with Tip Wirrick in a brick building south of Market, and spent most of his time in the studio, at the gym, and having sex. "He really didn't have much of a social life," said Frank Loverde, who worked with Patrick. "It was just music and the baths, music and the baths."

The two enterprises were linked, of course, and they fed each other. Patrick called his publishing company Masculine Music. Patrick's first male fantasy figure was Lloyd Bridges as a hunky frogman on the late-1950s TV series *Sea Hunt*. One night, he and his friend Jo-Carol Block (later, Jo-Carol Davidson) went in and recorded a song called "Sea Hunt"—she sang the siren song of a mermaid—in honor of Lloyd Bridges's sexy chest. Patrick and Sylvester talked about making records that would be "about hanging around in deep, dark places doing these nasty, lewd, wonderful things." Patrick wrote a song called "Make It Come Hard," and he and Sylvester would play it, sing along, and laugh. "It was about sucking cock in the bathroom, the baths, the holes," Sylvester said. They even made rough recordings in deep, dark places just for the fun of it.

With Marty Blecman, his Megatone cofounder, Patrick had written a tune called "Energy." They got high one afternoon in the studio and added an "M" in front of it. The song became a club hit for Megatone. (Later, Sylvester recorded vocals for a mix of it, too.) *The boys in the bar room livin' it up, shooting off energy,* girl singers sang. *The guys on the sidewalk work it on out, talkin' about menergy, menergy, menergy, men-er-gy.*

One of the girl singers on "Menergy" was Jo-Carol Block, who had moved to San Francisco a few years earlier, drawn to the city by her heart and by a brother who lived on food stamps with his pregnant girlfriend and some other hippies on Bush Street eating beans all day and consulting channelers. She'd joined the San Francisco Community Chorus, and then a three-girl, three-guy jazz group calling itself A Cappella Gold. One day in 1980, when Jo-Carol was twenty-five, her groupmate Michael Finden, who was also in Sylvester's band, said he had a gig for the three women, singing on "Menergy" for Cowley. They sang and started getting club gigs that actually paid them hundreds of dollars. Jo-Carol and her colleagues Lauren Carter and Carol McMacken adored Patrick, their "little blond doll," and he them. They'd show up at the studio, and he'd light up a joint. "Here, smoke this first," he'd say, "and we'll have fun."

As the Patrick Cowley Singers, Jo-Carol, Carol, and Lauren were getting paid to perform on top of bars at gay clubs in hot pants and makeup while beautiful men screamed, "Fabulous! Fabulous!" They were making good money and doing some "fast drugs," Jo-Carol said. They wore, she said, "slutty little outfits—jungle outfits with snakes, space costumes, female drag queen kind of stuff." One night, they stayed up all night at a gay bar, performing in their jungle-girl costumes, and went straight from there to an early morning A Cappella Gold performance at a local jazz station. They showed up in streaked makeup and outfits that, while still slutty, didn't look quite as fabulous in the daylight. That was the beginning of the end of the jazz group, but the Patrick Cowley Singers signed with Tim McKenna and started opening for Sylvester. It was, for Jo-Carol, "the big time."

Carol eventually left the Patrick Cowley Singers, and Jo-Carol and Lauren changed their name to Jo-Lo. Jo-Lo's first performance was at Sylvester's birthday party at a Russian River club called the Woods. Sylvester took them aside to impart to them his philosophy of performing. One: If the crowd isn't going along with you, make your own party and let them join you if they wish. Two: More cheeks. Three: More eyes.

The best advice is always that simple. Linda Imperial—cofounder, with Frank Loverde, of the group Loverde—sometimes performed with Sylvester. Sylvester reminded her of sunlight. When she doubted herself, he would say, "Just sing. Keep singing. Paint and sing. And never go out in public without sunglasses, a great hairdresser, and lipstick."

As *Megatron Man* moved up the dance charts in 1981, Patrick Cowley got sicker. He had been ill on and off ever since the 1979 tour with Sylvester to Brazil, when he got an ear infection. He was losing weight. Sylvester, like everyone else, figured it was something he'd eaten down there; the doctors had treated Patrick for specific infections, for parasites, for Bell's palsy, but nothing seemed to work.

In June 1981, a small article in *Morbidity and Mortality Weekly Report*, published by the U.S. Centers for Disease Control, reported five cases of *Pneumocystis carinii* pneumonia among young gay men in Los Angeles. In July, *The New York Times* reported that forty-one men, mostly in New York and San Francisco, had been diagnosed with a rare cancer called Kaposi's sarcoma, and that eight had died within two years of their diagnosis. "The reporting doctors said that most cases had involved homosexual men who have had multiple and frequent sexual encounters with different partners, as many as 10 sexual encounters each night up to four times a week," the *Times* reported. "Many of the patients have also been treated for viral infections such as herpes, cytomegalovirus and hepatitis B as well as parasitic infections such as amebiasis and giardiasis. Many patients also reported that they had used drugs such as amyl nitrate and LSD to heighten sexual pleasure." That fall, Patrick Cowley was admitted to the hospital with pneumonia; early in 1982, he wound up in intensive care at the U.C. Medical Center.

Sylvester visited him regularly at the hospital, to "read my Bible and just be with him." Doctors were calling his disease GRID, for gay-related immune deficiency, which a lot of people just called the gay cancer. Whatever his illness was, Patrick wasn't getting better; his family came out to San Francisco from Buffalo, since it looked as if he had reached his end. Patrick was screaming that he wanted to be unplugged, and his parents were considering the request. Then Sylvester walked in.

Marty Blecman sent him to "tell and promise Patrick anything just to give him some hope or something to live for." Sylvester held Patrick's hand and simply refused to take no for an answer. He told Patrick that everyone was waiting on them to do another project together, and that he would just have to try harder. "I'm not having it anymore," he said. "Get your ass up out of bed so we can go to work." Patrick was released from the hospital a few days later.

When Patrick left the hospital, he went to stay with his best friend, Paul Parker (whose dance hit "Right on Target" he had written and produced), and Paul's boyfriend, Ken Crivello. Their apartment was up several flights, so Paul would throw Patrick on his back and walk up the seventy-two steps. Paul and Ken nursed Patrick from eighty pounds back up to around a hundred and ten. When he was well enough, Sylvester stopped by to pick him up and bring him over to Megatone, also known as Marty Blecman's house, on his moped. Patrick was like Lazarus with a scarf. They went to work.

Sylvester wrote lyrics and Patrick wrote music, and they made a record for about five hundred dollars. The song they made, "Do Ya Wanna Funk," is a traditional Sylvester-Patrick song. Sylvester's gospel-falsetto floated over cowbells and Patrick's San Francisco gay-boy synthesizers; the lyrical come-on made clear the equation of funking and fucking. Patrick did the hand claps. You could imagine people gyrating up to each other singing *do you wanna funk, let me show you how, do you wanna funk with me.* It was a question with no question mark.

When "Do Ya Wanna Funk" was released on the Fourth of July, 1982, it looked as if Sylvester was rising again, too. The song went to the top of the dance charts, crossed over to the pop charts in many countries, and the next year was featured on a Jane Fonda workout tape and the soundtrack of Eddie Murphy's *Trading Places*, even though Sylvester complained that Murphy was "crass."

◦   ◦   ◦

After the blond-wig-I-ain't-changing-shit incident, Sylvester said, Fantasy Records had put him "on suspension"—though it was probably a less formal arrangement in which each left the other alone, biding their time. When his contract finally ran out, Sylvester left for good.

He was through with Harvey Fuqua and Nancy Pitts, too. They did not part amicably. The dispute between them was a long time in the making, as for years Sylvester watched others move away from Fuqua and Pitts. "When we started, we were just out of the church," Izora Rhodes Armstead says of her and Martha. "Sylvester was flamboyant and we was wild little girls. You wanted to trust people." By 1981, the Tons' trust of Fuqua and Pitts had more or less eroded. "We was doing all those shows, and every show we did we got five hundred dollars, which was a nice penny in those days," says Armstead. "But we got fucked over. No matter what we brought in, it was always five hundred dollars."

From quite early on, several of Sylvester's band members had also suspected that they were not getting their financial due from Honey Productions. For one thing, even when they were touring with a hit album, Marc Baum says, "the money was always just okay." When James Wirrick got his start with them at nineteen years old, he says, Ted Rosenblatt, the attorney representing Harvey Fuqua, Nancy Pitts, and Honey Productions, had told him, "We're going to take care of your publishing." Wirrick had happily agreed, and felt rich getting checks for a few hundred dollars. But when "Mighty Real" went gold and he was not seeing much more money than before, he was savvy enough to poke around. In 1978, Wirrick, Michael Finden, and Patrick Cowley hired a lawyer, Gerald Weiner, to see if they were being properly paid for songs they had written. "We tracked the problem down to Ted Rosenblatt," Weiner says. "He had been claiming their interest in the publishing, with no paperwork from any of the writers. We found out he collected a whole bunch of money. Some of it he had taken for himself, some of it he had paid over to Harvey and Nancy, and almost none of it to the writers." After some legal wrangling, Wirrick, Cowley, and Finden settled with Rosenblatt, who handed over a cash sum and all of their publishing.

No action was taken against Fuqua and Pitts, and nothing tied them to any wrongdoing. Still, band members harbored vague suspicions—of sloppiness or greed or both—about Fuqua and Pitts. Singer Linda Imperial, who also worked with them, described the pair as "old school gimme, gimme, gimme, gimme, gimme." Frazier suspected that "the whole crew was just using Sylvester to line their pockets"; Baum describes the two as "the gangsters of the whole scene." Despite the affection and respect many of the musicians had for Fuqua, he was known as a "cut corners, fix it later" kind of guy, David Frazier says. For her part, Pitts was "not a well-liked individual," says Frazier. Baum recalled her as "pissy, always in a bad temper"; Weiner, the lawyer, recalled that while "Harvey was a musician, and I don't think he thought that much about money, that's all Nancy thought about."

For several years, as long as his own pockets were lined, Sylvester had not been concerned about contracts or percentages. "If you put something in front of him and told him to sign it, he'd sign it," says Weiner, the attorney. "He didn't care to read it or have it explained to him. If he had money in his pocket, he was happy." Eventually, though, Sylvester too turned to Weiner, and filed a lawsuit against "Harvey Fuqua et al" in November 1982. Nancy Pitts suggests that he did so because he was under the influence of "a lot of people in the background, friends and what have you, the San Francisco crowd." She speaks of "outside sources" who wanted "a piece of the pie," who had "no knowledge and experience in the business" but "felt that they could do no more for him than we could do," who were "plotting and planning" and "feeding him information" and telling him it was time to move on. "He wanted to make a change, and you can't just come and say 'I am going to make a change' if you have a contract," says Pitts. "Any time an artist wants to get out of a contract, there is always going to be a lawsuit." Weiner himself says that he was brought in "to help get rid of Harvey Fuqua," not only because Fuqua wasn't paying according to contract, but because the existing production contract was "really bad."*

Whatever Sylvester's motivations, Weiner did not have too difficult a time finding evidence that Fuqua and Pitts owed Sylvester money. "I don't think they even bothered to account," he says. "They just gave him some money, never accounted. It was all just one big candy jar." Sylvester sued. "Nobody ever stole a dime from Sylvester," says Nancy Pitts. "Sylvester

---

*Harvey Fuqua did not return numerous calls, letters, and faxes requesting an interview for this book, although his son Michael did call to say that Mr. Fuqua would consider an interview in return for "residuals."

loved to live a lavish life. When you are living the lavish life, that's coming off the top of your royalty. Harvey did not collect royalties and not pay on them. Sylvester got every penny that was due him. Everything was paid out, and not only that, Sylvester got a salary, and in addition to that salary all of his expenses were covered and paid out of his money. Nobody ever stole a dime from Sylvester. As a matter of fact, more was given to Sylvester, because when Sylvester came to us, Sylvester was penniless."

In June 1983, however, the California Superior Court for the County of Alameda reached a somewhat different conclusion, and Sylvester obtained a judgment of $218,112.50 against Harvey Fuqua and Nancy Pitts. Neither was able to actually pay that amount, and eventually, Weiner says, "we gave up trying to collect." (In August 1985, Fuqua and Pitts each signed final settlement agreements: Fuqua agreed to pay Sylvester twenty thousand dollars, and both he and Pitts agreed to transfer to him all rights to the publishing companies Beekeeper Music, Borzoi Music, Beeswax Music, and Tipsyl, along with all rights to Honey Productions and Honey Records. These joined Sylvester's own publishing company, which a few years before, in a succinct statement of personal philosophy, he'd named Sequins at Noon.) Sylvester wouldn't even let his friends utter Harvey Fuqua's name.

"I was hurt," says Nancy Pitts of Sylvester's difficult leave-taking. "That was my baby. But I can't fight all of Castro. I can't fight everybody."

Sylvester would decide who got a piece of his pie. As his manager he hired Timmy McKenna, his old Castro friend and tour manager. This was a small-world choice rather than a big-world one: Tim was most plugged in to the club circuit, not so much to the larger industry. He and Sylvester had traveled in the same gay San Francisco world for years, living in and around the Castro; Tim had even once dated Michael Rayner. Tim was a no-nonsense businessman, and knew that Sylvester would spend any money that was in his pocket. Most of all, Sylvester trusted him, like family.

Tim told Sylvester he needed to buy something big that would hold its value, so Sylvester purchased a green Jaguar. It was in the shop a lot, but when it was healthy and on the street, the car looked stunning, especially with fur and sunglasses.

✿   ✿   ✿

A really good dress could clarify the direction of Sylvester's life even when he wasn't the one trying to wear it. In late 1981, James Wirrick had come up with some good songs, which John Hedges was going to produce and Marty Blecman was going to release on Megatone. They'd hired a singer named Gwen Jonae to record them, but when she demanded a five-thousand-dollar beaded gown for the cover, negotiations broke down. In the fall of 1982, they had a record but no singer.

Marty and John were cranky, so they went to the I-Beam for a drink. "Out of the blue," John Hedges recalls, "Sylvester walked into the bar." They hugged and kissed hello and chatted. Marty and John had mixed a lot of Sylvester's music—the *Stars* album for Fantasy, among others. They'd all gotten high on Quaaludes together at the Plaza Hotel in New York, lying on the floor and solving all the world's problems. Marty explained about the dress and the tracks and the crankiness, and Sylvester said he'd be interested in hearing the songs. By the end of the day, he had agreed to do the *All I Need* album, with "Do Ya Wanna Funk" as an anchor. If he needed a beaded gown, everyone knew he had plenty in his closet.

Megatone was hardly a major label, and on one level Sylvester was taking what was available, retreating and retrenching. After Fantasy, with no hits in a few years and the stale scent of disco lingering around him, he was not all that interesting to major record labels. He'd spent much of his money and his lawsuit against Fuqua and Pitts was just beginning. But Sylvester could certainly have *tried* to get himself back into the big time: he could have dumped his small-time manager, Tim McKenna, moved to New York or Los Angeles, put his finger on another pulse. After Fantasy, he seemed to want a different kind of life. "There's nothing worse than a fallen star, when the light burns out and you still have these illusions," he said in 1982. If living without illusions meant performing on a smaller stage, so be it. He wanted control, he wanted to be home in San Francisco, he wanted freedom, he wanted to shop, he wanted to be in love, and he wanted to be able to "still crawl around and sleaze with the best of them." Megatone—like Sylvester, homegrown and gay as could be—offered stardom without illusions. On *All I Need*, Sylvester thanked Timmy McKenna ("the manager of the 80s") and Tip Wirrick and John Hedges for choosing him, and dedicated a song to Marty Blecman and the Megatone staff. "I'm so happy to finally have a home," he wrote.

At the studio where Sylvester recorded, Hedges recalls, cocaine was sometimes laid out on empty reel-to-reel containers, like a cheese platter. Sylvester often brought his bag of diamonds for show-and-tell. The songs James Wirrick had written for the album—he played synthesizers and guitars for all of them except "Do Ya Wanna Funk"—were mostly fast, New Wavey dance-rock songs, with an occasional guitar solo, and unchallenging lyrics, such as "I'm hard up for your love" and "Don't stop, you're movin' me." On some songs, Jeanie Tracy and Martha Wash sang background. Sylvester's high voice, coupled with the remote and artificial sounds of the synthesizers, seemed to come from a similar but slightly distant world. The cover illustration by Mark Amerika was a profile portrait of Sylvester as an Egyptian prince/ss: black hair flowing like a waterfall behind him; a green eye accentuated by geometric makeup; a large silver Wonder Woman earring, red lipstick, and nail polish. In the painting, Sylvester was wearing bangles and a thumb ring recognizable to his friends, and holding a lit cigarette. It looked like his brand, too.

Sylvester would "scratch and claw and threaten suicide," he said, to get ballads on his Megatone albums, but he was otherwise at home in the San Francisco dance music scene. Tim McKenna could get him lucrative gigs in Europe and Mexico and here and there around the States, earning enough money to shop and pay the mortgage. The rest of the time he could live the San Francisco life, doing nothing on some days and being unusual on others. When he described his new style to *New Musical Express* that year, you could hear a bit of Dooni and a smidgen of Cockette, and a touch of the elation you feel when stowed-away parts of yourself are reawakened: "I can still do a little glitter, but it's a lot more tasteful, like little T-shirts. My hair is blond, it may be blue tomorrow, that sort of thing; little squashed boots, wrap-around sunglasses. At some point I'm going to wear a sequined mini-skirt. I don't know why, but I just have a feeling that I *should*—over pants, of course."

In the first few years of the 1980s, the acts that grew out of the San Francisco gay dance world, such as Jo-Lo, Loverde, and Paul Parker, routinely took their shows out on the mostly gay club circuit where Sylvester—even when his Fantasy career was stalling—was the reigning queen. "Sylvester was like a guardian angel to us or something," Lauren Carter said in *Tribal Rites*. On Valentine's Day, 1982, Sylvester, Jo-Lo, and the Weather Girls were all in New York. Between them, they had gay New York pretty much covered. Sylvester had taken one look at Jo-Carol's and Lauren's outfits and shaken his head. "That's not the right look," he'd said. "You have to go shopping." He'd sent them out to buy something classic. They'd found men's white dinner jackets at a used-clothing store in the Village; he'd sent them out again, to get black pants and corset-bras, which they found at Macy's. They opened that night with an a cappella version of "My Funny Valentine," backlit, their backs to the audience. Thousands of men listened quietly, and then each of the women raised an arm as the stage started filling up with smoke and the space-music of "Menergy" started up. They turned around one by one and danced in the light, smoke, and whooping screams.

"The world was at our feet for an hour or two," said Jo-Lo's Lauren Carter.

Out on the circuit, Sylvester and the other San Francisco dance stars often ran into each other and went clubbing together—Paul Parker and Ken Crivello would knock on Sylvester's door at noon to go to brunch the morning after, or Jo-Carol and Sylvester would go shopping. Often they would play at a club within a week or two of each other. Once, a month after Sylvester had played a "Silver Party" in Chicago, Paul Parker came in to do a "Gold Party." Arriving at airports, he and Ken would each try to be the first to spot the person picking them up. In Chicago, Paul won, pointing to a guy in shorts, red and yellow kneesocks, and a raccoon chubby. The young man, their driver, told them how much he'd loved Sylvester, who'd been there the month before. He said Sylvester had been wearing a top made of mirrors. The next time they saw that child was at the Gold Party, where Paul sang "Right on Target." The young man was wearing little pieces of mirror glued to a mesh tank top. He had to leave after twenty minutes, though, because the mirrors were cutting into him. He took off the tank top and ran out of the club dripping blood.

One night in 1982, back from a club tour, Jo-Carol Block and Lauren Carter went into the studio, smoked a joint, and listened as Patrick introduced them to his new LP, *Mind Warp*. He showed them the words they were to sing, from songs with titles like "They Came at Night," "Mutant Man," and "Going Home." He wanted them to sing about intruders who strike when you're alone, who made their move on the human race, who are a voice behind your eyes. He wanted them to sing about a voice that spoke to him in an ancient tongue he couldn't recognize, calling out a warning. He wanted them to sing about an anemic red sun, a greenish glow, chemical contractions in a vortex spinning around, planets falling down. He wanted them to sing lines like "Uh-oh, uh-oh, beware of darkness."

"I'm not singing this shit," Jo-Carol said.

"Yes, you are," he said. "You're going to sing it just the way I wrote it."

Patrick directed the engineering while reclining on a couch in the studio. People propped him up by the synthesizer so he could work. He invited David Frazier to play on the album; usually, David would name Patrick an outrageous price, and then Patrick would act irate, and then they'd haggle for a while. This time, when David named his ridiculous price, Patrick agreed without a blink. They called *Mind Warp* the "death record."

That fall, the Megatone crowd organized a tribute to Patrick at the Galleria. Sylvester, his hair cut short and bleached white, came plowing through a big banner at the start of the show to the delight of several floors of screamers, and sang "Don't Stop." Jo-Carol and Lauren sang "They Came at Night," moving to steps taught to them by one of the choreographers from the TV show *Dance Fever*. Patrick, now an old man, watched from a wheelchair. At the age of thirty-two, he was about to be one of the first few hundred people killed in the United States by the just-named acquired immune deficiency syndrome. Several years were to pass before President Ronald Reagan mentioned AIDS in public, although his press secretary, Larry Speakes, joked about "AIDS, or whatever it is," that October. Asked whether the president knew anything about the "gay plague," Speakes commented, to laughter among the press corps, "I don't have it— do you?" In San Francisco a few months earlier, a group calling itself the Kaposi's Sarcoma Foundation had opened an office in a small flat in the Castro, right near the Elephant Walk; client intakes were conducted in the bathroom, with breaks when someone needed to use the toilet.

At the party for Patrick Cowley, people danced. The Galleria smelled of poppers and sweat. "Those stupid queens," Patrick said, looking down at the crowd.

"What really destroyed me was how he became so bitter," Sylvester later said. "All of the plans we made for future projects were getting so far out of reach for him." Sylvester went to visit Patrick the day before leaving for a European tour. Patrick was in a foul mood, and mean to Sylvester. "Patrick, I'm not going to allow this to taint the way I feel or what I have to say to you, because I love you," Sylvester recalled saying. "And we're gonna try to pull it all together. If you can't do it now, just wait and then we'll really do it. We'll just really do it." Patrick didn't say anything, but he looked at Sylvester with his big blue eyes, and Sylvester thought he detected a smile.

A few days later, Sylvester was in England, and Patrick was on his deathbed, barely conscious. His friend Ken Crivello asked visitors to keep their voices down. "No, no, no, no," Patrick said from his room. "Leave the door open. I want to hear voices. I want to hear everything. I want to go into what their voices are thinking."

On November 12, 1982, Sylvester was in London, scheduled to perform at a club called Heaven, when he got a phone call telling him that Patrick had died. Sylvester relayed the news to the crowd gathered that night in Heaven, and then, as a tribute, performed "Do Ya Wanna Funk."

After Patrick's death, before people really knew how the virus was transmitted and how to prevent its spread, Sylvester was asked what he would like to say to the gay community about AIDS. "Get out of the fast lane for a few minutes. Be just a little more aware of your body. Move over to the slow lane for a couple of days," he said. "Don't worry, honey, the party will still be there when you get back."

Audrey Joseph, a tough Jewish girl from Brooklyn and a big deal in the dance music world, had arrived in San Francisco just before Patrick died. She knew Marty Blecman, John Hedges, and Patrick Cowley from her days as a disco record promoter in the 1970s. In 1982, she had left her high-powered job at Arista Records to get her head together, and that September called Marty Blecman from Portland, Oregon. She'd better get down to San Francisco in a hurry, he'd told her.

Audrey agreed to watch over Megatone while Marty took Patrick's body back to Buffalo, but when he returned she was going to pick up and head to Yosemite and then back to New York. Sylvester, whom she'd only just met but who was starting to make a sister out of her, told her she couldn't leave. The strength of his conviction convinced her to stay.

Audrey promoted the *All I Need* album, whose "Don't Stop" made it up to Number 3 on the *Billboard* dance charts, sitting for a while just below Michael Jackson's "Billie Jean." Audrey also produced a video for Sylvester's

"Hard Up," which became the third video by a black artist to appear on MTV. They shot (but didn't use) scenes in which Sylvester was carried around by muscle boys, including a well-known local porn star whose large member was clearly visible in his short shorts as Sylvester sang "I'm hard up for you." In the end, they went with a cleaned-up ancient-Egypt theme, not because the song had any discernible connection to ancient Egypt but because of the Sylvester-as-Cleopatra album cover. In the video, Sylvester was dressed as an Egyptian princess some of the time; at other times he danced in a striped shirt, near conspicuously low-budget pyramid cutouts; there were King Tuttish props and dancers holding their arms like live-action hieroglyphics. Sylvester was terrified of snakes, but he agreed that they would be too fabulous, so Audrey found some and wrapped them around his hands. In some shots, Sylvester danced with them.

Audrey wound up moving into Patrick Cowley's old house. Not knowing what AIDS was, the landlords had fumigated it twice. Not long after, Audrey's neighbor had rung the bell and asked for a hose. "Stay in the house," she'd told Audrey, who hates bugs. Audrey had watched from a window as her neighbor hosed down the two-story house, which was entirely covered with ants. Exterminators came but the ants returned. "The house was fucking haunted," says Audrey. One set of bugs would be exterminated, only to be replaced the next week by a different species of intruder: carpenter beetles, bees, wasps.

On New Year's Eve, Eartha Kitt was performing at the Trocadero. "We're going out in drag," Sylvester told Audrey. "So what's new for you?" she said, Jewishly. "Oh, no, no, I mean *drag*, honey," Sylvester said. "I'm going to dress in a tuxedo and tie. I'm going to dress you like a *girl*." He bought her a black dress with a plunging neckline and a plunging back, and high heels with rhinestones; loaned her a diamond necklace and bracelet; did her hair and makeup. He brought a top hat and cane to go with his tux, and off they went to see Miss Eartha Kitt. "I looked like a drag queen," says Audrey, who so rarely wore heels that the shoes didn't last the night, "and he looked like a dyke dressed like a boy."

Audrey Joseph didn't make it to Yosemite until some time in the 1990s.

Sylvester had dedicated the song "All I Need" to his boyfriend at the time—after Michael, after John—a hairdresser in his early twenties named

Tom Daniels. In 1982, Tom had been living with a few friends on Fell Street, and since all of them had May birthdays they'd decided to throw a big party. A friend of one of the roommates invited Sylvester. Tom had spoken to him briefly but hadn't paid him much mind.

The next day, Sylvester invited a crowd of people to his house for brunch, and Tom went along. "It was all a setup to get me to his house," says Tom. He was charmed and flattered. He liked Sylvester's face, pretty and glowing, and though he was ambivalent about queeniness, in private he found Sylvester "quiet and masculine." Tom was not so much smitten as easily persuaded. "For me, it was the first time someone was really genuinely interested in me and really was loving and sweet and accommodating," says Tom, sounding not unlike the men who had come before him. He stayed the night, and within a month he was living at the house on Corbett amid the deco and the gold.

Sylvester traveled quite a bit—"collecting the pennies," as he called it, to support his ordinary fabulousness. At home, he was silly and content. To make Tom laugh, he would tra-la-la badly and speak pidgin French. He would sit on the floor in front of the television for what seemed like days while a hairdresser weaved and braided his hair. He and Tom watched movies. They rarely cooked, but they drank a lot. Friends would come over and they would all play in the drag room, pulling gowns and wigs out of the pile and dressing up for hours. Periodically, Sylvester's jeweler, "a tiny little queen," would show up with a little satchel containing a couple of hundred thousand dollars' worth of jewelry, and Tom and Sylvester would paw through, occasionally buying a piece if it was marvelous enough. They dropped acid now and then, and did cocaine on special occasions. They lounged around in fur and jewels.

They watched their terrier, Terry, eat everything she encountered, chase their borzoi up and down the stairs, and knock into a two-foot perfume bottle that seemed, in the acid-trip haze of that day, to take half an hour to fall over and crack into a hundred rancid pieces. On free weekends, along with much of the Castro, they often drove the Jaguar up to the Russian River.

Sylvester would come back from a trip with money and unpredictable hair; shortly, the money would be spent and the hair redone. All payments came through Tim; after the bills were paid, Tim would dole out money to Sylvester. When he had money, Sylvester threw it around, and when he didn't he and Tom would go out anyway. He liked to walk around the

Castro with his remaining borzoi, despite its habit of shitting uncontrollably. "Let's go live on the legend," Sylvester might say at night, and they'd dress up and collect free cocktails around town. For sport, Sylvester would find badly dressed homosexuals and hand them a "Fashion Citation" sheet he'd printed up. Violations included Polyester, Leg Warmers, Hair Pieces, Bell Bottoms, Wide Lapels, Intolerable Shoes, Clone Wear, Fake Fur, Bad Grooming, Bad Coloration, and General Wrongness.

When he went out of town, Sylvester usually left Tom some money; he didn't want Tom to work. "He wanted someone to just be around, especially with his home, to hang in the house all day and all night," Tom says. "He wanted someone who was around at his schedule." Within a year, sex had pretty much evaporated, and though they were supposed to be monogamous Tom had heard stories about what Sylvester did out on tour. Tom got a job, and about six months later took the weak man's path out of the relationship: while Sylvester was on tour in Europe, Tom found himself a new boyfriend, a man named Conrad, who owned a sleazy hotel on Sutter and Gough. Sylvester canceled the rest of his tour and came right home, but Tom had already moved in with the new guy.

Sylvester was, as he would say, too through, and he was not afraid to tell all about it. "He had cut off all his hair because some *trick* he met at the baths told him that he'd be really hot if he went to the gym and pumped himself up and turned into a man instead of a queen," Sylvester told *The Advocate*. "*I* had to go because I wasn't butch enough." Sylvester cut off his hair and tried black leather and Levi's 501 jeans, but felt like a fool. "Fuck this," he thought. "I'm not going to bother with this. I must spend $60,000 a year on clothes, and I'm *not* going to reduce myself to 501s."

Instead, bursting into extreme divativity, Sylvester flew to Florida, chartered a yacht, and spent "thousands of dollars being a crazy queen." He sailed around, drank and partied, and ordered "ridiculous amounts of food." He sent Tom postcard after postcard, trying to win him back, and when that didn't work, he released his own version of "Band of Gold," the classic Freda Payne song about being left in a lonely room with nothing but memories of what love could be and a band of gold. He made sure it got back to Tom that the song was meant for him.

13.

WHAT'S A QUEEN TO DO?

"People still look to me as some sort of spokesman," Sylvester told *New Musical Express* in 1982, "but I think my career has transcended the gay movement. I mean, my sexuality has nothing to do with my music. When I'm fucking I'm not thinking about singing and vice versa." True enough: it's silly and small-minded to be that reductive about music. But then again he was also recording on the gayest record label on earth, and performing much of the time for people for whom music and sexuality were as entwined as the roots of an old tree.

If the truth be told, Sylvester was right then becoming more of a spokesman, not less; it was just that he was not a spokesman for gayness per se. His causes hadn't changed—freedom, unity, and fabulousness— but gay life had become less hospitable to them. As it had become less closeted and more organized, gay San Francisco—the "gay movement" in general, really—had also become more narrowly focused, divisive, and unimaginative. Sylvester wanted no part of that. While in the past he had taken the above-it-all stance of a star, the more Sylvester committed to a regular life within the San Francisco gay community, the more vocal he became about the way some gay men were working his nerves. "I get more shit from queens than I get from anybody else," he told *Christopher Street* in 1982. "I get this conformist shit from queens all the time. They always want to read me. They always want me to do it their way. I am not going to conform to the gay lifestyle as they see it and that's for sure—that's the very last thing that I want to do."

A lot of gay men, Sylvester complained, had gotten "all cloned out and down on people being loud, extravagant or different." They had taken all the fun and the madness out of being gay. They seemed to be trying to be straight, and they were not about to get him to follow suit. "Miles Davis recently said that if he woke up white one morning, he would kill himself," Sylvester said. "Well, if I woke up straight, I'd probably do the same thing. If I were straight, I couldn't wear pearls and diamonds and things, and be fabulous, and get away with all kinds of crazy things." (Plus, he said, being extravagant and different got him exactly what the clones all wanted: men. "The more I put on, and the more outrageous I am," Sylvester said, "the more fabulous boys I meet.") Sylvester said he was fed up with men who threw on mustaches and boots and then thought they were better than everyone else. As his breakup with Tom Daniels had taught him, the butch ideology was not funny. "What *is* butch, sister?" he asked. It was a question he'd been asking for years, but now he posed it not as a parlor game but as a public reprimand. "I mean, just because you can lift a sofa to vacuum under the rug, does that make you butch? They take care of their bodies, their hair and their clothes, but *honey,* they're still queens."

Sylvester had not worked as hard as he had to claim his space in the world—leaving his church, and his record label, to be real—just to take shit from the very people who had every reason to know better. "You don't go out in the world demanding your rights when within the community you don't give them," he said at the beginning of an energetic diatribe against "clones" and "this heavy homosexual thing," fueled by a lifetime of experience with self-righteous hypocrites and conformity bullies. "I say *fuck* them. I don't care. You don't go out and ask the world to give you everything that you think you deserve when within the community you have the leather queens who don't like the jean queens and the black queens who don't like the white queens, and the queens who don't like beards, and lesbian women who don't want to be gay-identified, and this bullshit and that bullshit. The community itself is so fucked up that I refuse to be bothered. Let me give you an example of how our community fucks itself over. When I go places and I see they are carding people at the door, or they are turning women away because they are wearing open-toed shoes, but they don't card me or turn away Diana Ross with open-toed shoes, I stop right there and say, 'If you are carding people at the door, you card me too.' It seems ridiculous that nine times out of ten you can be accepted on the job even when people know you are gay when you can't be accepted in a gay bar because you have a Lacoste shirt on. It's discrimination within discrimination that I hate the most. We've got to clean up our own house first." He stopped shows, he said, if he heard that people were being hassled at the door. "My shows are all E.O.Q," he said. "Equal Opportunity Queen."

The first Gay Games were organized in San Francisco that summer of 1982, with the former Olympic athlete Tom Waddell in the lead. The planners were looking for a performer who could set Kezar Stadium to flaming. Many people assumed that would be Sylvester. Not only had he served as gay San Francisco's ambassador to American culture, but he "gave his talent away quite freely," as Bob Ross, the founder and publisher of the gay *Bay Area Reporter*, put it. "Sylvester never ceased being a part of the community," says Allen White, a longtime writer for the paper. "He was always available to the community." He had done one of the first benefits for the Kaposi's Sarcoma Foundation—later the San Francisco AIDS Foundation—and many more fund-raisers, including a stint with Allen White as a celebrity judge at the Castro Dog Show. "He had earned the right to be the star of that Gay Games show," says White. But Sylvester was never asked. The organizers hired Tina Turner, who wore a little red Bob Mackie fringe dress that could have come right out of Sylvester's closet.

Sylvester was not hopeful about the future. "The only thing that will unite people is a threat," he said. "Anita Bryant and the Briggs Initiative motivated people to get over their bullshit and unite. But as soon as the threats were dealt with, the same separatist bullshit started all over." Be careful what you wish for.

When Sylvester wanted to escape the nonsense he went over to Tony and Nitsa Elite's house on Twin Peaks. The Elites were a big breath of normal in a neighborhood of anomalies: two parents, one of each sex; two little girls; cookies. In the early eighties, they hosted *Dynasty* parties on Wednesday nights. They were a surrogate family for more than a few people who'd left behind their original families or been tossed out of them.

Just before *Step II* was released, Nitsa Elite had hired Sylvester and the Two Tons to sing at her house for Tony's fortieth birthday, and they had all been friends since. Tony, an M.D., had been the unofficial band doctor for a while; the Elites' house became Sylvester's unofficial retreat, and Tony and Nitsa pretty much adopted him.

Sylvester came over whenever he felt the urge. The Elite girls, Alexandra and Kristiana, thought of Sylvester, Alexandra says, as "kind of an uncle." (While many people called the girls Alex and Kris, Sylvester preferred the panache of their full names.) When Sylvester showed up, the girls would go crazy. He might be wearing something uneventful, or he might be all made up, bigger than life in his huge furry white coat. On occasion, he brought wigs. The girls knew all about gay people and even about drag. "Sometimes people like to dress up this way to express who they are inside," their parents had told them. "Sometimes we need to do extra things to help people understand who we are."

When Alex and Kris were six and four, their parents liked to record them singing on a cassette player and send the tape to family in Greece. The girls refused to sing anything but Sylvester songs, so Tony would put on a Sylvester album and they'd sing. They knew all the melodies by heart, but the lyrics were beyond them. "I feel real" came out something like "I beeoo beeoo," and they'd repeat the phrase for the whole song. After a number, they would whisper into the microphone things they knew they shouldn't say aloud. "Behind his music, we could just let it out," says Alex.

When they got a little bit older, the girls would dance for Sylvester. Alexandra was the choreographer, and she tackled her routines with great seriousness while Kristiana tried to follow along, bouncing and shimmying and watching Alex's feet. Sylvester would sit on the couch, resting his chin on his hands and trying not to laugh. "It's like we wanted to give him something back," says Alex. "I don't know what it was, but he needed something from us, and I didn't know how to give it. So we just performed." After each performance, Sylvester would applaud and take his leave, and they would hear serious, incomprehensible grown-up talk coming from the next room.

On days when she and Kristiana were not singing or dancing for Sylvester, Alex just stood back and watched him. "He just took up the whole room with his energy," she says. "You can't ignore Sylvester. You can't avoid him. He was just right there. He absorbed the whole room when he would walk in, and I loved to watch that." She sensed a mysterious heaviness underneath the energy, pain painted over with brightness, and she watched him with curiosity and admiration.

The Elites were Greek Orthodox, and for all their openness and warmth, the girls were raised "having to do everything right, having to be perfect." When Sylvester was in the room, Alex felt her options open up. She felt his freeness wash over her. "I see this man who does whatever the hell he wants, out of so much struggle and pain," she says, "and there was a part of my spirit that wanted to be able to say, you know, 'Fuck you all. I'm doing what I want to do.'" She loved to wrap herself in the warmth of Sylvester's wildness and possibility. After a few minutes, someone usually told her it was time to leave the room.

Sylvester had gone to church now and then over the years—when he was in Los Angeles, his mother always took him back to Palm Lane—but he had never really returned to organized religion. Instead, he'd made of himself a sort of portable ministry that he set up on stages and dance floors; he'd prayed before shows, by himself in a quiet spot, and sung hymns as warm-ups with other singers, many of whom grew up in the Church of God in Christ or a similar tradition. Of course, on a good night, when it was not just him and a tape but him and some other church singers and some tambourines, his performances could turn into a revival meeting. He had his own flock.

From time to time in the early 1980s, Sylvester would drop into the Love Center Church in East Oakland for a service, wearing a hat like an upside-down fishbowl—his "Sunday drag," he called it. Jeanie Tracy had introduced him to the place, and he kept going back. By 1982, when he sang at a benefit for the church's scholarship fund, he had become a regular churchgoer, just like his mother. The service, he said a couple of years later, "carries me through the week." It is not clear just why Sylvester began to rehouse his spirituality in an actual Christian building, though it might not be a coincidence that he did so around the time of Patrick Cowley's death. That the sanctuary at Love Center was painted peach, trimmed in gold and turquoise, and illuminated by glass and brass sconces might also have been a factor.

In any case, Sylvester cottoned quickly to the place, partly because it was a singing place but one where nobody expected *him* to sing, and when he did nobody made a big deal of it. That he was a semi-famous singer did not go unnoticed, but it was nothing new to the Love Center crowd. Love Center's founder, the Reverend Walter Hawkins, was one member of the well-known longtime gospel-singing Hawkins family. His older brother Edwin had directed the Edwin Hawkins Singers to a crossover pop hit with "Oh, Happy Day" in the 1960s; Walter Hawkins and the Love Center Choir had made music that spent weeks on Billboard's Top 40 gospel charts, had been nominated for Grammys, and had won awards from

Billboard, Cashbox, Record World, and the Gospel Music Association. At Love Center, Sylvester just sang what he felt when he felt like it.

Love Center was also a bit like a Palm Lane for outcasts. Both Reverend Hawkins and Yvette Flunder, who was the associate pastor, grew up, as Sylvester did, in the Church of God in Christ. In that world, Walter Hawkins says, the "total experience was in the four walls of the church and everything else was a no-no." He watched a lot of young people get fed up with the church—"not so much that they didn't have a love for God or a yearning to know God better, but that they couldn't do it within the confines of the church." For a while, Hawkins was one of those who left church, but as he grew older he started looking for a way to bring together "all those young people who I knew could not survive in a traditional church setting." What started as a Bible study group at his mother's house had by 1973 become a church. His job, Walter figured, was to "take off all of these restrictions and allow people to just come and experience being exposed to the Word of God." As the hymn says, "While on others Thou art calling, do not pass me by." Like Sylvester, Reverend Hawkins wanted to make sure that the children who'd felt passed by were exposed to the flame. As his own pastor used to say, "You can't stand around fire and not be burnt."

Love Center's policy of not passing people by translated into a pretty wide-ranging, unusual congregation, dominated by exiles returning to the church. You came as you were. Once, Revered Hawkins recalls, a young woman came to the church and started talking about her background as a prostitute. "Oh, please, girl, I can tell you some things," one of the other women said, with a wave that said she'd heard it all already. "If you are looking to shock us, that won't happen, not here." They took the same attitude to Sylvester. His strangeness, when it was even noticed, was beloved.

One day, Sylvester stopped by to talk with Yvette Flunder. "Girl, we need some fried catfish," Sylvester told her. This was not so unusual; it seemed that every time Sylvester saw Yvette, he wanted fried something. While they ate, he talked to her about being pushed out of church as a kid. "He was angry at the way he had been handled by the church," Dr. Flunder told the filmmaker Stephen Winter, "and at the same time he had a sense of leftover guilt and shame from his childhood, and more importantly, guilt and shame for being as flamboyant a gay man and a Christian as he was." He wanted to have "assurance," he told her, of his relationship with God. "God is not the church and the church is not God," she reminded him.*

On his albums, Sylvester took to thanking "my Love Center family," and Love Center members like Lynette Hawkins—Edwin and Walter's little sister—and Daryl Coley began appearing as background singers. God moved way up in the acknowledgments, too: "First, I thank God for bringing me this far in life and career and not leaving me," Sylvester wrote on the notes to *All I Need.* "He is first in my life." On his final album, a few years later, Lynette and Tramaine Hawkins—Tramaine was Walter's Grammy-winning ex-wife—and the whole Love Center Choir would sing. Sylvester's album notes quoted Psalm 117: "O praise the Lord, all ye nations: praise him, all ye people. For His merciful kindness is great toward us: and the truth of the Lord endureth forever. Praise ye the Lord."

Once, Walter Hawkins rode on the back of Sylvester's moped to watch him perform at Trocadero Transfer. It seemed a little crazy, but in a way the scene reminded him of Love Center: "a bunch of people who are oppressed and looked down upon, feeling 'This is our place, this is our haven, this is our sanctuary, and he is one of us. We can just let it go.'" Sylvester, Reverend Hawkins thought, was freeing people. In his music and performances, Sylvester did at Trocadero what Hawkins did at the church: "He made a statement that there is a love in God that embraces anybody who wants to come."

When he did choose to sing at Love Center, Sylvester often picked the hymn "He'll Understand." Walter Hawkins was struck less by Sylvester's technical skills as a singer than by the conviction he brought to the song, as if he were reminding himself of something. "He preached a message," Hawkins says. Sylvester recorded "He'll Understand" on his next album, *Call Me,* sandwiched between a dance song and a ballad. *When I come to the end of my journey, weary of life, and the battle is won, carrying the staff and the cross of redemption,* the song goes, *He'll understand and say, "Well done."*

*In 1991, Yvette Flunder would open City of Refuge, a "radically inclusive" ministry meant especially to welcome lesbian, gay, bisexual, and transgendered people and any others "who have felt shut out, isolated and alone in their desire to be fully themselves and fully Christian."

Sylvester, single again, spent a lot of time out and about in San Francisco in 1983, but he seemed to be more and more on the lookout for people who refused to be bothered with conformity and exclusiveness. Sylvester was actually quite shy about approaching men at bars, but usually he didn't have to do the approaching. Jason Williams, the "grand sissy" who had admired him for a decade, was shy, too. Jason would see Sylvester at bars like the Midnight Sun, where sometimes they'd play Sylvester videos on the big screens at each end of the bar. He and Sylvester always smiled and said hello. One night at the Midnight Sun, Jason, assisted by a cocktail, finally got up the nerve to talk to Sylvester. "I really would like to know you," he said, and asked Sylvester out for coffee. He gave Sylvester his phone number. Sylvester promised to call, but like most men who make such promises, he didn't. When they ran into each other a few days later, Jason was ready to cut Sylvester up with his tongue and give as much sissy-tude as necessary.

"Relax, Jason, it's not what you think," Sylvester said, claiming, as men often do, that he had been out of town. "I'll call you." Soon Sylvester did call, and they sat up at Jason's house until two in the morning talking about music, fashion, and jewelry. It felt like a romance. The first time Jason went over to Sylvester's house—three floors, with its own drag room and music room—they sat in the middle of Sylvester's bed and played in his jewelry box. Sylvester, Jason noticed, had a shelf with all his awards, including a French one in the shape of the Eiffel Tower. He also had a magic genie lamp that he rubbed to make wishes come true.

Sylvester went out on tour a few days later, but he called Jason every day from the road, courting. "Have you been getting rid of every other man in your life?" he said in one call. "'Cause I'm comin' home and you gonna be *mine*." He sent a greeting card with a cartoon of a big-dicked, clone-ish, mustachioed white man straddling a satisfied black man in bed: "Jason," he wrote. "This card was so wonderful. It's a picture of me and you! See. We fit well together. Don't we! I can't wait to get you in this posi-tion. I just know we will be too fabulous together. Many a queen will be too through with us. But fuck them, 'cause we'll be too happy together. I'm loving you more each day."

That turned out to be another short-lived fantasy. Jason was not that man at all, and he didn't like that position. "I was this little swishy thing that everyone thought was a bottom, but I wasn't," he says. After a couple of dates, they realized they'd work better as sisters than as lovers. "Usually, if I have a boyfriend or a date and we break up, they don't just leave town, they leave the *country*," says Jason. But Sylvester didn't leave, and Jason didn't recommend, as he usually did in such situations, that Sylvester consider moving to another state. Instead, they played music for each other and searched together for beautiful things. They were fabulous and happy together, two grand sissy tops in beautiful jewelry, and many a queen was too through with them.

When Sylvester went out on tours, Jason would await his postcards. From London, a picture of Prince Edward: "I'm in need of a man. Perhaps a man like this one!" From Atlanta, a picture of Orton Plantation and Gardens: "Jason, I could just see you here in your hoop skirt." From Lisbon, a picture of the Jeronimos Monastery: "I think I'll buy it for a summer home." From Puerto Rico, a picture of the Morro Castle: "Boys, Boys, Boys! Sylvester." Sometimes Jason would just get a note on hotel stationery, telling him how happy he made Sylvester "being just as wonderful as you can be," and once he received a card of a woman in a black hat, black gloves, pearls, and a fur-hemmed black coat, waving from the steps of a decaying railroad car, holding two borzois on a leash.

One of the songs Sylvester recorded for *Call Me* was "One Night Only," a ballad from *Dreamgirls: One night is all I have to give, and in the morning the dream will be gone.* That pretty much summed up his life, Sylvester said. "I can make it for one night," he said. "I think one-night stands are awful, but just like the glory holes and the fuck rooms, I think they serve a purpose." Sylvester, having not quite found a Mr. Right, had no objections to Mr. Right Now, as the cliché went. Once, Sylvester was getting ready to go out with his favorite type of boy: short, white, hot, and blue-eyed. This one had received extra points for being bow-legged and from out of town. "Sylvester," Jason said, "he only wants to sleep with you because you're Sylvester." Sylvester shrugged. "That's fine," he said, "I just want to fuck him." If you were going to live on the legend, you might as well get more than a cocktail.

Jason liked to watch Sylvester work in the studio, cutting his next album, usually late at night. Sylvester would sing the same notes for hours until he got them right. The falsetto didn't always come easily, and sometimes Sylvester would hold his throat with one hand and hold a finger from the other hand in the air; as the finger moved up, so would his voice. If the

notes weren't coming out right, he'd excuse himself to go smoke a cigarette—usually Salems, or sometimes Benson & Hedges for old times'
sake. He'd return, and the voice would just blast right out of his lungs. On
the ride home, he and Jason would listen to what he'd recorded and
decide what might need fixing. When a song was done, they'd listen to it
at the house of one of Jason's friends, who had a phenomenal sound system, and if they liked it they'd break it at the I-Beam over the weekend.

Like all Sylvester's Megatone albums, *Call Me* was made on the cheap,
using mostly synthesizers and voices; it sounded much like the album
before it, and the one after. In addition to "One Night Only," the hymn
"He'll Understand," and the get-even "Band of Gold," Sylvester recorded
a series of songs in which he sang over a hyperactive, robotic, Patrick
Cowley–derived San Francisco sound. The most successful song from the
album briefly broke into the dance Top 20: "Trouble in Paradise," which
Sylvester cowrote. It was ostensibly a song about a relationship falling
apart, but there was something eerie about the refrain. Sylvester sometimes called it "my AIDS message to San Francisco."

"The sexual revolution has begun to devour its children," Patrick Buchanan
wrote in 1983, mixing false pity with barely concealed told-you-so glee.
Buchanan believed, of course, that AIDS was the logical outcome of sexual
freedom and gay rights; many good people knew, even back then, that this
idea was at best stupid. But he was right in description if not in analysis:
about the devouring of the children; about the implosion of the sexual revolution. That year, Randy Shilts reported, one researcher estimated that "in
some cohorts of gay men in San Francisco, AIDS incidence rates in the
thirty- and forty-year-old groups are now of the order of 1 to 2 percent."
Soon, people would be nostalgic for those rates.

It was hard to be "pro-sex," to advocate the throwing-off of prudish,
vanilla norms, when sexual contact—by 1983 known to be one means of
transmission—was becoming so closely associated with dying. In the seventies, the writer John Rechy had praised the "sexual outlaw" as a revolutionary figure; sexual adventure and experimentation had come to seem
almost a duty for a lot of urban gay men. As one man remarked to the
writer Dennis Altman, "Whenever I threw my legs in the air, I thought
I was doing my bit for gay liberation." Early AIDS reports treated
these same values and practices—especially multiple partners and public

sex—as lethal. (It took a while for doctors and public health officials, and everyone else, to recognize that, as Altman put it, "the relevant question was what acts were performed, not where or with how many.")

Bathhouses, the central symbols and spaces of "promiscuity," were the focus of much energetic debate. In San Francisco in 1983, as the city government and public health officials struggled with the question of whether to close bathhouses, the organized gay community was bitterly divided. Those who called for the closings as a public health measure were denounced as sexual fascists, moralistic traitors setting back the last two decades of sexual liberation; those who insisted on keeping them open were accused of being reckless murderers or of having their heads in the sand, or were portrayed as the hapless allies of greedy bathhouse owners. The children of the sexual revolution, at least some of them, had begun to devour each other.

Of course, AIDS united as much as it divided. As Sylvester had suggested, the new threat encouraged a lot of people to "get over their bull-shit," brought them together into AIDS organizations, marches and candlelight vigils, and informal caretaking routines. The dancer Rita Rockett, for instance, threw brunches on Sundays in Ward 5B, the AIDS ward at San Francisco General Hospital. She had started out delivering meals and doing errands for her friends when they took sick—the first of three complete circles of friends she lost to AIDS—and when they moved to the hospital, so did she. Every other Sunday was Rita Rockett Day at San Francisco General. Rockett cooked and fed the residents of the ward. Sometimes there was music, or tap dancing, or a comedian. Occasionally, Rockett threw a pajama party, and she celebrated so many holidays at the hospital that someone once likened her to a Bob Hope special. She had a mailbox on the ward.

By late 1983, most San Francisco gay men and lesbians knew someone, or knew someone who knew someone, who had entered Ward 5B. It was full up, and a hub of volunteer activity. More people died there than in any other ward, and "more diseases raged in a typical 5B patient's body than could be found in an entire ward in any other part of the hospital." Thanks to people like Rita Rockett, 5B had also quickly become "the most enter-taining unit in the hospital," Shilts wrote, and there was a waiting list: "Well-heeled, respectable gay men clamored to get in."

On some Sundays, Sylvester would call up Rita Rockett at Ward 5B. "What are you cooking this week, girl?" he would say on the phone.

"Maybe I'm coming for lunch." They had known each other since 1976: Rita had cocktail-waitressed at the Palms, where Sylvester and his band performed. Over the years, Rockett says, he had become "one of my best girlfriends." He treated her "like a movie star." Sometimes they went to the Russian River together, sometimes shopping, sometimes to get their hair done.

Sylvester would show up at San Francisco General in sweatpants and very little jewelry. He would sit with Rita in the lounge on the sunny western end of the ward—renamed the Rita Rockett Lounge—and talk to people and help serve brunch. He and Rita brought out the food as if they were working in the finest restaurant in town.

When Sylvester told Jason that he was planning a ten-year retrospective concert called "One Night Only" at the Castro Theatre for February 1984—he'd actually been performing longer than ten years, but could see no good reason to advertise that fact—Jason had two requests. "I want the entire third row," he said, "and I want one song."

"Okay, queen, which song?" Sylvester said. Jason requested "Here Is My Love," one of the songs Sylvester had written for *Too Hot to Sleep* and sung in his deep register. Sylvester refused, over and over: no one knew the song, no one had bought that album, and so on. Jason did not ask for much, but when he did he kept on asking. Sylvester had denied his previous request, which was to borrow a pair of turquoise Indian earrings. Jason decided he would stop at nothing to hear that song live in the Castro Theatre.

They were at a standoff until one day, holding on to Sylvester on the back of his scooter as they drove down Howard Street on the way to a fur sale, Jason played what he knew was his last card.

"Sylvester, I'll give up the booty if you'll sing it," he said.

Sylvester swerved the scooter and pulled over. "Queen, you'll kill us talking like that," he said. "You better not fuck with me. You really want the song that bad? You'd open the jewel box?"

"Yes, ma'am," Jason said, and didn't mention it again.

There had been just a couple of live acts booked at the Castro in some forty years. "I'm fine," Sylvester told a reporter a few days before the show, after a long rehearsal. "I'm having a nervous breakdown. I'm going to take a Valium in just a minute." The night of the concert, Jason sent him a

Western Union Mailgram composed mostly of Sylvester lyrics: DARLIN'
CAN'T WAIT DON'T STOP YOU MAKE ME FEEL KNOW YOU'RE GOING TO BE
FLAWLESS YOU ARE MY LOVE.

Although Sylvester hadn't performed in a major San Francisco venue
in nearly two years, the Castro Theatre didn't sell out, maybe because the
show was the same night as the local gay Cable Car Awards, at which several hundred gay musicians were performing "I Am What I Am" from *La
Cage aux Folles*. But in the multiracial audience at the Castro was Sylvester's
mom, in mink, along with all four of the Elites, most of Sylvester's other
friends, a lot of familiar-looking gay men, and a smattering of women.
They held programs with congratulatory advertisements from local estab-
lishments like the Trocadero Transfer, Leticia's Restaurant, Gramophone
Records, and the Elephant Walk. Sylvester had a fourteen-piece orchestra
and four vocalists—Jeanie Tracy and Martha Wash, from his old Fantasy
family, and Daryl Coley and Lynette Hawkins, from his new Love Center
family. The design was black and white. Sylvester's old boyfriend Michael
Rayner had arranged huge piles of white flowers next to black balloons on
each side of the stage. The orchestra wore black and white. The background singers wore white silky-looking outfits, and the bandleader played
a white violin. Sylvester, in a series of costume changes (gold sequins;
bright blue top over a silvery tunic; fuchsia sequined cape and fuchsia
feathered headdress), would provide the splash of color.

Sylvester did two shows, the second one at midnight. One reviewer
called the evening "retrograde," though "nostalgic" might have been both
kinder and more accurate. Sylvester sang for two hours, as album covers
and old photos flashed up on the screen. ("Look at me now," Sylvester
commented. "You can see we're talkin' major plastic surgery. And see
those teeth? Whoo, I got new teeth, too.") He pulled out his disco hits, his
gospel ballads, his Blue Thumb throaty rock, his torch songs, and tunes
from his new album, "Trouble in Paradise" and "Too Late to Turn Back
Now." He scatted on Billie Holiday's "Moonglow," and got the audience to
sing "You make me feel mighty real." After the intermission, Jesse Hamlin
reported in the *San Francisco Chronicle*, Sylvester walked onstage to sing
"Stormy Weather," wearing a gown, and a headdress with "a croissant-
shaped object resting majestically on top." With the strings behind him, he
sang the song "with the dramatic feeling and jazz phrasing you'd expect
from a Betty Carter or a Carmen McRae." He received two standing ovations and came back for two encores.

Jason Williams and his friends, as promised, had the third row at midnight. Jason wore a dinner jacket and lots of makeup and jewelry. They had all smoked pot and snorted some coke, and everyone was teasing Jason about the deal he'd made with Sylvester. Just when he'd given up wondering whether Sylvester was going to give him what he'd asked for, Sylvester, mid-song, waved at the conductor to stop. "Wait a minute, wait a minute. I don't want to do that song," he said, looking right at Jason. "Ya'll know my friend Jason?" he asked, and the whole third row screamed. "Okay, Jason, you're going to have to live up to your end of the bargain." He sang only a couple of lines of "Here Is My Love," but that was enough to thrill Jason to tears, and to keep the third-row children wondering for weeks whether Jason had finally given Sylvester the booty.

Almost anyone who had spent more than an hour with Sylvester knew that he could not hold on to money. "He would spend himself into oblivion," says Michael Bailey, who worked at Megatone Records. "He would be buying stuff for everybody," Audrey Joseph recalls, "buying dinners, buying clothes. He'd see a little bauble he liked and it was fifteen thousand dollars and he'd buy it." "Even in the lean years, honey, he still spent his money like water," says Jeanie Tracy.

Usually, Tim McKenna kept Sylvester on an allowance, but Sylvester was known now and then to make a scene and demand his money, and if that didn't work, to go behind Tim's back. Once, Sylvester's lawyers received a ten-thousand-dollar payment for him while Tim was on the road. "Send it to me," Sylvester said when he got wind of the money. It was his, Gerald Weiner, the lawyer, reasoned, so he sent it. When Tim McKenna called the next day, he went ballistic. "It's only been a day," Weiner protested. "It must still be there." Tim knew better. By now Sylvester would most likely have gotten a lampshade, a gadget, some clothes, a bedspread, and a new piece of jewelry.

Sylvester wasn't making all that much from his recordings, and though he still performed regularly at events around San Francisco, many of these were fund-raisers for AIDS organizations or local politicians, or events like Willie Brown's party for Democratic National Convention delegates in July 1984. (Sylvester got even the most uptight Democrats to shake some ass.) At home, as the music writer Joel Selvin put it to Tim McKenna at the time, Sylvester was like the little house on the corner that needed a coat of paint. In the larger world, he had been overshadowed by the kinds of musical acts he had helped make possible: androgynous, brown, sexy, shiny jump-suited Prince, whose "When Doves Cry" was the biggest hit of 1984; androgynous, pale, sweet, colorfully made-up Boy George, whose "Karma Chameleon" also hit big that year, one of five songs from Culture Club's debut album to make the Top 10 on the U.S. charts. Apparently, although Sylvester had been too much for the world just a few years before, he had quickly become a vaguely familiar face in the crowd.

Tim could still book Sylvester in small clubs, though now when he went to New York, it would often be for a gig in New Jersey. On tour, the personnel would be Sylvester, a manager, and a tape. In his heyday, Sylvester had sniffed that he would never sing to tracks, but a girl's got to collect her pennies; costs were low, so the money could still be good enough. He could get a few thousand dollars for a short set, and a trip to Europe could bring in tens of thousands of dollars. Sylvester would try to make Paris his last stop, so he could shop.

When Tim couldn't go out on tour—when Sylvester went to the U.K. in 1984, for instance—Michael Bailey often went instead. Michael was the oldest of seven children from a strict Salt Lake City Mormon family, and gay, and therefore a bit of a mess. When he moved to San Francisco, he discovered that crystal meth wiped out his shame, and spent many of the ensuing years in bathhouses, on drugs. At the same time, he worked at Moby Dick Records and then, when he was fired from that job, at Megatone, where his duties included running out for chicken wings when Sylvester and Jeanie were around. When Michael was fired by Megatone— he was doing too many drugs even for a drug-friendly company—Tim McKenna had hired him at his company, Borzoi Music Artists.

As Sylvester's righthand man on the U.K. tour in 1984, Michael Bailey had a few jobs: check the sound; push the button at the beginning of the show; push the button at the end of the show; retrieve the tape. He was also to get the cash up front and to wire the money to Tim before Sylvester could get his hands on it. Finally he was, Sylvester insisted, to dress in silk shirts and pants that showed off his ass; no more polo shirts with the collars up. "If you're going to represent me," he told Michael, a plump, curly-haired blond, "you have to dress the part."

Sylvester watched out for Michael. In Glasgow, Sylvester insisted on a rent boy, and when he was through, sent him over to Michael's room. At shows, he would point to the DJ booth and say, "Here is my friend, Michael. Michael, what would I do without you?" In Manchester, while the spotlight was briefly on Michael and the crowd was giving him a polite round of applause, Sylvester added, "Somebody please shag him tonight." Several people did.

The bandless road show was unglamorous, to say the least. Drunks tripped over extension cords; the tape would get stuck or be cued to the wrong place; an audience member might read a newspaper while the show was going on. Sylvester made do. If the electricity was gone, he sang a gospel song; if the tape was miscued, he glared at Michael and waited for him to reset it; if a newspaper was read, he snatched it out of the reader's hands and invited her to leave. In Glasgow, backed by his "embarrassingly cheapskate P.A. tape," one attendee reported, Sylvester "spent most of tonight's performance testing his seduction techniques on the predominantly male front row." He wore "an untidy hairstyle and black velour two-piece garment" on the empty, barely lit stage. He sang his hits, and then, when the backing tapes failed, "Marahuana" unaccompanied. His delivery, the writer said, suggested "a remarkable apathy," but he was "able to satisfy this sickeningly laudatory audience with cheap, one-line parodies of himself between songs" before disappearing to "become a mere blast from the past."

The audiences now did not really seem to want him to be anything but a reminder of the past. Once, in Florida, Sylvester decided not to wear much makeup or jewelry, the crowd being mostly older, straight Jews and Italians. After the first show, the manager came back to ask whether he was sick, and insisted that he put on the makeup and hair lest someone ask for his money back. "I can't do it!" Sylvester once screamed to Jason, getting ready to go on in one dodgy club. "They're gonna want me to growl and jump around and show my tits and sing those same damn songs. I can't do it again! *I'm tired of being her!*"

At other times, he *was* in the mood to be her but thought better of it. In 1984, Jason accompanied Sylvester to a gig at an auto show in San Jose. Sylvester's hair was short, but he was wearing a gauzy white blouse, much makeup, loads of jewelry, little summer sandals he'd bought in Europe, and toe rings. The people who went to auto shows did not tend to be the same people who bought Sylvester albums, and as soon as Jason and

Sylvester parked that afternoon, they panicked. "Jason, we gotta change the act," Sylvester said. They dashed to the bathroom, where he started throwing off jewelry and wiping off makeup, toning and blending. Jason watched him go out onstage. "Oh, God, there's the diva, that mad queen, and they've never heard of her," Jason thought, holding a towel so that Sylvester could dance over periodically and wipe off more makeup. He thought that gig might be the worst ever. "But in five minutes she pulled it together, and pulled the crowd with her," Jason says.

If there was one thing that Sylvester could draw on in lean years or trying moments—besides free cocktails at any bar in San Francisco—it was his commitment to majesty. When things were at their toughest or ugliest, Sylvester would often turn to a good friend and scrunch up his mouth. "What's a queen to do?" he would say. He would pause as he brought his right hand spiraling up into the small-circled, two-fingered wave of the queen, green rings turned into the light, then raise his chin and give a sideways glance before answering his own question: "Be royal." And off he would go. "Be royal" was a command to himself, an acknowledgment of his legacy, and a credo. It was "A man's got to do what a man's got to do," and "The show must go on." It was also "This too shall pass," and "Never let them see you sweat," and "Do unto others."

On one of his trips to New York City, Sylvester was booked to perform at the Teenage Black American Pageant at Town Hall. Tom Martin and Ed Shepard went with him. "They had these two tiny little speakers, and the only tickets they had sold were to parents and friends of the teenagers," says Tom. Sylvester had at his disposal only his little cassette, the two tiny speakers, and a small microphone on a wire. He wore black heels. Sylvester looked at Tom and Ed, and they looked at him. They all looked at the contestants. "What's a queen to do?" Sylvester said, and they all raised their hands into Her Majesty's wave. "Be royal," called Tom and Ed, and off Sylvester walked to give those teenagers and their parents a show they would take home with them.

On another of Sylvester's New York visits, the three friends went to a drag ball in the Bronx, in a prom-dance ballroom with plastic chandeliers, bright lightbulbs, tables with plaid tablecloths, and spiral staircases. There they encountered four Jheri-Curled Sylvester drag queens, each of whom wanted pictures with him. "What's a queen to do?" said Sylvester to Tom, and sat down to have his picture taken with the four other Sylvesters.

When it was time to mix down the final sounds and balances on a record, Megatone's owner, Marty Blecman, had learned to wave his credit card in front of Sylvester's face. Producers and engineers didn't really like Sylvester hanging around at that point. "He always wanted his vocals and his gospel girls louder than anything," says Ken Kessie, who mixed most of Sylvester's Megatone albums. Blecman's solution worked like a charm: Sylvester would take off with the credit card, says Kessie, "and we could mix in peace."

Kessie and Morey Goldstein were the major force behind Sylvester's 1984 release, *M-1015*. They wrote three of the songs on the album; they produced, programmed, and played keyboards on four. Goldstein played the sax, with Tip Wirrick on guitar and keyboards, the future *American Idol* judge Randy Jackson on bass, and a guy named Bongo Bob on percussion. "We were young and full of ourselves, and we couldn't imagine any way our tunes could be improved," says Kessie. Sylvester changed every song they presented. "He would just belt out his version, totally stylized, and totally make the song his own," Kessie says. "And there was no arguing with him. If you worked with him you did it his way. He was unstoppable." At the time, Kessie and Goldstein were dejected— though Marty Blecman would just give them a knowing shrug and a raised eyebrow—but, in retrospect, Kessie suggests that "we just weren't wise enough to recognize true artistry."

The album had a few stirring dance tracks—with Martha Wash back on backgrounds and with musicians playing real instruments, some of the songs sounded less machine-made than Sylvester's other recent work. In the context of 1984 gay life, though, *M-1015* was exhausting and somehow exhausted, like a marathon runner putting out his last strength to reach the finish line. The dance songs, none of which Sylvester wrote, were more pumping than ever. Their sound, which had come to be known as Hi NRG—even the name sounded like a designer drug—was frenetic. "We tried to make it sexy," Ken Kessie says of one of the songs, "How Do You Like Your Love," which included backgrounds from Michael Cooper, the lead singer of Con Funk Shun. "But the racing tempo just sounds nervous." A lot of the songs resembled "Maniac" from 1983's *Flashdance,* to which Jennifer Beals, her sweatshirt falling off one shoulder and sweat flying everywhere, had pumped her legs really, really fast; they had the sound of trying too hard, of desperation, of running from something.

Sylvester would tell you, if you asked, that his music rarely had a message other than something like "Let's party and have a good time." Still, he had an uncanny knack for capturing in the most shallow dance songs what it was like to be where he was, when he was. *I believe in the boogie,* Sylvester sang on his *M-1015* cover of "Lovin' Is Really My Game," *but the boogie don't believe in me.* That was a fairly accurate assessment. Even the ongoing warmth and fervor of Sylvester's falsetto, which could breathe life into the most artificial and familiar of thumping, could not make the San Francisco sound's upbeat attitude seem really alive anymore.

In San Francisco in 1984, people were still dancing, still dancing in ecstatic hordes, and it must have been a comfort to still be dancing to Sylvester's voice, as if the sound kept life recognizable. On an *M-1015* dance song, "Sex," Sylvester sang: *I'll give you my hand, you'll show me what to do, you make it hard.* Other songs covered similar ground: *Hot, cool, rough or smooth, how do you like your love?* he asked. And: *You've been dancing all night long with so many other guys. Make some room, 'cause I'm coming through, taking love taking love into my own hands.* That all sounded like old times, raunchy and wistful. Sylvester had always been part of what Barry Walters calls the "melancholy party tradition," able to get across "both the joy of the party and the horror that lies behind it," both "the delirious escape the party gave you and the fear of what you're trying to avoid." He was not going to be the one to stop the party. But something barely perceptible had shifted in the balance, as if the music had to work just a little bit harder to keep the dancers from the horror and the fear: the people who left the party now were probably not coming back.

The most remarkable tune from the album, "Take Me to Heaven"—a traditional Sylvester gospel-dance-synthesizer piece that broke into the dance Top 10—evoked a familiar equation of sex, drugs, dancing, and religious ecstasy. Into the mix, appropriately, it added death. It began with oohing and a hymn: *Now I lay me down to sleep, pray the Lord for someone to keep. Fill me up, love me forever. Take me to heaven.* Then the beat picked up, the hectic synthesizer kicked in, and Sylvester sang about hitting the dance floor and getting higher. Sylvester sang to a lover, to a dance-floor cutie, or to God—asking, commanding—*Why don't you take me, take me to heaven.* In the middle of the song, he repeated that refrain over and over, building and preaching it over big, strong chord changes. If you closed your eyes on the dance floor and sang along (*Higher! Higher! Higher!*), you entered Sylvester's curious bubble of elation, surrender, comfort, nostalgia, grief, and faith. Even if you didn't believe in heaven, you might be thinking about how much you missed someone, or would miss them, or how much longer you hoped you could stay here on earth.

14.

WHY DON'T YOU TAKE ME

"Don't I look full-on Indian tonight?" Sylvester asked Jason Williams, getting ready for yet another Gift Center party in the summer of 1984. Sylvester's look for the night was intended to accentuate whatever Native American blood he might claim; all black people, he told Jason, like to say they have Indian blood in them. His outfit was sort of Cher circa 1977: an ankle-length wraparound leather skirt; a large belt with an eagle's head made of rhinestones; turquoise necklace, bracelets, and earrings; hair pulled back tight across his head.

"Why, yes, you do," said Jason. "You look just like a squaw."

"You're just jealous," Sylvester said, since he was wearing the jewelry he had refused to let Jason wear. "You want to wear the earrings, but you can't. They are too nelly on you."

"Honey, talk about the pot calling the kettle beige," Jason said. "If I'm feminine, what are you?"

Sylvester raised his eyebrows. "I am Sylvester," he said.

After his set that night, Sylvester toweled off and stood with Jason Williams surveying the crowd. They noticed a handsome blond man, six foot two and eyes of blue, in a Hawaiian shirt. Sylvester was in a shy mood, so Jason approached the man. "You're really handsome and we love the way you're dressed, and my friend would like to meet you," Jason said, adapting a classic high-school-girl move. "Would you please come with me?"

Sylvester and the man, whose name was Rick Cranmer, chatted, and Sylvester asked for a date. He wasn't Sylvester's type—not short, not fast, not awed—but something seemed to click. "I'm going to court him," he told Jason. Sylvester picked Rick up the next night in his green Jaguar and took him to his favorite Greek restaurant. It was at least three days before Rick and Sylvester even had sex, and at least six months before they were living together. Rick, it turned out, had a good brain and excellent penmanship. He had a dinnerware set from the 1940s, clear glass patterned with perfect circles, which pretty much clinched the deal for Sylvester. They became deeply coupled—"husbands," Rita Rockett says.

Many of the features of Sylvester's relationship with Rick echoed his earlier ones. They weren't monogamous, for instance, in part because Sylvester spent so much time out on the road, and in part because, like most of their friends, they did not consider recreational sex and commitment to be incompatible. "Ricky's going to do what he needs to do, and I'm going to do what I need to do," Sylvester told Jason. Unlike Sylvester's previous boyfriends, though, Rick did not need bolstering, emotionally or financially. He had his own. He had a good job as an architect, and drew male nudes at home. If Sylvester was often somehow in the air, Rick was usually on solid ground. He was, Sylvester said, "magic."

Sylvester and Rick moved into an apartment a bit higher up in the hills, which was properly theirs together rather than just Sylvester's alone. The place was sleek, modern, spacious, painted mostly white; it had its own elevator, and a balcony off the back. On one floor was a powder room that Sylvester decorated as a tribute to the living legend Divine, whom Sylvester knew slightly from the early seventies, with framed, autographed glossies and movie posters, including one of Divine working a leopard print dress. Sylvester and Rick threw grand parties at their grand apartment on Grand View. If the occasion was a cocktail party, you knew not to show up in jeans; if you somehow found yourself drinking champagne out of a plastic cup, one of them would quietly replace it with a proper crystal glass.

Rick could play like a girl. Once, he showed up at Trocadero in an ordinary man's outfit and his hair up in three ponytails, like a very tall doll. He just wanted his long hair up and out of his face, he said, and he'd seen this hairdo on the Jetsons. "It's hard on the ones that want to go to bed with me," he told Jason, who was nearly peeing in his pants at the sight. "They've been hot on me for a while, and now they don't know what to do with me." Around Halloween, at the annual Muscle Systems party—given by a gym commonly referred to as Muscle Sissies—everyone was required to be in drag and then run around the Castro being crazy. Sylvester arrived in what they called his Dominique Deveraux drag, named for Diahann Carroll's high-glamour character on *Dynasty*: big hair, classic face, long pink fingernails that matched his lipstick, long black gown, flashy necklace and earrings, full bosom, fur. Jason wore a pink-and-black-striped sequined jacket over a smart black dress, bright red fingernails that matched his lipstick, false eyelashes, and a wide sandy wig: he was Linda Evans with a mustache. But Rick took the cake. He showed up as if he'd just gotten off work down on Montgomery Street: a navy business suit, blond hair and blue eye shadow, tennis shoes on his feet, and slung over his shoulder a briefcase-bag stuffed with work pumps, *The Wall Street Journal*, and a baguette. He was quite ridiculous.

In the movie of Sylvester's life, Rick would have been the answer to his prayers, his one true love, the lover man he finally found, but the truth is not so black and white. Some say they lied to each other and argued over home design, and had affairs that were more than casual. A relationship with a peer can try your patience. "It was an adult relationship, and far more complicated than I would wish on anyone, but it was working and they were working at it," says Jason Williams. "Even when they were fighting or there was tension, you could see, you could feel: it worked." There's no telling where the relationship would have gone, given more time, but Sylvester seemed to be as close to in love as he'd ever been.

Part of Rick's brand of Midwestern elegance was a personal privacy that bordered on secretiveness; Sylvester, although private, was not much for secrecy. Rick hadn't told his parents he was gay—though Sylvester once showed up at their door in Michigan with a video camera, introduced himself as Rick's "roommate," and came home to San Francisco with videotapes of himself with the thoroughly charmed senior Cranmers. When Sylvester's sister Bernadette came to visit, Rick stayed in the background. He would join them for breakfast and sometimes dinner, and he was a beautiful host, leaving a little piece of candy on Bernadette's bed. But he didn't seem to want to intrude. "No one knew Rick that well," she says.

Sylvester first turned forty in 1985, when he was thirty-eight. He wanted to go ahead and get that milestone out of the way while he still looked good. And he did not see the point in shaving off years when the reverse made so much more sense. He knew his guests would walk away saying, "Girl, he looks so young I simply cannot *believe* he is forty." His youthful looks were all natural, he once said, "except for a few things I had changed, like I had plastic surgery done to change the shape of my nose and cheekbones, and I'm going to have work done on the shape of my eyes." Besides, he liked to say, he was timeless.

On his birthday, Sylvester could sing what he wanted rather than what others wanted him to sing. "Yes, it's true, the doll is forty years old today," he said at his first fortieth-birthday performance at Trocadero, though of course it was not true at all. "Do I look okay?" He turned a bit to give the audience a fuller view. He was in high drag that night. Over a black gown he wore a long white cape lined with gold tinsel, and a gold fabric flower on one shoulder; he brought his long, long golden nails up to his large black wig, under which dangled big earrings in the shape of stars. "It's not even about the drag, okay, it's about total illusion," he said.

He was loaded that night, he later recalled, and it took him a while to find his voice. "I know this might be a little different for some of you, and those of you on speed, you'll just have to calm down for a minute," he told the crowd. "Think about Paris in the twenties, New York in the thirties, San Francisco in the forties. I know you can do that." He sang Cole Porter's "Night and Day," a jazzy "Cabaret," and some Billie Holiday. Later, the band played "Happy Birthday," and Sylvester stuck his face into a humongous birthday cake and said good night. "I'm going to go change into my butchest drag," he said.

He worked that birthday like a snake oil salesman. Timmy McKenna offered clubs a "fortieth birthday discount," and Sylvester celebrated on various dates across the country, sticking his face in many a big cake.

By the next time Sylvester celebrated his fortieth birthday—he was thirty-nine—boyhood dreams seemed again to be coming true. Between the two birthdays, the producer Narada Michael Walden had invited Sylvester and Jeanie Tracy to sing on Aretha Franklin's latest album. There he was, the boy who'd screeched over Aretha at Disquotay parties, singing in the background on "Freeway of Love."

His latest Megatone-produced album, *Mutual Attraction,* had been licensed and released by Warner Bros. The Warner Bros. licensing agreement afforded more resources for production, so the sound of the album was cleaner and more professional than its predecessors. But the *Mutual Attraction* album was also more than ever a family affair. On Sylvester's churched-up version of Stevie Wonder's "Living for the City," Walter Hawkins played piano, Tramaine and Lynette Hawkins Stephens sang with Jeanie—who sang on most of the rest of the songs, too—and the Love Center Choir. (Even the producers weren't so sure the song worked.

"Attempting Stevie Wonder was way over our heads," says Ken Kessie.) In the video for the song, Letha mopped the floor while Sylvester's voice sang about the mother who scrubs the floors for many and hardly makes a penny; his adopted sister Tammy was in it, too.

James Wirrick, who for quite a long time had felt like "old news" in Sylvester's life, was back with a song he wrote, produced, and played on, "Sooner or Later." Jerry Kirby, who had been one of Sylvester's background singers in the mid-1970s, was back, too, on two songs. On a strange cover of George Gershwin's "Summertime"—done to an eighties beat that sounded a bit like Soft Cell's cover of "Tainted Love"—Rick sang background vocals. Sylvester handed out "fashion citations" to the straight engineers and producers, who worked in jeans, sneakers, and T-shirts.

Reviews of *Mutual Attraction* were decidedly mixed. A *Creem* writer praised Sylvester as a "true original" who "hasn't had the crossover success that is his due," calling the album a "first-rate overview of his versatility," while *Sounds* called it "dismal," placing Sylvester "in the pending file until the next time." A *Melody Maker* reviewer snarkily remarked that "in his mind, and in one or two discotheques, Sylvester is a superstar," but that "the neutered Narcissus" had made a record that "isn't atrocious" and includes "undeniably classy dance music with the occasional tart incongruity stirred in." One of the singles, "Someone Like You," was quickly moving up the dance charts and getting mainstream radio airplay. It was a funky piece of bubble gum. "We were trying to grab that 'Freeway of Love' vibe from Aretha," says Kessie. In the middle of the song, Sylvester did a talky little bit about picking up a newspaper and seeing an ad that had everything he wanted. "I couldn't believe it," he said, deep-voiced, as the synthesizers bounced beneath him. "It really freaked me out." Then he swooped back up into falsetto, with punctuation from himself, Jerry, and Jeanie: *Baby! Said I always wanted. Baby! Said I always needed. Baby! Said I always wanted: Someone like you!*

"Someone Like You" went to Number 1 on the *Billboard* dance charts. He was slated to tour with a live band. Sylvester, as *Billboard* put it, was bouncing back.

Warner Bros. managed to get Sylvester booked for New Year's Eve on *The Late Show Starring Joan Rivers*. Sylvester had called in James Wirrick to play guitar and lead the band, and asked Jeanie Tracy and Martha Wash to sing backup. Martha was too busy with her Weather Girls gigs, so Sylvester asked Charlene Moore, a friend of Martha's he'd met at a party—another big girl who could sing. "Bring your drag now," he said when he hired her. Charlene learned her part and bought a brand-new blue sequined dress. Sylvester was very pleased. "Wear that," he said. "You look tough in that."

At the sound check in the studio in Los Angeles, Jeanie and Charlene practiced their little dance steps in the mirrors on either side of the stage. From the green room, Rick, along for the ride, watched Sylvester, Jeanie, Charlene, and the band perform "Someone Like You." Sylvester wore his high-blown red wig and a black suit with big shoulder pads. He was fighting a cold, but the song went over just fine.

James Wirrick's parents, off with golfing friends for New Year's, were thrilled that he was going to be on *The Late Show*. "Trust me, Mom," James said, "you *don't* want to watch this with your friends." When she saw the tape later, she thanked him for the good call. "I knew that he was going to come out and really flame," James says.

Flame he did. That was the night Sylvester, chatting with Joan Rivers and Charles Nelson Reilly, would announce to Joan Rivers that he was not a drag queen ("I'm Sylvester!") and recount the conversation with his mother, who had told him as a child that he couldn't dress up ("And she said, 'You're very strange,' and I said, 'That's okay'"). But first he would wave his diamonds in the air. "Look at your jewelry," Rivers said, with an "Ach!" thrown in to show how jealous and impressed she was.

"That's my wedding set," Sylvester said. Joan asked whom he was married to, and with a chuckle he answered, "Uh, Rick." As the audience whooped it up, Sylvester opened his eyes wide, then put his hands to his face.

"I'm sorry," he said, cringing. "Rick's parents are watching."

Rivers turned to the camera to address Rick's parents. "Surprise!" she said. Joan Rivers asked Rick's last name, and when she couldn't quite catch it, Sylvester spelled it out, slowly, letter by letter, as if it might be a secret he was tired of keeping.

The same year that Sylvester seemed to be reclaiming a battered throne, 12,016 people died of AIDS in the United States, about twice as many as had been killed by it the year before. The government predicted that the number would increase tenfold within five years.

"Everyone died," says the singer Linda Imperial of the latter 1980s, and so it seemed to many people in the thick of things in San Francisco. Many had left families that couldn't love them, only to bury nearly everyone who ever *had* loved them. The address books of most longtime gay San Franciscans became pages of crossings-out. "All the kids I knew in the seventies were no longer there in the eighties," said Marapasa. "Every time you would ask about someone, they were gone."

Eight out of nine of the coworkers who'd watched Michael Rayner walk into the Alta Plaza in Sylvester's fox coat died. Nearly everyone the producer John Hedges knew from the dance music scene died, including almost everyone from Megatone. "It killed our customers, it killed our artists, it killed our founders," he says. "It was kind of a three-year or four-year blur, and then everybody was gone." Some people had a hard time remembering who was dead and who was alive. At the Café Flore, where they had once plotted their next battle against the clones, the poet Aaron Shurin and his friends would now open the gay papers to the enlarged obituary section to see who'd died that week—a game, as Shurin describes it, "to see how much sorrow one can translate into endurance."

By 1986, the Castro had become almost seedy. Restaurants were emptier; clubs were emptier. There were blocks and blocks of empty parking spaces. People stayed in a lot. No one really knew what to say.

Tahara, who as a Cockette had been one of Sylvester's roommates, left San Francisco in 1981 and came back six years later. "When I left," he says, "there were three parties a week, and there was always a room where there was an orgy going on, and drugs. It was just raging. The streets were so full on weekends, the cars wouldn't be able to drive down Castro Street. When I came back, there was nobody there. You could walk down the street with your arms out. Everybody looked sad or old, and everybody was afraid of parties. I was going to a funeral every week."

"There wasn't a language to absorb it, there wasn't a language to clarify it," says Aaron Shurin. When people describe that period, they almost instinctively turn to metaphors. "It was a fucking extermination," says Joel Selvin. "It was a war," says Rita Rockett. "The Castro became like a museum," the reporter Allen White says. Robert Pintozzi, who for a while had been Sylvester's right-hand man and had dropped acid with him in the dressing room at the Opera House in 1979, had been living near the corner of Castro and Nineteenth Streets for a decade. Now he had to steel himself before he left the house. Going around the corner to the grocery store could be easy—walk, get a quart of milk and some bananas, come home—or it could be brutal. "You would just never know," he says. He'd turn the corner and have to stifle a gasp at the sight of someone he hadn't seen in a couple of months. Or he'd get that same look from people who thought *he* might have died. Or someone would just flat-out say, "I heard you were dead," and he'd smile and answer, "Thank God, girl, I'm not dead yet."

Dying people were cared for by sick people who, having viewed up close what might be in store for them (slow wasting and/or swift descent; diarrhea and/or constipation; skin lesions and/or blindness and/or dementia), reached the front of the line and became dying people. Some staged final moments, their own or someone else's. Aaron Shurin knew a man who made a tape for his dying lover that included Yoko Ono, K. D. Lang, Kiri Te Kanawa singing Schubert, Montserrat Caballé singing Bellini, and Elisabeth Schwarzkopf singing Strauss; he marked it "Honeybear's Memorial" in blue pen, and played it before his lover's ashes were scattered. He also knew a man who, hemorrhaging to death, asked his lover to carry him into the garden so that he could "bleed into the earth."

Living people had their hearts broken many times over, and carried shrapnel stories from one memorial service to another. A woman carried the ashes of a friend around town in a Gucci bag. A man convinced his lover to let go into death by reminding him of what it had once felt like to let his rectum relax around a fist. There was the man who gave douches to a young friend constipated from morphine, and a woman who brushed the teeth of a friend who had gone blind and mute at thirty. A man bathed his lover, whose wasting had left flaccid skin behind, and watched as the water collected in the folds of what had once held hard flesh.

"Everything had to be made from the ground up," Aaron Shurin says. "Every institution and collective act, in terms of aid and succor and elegy, had to be invented. It all had to be invented, and it took years and years of communal effort." Of course, San Francisco communities, the lesbian and gay community in particular, came up with beautiful inventions of aid and succor and elegy, and then of angry politics as well. People still went dancing, went to movies, made dinner, and not everyone's life was dominated by AIDS and death. Still, Aaron and a lot of others worried that the decade of Cockettes and Sylvesters, of boundary jumping and sex as revolution—the "one little decade of fabulous exploration," Shurin calls it—was being shut down, and that there would be no one left even to tell the stories.

Back at the Grand View apartment after a summer night of dancing in 1986—Sylvester was out of town—Jason Williams saw Rick Cranmer emerge from the shower. He looked unusually skinny.

"Ricky, have you lost weight?" Jason asked, which among gay men at the time was an oblique way of asking whether someone had AIDS.

"Yeah, a little bit," Rick said. He told Jason, at great length, that it was just because of job pressure and relationship troubles—Rick was frustrated, he said, with all of Sylvester's traveling, and his own affair with a gorgeous alcoholic had taken some unexpected turns. "He was smooth as silk," says Jason, "and I knew I was being lied to, that he was sheltering me." Later, Jason found out that he was also being lied to about the extent of Rick's drug intake. They all did some drugs, but it turned out that Rick was doing "huge quantities, all weekend," the way some people do when there's something they want to erase or exorcise.

A few months later, Jason was getting ready for a trip to Hawaii, and Rick invited him over. Sylvester was out of town again. Rick gave Jason some compilation tapes he had made, and then he went into his closet and pulled out several Hawaiian shirts, offering them to Jason. One of them, Jason thought, was the ugliest thing he'd ever seen. Jason declined, but Rick insisted. Jason was very uncomfortable taking all those shirts, though at the time he was not quite sure why.

People had started to talk, after parties or warm-weather events, about how thin Ricky looked. If Sylvester saw the clues, he did not allow them into his consciousness. In early 1987, their friend and dentist Steve Foresse ("a brilliant dentist, but he had major drug problems," says Jason) sat Rick and Sylvester down. He had given them both their beautiful smiles. That day, he told them he'd detected thrush—a yeast infection— in Rick's mouth, but they hadn't seemed to want to hear what that meant.

A British reporter wondered aloud in early 1987 whether Sylvester's "suspiciously svelte" look on the cover of *Mutual Attraction* indicated that he was sick. Sylvester told her it was "a self-improvement program" to "make myself as gorgeous as I can." This program involved the gym and support from his lover and cook, so that he could look wonderful in a bathing suit on his upcoming cruise-ship vacation.

By then, researchers had determined that the human immunodeficiency

virus attacked the immune system, and AIDS organizations were encour-
aging people to get tested, though treatments were few. Sylvester never
wanted to get tested for the virus, mainly because it seemed pointless; he
already knew the odds, and anyway there wasn't anything much to do
about the results, this being 1987. "It's not that I didn't want to think the
worst, because I've been a queen long enough," Sylvester said the next
year. "I didn't need to take the AIDS antibody test. Why would I waste
those ninety dollars when I could go shopping?"

In late August 1987, Rick was admitted to San Francisco General. He had
not told Sylvester, or Jason, or maybe anyone at all, that he was sick.
Sylvester was out of town, no doubt relieved to have a break from a rocky
phase of their relationship, but he came home right away.

"Why didn't I know?" Sylvester asked Jason. "Why didn't he tell me?"

Rick, thin as a rail, had a private room. Several of his friends, along with
his parents—who had flown in from Michigan—stayed by his bed and
prayed at the hospital chapel. On the evening of September 4, 1987, the
doctors told Sylvester, Jason, and Rick's parents that there was nothing
they could do for Rick except give him morphine. "Syl turned into a person I'd never seen before," Jason said. He read the Bible and rocked in his
chair, saying over and over, "Ricky's dying, Ricky's dying." The doctors
finally took Rick off life support and sent everyone home. "Jason, don't
stay here," Sylvester told Jason sharply, but Jason and his friend Dennis
stayed behind and watched Rick's breathing slow down and then cease.
He was thirty. Rick had gone very, very quickly. "He was here one moment
and gone the next," Sylvester said.

Back at the house that night, people poured themselves drinks, but
there were long periods of awkward silence. Sylvester sat in a chair,
wrapped in sweaters and blankets, and read his Bible. He looked very old.

The next night, he was scheduled to perform at a victory party for the
Gay Softball World Series at One Market Plaza. It was a strange place for a
party, the marble-floored lobby of a business building; it was a stranger
night to perform, just after the death of a lover. Sylvester had thought about
leaving town, but decided instead to sing. "I know that it killed him to do
that show, but it was what Rick would have wanted, and he had to do it,"
says Jason Williams. "He never would have lived with himself if he hadn't."
That night, Jason and the few other people who knew about Rick's death

kept quiet about it to the partygoers they knew. "They were all on drugs," says Jason, "and we were just trying to keep our shit together and see what we could do for the diva, because she could barely walk. I was worried he would really have to be locked up or he would kill himself. He was gone."

Sylvester arrived late; when he took the stage, the crowd of lesbian and gay softball players and their admirers cheered as though in old times. After a couple of upbeat songs, Sylvester stopped and wiped his eyes. He told the crowd, quietly, that Rick had died the night before, and sang "You Are My Friend."

The next day, September 6, was Sylvester's birthday, the very last time Sylvester turned forty. A party had been planned at the I-Beam and the line to get in snaked down Haight Street; the bar staff walked down the line distributing birthday cake. The theme of the party, named for a song from the *All I Need* album, was "Don't Stop." From the I-Beam stage, wearing a hand-woven suede shirt, Sylvester confirmed what most people already knew. "My lover died Friday night, and I loved him so," Sylvester said, "and if he was here he would love you." He sang and they danced. *Don't stop. Baby, don't stop. Don't stop, you're movin' me.*

Sylvester called Yvette Flunder the next week and asked her to come over. She brought along some fried fish. Rick had been cremated, and Sylvester had gone shopping for a golden urn. When she got to the apartment, Sylvester was sitting in the dining room, holding the box that contained Rick's ashes, getting ready to transfer the remains into the urn. For the time being, he must have been all cried out. He was moving the box back and forth, listening. "What is that sound?" he whispered to Yvette. "Somethin' rattlin' inside this thing."

"It's probably a piece of bone or a toe tag," she said. They sat quietly, letting some time pass.

Before Sylvester knew for sure that he, too, had AIDS, when he was just coughing and having some labored breathing, he went into the studio and recorded the vocals for a few songs that were to be on his next Warner Bros. album—a record that would remain unfinished. Sylvester and Jeanie were playing around with some songs. His voice was there, but it didn't sound right to him. "The inspiration, the thing that makes you be fabulous," just wasn't coming. "Sister Jeanie, my chops ain't right, honey," he said. "I can't seem to make them runs complete."

"Chil', you know you can sing," Jeanie said. "You better open up your mouth and sing."

Among the songs Sylvester recorded was one that he had wanted to record as long as he could remember, a "beautiful, beautiful, beautiful song" called "When the World Turns Blue," written by Joe Sample and Will Jennings. He had performed it at his Castro Theatre retrospective in 1984, bathed in blue light. It's a sad jazz song, with slow piano, the kind you can imagine hearing on a movie soundtrack while a lonely woman nurses a cocktail in a bar. *When the world turns blue, somewhere after you, I'll just have to handle it with all I know how to do. When the world turns blue,* he sang, *you will turn into rhythm, words and melody that show the power anew.* He might have taken a break to cough and catch his breath. *And when we are gone the song will live on. Some stranger will hear and he'll say "This is just how I feel. Every line, every moment is true."* He was pleased to have finally recorded it, even though, he said, "the vocals are shit."

Letha Hurd wanted her son to leave the city. As they had for many people, San Francisco and AIDS had become synonymous for Mrs. Hurd, and moving away seemed like something a person should do for his health. Sylvester never considered it. He loved the city, and the city loved him back. He did not tell Letha that he thought it was probably too late, anyway.

Since right after Rick died, Bernadette had known that Sylvester probably had AIDS, but he had sworn her to secrecy. "You are not to ever cry," Sylvester told her; though she did cry, a lot, she also shared with Sylvester the conviction that laughter in the face of death made just as much sense. When he'd first told her, they had talked not only about death but also about makeup. Bernadette had offered to do his makeup for his memorial. "I don't know," he said, skeptically. "We have to practice." After she'd tried her hand on his face, Sylvester looked in the mirror and said, "Oh, no, Miss Thing, this is not going to work. Girl, with that kind of makeup, they gonna have to keep the casket closed. They're gonna have to close it real tight."*

Bernadette helped Sylvester go through his things when he moved from Grand View to a smaller, less expensive, more accessible apartment. Just as he had ascended the hills of San Francisco in the middle of his life, Sylvester came down to the flatlands toward the end. His new apartment was in a modern three-story building on Collingwood near Eighteenth Street, just up from where he'd performed at the Elephant Walk. It had

*Bernadette is now a jewelry maker and makeup artist.

two bedrooms, a sliding glass door opening to a small balcony, and wall-to-wall carpeting. Some might call it modest, or even nondescript. On the walls, Sylvester hung his gold records, his collection of gloves, and his Keith Haring "Free South Africa" piece—he had befriended the artist years before in New York, and Haring had illustrated the cover of the "Someone Like You" 12-inch. In the living room, he placed white sofas and a plant. He kept his big TV, but downscaled to a Honda sedan.

"Well, this is a beautiful gold box," Bernadette commented, on the day she was helping him pack for the move. She took a gold box from a corner of the closet and opened it. "What is this? Who has these fireplace ashes in here?" she asked. "Bernadette, I'm going to tell you to put that down," Sylvester said. "I'm going to tell you to put it down, and then I'll tell you what it is." When she set it down, Sylvester informed Bernadette that she had been holding a box of Rick, and they laughed until they cried.

Without actually telling them, Sylvester started to let other people know what he now assumed to be true, that he had what he called the plague. Walking to dinner in the Castro one night with his new friend Dean D'Onofrio, a model in his early twenties with whom he had been carrying on a flirtation, Sylvester caught his image in a storefront window. "Damn, I look good," he said. "I've lost so much weight." Dean agreed that Sylvester did look really good. "But you know what," Sylvester said, "this isn't the way I wanted to lose it." Yvette Flunder figured it out when he told her over the phone about going to the gym and seeing an herbalist and eating some good boiled chicken. Only mortal illness could explain a fried-chicken man eating boiled chicken.

That fall and winter of 1987, not well enough for a full tour, Sylvester tried his best to keep working: money was tight. Tim McKenna occasionally still booked him at clubs around the Bay Area, but Sylvester was increasingly nervous about performing, as if he could no longer be certain his voice would come through for him. Achy, he sometimes took painkillers, which could sap the energy of a performance.

There were still small pleasures to be found, and small moments of majesty. Early that year, Sylvester and Dean D'Onofrio went down one weekend to San Jose, where Sylvester was to play at a club called St. John's. On the way, they stopped in at a Macy's, where Sylvester tried on clothes in the women's dressing room while a flabbergasted saleswoman and a bunch of star-struck Macy's queens skittered around to find him the right thing. In San Jose they settled in at the Fairmont, a new luxury hotel built to look like an old one. On their way out to the club, they peeked into the Fairmont ballroom and saw a ten-piece, forties-style swing band and dressed-up, swing-dancing couples. Sylvester was in full face makeup and black tights—not the right attire for a forties night—but he laughed at the sight with as much pleasure as if the show were meant for him. At St. John's that night, Dean thought, he sounded just right.

A month later, Sylvester had sinus surgery, and after that he started to have fevers. In early December, at the end of a short tour, he performed at an AIDS benefit in Philadelphia. By the time his set was over, he was having trouble catching his breath. He flew back to San Francisco and was hospitalized with what doctors called a sinus infection.

On one of the days Jeanie went to the hospital, Sylvester broke down and cried in her arms. The only other time Jeanie had seen Sylvester cry she'd envied the tears: *We love each other, y'all,* he'd said onstage at the Opera House, sniffling with Martha and Izora. *These women can sing, y'all.* "I tried so hard," he now said, sobbing.

When Martha Wash came out from New York to visit Sylvester in the hospital, Jeanie told her very sternly not to cry. "Just hold it until you finish," she said. Martha went in and dished and laughed noisily with Sylvester, and as soon as she shut the door behind her she broke down and wept.

Sylvester weighed around a hundred and forty pounds when he left the hospital. Jeanie took care of him most days, singing for his spirit and cooking peach cobbler and macaroni and cheese for his body, but, overwhelmed and burnt out, she told him she had to cut back to three days a week and suggested that he call his mother. Sylvester resisted: "I don't want my mother to go through it." "She's gonna go through it anyway, so you might as well have her here," Jeanie told him. "I am not your mother. I am your sister. I can't do what your mother can do for you. This is the time that you need her, and she needs you." Jeanie had a way of getting Sylvester to do stuff: she'd raise an idea with him, and a few days later he'd present it to her as if it had been his in the first place.

The next day, he called. "Sister Jeanie," he said, "girl, my mother's coming."

When Letha Hurd arrived, Sylvester finally told her he had been diagnosed with AIDS. She "didn't know very much about HIV, because that wasn't the thing that's normally discussed in black families," she said later, but she had suspected that her son was suffering from something more serious than a sinus infection.

Mrs. Hurd settled in for a stay. "Y'all got him spoiled," she said to Jeanie when she'd been there a little while. "You *know* he was that way before he got sick, and whose fault is that?" Jeanie teased back. Letha Hurd tended her baby until he was back on his feet, and then went home to Los Angeles.

A few months later, Sylvester accompanied Jeanie to the Dog Show, where she was performing, and she asked him to join her for a song. "Girl, I'm scared," he said. "I'm scared I don't have no voice." Jeanie told him he'd never know if he didn't try it out in front of everybody. In the middle of her performance, during a musical interlude, she went down off the stage. "Would you do it for me?" she asked. She saw fear she'd never seen before in Sylvester's face. "Just do it, just do it, please," she said. "Just once more, just do it. Just let out a squall." The last time she'd had to beg him to sing had been at her wedding two years earlier, where after much prodding he had agreed not only to design her dress, loan her his jewels, and fix her hair, but also to perform at the ceremony: *I love the Lord,* he had sung, *Long as I live, and troubles rise, I hasten to his throne.*

At the Dog Show, Sylvester took a breath and let loose a *haaaaooooooh* screech, and the crowd screamed in recognition or surprise or both. Jeanie hugged and kissed him and bounced back up to the stage. "Sylvester, y'all!" she called to the crowd.

In May 1988, after a hospital stay for Pneumocystis pneumonia, Sylvester drafted his will. He left his silver and crystal to his sisters and mother, his deco furniture to Jeanie, his record collection to a friend named Jimmie, his ceramics to his old Los Angeles friend and hairstylist Barron Matalon. He left his "diamond and sapphire ring that turns into a pair of clips," as the will puts it, to Kristiana and Alexandra Elite, one clip per girl. He left his royalties to Tim McKenna for a year, and then, "at Tim's death, or after one year, whichever comes first," to the AIDS Emergency Fund of San Francisco and the Rita Rockett Food Program. (Tim McKenna would die in January 1990.) To Jason Williams he left his box of ivory, silver, and gold.

There was even less left to will than he believed. Despite Sylvester's good intentions, the AIDS programs would never see a nickel. According to Roger Gross, the lawyer who prepared the will, Sylvester would leave his life essentially broke. He had long since started selling off the dresses he and his background singers had worn over the years, mostly to drag queens. He had been hocking jewelry on an as-needed basis at a shop down in the Mission, and picking pieces up a week later when he had some money; even on television with Joan Rivers he'd talked about selling a prized Jean Harlow ring. He had borrowed heavily against his copyrights and royalties so he could shop. A couple of months before he died, when Gross, the lawyer, went to visit him in the hospital, Sylvester was watching the Home Shopping Network, and not passively: "He was shopping while he was dying," says Gross.

One day that year, Jason noticed that the five-thousand-dollar, custom-made, floor-length mink coat Tim McKenna had given Sylvester one Christmas was not in its usual place of honor. It had been stolen, Sylvester told him: "I came in and threw it on the sofa, and the sliding glass doors were open." This seemed improbable—Sylvester rarely left doors open, and anyway he didn't live on the ground floor, so Jason and Jeanie thought he had probably sold the coat. "He didn't want anybody, especially me, to know that he didn't have any money," Jason says. Sometimes, friends slipped money into Sylvester's bedside table, or Tim McKenna would simply pay a bill out of his own pocket.

It wasn't long before Sylvester started calling in friends and giving them things, tailoring the gift to the friend. He gave Michael Rayner an art deco armoire; he gave Sister Jeanie some black baby dolls, some 1940s April in Paris perfume bottles with perfume still in them, a sweater made by the actor Michael Landon, and his Keith Haring poster. He gave Alexandra Elite, who had just started high school, a pair of antique lace gloves, telling her they were for her wedding. "I'm not getting married for a long time, Sylvester," Alex said. "Well, you know," he replied, "I'll be there."

He had given his mother one silk kimono and another to Jeanie, and he left the red kimono hanging on the wall in the living room. "I want to be buried in that," he told Letha Hurd and Yvette Flunder.

Another day, he called Yvette to announce, "I've got some things to give you." They were some vases and a candelabra; a throw with the Gucci name all over it; and his wool shawl with sable tails on the ends. The shawl was the most significant: he always liked to glam up his sisters—"It looks like you," he said—and Yvette Flunder isn't much of a froufrou dresser. Sylvester probably liked to imagine her dripping with sable tails. "It isn't something that I would wear," she says, "but it's warm, and it's something that he wanted me to wear, and it makes me remember." He gave away so much that by the end he didn't have much more than a hospital bed in his apartment. "I knew when he started giving away stuff that he had decided that he was dying, and he did not want people coming up in there taking what they want," Yvette says.

You can't take your belongings with you when you die, but there's nothing that says you have to hand over your yearning before you're ready. "I need a boyfriend so bad," Sylvester told Barry Walters. "I've been in mourning for a year now, and haven't had sex for longer than that. It would be so nice to have somebody to wake up to in the morning. But where am I gonna find a boyfriend, hobblin' around and lookin' strange?"

June is not generally the sunniest month in San Francisco, but the sun always seems to come out for Gay Day. So it did on June 26, 1988, the day of Sylvester's last Gay Freedom Day parade on earth.

Sylvester declined an invitation to serve as grand marshal: he had just gotten out of the hospital and, besides, he had not yet officially announced that he had AIDS, although a lot of people had guessed. That Sunday morning, Tim McKenna, Jason Williams, Tony Elite, and a few other friends were gathered at Sylvester's apartment, waiting to see if he was up for going to the parade. Tim McKenna had informed the parade committee earlier in the week that Sylvester might participate, and that he wanted to march with the People With AIDS contingent. He'd also issued a statement that morning in which Sylvester called on his friends to "support the many worthy AIDS-related organizations" and proclaimed that "the love between us all is so important in this crisis."

The sun was coming out.

Sylvester put on a large black hat, white pants, and a blue denim jacket with long suede fringes. "Get me in my wheelchair," he said to Tony Elite.

His friends packed Sylvester and his chair into the car, and Jason drove them down to Market Street. Toward the head of the parade was Art Agnos, the first San Francisco mayor to participate in a Gay Pride parade. Dense crowds lined Market Street; in later years, there would be barricades on the sidelines, but in 1988 there was no barrier between marchers and spectators. Tony and Nitsa wheeled Sylvester out to the street, and Tim took the chair.

Sylvester was anxious before the parade started, Tim McKenna said afterward, "but once we started to move, everything changed, and it was wonderful." Tim pushed the wheelchair in front of the People With AIDS banner; he had already lost his lover to AIDS two years before, and was looking a bit gaunt himself. Jeanie Tracy was riding in a pink '59 Cadillac just behind. Sylvester smiled and waved a glove, like a queen. He carried a balloon in his lap. "It was such a small thing, for one person to be pushed in a wheelchair," the reporter Allen White says, "but it was so real."

A lot of people didn't recognize Sylvester at first, what with the hat, the wheelchair, the emaciation, but then the response moved through the crowd like spooky waves lapping Market Street. "It's Sylvester," you'd hear, and cheers would begin. "It's Sylvester." Then silence or the sudden intake of breath as he approached. "Obviously he was very sick, obviously he had AIDS, obviously he was dying," says Tony Elite. "You'd see people put their hands on their mouths, tears." "Sylvester!," cheers, breaths, "Sylvester!," silence, cheers, silence, breaths, "Sylvester!," cheers. "It was so strange," says Jeanie Tracy.

Some were surely buoyed by his presence. "Sylvester is, as he was then, one of the few gay celebrities who never renounced his gayness along the ladder of success," Armistead Maupin said after the parade. "He's allow-ing us to celebrate his life before his death, and I don't know a single star who has the integrity to do that. In sickness and in health, Sylvester has carried on with the identical spirit." Sylvester was never interested in hid-ing. He was loyal to himself, to the place he'd made his home, and to the people who had helped him celebrate the strange and the fabulous. His parade appearance had a quiet majesty—"What's a queen to do?"—and he had clearly given thought to his attire.

Still, no matter how many shriveled forty-year-olds you had seen, no matter how many thirty-year-old friends you'd watched become demented, seeing Sylvester that day—he of the headdresses, now smiling out from beneath a too-big hat; the bouncing, hefty goddess now an old man softly waving a glove from a wheelchair—might have opened up yet another big hole where you thought there was only vacant space. It's not that you hadn't seen this before, or that Sylvester was a saint while the other dead, your own dead, were unworthy. Sylvester was exactly like every other person with AIDS a spectator might have known: giving things away, trying to hold on, saying good-byes, planning his ending. He would be another panel on the AIDS Memorial Quilt. But there was something especially painful about watching a symbol of audacity roll by, a symbol of helplessness.

Sylvester had been speaking publicly about AIDS in his I'm-not-really-political political manner for years. He'd taken to attaching safe-sex booklets to the backs of his autographed photos, and he'd complained to reporters about still seeing "kids out there doing the nasties." After his appearance at the parade, he talked with more frequency and authority about AIDS—now using his own illness, and his status as the first black celebrity with AIDS, as a hook. "It bothers me that AIDS is still thought of as a gay, white male disease," Sylvester told the *Los Angeles Times* in September, citing statistics to the contrary. "The black community is at the bottom of the line when it comes to getting information, even when we've been so hard hit by this disease." He spoke matter-of-factly about his symptoms, his sex life, and his attitude toward death to the African-American magazine *Rhythm & Business.* "I don't regret a thing," he said, though he did allow that he missed shopping and going out to movies and lunch, and that he was upset that his clothes no longer fit. Sometimes, tired of talking, he kept it simple. "I'm dying, and it's not pretty," Sylvester told *The Advocate.* "That's it."

Sylvester had twice heard rumors that he was already dead. "Until I call you up and tell you I'm dead," he told a reporter, "don't believe it."

A lot of strangers seemed to want to say good-bye to Sylvester in some public, grateful, cheering manner, and there were quite a few opportunities. A couple of months after Gay Pride, at a Dreamland party to celebrate the release of *Tribal Rites*—a book about the San Francisco dance scene—Sylvester sat on the balcony, in a black tuxedo and yards of pearls. Trees had been set inside the club, deep green against the white walls. An announcement was made that Sylvester was a special guest that night, and at around ten o'clock, the DJ played "Mighty Real." After the song ended, the crowd was left in silence and the only light came from the balcony. "The crowd began to applaud," wrote Allen White, who was there. "The applause built in intensity as they started to scream and yell." After minutes of noise, Sylvester looked down and gave a nod to the crowd and a sweep of the hand that "was vintage Queen Elizabeth." The next week, he called Tom Martin in New York. "Tom," he said, "I had my heels on. And I danced." That may have been a fiction offered as a gift to Tom, since by then Sylvester was having trouble with his feet and legs.

The theme of the 15th Annual Castro Street Fair, in October, was "A Tribute to Sylvester." About seventy thousand people filled the streets. The sun broke through the clouds at three in the afternoon. The year before, Sylvester had hosted a champagne breakfast in his three-level house on Grand View; the first on the block to have a video camera—a big, heavy, over-the-shoulder contraption the size of two shoe boxes—he had filmed people all day. This year, he was too weak to leave his apartment around the corner from the festivities.

In front of a huge picture of Sylvester, various city figures read tributes, including Supervisors Carol Ruth Silver and Harry Britt, who had read the declaration of Sylvester Day at the Opera House nine years before. Booths sold Sylvester posters and T-shirts. Word got out that the subject of all this veneration was at home, nearby, too sick to revel. The crowd chanted "We love you, Sylvester!" and then just "Sylvester!" over and over, together and loud, in the direction of Collingwood Street. Friends say that Sylvester could hear his name roaring across the neighborhood and right up into his bedroom window.

15.

THE RED KIMONO

sweet birds sang: *there is trouble in paradise today.* and we
    sweated each other away: shirtless
you and I afforded ourselves: a land traversed many times. nights
    of undoing
lover divine and perfect comrade. *I always wanted someone like*
    you. now the ground is braking

visitation is brief but exact. smiles grow a little sharper. no more
    expectations
ears in lips and no more wit. *and I'm still real hot then you kiss me*
    there. we toy in earnest
slow tyranny of moonlight: dead boys make the sweetest lovers. if
    they could all be finale

they pass too quickly out of breath. *I feel real when you touch me.*
    the night is an open "o"
erased metropolis reassembled: the anatomy remembers where it
    came from. up as if from subways
reveries are rivers: *why don't you take me to heaven?* the shiny
    buckle unfastens at last

        —D. A. Powell, "[first fugue]"

"I think the day I die, I'll be sitting somewhere, in some nice comfortable
spot, and die," Sylvester told his old friend the ex-Cockette Martin Worman,
in December 1988. Months before, he recalled, he had been in Philadelphia, sitting around with Tim McKenna and his "good friends" the singers

Phyllis Hyman and Jocelyn Brown, talking and dishing. "I said, 'I love you all,' and I kissed them all and in about two minutes I was asleep. I mean *asleep.* I had my black mink coat draped over my shoulders. I was just sitting there asleep. Timmy says, 'I think she's gone.' I always told Timmy, he always knew, that if I went, to put me in my mink coat, I was going to try to put myself in a nice position. Just pick me up and put me in the hearse. Just put me in the metal box, ship my body home to San Francisco. It's all I wanted."

Most of the late fall of 1988, Sylvester spent at home in San Francisco in bed, on the phone, or greeting a steady stream of visitors. When Marapasa came to see him, bearing memories of Disquotay days, Sylvester was still walking but his hair had gone from kinky to straight. He threw up several times while she was there, but told her he was getting ready for his dinner, which was to be pork chops and pound cake.

"Child, how can you be up in here eating pork chops and pound cake?" Marapasa declared. "You *need* to be eating some brown rice and vegetables." He said, "I ate brown rice back in the sixties and I don't like it. I am eating what I want to eat." The last Marapasa saw of Sylvester, he was having his pork chops and pound cake.

In the last couple of months of Sylvester's life, lots of people came through that Collingwood apartment to pay their respects: Tom Daniels, his ex-boyfriend-turned-friend, who listened to his complaints; David Frazier, his bandmate from a decade before, who held his hand; Michael Rayner, who sat and ate pizza with him and joked about Sylvester's gray hair. Tammi, from Disquotay days, flew in from New York, and she and another ex-Disquotay, Jackie Hoyle, came by; while Tammi put lotion on Sylvester's ashy skin, the three of them, Jackie says, "threw out a couple of quirks about good times," like when Dooni and Tammi used to study *Vogue* as if it were the Holy Bible. Giana from Elephant Walk days visited from New York in November, cooked Sylvester fettucine with white clam sauce, and joked with him about their love lives. "Girl, I know I still look good," he said, though they both knew he looked like shit, could barely walk, and was taking more pills than you'd ever seen in your life. "I could get me a new husband, can't I, girl?"

He loved to kid with visitors about his appearance, playing the role of the fallen diva unable to let go of her vanity. "My hair is a mess, and my makeup," he said to Rita Rockett. "Don't worry," Rita replied, melodramatically, "we will be gone from this life soon, and we will all be together, and we won't have to worry about hair and makeup ever again."

"Girl, don't make me laugh," Sylvester said, laughing. "I will lose my oxygen. Girl, I'm going to miss you."

"Girl, I'm going to miss you," Rita said, "but they need some music up there. I'm going to miss you, but honey, you are going to be singing so loud I will hear you. You will be cracking windows from up there."

Jeanie Tracy always knew when things had slowed down over at Collingwood. She spent three or four days a week there; on nearly every one of the other days, she'd return home to several messages from Sylvester on her answering machine. By now, his voice was slowed down, deeper and scratchier than before. "Jeanie," he'd drawl, "where are you, girl?" For years to come, when the phone rang, Jeanie would sometimes find herself thinking it was Sylvester, not gone, calling from some town out on the road just to say, "Hey, girl!"

Thanks to Jeanie, even Patti LaBelle stopped by. Sylvester had always gone to see her when she was performing in town, and a few years before she'd invited him onstage to sing "You Are My Friend" with her, claiming him from the stage as one of her girlfriends. Once, after a show at the Warfield, she had admired Sylvester's single, custom-made, three-hundred-dollar, shoulder-length sparkly earring, which had been delivered to him that very day, so he'd given it to her. "He was way out there, and that's what I loved about him," she says. "He said, 'Take me or leave me,' and most people took him." He sounded something like her, she thought, and often "looked like a grown-up Patti LaBelle." "Whenever I met him it was pleasant to my eyes," she says, "to see him all made up, looking better than me."

The last time she saw him, though, Sylvester looked nothing like her. Jeanie Tracy had told her he was ill, laying it on thick because she knew how much Sylvester admired Patti. "Patti, go see him," she said. "I'll pick you up. Patti, oh, I'm so glad you're going to do it, oh, my God. Sylvester loves you so much, and you know, he's been abandoned, and I really feel like if you go it's going to boost him. You might give him some more time to live. Just let him live a little longer, Patti. If you do this, oh my God. Sometimes we have to be more than singers. Sometimes we have to be missionaries." Patti expressed concerns that it might hurt her singing that night. "You gonna sing better! You gonna sing *better*!" Jeanie said. "I'm gonna do this!" said Patti LaBelle.

Jeanie gave her the same orders she'd given Martha Wash: just go in there and give him the latest dirt; don't tell him he looks terrible, even though he's not going to look like Sylvester; don't cry until you're out of his sight. Patti LaBelle and Sylvester chatted for an hour, diva to diva. Sylvester got her telling the story of the time a faint-feeling Diana Ross had asked Patti LaBelle to help out on a song, and LaBelle had so nearly stolen the show right out from under Diana Ross that people took to joking, "Don't ask Miss Patti to help you do *nothing*." In the snapshot from the visit, Patti LaBelle is leaning into Sylvester on a big white chair, her hand on his sweatpants leg and his hand around her waist, both smiling big; Sylvester's eyes are bright.

"You did good," Jeanie told her when Patti LaBelle came back out to the car. "He just looks like a little old man," Patti LaBelle said. She asked Jeanie to slow down the car and take the long way, even if it meant that she'd be late for her own show.

The next time Patti LaBelle was in town, a month or two after Sylvester had moved on, Jeanie gave her a little gold boxy pocketbook that had belonged to him. "I'm going to put my tears in this little box," Jeanie remembers Patti LaBelle saying, though in the end she put in coins instead. Sylvester's gold purse is still carried from place to place by Miss Patti LaBelle.

Sylvester had neuropathy in late 1988. He could barely walk, and most touch caused him pain, but he loved to be touched. Tony Elite would sit and gently rub his legs, and when that became too painful, stroke his skin, and when that became too painful, just sit with him.

Tony and Nitsa took Alexandra and Kristiana to be with Sylvester, who had talked about wanting him to make up their faces one more time. "It was always weird when I would see Sylvester without his wig," Alexandra says. "He almost always had some hairpiece on when he came over to our house." In his dying days, when he knew the girls were coming, he'd say to Tony, "Give me my makeup. I want to put something on." But there was only so much he could do. On this day, he was in bed, and his hair was very short and wispy, his face gaunt, eyes sunken, flesh wasted almost to the bone. The bedroom faced the street, and in Alex's memory it was also dark. Sylvester seemed absent, and then suddenly looked at the girls with clarity and started to cry. "I'm going to miss you guys so much," he said, and then he started talking about things the girls couldn't understand, saying things the adults probably didn't understand either. The girls left the room frightened and crying. For two or three days, Alex came in and out of the apartment, falling asleep on the couch and then going into the bedroom just to look at Sylvester.

"I haven't really been a bad person, have I?" Sylvester asked Yvette Flunder on one of her visits. She figured he meant all that sex and carrying on. "Syl, I don't think so," she said. "If that's what's been going through your head, today's the day you gotta stop it. Folks don't measure that way with God. What I know of you, most of your life you've been trying to find somewhere to light, somewhere to call home. You loved people and you gave to God." They prayed together. It took him a little while, Sylvester said not long after, but he'd settled himself and settled his life. "Honey, I've done it all—been, had, lost and given away everything," he told a *San Francisco Sentinel* reporter, "but my life has always been spared. And believe me, I have been in some situations, honey, that were dangerous. But through it all, God has been good to me. In my stupidity, my awfulness—you know, ranting, raving and carrying on—he has always taken care of me." He didn't want to be morbid, he said, just realistic. "I've been a mad queen," he told Marty Blecman, who was trying to get him to try AZT, the first anti-HIV drug, approved by the U.S. Food and Drug Administration the year before. Sylvester wasn't interested; AZT, which was highly toxic, had almost killed Tim McKenna, and besides, everyone knew it produced the pancake-flat buttocks known around the neighborhood as "AZT ass." Sylvester said, "This is in God's hands." He had no regrets. "The Lord has a lot to do with it," he said. "When he says I'm ready to go, then it's time to go." He hoped he wouldn't be in a lot more pain, but he would be fine, Sylvester said, because his spirit was fine.

Sylvester called close friends into his room to make sure they knew he loved them, and to give them some comfort. He called in Jason Williams in early December. "This is going to be one of our last times," said Sylvester, now shrunken to around a hundred and ten pounds, as Jason carefully cut his fingernails. Jason was crying. "I don't want you to cry anymore, 'cause I'm going to be all right," Sylvester said. "I love you, so promise me no crying. I'm gonna be all right, but you've got to be all right, too." A few days later, Sylvester lost control of his bowels, and insisted that

Jason immediately leave the room. A few days after that, Jason tried to help him pull the shoes off his swollen feet, and when Sylvester screamed in pain, Jason burst into tears. It is possible only up to a point to keep from crying and be all right.

"I don't ever want to be a burden to anyone," Sylvester told Martin Worman, who was interviewing him for his Cockettes dissertation a few weeks before Sylvester died. "Close your eyes with me. I'll know you're there. Just go to sleep. I had this whole thing planned out. I just want to go to sleep. Because I know where I've been, and I know what I've done. I just want to go to sleep, peacefully, quietly. My mother knows. You see, everyone knows. It's all taken care of. All done. All my business is done." Then he asked for his urinal.

Letha Hurd got the whole family together for Thanksgiving at Sylvester's house. Sylvester's grandmother, nieces, sister, brothers, and nephews— pretty much everyone except Bernadette, who was ill that November. She talked to her brother on the phone, and against instructions cried because she couldn't be there. Sylvester's grandmother JuJu cooked an old-fashioned turkey dinner. After Thanksgiving, Letha stayed with Sylvester. "He knew he was going to die," she said later. "We laughed and talked and I spent nights with him. We talked about the past, when he was little, all the things he did, silly things, and we laughed about it."

"Mom, tell Bernadette to hurry," Sylvester said to Letha a couple of weeks before Christmas. "Oh, you're just trying to stay alive for Bernadette?" Letha said. "Yeah," he said, "I'm waitin' on Bernadette." Letha called Bernadette to tell her to come up as soon as she was healthy enough to fly. "Now you know I only fly if somebody's dying," Bernadette, who has a fear of flying, said to Sylvester. "Now are you *sure* you're dying? Don't miraculously all of a sudden get healed." They laughed. "No, I'm dying," he said. "Get here fast."

When Bernadette arrived at Collingwood Street, Sylvester woke up out of a near coma. He had a hankering for chocolate chip cookies, so they sat up eating cookies and watching black-and-white movies on TV, the way they used to when she was a little girl, until he faded out. Bernadette slept in the room with him. When he snapped back into alertness hours later, it was to tell his mother he had a taste for french fries. There were no pota- toes in the house, so Letha went out and bought some and fried them up.

The three of them sat eating french fries at one-thirty in the morning, Bernadette and Sylvester laughing about the bird funerals they'd conducted as kids. Sylvester spent much of the next day watching cooking shows, which inspired another sudden craving, for some baked beans. Bernadette and Jeanie, who was back over by then, went out for some beans. "If I bake these beans, you better eat them," Jeanie said, and baked them up. One bite was all he could handle, but it looked to Jeanie like those were the best baked beans she'd ever cooked.

A few days later, Sylvester called Jeanie over to his bedside. "Girl, I'm going under the morphine," he told her. Jeanie kept herself together. He gave her a familiar little half-smirk, curling up one side of his mouth in a way that said, "Okay, this is it. Here we go." Jeanie said, "I know, chil', I know. It's okay, though."

Letha Hurd insisted on administering the morphine. The nurses on hand were not happy. "They want to tell *me* how much to give him, but I'm telling *them*," Mrs. Hurd told Jeanie. She wanted him to go himself, not be dispatched by a drug. "I just want him not to be in pain," she said. "I don't want them sending him to the other side before his time. They don't like it, but that's just too bad."

Jeanie spent what turned out to be Sylvester's last day with Bernadette and Letha and Sylvester at the house. That evening, before she went home, she went in to say good night to Sylvester. "I love you," she said. He was too asleep, or drugged, or occupied by his transition to another place to talk, but he said, "Mmmm," so she knew he'd heard her.

Sylvester loved his television, so when, on the night of December 16, 1988, he asked Letha to turn off the TV, she knew he was reaching the end. She and Bernadette and the nurse sat up all night and into Friday morning. "He told me he's not going to die with you in the room with him," the nurse told Bernadette. Letha, looking back later, thought that must have been true. "He never said anything," Letha recalled. "He just lay there. I never got the feeling that he wanted us to leave the room, but he wouldn't go anyplace until we left out the room." Letha went into the kitchen to get a cup of coffee, and Bernadette joined her. They were gone only a few minutes, but when Bernadette walked back into the bedroom, it smelled different—"not a bad smell, it was just an unusual, unfamiliar smell"—and she knew Sylvester was gone. She brought her mother in, and Letha gave her son a kiss, and they sat one more time, the three of them. The nurse closed Sylvester's open eyes.

While they were waiting for the undertakers to come, Letha fixed breakfast. "You killed him, Ma," Bernadette said. "It was those chocolate-chip cookies. You know you can't bake. You did it with the chocolate and the french fries." Letha and Bernadette went back in with Sylvester, and sat looking at pictures, laughing and talking. Sylvester's tall body posed something of a challenge to the undertakers: the sheet fell off when they were trying to get him through the doorway, they couldn't figure out how to get his body into the elevator, and at one point they accidentally propped him up in the hallway upside down. Letha and Bernadette were in tears. "It was total comedy," says Bernadette.

Sylvester James knew how to make an entrance, and he knew how to make an exit. His memorial service played like a grand diva's finale in an old movie, mainly because he had directed it. Some in the family had wanted the casket to be closed, but Sylvester had requested otherwise. "He wanted to be seen," said Tony Elite. "He wanted to be *viewed*." He left more specific instructions, too. Just a few hours before he passed, he told his mother he wanted a pearl-colored casket with gold trim, since he thought a white one would make him look as if he were lying in a big white refrigerator. He wanted Jeanie Tracy to sing something—as long as it wasn't "Touch Somebody's Life," which worked his nerves.

"He told the choir to sing like they'd never sung before," his mother told the filmmaker Tim Smyth. Memorial color scheme, red, white, gold. Candelabras on both sides of the casket. Too many flowers, and lots and lots of singing. As for hair and makeup, he told Yvette Flunder, "Girl, make me fabulous. Do you understand? *Fabulous.*" Just in case, he gave her detailed instructions. At Sylvester's request, Yvette enlisted the help of Marcus, a cosmetologist who was a Love Center member. Sylvester's hair was pretty much gone, but Yvette and Marcus used a new hair-glue technique. "We put some flaming red hair all around his crown and brought the hairline in and worked the rest so it fit," Yvette said. She had promised him bright red lipstick to match the kimono, but Mrs. Hurd asked her to tone it down. They compromised, wiping off the red lipstick and replacing it with a peachy orange. "It worked for him," says Yvette Flunder, "and he was looking pleased, because it kept Mama from having a cow and still made him Sylvester." Now he himself matched the Love Center.

Kreemah Ritz's sense of time was frequently softened by a cloud of pot smoke, and by the time he and a friend arrived at the Love Center, limousines were triple-parked and the street was blocked off. The church was in a big converted theater in a fairly run-down section of Oakland, and you half-expected to see Sylvester's name on the marquee. That seemed appropriate enough for the occasion, Kreemah thought, and so did the dominant color of the place, a peach paint that Kreemah thought of as "titty pink." Inside, it was standing room only. The balcony was packed, so Kreemah and his friend slowly made their way through the crowd down below. He caught sight of a smattering of ex-Cockettes, who though they still looked unusual enough seemed to be aging into something tamer and maybe a little sadder than the hippie-anarchist, sexually wild, drugs-and-old-musicals-loving, thrift-store-drag-and-glitter-wearing troubadours they'd been. Kreemah spotted an empty space toward the front, and they squeezed in, he swears, right next to Aretha Franklin. The Love Center choir was in purple, and the pastors were in magenta. Flowers crowded and ribbons streamed the place: red, white, gold. Four tall, weeping transsexuals in black hats and black veils stood at the side, dabbing at their eyes with kerchiefs. Some of Sylvester's fans sobbed and cried as if they had known him. A few people asked at the door whether there was a cover charge.

Michael Rayner drove by himself across the Bay Bridge. He had changed clothes five times before he left the house that day, as if committing to an outfit would mean committing to Sylvester's death. He went back and forth with himself about what kind of flowers to bring, and settled on a single rose with a glittery ribbon. Leslie Stoval drove the KMEL van over to Love Center and stood at the back, too devastated to talk to anyone. Robert Pintozzi held up Jason Williams, who was so stricken he could hardly walk. They sat with Tim McKenna, who didn't look well, just behind Mrs. Letha Hurd and her family, who sat in the front row in front of the coffin. Harvey Fuqua was there. "The house was filled with Sylvesters, to the rafters," Yvette Flunder recalls, "queens of every color and culture." James Wirrick saw band members he hadn't seen in years, and sat next to his friend Marty Blecman. Alex and Kristiana Elite sat nearby with their parents, Tony and Nitsa, red-eyed and dazed. Alex Elite felt a "crumbling" inside of her. Something like: *What are we going to do now?*

Many people in the room, too, must have sensed the collapse of something bigger, which Sylvester embodied but did not create: a respect for the uniting freedom of fabulousness, for the power of audacity over conformity. Gratitude mixed with despair. How do you go on when a sequin in the right light is no longer enough?

"Tragedy is *not* a punishment from God," the Reverend Walter Hawkins preached to the applauding crowd. He had already buried many of the Love Center's dead. "AIDS is *not* God's punishment." Very few people there thought otherwise, but it was still nice to hear it said in a church. For those present who weren't already too burnt out from memorials to face yet another, Sylvester's was only one of several they'd be attending that month. Of the ten honorary pallbearers listed on the program, four would die from AIDS within the next few years: Timmy McKenna, Sylvester's close friend and manager; Steve Foresse, his friend and dentist and the man who informally diagnosed both Sylvester and Rick; Barron Matalon, Sylvester's old Los Angeles friend and hairdresser; Marty Blecman, who had brought him in to Megatone. Many attendees had probably given thought to their own memorials; maybe they were picking up pointers.

The magenta preachers preached, and the purple choir sang "I'll Fly Away" and "Going Up Yonder." Jeanie Tracy sang the tune Sylvester had often performed as a little boy in a suit on a milk crate, dismissing church with his sweet high voice. *When our work here is done and the life-crown is won, and our troubles and trials are o'er, all our sorrow will end, and our voices will blend, with the loved ones who've gone on before,* Jeanie sang, trying not to look at Sylvester's casket. *Never grow old, never grow old, in a land where we'll never grow old.* Timmy McKenna tried to speak but all he could get out was one sentence: "If I had to know just one person in my lifetime, it would be Sylvester." Jeanie managed to tell some stories, and Izora's sister read a letter from Izora, who was laid up after an accident. People laughed at the stories; the crying came in refrains. His sisters could remember when Sylvester had stood with them around another casket—gilded, rhinestoned, lined with lace—and preached and sung and made them cry for the death of a neighborhood bird.

It was less than a week until Christmas. Before Walter Hawkins's eulogy and sermon, Tony Elite put on a tape of Sylvester singing Christmas songs in blues-gospel style. "In these times of trouble and strife," Sylvester's soft, deep voice first spoke, "we bring these songs of love and hope." Then, as he had been doing forever, Sylvester leaped up into falsetto—*O, holy night, the stars are brightly shining*—punctuated with little yelps and by Jeanie and Maurice, the C.O.G.I.C. singers, on background. *Joy to the world,* he sang. When he spoke his last words, "Merry Christmas," most people in the church were overcome. "Mmm-hmm, you see," Izora Armstead pointed out later, "he upstaged *Christmas.*"

Some people complained afterward that the service was too long and too preachy, but that was what Sylvester had said he wanted. As much as Sylvester wanted to exit movie-fabulous, he wanted to have church. "Be yourself and do what you do on Sundays," he'd told Reverend Hawkins. He told Tony Elite that he was going to use the occasion to take people who almost never set foot in church and give them "a sermon and the whole nine yards." He made sure they got a straight-up Pentecostal church service, with sermons, prayers, songs, testifying, tambourines, and praising of Jesus. "If Sylvester was here," Walter Hawkins told the crowd, "he would not want us to be quiet." The church was full of music and racial impurity and gender confusion. Some people who were there remember churchgoers speaking in tongues.

In fact, Sylvester was as much the preacher at his memorial as he was the glamorous corpse. His instructions for the body, the decorations, and the music were as much about creating a final sermon as starring in the last scene. For Sylvester, of course, a sermon and a scene were pretty much the same thing. "Girl, we had *service,*" Sylvester would sometimes say to the Tons back in the day, when they'd sung well enough to summon God. When Sylvester had service, you could barely tell dancing from prayer, celebration from sadness, man from woman, sex from soul, the movie fantasy from the ordinary life. "It was just all emotions mixed together," said Dean D'Onofrio of the service. "It was totally mixed up." In his glued-on hair and red kimono, he had brought a ragtag, everything-but-the-kitchen-sink stew of humans into a peachy-pink room that matched his lipstick: ex-lovers, family members, high-powered music producers and performers, Tenderloin drag queens, friends from his life in the Castro, disco fans who barely knew him, grown-up Cockettes, radical AIDS activists, all colors and genders and ages, all of whom saw him as somehow related to them. "You know," Sylvester used to say, "to have a beautiful garden, you've got to have many kinds of flowers."

"He was there," folks said afterward. "We had some *serious* church around him," Yvette Flunder said later. "I swear he got up and danced with us," says Rita Rockett. Many hope that he haunts them still.

Sylvester's body would soon be wheeled out to a round of "When the Saints Go Marching In," and then taken down south to the family plot in Inglewood Cemetery, over which the planes fly low on their way into LAX. Before that, as the service wound down, a line of mourners filed quietly by the open casket. If they hadn't seen the emaciated, gray version of Sylvester over the past months, they had seen other friends wasting away, and most people were prepared for a jolt.

"How do you want to be remembered?" the late radio DJ Frankie Crocker had asked Sylvester nearly a decade earlier, back when that was just a light, innocent lob of a question about a distant future. "For being fabulous," Sylvester had answered without hesitation.

And so it was.

Sylvester's hair was bright red and his lips painted pink and his brown face made up tastefully for an evening occasion, his tall body wrapped in a gold-embroidered red kimono. Everyone agreed he looked like Sylvester. They agreed he would be pleased to be such a sight to behold. He looked like a sleeping little boy, dreaming himself into being. He looked slim, with the body of the teenaged Dooni who had banged tambourines and roller-skated—so ridiculous, so unafraid—down a South Central street. He looked like a film star or a princess, taken tragically before her time.

Flawless, on a Monday.

NOTES

Although it is also something of a fable, this book is a work of nonfiction, based primarily on interviews with people who knew Sylvester or who had insights into his music and performance, and from the public record (newspaper and magazine coverage, primarily). Unless otherwise indicated in the text or below, the stories and quotes in the book come directly from interviews. People's memories are often fuzzy, idiosyncratic, and inaccurate, so whenever possible I checked sources against one another. I also routinely indicate where I am recounting memories, as a reminder to readers of the sort of "data" they are getting. When I say that someone "thought" this or that, or "felt" this or that, the person in question told me, or said on the record, that he or she thought or felt it; when I use words like "may" or "might," I do so to indicate that I'm imagining a feeling, and inviting the reader to do so.

Three excellent overviews of Sylvester's life have informed this book from the start and provided the background: Jake Austen's comprehensive, well-researched "Mighty Real: Sylvester's Story," in *Roctober* 19 (Summer 1997); Barry Walters's smart *San Francisco Examiner* articles, "San Francisco's Disco Diva" (originally published as "Stayin' Alive" in the *Village Voice*) and "He Captured the Ecstasy of Disco" from November 20, 1988; and Jack McDonough's entry on Sylvester in *San Francisco Rock* (San Francisco: Chronicle Books, 1985). Detailed notes on sources for each chapter follow.

Sylvester's albums, of course, are also sources throughout the book. They are *Scratch My Flower* (Blue Thumb, 1973); *Bazaar* (Blue Thumb, 1973); *Sylvester* (Fantasy, 1977); *Step II* (Fantasy, 1978); *Stars* (Fantasy, 1979); *Living Proof* (Fantasy, 1979); *Sell My Soul* (Fantasy, 1980); *Too Hot to Sleep* (Fantasy, 1981); *All I Need* (Megatone, 1981); *Call Me* (Megatone, 1983); *M-1015* (Megatone, 1984); and *Mutual Attraction* (Megatone/ Warner Bros., 1987).

1. GET READY FOR ME

The Essex Hemphill poem that supplies the epigraph appears in his *Ceremonies* (New York: Plume, 1992). The descriptions of Dooni, the Disquotays, and their compatriots are drawn from interviews with Duchess, Jackie Hoyle, Marapasa, Tiki Lofton, Diane Morehead, and "Tammi" (a pseudonym for a former Disquotay). Information about Etta James and her friendships with Miss Dakota and Lady Java is from her autobiography, *Rage to Survive: The Etta James Story* (Cambridge, Mass.: Da Capo, 1998), written with David Ritz. Information about Lady Java is also drawn from an article by Joshua Freker, "The Work of the ACLU: Linking Gender Identity and Gay Rights" (http://archive.aclu.org/issues/ gay/transgen_equal.html, 2000). Other details from Dooni's childhood come from an interview with Sylvester's sister Bernadette Brown; the descriptions of later Sylvester moments draw on interviews with Michael Bailey and Marc Baum, and from a letter to the *San Francisco Chronicle* written by Paul Wynne (December 24, 1988).

2. LIKE AN ANGEL CAME DOWN, HONEY

The descriptions in this chapter of Sylvester's early family life are drawn from interviews with family members Bernadette Brown, Bernadine Stevens, Robert Hurd, Tammy Hurd, Larry James, and Esau Joyner, and with his friends Yvette Flunder and Dreda Slaughter; I also relied on an interview by the filmmaker Tim Smyth with Sylvester's late mother, Letha Hurd. Information and quotes about Sylvester's sexual experiences at the church come from Lee Hildebrand's liner notes essay on the 1999 Fantasy Records reissue of *Sylvester* and *Too Hot to Sleep* and from Barry Walters's "San Francisco's Disco Diva" (*San Francisco Examiner*, November 20, 1988). Other published sources include Casey Carey, "Sylvester," *Inside Gossip* (December 1978); an interview with Sylvester conducted by Frankie Crocker on the radio station WBLS (circa 1979; transcript provided by Fantasy Records); an interview with Sylvester conducted by

Connie Johnson for *Black Stars* (circa 1981; transcript provided by Fantasy Records); "Sylvester," *Pink Trash* (September 1977); and Fantasy Records biographies of Sylvester from June 1977 and June 1978.

The discussion of gospel music and holiness churches draws on James Baldwin, *Go Tell It on the Mountain* (New York: Laurel, 1952); Michael Eric Dyson, *Race Rules* (Reading, Mass.: Addison-Wesley, 1996); Samuel A. Floyd, Jr., *The Power of Black Music* (New York: Oxford University Press, 1995); Anthony Heilbut, *The Gospel Sound*, 6th ed. (New York: Limelight, 2002); E. Patrick Johnson, "Feeling the Spirit in the Dark," in Delroy Constantine-Simms, ed., *The Greatest Taboo: Homosexuality in Black Communities* (Los Angeles: Alyson Books, 2000); Arthur Kempton, *Boogaloo* (New York: Pantheon, 2003); Guthrie P. Ramsey, *Race Music* (Berkeley: University of California Press, 2003); and Craig Werner, *A Change Is Gonna Come* (New York: Plume, 1998). George Crawford's remark is taken from Ramsey's *Race Music*. The section on church hats is informed and inspired by *Crowns*, by Michael Cunningham and Craig Marberry (New York: Doubleday, 2000).

The brief descriptions of South Central Los Angeles neighborhoods, population shifts, police behaviors, and the Watts riots are drawn from Josh Sides, *L.A. City Limits: African American Los Angeles from the Great Depression to the Present* (Berkeley: University of California Press, 2003); and from Alejandro Alonso, *Territoriality Among African American Street Gangs in Los Angeles* (Ph.D. dissertation, Department of Geography, University of Southern California, 1999). The brief descriptions of the early gay and lesbian movement in Los Angeles are drawn from Harry Hay, *Radically Gay*, edited by Will Roscoe (Boston: Beacon, 1996), and Moira Rachel Kenny's *Mapping Gay L.A.* (Philadelphia: Temple University Press, 2001).

For my account of Disquotay life, I have drawn on interviews with Duchess, Jackie Hoyle, Tiki Lofton, Marapasa, Diane Moorehead, and "Tammi." The details of Sylvester's arrest record appear in Superior Court of the State of California for the County of Los Angeles, Case No. A237130 (1968). Miscellaneous tidbits in this chapter also come from interviews with Robert Kingson and Kreemah Ritz.

3. SEQUINS AT NOON

For the story of the Cockettes, Sylvester among them, I have relied on interviews with Fayette Hauser, Scrumbly Koldwin, Peter Mintun, Sebastian Miron, Kreemah Ritz, Joel Selvin, John Waters, Jann Wenner, and Tahara J. W. Windsor; Martin Worman's unpublished, partially completed New York University dissertation, "Midnight Masquerade: A History of the Cockettes"; Worman's interview with Sylvester, conducted on November 18, 1988; footage of interviews conducted by Bill Weber and David Weissman with Reggie Dunnigan, Goldie Glitters, Fayette Hauser, Scrumbly Koldwin, Peter Mintun, Sweet Pam, Kreemah Ritz, Rumi, and John Waters; and Bill Weber and David Weissman's documentary film *The Cockettes*. Details about Hibiscus in particular are drawn from Worman's dissertation work (including the remarks by Irving Rosenthal); Horacio Silva, "Karma Chameleon," *The New York Times* (August 16, 2003); and Mark Thompson's "Children of Paradise: A Brief History of Queens," in *Out in Culture,* edited by Corey Creekmur and Alexander Doty (Durham, N.C.: Duke University Press, 1995).

Published articles from which I've drawn Cockettes-related descriptions and quotes are Barbara Falconer, "The Cockettes of San Francisco," *Earth* (October 1971); Maureen Orth, "History of a Hype," *Village Voice* (November 25, 1971); Jon Stewart, "From the Cockettes with Love and Squalor," *Ramparts* (December 1971); John Waters, *Shock Value* (New York: Thunder's Mouth Press, 1995); Joan Wiener, "Cockettes," *Rags* (August 1970); Maitland Zane, "Les Cockettes de San Francisco," *Rolling Stone* (October 14, 1971). Sylvester's thoughts about black music and black stars are taken from Casey Carey's *Inside Gossip* story; Sylvester's interview with Frankie Crocker on WBLS (circa 1979); Archie Ivy, "'I'll Do What Makes Me Happy,'" *Soul* (March 18, 1974); Patrick and Barbara Salvo, "Sylvester," in *Sepia* (November 1974); and Maitland Zane's *Rolling Stone* article.

On the Diggers and Kaliflower, I draw from the Digger Archives, at www.diggers.org. The quotations from the Sexual Freedom League are taken from Jefferson Poland and Sam Sloan, eds., *Sex Marchers* (Los Angeles: Elysium, 1968). The description of Sylvester's departure from Los Angeles is from Sharon Davis, "Sylvester, the Master of Divine Decadence," *Blues & Soul* (June 5–18, 1979); Robert Julian, "Mighty Real: Sylvester Reflects on a Golden Career," *San Francisco Sentinel* (September 2, 1988);

Dick Lupoff, "Sylvester: From Harlem Drag to the Hot Band," *The Night Times* (September 6–19, 1972); Douglas Price, "Sylvester," *The Advocate* (October 19, 1977); Patrick and Barbara Salvo's "Sylvester," in *Sepia*; Fantasy Records biographies of Sylvester from June 1977 and June 1978; and interviews with Bernadette Brown and Marapasa. The discussion of early gay life in San Francisco draws on John D'Emilio's *Sexual Politics, Sexual Communities* (Chicago: University of Chicago Press, 1983); Susan Stryker, "How the Castro Became San Francisco's Gay Neighborhood," in Winston Leyland, ed., *Out in the Castro* (San Francisco: Leyland Publications, 2002); Carl Wittman, "A Gay Manifesto," in Karla Jay and Allen Young, eds., *Out of the Closets* (New York: Pyramid, 1972); and interviews with Bob Ross, Aaron Shurin, and Randy Wallace.

4. JADED LADY

This chapter relies primarily on interviews with Fayette Hauser, Scrumbly Koldwin, Peter Mintun, Sebastian Miron, Kreemah Ritz, Joel Selvin, Pam Tent, John Waters, and Tahara J. W. Windsor; on Martin Worman's "Midnight Masquerade"; Worman's interview with Sylvester; on footage of interviews conducted with former Cockettes by Bill Weber and David Weissman, and on their film *The Cockettes*; on Pam Tent's *Midnight at the Palace: My Life as a Fabulous Cockette* (Boston: Alyson, 2004). Some descriptions of performances are taken from tape recordings (courtesy of Kreemah Ritz), documents such as notes and scripts (courtesy of Peter Mintun), and Mike Freedberg, "Tony Washington and Sylvester," *Soul* (September 26, 1977).

The discussion of blues music draws directly from Albert Murray, *Stomping the Blues* (Cambridge, Mass.: Da Capo Press, 2000 [1976]); Angela Y. Davis, *Blues Legacies and Black Feminism* (New York: Vintage, 1998); and Lena Horne and Richard Schickel, *Lena* (Garden City, N.Y.: Doubleday, 1965). It is also informed by Guthrie P. Ramsey's *Race Music* and Craig Werner's *A Change Is Gonna Come*.

5. BIG CITY BLUES

The Cockette stories come from interviews with Giana, Fayette Hauser, Scrumbly Koldwin, Michael Lyons, Peter Mintun, Sebastian Miron, Anita Pointer, Rex Reed, Kreemah Ritz, Pam Tent, and Tahara J. W. Windsor;

from Martin Worman's "Midnight Masquerade"; from Worman's interview with Sylvester; from the film *The Cockettes*; and from Pam Tent's *Midnight at the Palace*. In addition, information about the Cockettes' and Sylvester's time in New York are taken from Maureen Orth's *Village Voice* piece on "History of a Hype," along with: Anthony Driscoll's "Cockettes Crumble," *Berkeley Barb* (December 10–16, 1971); Barbara Falconer's "The Cockettes of San Francisco" in *Earth* magazine; "Theater: Coast Transvestite Troupe," *The New York Times* (November 9, 1971); Ernest Leogrande, "The Big Tough Apple," New York *Daily News* (November 9, 1971); Ed McCormack, "No, No Cockettes," *Changes* (circa December 1971; from author's personal collection); Sally Quinn, "The Cockettes: The Show Was a Drag," *The Washington Post* (November 9, 1971); and Maitland Zane's *Rolling Stone* article on "Les Cockettes de San Francisco."

The description of the New York underground, avant-garde, and drag scenes draws from George Chauncey's *Gay New York* (New York: Basic Books, 1995); Brennan Gerard, "Mapping Queer Worlds: Charles Ludlam and the Theater of the Ridiculous," unpublished paper, Department of Women's and Gender Studies, Yale University (2001); Wayne Koestenbaum's *Andy Warhol* (New York: Viking, 2001); Yvonne Sewall-Ruskin's *High on Rebellion: Inside the Underground at Max's Kansas City* (New York: Thunder's Mouth Press, 1995); Andy Warhol's *The Philosophy of Andy Warhol* (San Diego: Harvest, 1977); and www.warholstars.org. The remarks by Robert Stone are from his article "The Prince of Possibility," *The New Yorker* (June 14 and 21, 2004).

6. SCRATCH MY FLOWER

The stories and reporting in this chapter come from interviews with Hot Band members Travis Fullerton, Kerry Hatch, and Chris Mostert; "Cassie" (a pseudonym for the wife of one of the band members); Michael Lyons; Marapasa; Peter Mintun; Anita Pointer; Angel Reyes; Joel Selvin; Jann Wenner.

In addition, quotes and stories are drawn from these published sources: Jake Austen, "Mighty Real," *Roctober* (Summer 1997); "Ballad of the Blue Thumb Gang," www.vervemusicgroup.com; Lester Bangs, "Alice Cooper, All American," *Creem* (January 1972); Richard Cromelin, "Sylvester's Victory," *Melody Maker* (December 2, 1972); Cameron Crowe, "Ground Control to Davy Jones," *Rolling Stone* (February 1976); Jerry De

Gracia and Jon Seifer, "A Decade of Faaabulous Falsetto," *Bay Area Reporter* (January 10, 1984); Bill DeYoung, "The Story of Blue Thumb Records," *Goldmine* 412 (May 10, 1996); Russell Gersten, "Sylvester," *Rolling Stone* (October 6, 1977); Barney Hoskyns, *Glam!* (New York: Pocket, 1998); Barney Hoskyns, "Woofers and Tweeters," *New Musical Express* (September 25, 1982); Dennis Hunt, "Sylvester Minus Charisma," *Los Angeles Times* (December 6, 1974); Dennis Hunt, "Sylvester Out-rocks Top-Billed Preston," *Los Angeles Times* (January 15, 1974); Archie Ivy, "'I'll Do What Makes Me Happy,'" *Soul* (March 18, 1974); Michelle Kidd, "Makin' It" (publication and date unknown; from author's personal collection); Michele Lomax, "'A Joyful Noise Unto the Lord'" (January 12, 1974; publication unknown; from author's personal collection); Dick Lupoff, "Sylvester: From Harlem Drag to the Hot Band," *The Night Times* (September 6–19, 1972); McFadden, Strauss & Irwin, Inc., Public Relations, "Biography: Sylvester and the Hot Band" (circa 1974); "Random Notes," *Rolling Stone* (July 4, 1974); Patrick and Barbara Salvo, "Sylvester," *Sepia* (November 1974); Ben Sidran's memoir, *Ben Sidran: A Life in the Music* (New York: Taylor, 2003); "Sylvester & Hot Band," *Variety* (November 21, 1973); Voco's liner notes for *Lights Out: San Francisco* (Blue Thumb Records, 1972); John L. Wasserman, "The Gravy Train Doesn't Stop Here," *San Francisco Chronicle* (February 7, 1972); John L. Wasserman, "The Deafening, Defiant Sylvester," *San Francisco Chronicle* (August 12, 1972); John L. Wasserman, "The Meek Shall Not Inherit the Earth," *San Francisco Chronicle* (August 15, 1973).

7. SUNDAYS AT THE ELEPHANT WALK

This chapter draws primarily on interviews with Izora Rhodes Armstead, John Dunstan, Yvette Flunder, David Frazier, Giana, Terri Hinte, LZ Love, Marapasa, Nancy Pitts, Dan Reich, Aaron Shurin, Leslie Stoval, Brent Thomson, Martha Wash, Jason Williams, and James Wirrick.

Additional background, details, and quotes are from Amiri Baraka, "The Changing Same," in William J. Harris, ed., *The Leroi Jones/Amiri Baraka Reader* (New York: Thunder's Mouth Press, 1991); De Gracia and Seifer's 1984 *Bay Area Reporter* article "A Decade of Faaabulous Falsetto"; "Disco File," *Record World* (July 23, 1977); Philip Elwood, "Sylvester: A Turn in the Right Direction," *San Francisco Examiner* (July 21, 1977); Mike Freedberg, "Tony Washington and Sylvester," *Soul* (September 26,

1977); Gersten's *Rolling Stone* review of *Sylvester*; "How an Ex-Cockette Named Ruby Blue Became Sylvester," *Blues & Soul* (December 6–19, 1977); Etta James and David Ritz, *Rage to Survive*; Julian's 1988 *San Francisco Sentinel* piece, "Mighty Real"; D. Lawless, "Sylvester," *San Francisco Sentinel* (June 2, 1978); "The Legendary Harvey Fuqua," on www.harveyfuqua.net; Price's 1977 *Advocate* interview with Sylvester; Joel Selvin, "Sylvester's Potent Combination," *San Francisco Chronicle* (July 22, 1977); "*Sylvester*," *Billboard* (July 23, 1977); "Sylvester: *Sylvester*," *San Francisco Chronicle* (July 24, 1977); "Sylvester," *Rolling Stone* (September 8, 1977); Barry Walters's 1988 *San Francisco Chronicle* pieces; Cliff White, "Harvey Fuqua: The Man Behind Sylvester," *Black Music & Jazz Review* (November 1978); Peter Stein's documentary film *The Castro* (KQED, 1997); the transcript of Sylvester's interview with Frankie Crocker on WBLS; Fantasy Records biographies of Sylvester, the Two Tons, and the band (June 1977, August 1977, December 1980).

My discussion of the Castro draws on Blackberri's "Andy's—Center of the Universe," Frank Robinson's "Castro Street," and Susan Stryker's "How the Castro Became San Francisco's Gay Neighborhood," all in *Out in the Castro*, edited by Winston Leyland (San Francisco: Leyland Publications, 2002); Frances FitzGerald, *Cities on a Hill* (New York: Simon & Schuster, 1981); Randy Shilts, *The Mayor of Castro Street* (New York: St. Martin's Press, 1982); "Uncle Donald's Castro Street," at www.thecastro.net; Edmund White, *States of Desire* (New York: Dutton, 1980).

8. I FEEL REAL

This chapter draws on interviews with band members Marc Baum, Kelvin Dixon, Robert Kingson, and James Wirrick; with Izora Armstead and Martha Wash; with Nancy Pitts; with Sylvester's friends Linda Imperial, Marapasa, John Maley, Tom Martin, Ed Shepard, and Bruce Vilanch; with Fantasy Records staff members Phil Bray, Phil Carroll, Terri Hinte, and Jamie Putnam; and with the writers Vince Aletti and Barry Walters. I also make use of interviews conducted by David Diebold for his book *Tribal Rites: San Francisco's Dance Music Phenomenon* (Northridge, Calif.: Time Warp Publishing, 1986).

Information about Sylvester, including remarks attributed to him, also comes from John Abbey, "Sylvester: The Second Step," *Blues & Soul* (October 1978); John Abbey, "Sylvester: The Living Proof of Disco's

Heat," *Blues & Soul* (November 20–December 3, 1979); Susan Barnes, "Can Fantasy Records Break into the Big Time?" *San Francisco Bay Guardian* (July 6, 1978); Michael Branton, "Step Two: Disco Dandy Lured to Hollywood," *City Adventure* (June 1978); Michael Branton, "Sylvester Finds Heart in San Francisco," *Rolling Stone* (April 19, 1979); Carey's 1978 *Inside Gossip* story; Frankie Crocker's WBLS interview; Sharon Davis, "Sylvester: The Master of Divine Decadence," *Blues & Soul* (June 5–18, 1979); Sharon Davis, "Truckin' with Sylvester," *Blues & Soul* (September 12–25, 1978); De Gracia and Seifer's 1984 *Bay Area Reporter* piece; "Disco Forum V," *Billboard* (March 24, 1979); Fantasy Records press releases, "On the Road with Sylvester" (October 31, 1978) and "Sylvester's Giant Overseas Hit Arrives in the USA!" (November 30, 1978); Fantasy Records, "Disco News" (March 27, 1979); Bob Grossweiner, "Sylvester Lives in His Fantasy," *Good Times* (January 15, 1979); Lynn Hirshberg, "Sylvester: The Word Is 'Fabulous'!!" *BAM* (November 21, 1980); Knight-Ridder News Service, "Disco Star Sylvester Wants to Be a Back-up Singer" (May 18, 1979); Liz Lufkin, "Sylvester: Fire in the Disco," *BAM Magazine* (November 17, 1978); Disk O. Mann, "'Hot Shot' Gets Cooled by Sylvester," *Jackson* (Michigan) *Citizen Patriot* (August 31, 1978); Dick Nusser, "Sylvester's Tour No Chore," *Billboard* (November 18, 1978); Frank Sanello, "Interview: Sylvester," *Just L.A.* (August 1979); Davitt Sigerson, "This Man Was Singing About It Years Before Tom Robinson," *Sounds* (August 26, 1978); "Soul Star of the Month," *Song Hits* (February 1979); Ruthe Stein, "What's Left After Outrage," *San Francisco Chronicle* (July 8, 1978); Guy Trebay, "I, a Man: Sylvester's Story," *Village Voice* (August 19, 1981); Barry Walters's 1988 *Chronicle* pieces; Ken Williams, "Sylvester Steams from This Cool Reception," *Hollywood* (Florida) *Sun-Tattler* (April 20, 1979).

Reviews of *Step II* and of performances recounted in this chapter include Vince Aletti, "Disco File," *Record World* (June 17, 1978); Vince Aletti, "Sylvester Isn't Strange at All," *Village Voice* (December 18, 1979); Geoff Brown, "Sylvester: Hammersmith Odeon," *Black Music & Jazz Review* (January 1979); Robert Christgau, "Sylvester Is a Star," *Village Voice* (June 11, 1979); Richard Cromelin, "Sylvester: Disco, Soul at the Roxy," *Los Angeles Times* (December 23, 1978); Simon Frith, "No Business Like Show Business," *Melody Maker* (July 7, 1979); Pablo Yoruba Guzman, "Saturday Night Sashay," New York *Daily News* (May 27, 1979); John Rockwell, "Sylvester Takes His Exotica to Roseland," *The New York*

Times (May 25, 1979); Don Shewey, "Step II," *Rolling Stone* (December 14, 1978); Ken Tucker, "Sylvester: Delicate Disco Diva," *Los Angeles Herald Examiner* (December 23, 1978).

The descriptions of national and local politics, the Milk and Moscone assassinations, and quotes from Harvey Milk draw on Randy Shilts's *The Mayor of Castro Street* and Frank Robinson's "Castro Street," in Leyland's *Out in the Castro;* the brief description of the rainbow flag comes from Gilbert Baker, "The Rainbow Flag," in Leyland's *Out in the Castro*. The quotes about being "real" are from Margery Williams, *The Velveteen Rabbit* (New York: Doubleday, 1958).

The discussion of disco in this chapter and the following ones draws from John-Manuel Andriote, *Hot Stuff: A Brief History of Disco* (New York: HarperEntertainment, 2001); Mel Cheren, *Keep On Dancin'* (New York: 24 Hours for Life, Inc., 2000); "Disco Takes Over," *Newsweek* (April 2, 1979); Richard Dyer, "In Defense of Disco," in Alexander Doty and Corey Creekmur, eds., *Out in Culture* (Durham, N.C.: Duke University Press, 1995); Mikal Gilmore, "Disco," *Rolling Stone* (April 19, 1979); Albert Goldman, *Disco* (New York: Hawthorn Books, 1978); James Henke, "Record Companies Dancing to a Billion-Dollar Tune," *Rolling Stone* (April 19, 1979); Stephen Holden, "The Evolution of a Dance Craze," *Rolling Stone* (April 19, 1979); Andrew Holleran, "Dancing," *Christopher Street* (December 1982); Alan Jones and Jussi Kantonen, *Saturday Night Forever: The Story of Disco* (Chicago: A Capella, 2000); Darren Keast, "Feeling Mighty Real: How Disco Changed the Face of Local Dance Music," *SF Weekly* (August 16–22, 2000); Michael Segell, "Studio 54: Steve Rubell's Disco Disneyland," *Rolling Stone* (April 19, 1979); and Anthony Thomas, "The House the Kids Built: The Gay Black Imprint on American Dance Music," in Alexander Doty and Corey Creekmur, eds., *Out in Culture*. The Grace Jones descriptions and quotes are from Jones and Kantonen, *Saturday Night Forever,* and Krista Thomson, "Post-Colonial Performance and Installation Art," at http://www.emory.edu/English/Bahri/P&IArt.html. The material about the Village People is drawn from Andriote's *Hot Stuff;* the Jones and Kantonen book; Steven Gaines, "Jacques Morali: Man of the People," *New York* (September 25, 1978); and Abe Peck, "The Face of Disco: Macho Men with Their Tongues in Their Cheeks," *Rolling Stone* (April 19, 1979).

9. FLAME (ON THE DANCE FLOOR)

This chapter draws on interviews with Vince Aletti, Izora Armstead, Marc Baum, Howard Bloom, Phil Bray, Phil Carroll, Kelvin Dixon, Yvette Flunder, John Hedges, Terri Hinte, Robert Kingson, Michael Lyons, John Maley, Tom Martin, Steven Opstad, Robert Pintozzi, Jamie Putnam, Ed Shepard, Jeanie Tracy, Bruce Vilanch, Martha Wash, Barry Walters, and James Wirrick. I have also relied on Susan Barnes's "Can Fantasy Records Break Into the Big Time?" *San Francisco Bay Guardian* (July 6, 1978); Christgau's "Sylvester Is a Star"; Sharon Davis, "Sylvester: Master of Divine Decadence," *Blues & Soul* (June 5–18, 1979); "Disco King's Goal—To Do Nothing," *Willoughby* (Ohio) *News-Herald* (May 18, 1979); Diebold's *Tribal Rites*; Mike Freedburg, "Shy Guy Falsettos," *Musician* (August, 1979); Simon Frith's "No Business Like Show Business," *Melody Maker* (July 9, 1979); Lee Hildebrand's *Too Hot to Sleep* liner notes; Davitt Sigerson's "This Man Was Singing," *Sounds* (August 26, 1978); Ruthe Stein, "The Bigger the Better," *San Francisco Chronicle* (June 27, 1980); "Sylvester's Transition," *Blues & Soul* (March 11–24, 1980); Paul Wynne's letter to the *San Francisco Chronicle* (December 24, 1988). The discussion of the erotic quality of services owes much to Michael Eric Dyson's *Race Matters*, and E. Patrick Johnson's "Feeling the Spirit in the Dark," in D. Constantine-Simms, ed., *The Greatest Taboo* (Los Angeles: Alyson, 2000); the references to dancing in church and at Studio 54 come from James Baldwin's *Go Tell It on the Mountain* and Albert Goldman's *Disco*. The discussion of gay discos draws on Mel Cheren's *Keep on Dancin'* (New York: 24 Hours for Life, Inc., 2000); Andrew Holleran's *Dancer from the Dance* (New York: Plume, 1986 [1978]); Jones and Kantonen's *Saturday Night Forever*; and reminiscences about 12 West at http://home.att.net/~playguitar1/TW3html, and about the Garage at http://users.tellurian.net/garage2.

10. EVERYBODY IS ONE

This chapter makes use of interviews with Izora Armstead, Phil Bray, Bernadette Brown, Phil Carroll, Kelvin Dixon, Yvette Flunder, Giana, John Hedges, Terri Hinte, Robert Kingson, John Maley, Marapasa, Peter Mintun, Nancy Pitts, Robert Pintozzi, Jamie Putnam, Michael Rayner,

Joel Selvin, Leslie Stoval, Jeanie Tracy, Bruce Vilanch, Martha Wash, Jason Williams, and James Wirrick. Other sources of Sylvester stories, and reviews of albums and performances, include Letha Hurd's interview with Tim Smyth; Sylvester's interview with Frankie Crocker on WBLS; John Abbey's "Living Proof" interview in *Blues & Soul*; Jake Austen's "Mighty Real," *Roctober* (Summer 1997); Brad Balfour, "Keep On Dancin'," *Cue New York* (July 6, 1979); Brian Chin, "Disco File," *Record World* (March 10, 1979; November 17, 1979); Crispin Cioe, "Sylvester: Stars," *High Fidelity* (July 1979); Didier Delaunoy, "Record Data," *New York Black American* (December 12, 1979); Diebold's *Tribal Rites* interviews; Mike Freedberg, "Sylvester: Living Proof," *Boston Phoenix* (November 27, 1979); Freedburg's "Shy Guy Falsettos"; David Hendley, "Sylvester, The Venue," *Sounds* (July 14, 1979); Lynn Hirshberg, "Sylvester," *BAM* (November 21, 1980); George Lane, "Shades of Blue," *Bay State Banner* (May 3, 1979); Barry Lederer, "Disco Mix," *Billboard* (March 17, 1979); Rick Mitz, "Sounds," *Gentlemen's Quarterly* (February 1980); Dick Nusser, "Sylvester: Rose-land," *Billboard* (June 9, 1979); Bob Stuber, "Big Crowd for Dionne Warwick," *San Mateo* (California) *Times* (November 15, 1979); "Swingin' Sounds," *Tiger Beat* (February 1980); "Sylvester: Step Three," *Blues & Soul* (March 13–26, 1979); Ken Tucker, "Sylvester Revels on Clever 'Stars,'" *Los Angeles Herald Examiner* (May 13, 1979); Richard Williams, "Soul Sister—Brown Sugar," *Melody Maker* (June 30, 1979).

My description of the Opera House performance draws on interviews, the *Living Proof* album, and Philip Elwood, "Disco at the Opera House," *San Francisco Examiner* (March 13, 1979); Joel Selvin, "The Night Sylvester Became a Disco Star," *San Francisco Chronicle* (March 14, 1979). Armistead Maupin's remarks appear in his "The City That Dare Not Speak Its Name," *Blueboy* (September 1980). The description of the Dan White trial and its aftermath are drawn Randy Shilts's *The Mayor of Castro Street,* and from Rob Epstein and Robert Schmiechen's 1984 documentary *The Times of Harvey Milk.*

11. SELL MY SOUL

This chapter is based on interviews with Vince Aletti, Izora Armstead, Marc Baum, Phil Bray, Phil Carroll, Kelvin Dixon, David Frazier, Yvette Flunder, John Hedges, Terri Hinte, Linda Imperial, Robert Kingson, John

Maley, Tom Martin, Robert Pintozzi, Nancy Pitts, Jamie Putnam, Michael Rayner, Ed Shepard, Jeanie Tracy, Bruce Vilanch, Martha Wash, Barry Walters, and James Wirrick. Additionally, I have used Ian Cranna, "Sylvester: Sell My Soul/Too Hot to Sleep" (publication and date unknown; from author's personal collection); James Earl Hardy, "Sylvester: Living Proof," http://www.africana.com/articles/daily/mu20040608sylvester.asp; Mike Freedberg, "Sylvester Gets (Too) Specific," *Village Voice* (October 15, 1980); Sylvester's interview with Connie Johnson (circa 1981; transcript provided by Fantasy Records); Robert Julian, "Mighty Real," *San Francisco Sentinel* (September 2, 1988); Joel Selvin, "Castles, Churches for a Star," *San Francisco Chronicle* (November 26, 1980); Conrad Silvert, "The Coming Out of the 'New' Sylvester," *San Francisco Chronicle* (June 5, 1981); "Sylvester (Felt Forum)," *Variety* (March 19, 1980); "Sylvester: Thrills Without Frills," *Blues & Soul* (August 11–24, 1981); "Sylvester's Transition" in *Blues & Soul*; Guy Trebay, "Talking Heads: Is It True Tons Have More Fun?" *Village Voice* (February 11–17, 1981); "The Two Tons," *Ebony* (June 1981); Trebay's "I, a Man"; Barry Walters's "San Francisco's Disco Diva," *San Francisco Examiner* (November 20, 1988); "What the Stars Want for Christmas," *Black Stars* (December 1979).

My descriptions of the antidisco backlash draw on Andriote's *Hot Stuff*; Peter Braunstein, "The Last Days of Gay Disco," *Village Voice* (June 24–30, 1998); Cheren's *Keep On Dancin'*; Jones and Kantonen's *Saturday Night Forever*; and the Disco Demolition sites http://www.geocities.com/SoHo/Den/3001/do/demolition.html, http://whitesoxinteractive.com/History&Glory/DiscoDemolition.htm, and http://www.outernetweb.com/focal/disco/photos/index.html. For the resistance to jazz, see Ann Douglas, *Terrible Honesty: Mongrel Manhattan in the 1920s* (New York: Farrar, Straus and Giroux, 1995); Maria Agui Carter and Calvin Lindsay Jr., "The Devil's Music," from the PBS *Culture Shock* series (2000).

The story of Sylvester's arrest draws on interviews and "Crime Wave Rocks Gotham City," *Black Music and Jazz Review* (April 1980); Tito Davila, "The Check That Bounced to a Disco Beat," UPI wire story (March 17, 1980); Fantasy Records press releases (March 19, 1980; April 24, 1980); "Fraud Charges Against Sylvester Are Dropped," *Aquarian* (May 7–14, 1980); "Random Notes," *Rolling Stone* (May 1, 1980; June 12, 1980); "Rock/Disco Superstar Sylvester Denies Role in Grand Larceny," *Aquarian* (March 26, 1980); "Singer Sues Dealers Who Accused Him of Robbery,"

Jet (August 7, 1980); "Sylvester Cleared of Charges in N.Y. Arrest," *Jet* (May 15, 1980); "Sylvester 'Flips Out' Over Arrest in N.Y.," *Jet* (April 3, 1980); Sylvester's press statement (March 18, 1980); "Sylvester's Sour Note: N.Y. Arrest," *San Francisco Examiner* (March 15, 1980); Eli Teiber, "Cops Say Disco Superstar Danced Off with Stolen Coins," *New York Post* (March 15, 1980); Chris Vaughn, "Reporter Is Witness for Sylvester," *New York Amsterdam News* (March 22, 1980); report of Nat Laurendi, polygraphist (March 18, 1980; transcript provided by Fantasy Records).

12. LIVING ON THE LEGEND

Interview sources for this chapter are Izora Armstead, Marc Baum, Jerry Butler, Ken Crivello, Tom Daniels, Jo-Carol Davidson, David Frazier, John Hedges, Linda Imperial, Audrey Joseph, Mia Lucas, Terry Mahaffey, Tom Martin, Paul Parker, Nancy Pitts, Michael Rayner, Rita Rockett, Ed Shepard, Randy Wallace, Gerald Weiner, Jason Williams, and James Wirrick. Written sources include Adam Block, "Sylvester: There's Trouble in Paradise," *The Advocate* (December 8, 1983); Jerry De Gracia and Jon Seifer, "A Decade of Faaabulous Falsetto," *Bay Area Reporter* (January 10, 1984); Barney Hoskyns, "Woofers and Tweeters," *New Musical Express* (September 25, 1982); "Life After Disco," *Blues & Soul* (March 27–April 9, 1984); Tim McKenna, "Sylvester" (press biography, date unknown; from author's personal collection); Jan Carl Park, "The Party Will Still Be There When You Get Back: A Conversation with Sylvester," *Christopher Street* (December 1982); Joel Selvin "Castles, Churches for a Star," *San Francisco Chronicle* (November 26, 1980).

The discussion of the legal dispute also draws on documents filed in connection with *Sylvester James v. Harvey Fuqua et al.*, Case Number 565704, Superior Court for the County of Alameda, California. The discussion of the San Francisco club scene, the San Francisco sound, and Patrick Cowley draws primarily on Diebold's *Tribal Rites*; on Daniel Heinzmann's "Patrick Cowley," at http://pat.ma.cx/; and Darren Keast's "Feeling Mighty Real," *SF Weekly* (August 16–22, 2000). The discussion of the early AIDS epidemic draws on Randy Shilts, *And the Band Played On* (New York: Penguin, 1987); Lawrence K. Altman, "Rare Cancer Seen in 41 Homosexuals," *The New York Times* (July 3, 1981); "*Pneumocystis* Pneumonia—Los Angeles," *MMWR* (June 5, 1981).

13. WHAT'S A QUEEN TO DO?

In this chapter, I have relied on interviews with Michael Bailey, Alexandra Elite, Tony Elite, Yvette Flunder, Walter Hawkins, John Hedges, Audrey Joseph, Ken Kessie, Terry Mahaffey, Tom Martin, Paul Parker, Michael Rayner, Rita Rockett, Bob Ross, Joel Selvin, Ed Shepard, Gerry Weiner, Allen White, and Jason Williams. Additional sources include De Grazia and Seifer's "A Decade of Faaabulous Falsetto"; Hoskyns's "Woofers and Tweeters"; Adam Block's December 8, 1983, *Advocate* interview with Sylvester; John Dingwall, "Mighty Unreal" (publication and date unknown; from author's personal collection); Jan Carl Park's December 1982 *Christopher Street* interview with Sylvester; John Rechy, *The Sexual Outlaw: A Documentary* (New York: Grove Press, 1990 [1977]); Barry Walters's "San Francisco's Disco Diva"; Allen White, "Politics Packs a Punch at Delegates' Party Parties," *Bay Area Reporter* (July 19, 1984); "Last Will and Testament of Sylvester James" (San Francisco, May 27, 1988); and probate documents from the Superior Court of California, County of San Francisco, Case Number 253988 (June 19, 1990).

The AIDS background and quotes are from Dennis Altman, *AIDS in the Mind of America* (Garden City, N.Y.: Anchor, 1987); and Randy Shilts, *And the Band Played On.* My description of the Castro "Ten Year Retrospective" is aided by Jesse Hamlin, "A Deserved Hero's Welcome for Sylvester at the Castro," *San Francisco Chronicle* (February 6, 1984); Larry Kelp, "It'll Be a Celebration," *Oakland* (California) *Tribune* (February 1, 1984); Doris Worsham, "Sylvester Spectacle Leaves Audience Begging for More," *Oakland* (California) *Tribune* (February 6, 1984).

14. WHY DON'T YOU TAKE ME

This chapter is based primarily on interviews with Bernadette Brown, Ken Crivello, Dean D'Onofrio, Alexandra Elite, Tony Elite, Yvette Flunder, Roger Gross, John Hedges, Tammy Hurd, Linda Imperial, Ken Kessie, Marapasa, Charlene Moore, Paul Parker, Robert Pintozzi, Michael Rayner, Rita Rockett, Aaron Shurin, Jeanie Tracy, Martha Wash, Allen White, Tahara, Jason Williams, and James Wirrick.

Other quotes, details, and background come from Tim Smyth's interview with Letha Hurd; Adam Block, "The Sound of Silence," *Advocate* (January 31, 1989); "Castro Street Fair Pays Homage to Sylvester," *San*

Francisco Sentinel (October 7, 1988); Brian Chin, "Sylvester Bounces Back on Warner Bros.," *Billboard* (January 10, 1987); Darlene Donloe, "Sylvester's Fight with AIDS," *Rhythm & Business* (January 1989); Jim Feldman, "Sylvester: The Whole Tododadodado," *Creem* (June 1987); Andy Hurt, "Sylvester: Mutual Attraction," *Sounds* (date unknown; from author's personal collection); Connie Johnson, "Disco Singer Sylvester Confronts AIDS Without Any Regrets," *Los Angeles Times* (September 10, 1988); Julian's "Mighty Real" interview; Michele Kirsch, "Cruiser's Creed," *New Musical Express* (February 21, 1987); Dave Rimmer, "Sylvester: Mutual Attraction" (publication and date unknown; from author's personal collection); Chris Roberts, "Sylvester: Mutual Attraction," *Melody Maker* (January 31, 1987); Benjamin Heim Shepard, *White Nights and Ascending Shadows: An Oral History of the San Francisco AIDS Epidemic* (London: Cassell, 1997); Aaron Shurin, *Unbound: A Book of AIDS* (Los Angeles: Sun & Moon Press, 1997); "Sylvester Talks About His Battle with AIDS," *Jet* (November 28, 1988); Walters, "Disco Diva"; Allen White, "Sylvester Leads PWAs in Parade," *Bay Area Reporter* (June 30, 1988); Allen White, "'You Are My Friend: Sylvester Goes on with the Show the Night After His Lover Dies," *Bay Area Reporter* (September 10, 1987); Allen White, "You Make Me Feel Mighty Real!" *Bay Area Reporter* (August 11, 1988).

15. THE RED KIMONO

The poem that opens this chapter is from D. A. Powell's book *Tea* (Hanover, NH: Wesleyan University Press, 1998). The chapter draws on interviews with Bernadette Brown, Tom Daniels, Dean D'Onofrio, Alexandra Elite, Tony Elite, Yvette Flunder, David Frazier, Giana, Walter Hawkins, John Hedges, Jackie Hoyle, Ken Kessie, Patti LaBelle, Marapasa, Charlene Moore, Robert Pintozzi, Michael Rayner, Kreemah Ritz, Rita Rockett, Aaron Shurin, Leslie Stoval, "Tammi," Jeanie Tracy, Martha Wash, Allen White, Jason Williams, Tahara J. W. Windsor, and James Wirrick; Tim Smyth's interview with Letha Hurd; Martin Worman's interview with Sylvester; and Frankie Crocker's WBLS interview with Sylvester. Background and quotes are also drawn from "Singer Sylvester, 42, Dies of AIDS," *Jet* (January 9, 1989); "The Stage Lights Dim on 'Queen of Disco' Sylvester," *San Francisco Sentinel* (December 23, 1988); "Sylvester, Singer and Entertainer, Dies at 42," *The New York Times* (December 18, 1988); Robert Welkos, "Sylvester, 40; 'Disco Queen' Dies of AIDS," *Los Angeles Times* (December 19, 1988); "Sylvester, Flamboyant Gay Singer," *San Francisco Chronicle* (December 17, 1988); Allen White, "'Enquirer' Slams Sylvester," *Bay Area Reporter* (December 21, 1989); Allen White, "Sylvester: AIDS Claims Disco Diva," *Bay Area Reporter* (December 22, 1988); Allen White, "Sylvester's Manager, Tim McKenna, Dies," *Bay Area Reporter* (January 11, 1990).

INDEX

ABOUT THE AUTHOR

Joshua Gamson is a professor of sociology at the University of San Francisco and previously taught at Yale. His acclaimed book *Freaks Talk Back* is a dissection of American talk-show culture.